RELEASED FOR PUBLICATION

THEODORE ROOSEVELT

Released for Publication

SOME INSIDE POLITICAL HISTORY OF THEODORE ROOSEVELT AND HIS TIMES
1898–1918

BY

OSCAR KING DAVIS

*Formerly Washington Correspondent of the New York Times
and Secretary of the Progressive National Committee*

WITH ILLUSTRATIONS

BOSTON AND NEW YORK
HOUGHTON MIFFLIN COMPANY
The Riverside Press Cambridge
1925

The Riverside Press
CAMBRIDGE · MASSACHUSETTS
PRINTED IN THE U.S.A.

BY WAY OF EXPLANATION

THIS book has been written after a great deal of hesitation. It was undertaken only because of the repeated urgings of numerous friends, to whom, in intimate moments, some of the things here told had been narrated. In such relation of incidents in which one has taken part, or which he has observed personally, the rather frequent use of the first person, singular, seems neither offensively out of place nor evidence of exaggerated self-appraisal. But when it comes to putting these things down in black and white, for such public and enduring record as the bookmaker's art provides, it has given me, at least, more than a mere pause.

Moreover, these are only my personal recollections of some of the incidents in the busy, workaday life of an active newspaper man. I have put them down as I recall them, and they are presented solely in that guise. Many men are still living who either shared in some of these events or had opportunity to observe them closely. Their memories may, or may not, accord with mine.

Men are bound to differ in their recollection of events in which they have taken part or of which they have been close observers. At times it is possible, by conference and discussion, to reconcile such differences, and harmonize the recollections in one record. I have not attempted to do that. This is a book of my personal recollections, not the composite product of several memories.

Almost all of what I have written has to do, in one way or another, with Theodore Roosevelt, and the great political drama in which he was the leading actor. I count it as

one of the chief of the fortunate events of my life that I
was included by him in the number of those whom he described as his friends. With William H. Taft, another of
the prominent actors in the drama, I was also, for some
time, in close contact. The book sketches, in broad outline, my view of the inception, development, and culmina-
tion of the disaster that overthrew the Republican Party
in 1912.

In putting these recollections before the public in this
form, I make no claim of anything except that they present my view of Colonel Roosevelt. He was the subject of
that vigorous controversy which always accompanies the
leadership of a strong man who has the capacity to decide
and the courage to act. His political course, during the
last ten years of his life, carried such controversy to the
extreme of violence. Yet it was a thoroughly consistent
and understandable course. His death having, to some
extent, quieted this controversy, it may not be too much to
hope, now, that the presentation of this view of him is not
untimely.

These recollections deal, as a rule, only with political
and personal incidents. My contact with Mr. Roosevelt,
as President; as a campaigner for the Republican party in
1910; as a candidate for the Republican presidential nomination, in 1912; as the Progressive nominee for the presidency in that year, and, thereafter, to the time of his
death, was almost wholly on the side of political or public
affairs. The material on which I have drawn is simply my
memory, refreshed somewhat, in a few instances, by letters
from Mr. Roosevelt to me.

Such as it is, here is the book.

ILLUSTRATIONS

THEODORE ROOSEVELT   *Frontispiece*
  Photograph by Underwood & Underwood

WILLIAM E. BORAH   34
  Photograph by Paul Thompson

CHARLES EVANS HUGHES   46
  Photograph by Paul Thompson

ELIHU ROOT   54
  Photograph by Paul Thompson

WILLIAM HOWARD TAFT   94
  Photograph by Paul Thompson

CARR V. VAN ANDA   136
  Photograph by Underwood & Underwood

'AW, HANG THE CONSUMER!'   168
  From a cartoon by Herbert Johnson in the Philadelphia 'North
  American,' July 24, 1909

ROOSEVELT IN ACTION   208
  Photographed by Underwood & Underwood

FACSIMILE OF LETTER OF INTRODUCTION FROM THEODORE
  ROOSEVELT TO SECRETARY STIMSON   244

'PURSUED!'   258
  From a cartoon by Nelson Harding in the 'Brooklyn Daily Eagle,'
  November 27, 1911

JOSEPH M. DIXON   268
  Photograph by Paul Thompson, 1919

BAINBRIDGE COLBY   288
  Photograph by Paul Thompson

HERBERT S. HADLEY   304
    Photograph by Paul Thompson

GEORGE W. PERKINS   332
    Photograph by Paul Thompson

HIRAM W. JOHNSON   346
    Photograph by Paul Thompson

LEAF FROM ROOSEVELT'S TYPEWRITTEN SPEECH CARRIED
FOLDED IN HIS COAT POCKET AT MILWAUKEE AND
SHOWING HOLES MADE BY THE BULLET   382
    From the original owned by the author

RELEASED FOR PUBLICATION

RELEASED FOR PUBLICATION

I

In the early part of 1898 I was reading copy on the New York 'Sun' when, one night, there came to my desk a cable from Havana, saying that the commission then sitting there to investigate the explosion which had destroyed the battleship Maine on the night of February 15th would report that the ship had been blown up from the outside. I passed the message across the desk to my colleague, the late Frank Matthews, who was handling general telegraph copy, and he agreed with me that this news meant war with Spain.

Each desk man on the 'Sun' had one day, or night, off a week. When I went to the office on the night before my next night off, I took my gripsack with me, and after work that night, instead of returning home, I went over to Jersey City and took the four-o'clock train for Washington. At the capital I called on David S. Barry, then the Washington correspondent of the 'Sun,' and asked him to take me to Mr. Roosevelt, then Assistant Secretary of the Navy, whom I had never met, despite the fact that I was doing newspaper work during the time that he was Police Commissioner of New York City. We went up to the Navy Department and Barry introduced me to the Assistant Secretary. I told Mr. Roosevelt that I believed we were in for war with Spain, and he promptly agreed. I said I intended to ask the 'Sun' to send me with the fleet, but that if the 'Sun' did not send me, I intended to resign from it and enlist in the Navy. In case the 'Sun' should send me,

I wanted Mr. Roosevelt's assurance that he would give me letters of introduction to the fleet commander. That he readily gave me, and I took an afternoon train back to New York.

Two or three weeks later I put the case up to Chester Lord, then managing editor of the 'Sun,' the man who would give out the war assignments when the time came. I told him just what I had done, and that I had Mr. Roosevelt's promise to do what he could to get me with the fleet if the 'Sun' should send me. Mr. Lord did not say whether or not he was inclined to give me such an assignment, but along toward the end of March, when I was at home on a night off, I received a telegram from him asking me to come over to the office that night. When I got there, Mr. Lord showed me a confidential message from Mr. Barry saying that a squadron was to be assembled at Hampton Roads under command of Commodore Schley. He believed that this squadron would be sent to sea to meet Admiral Cervera who was expected to attempt to bring the Spanish fleet to Cuba. The location at Hampton Roads was picked so as to give Schley opportunity to go north or south according to the news from Cervera. There was a lot of talk going around at the time to the effect that Cervera might attempt an attack on some part of our northern coast. Mr. Lord asked me if I wanted to go with this squadron. When I said I surely did, he asked how soon I could start. I said there was a train for Washington at four o'clock the next morning, which I could take if I could get the necessary money. The business office being closed, it was a case of raise it among the men then in the office. I borrowed a hundred dollars, got back home and packed a grip, and caught that train.

Next morning, in Washington, Mr. Roosevelt was as

good as his word. He gave me letters himself and got others for me from Secretary Long, and that night I went down the Potomac River to Hampton Roads, with my credentials. By noon the next day I had had my interview with Commodore Schley, and was accepted as the 'Sun' correspondent with the Flying Squadron, which was yet to be assembled. The Commodore received me in the cabin of the flagship Brooklyn, which had already been stripped for war service. He read my letters slowly and then said:

'You want to go with me, do you?'

I said I surely did.

'Young man, you go with me. By God, I make you fight.'

Notwithstanding that promise I went with Schley — for several weeks. He took me out for two or three days of target practice and maneuvers off the Virginia Capes, and then sent me cruising up the New England coast in the old tinclad Columbia, which was assigned, with her sister ship, the Minneapolis, the duty of preventing the Spanish torpedo boats from blowing Bar Harbor and Hingham off the map.

We were in Portsmouth, New Hampshire, on Sunday, May 1st, and left that night for Portland, Maine. Going along the coast, pretty close inshore, early the next morning we passed an old chap in a dory who was tending lobster pots. As we swept by, hardly fifty yards from him, he stood up in his boat and swung his old coonskin cap around his head.

'Hurray!' he shouted, 'have ye heard the news?'

'What news?' we queried.

'Dewey whaled hell out of 'em!'

That's how we got the news of Dewey's victory in Manila Bay.

Protecting the New England coast from mythical Spanish torpedo boats was amusing, but not exciting, and nothing at all like what I had figured war at sea would be. So I got back to Hampton Roads and asked the Commodore to put me in another ship that was likely to be in on any fighting that might take place. This time I got the battleship Massachusetts, Captain Frank Higginson, which, after all, was coaling at Guantanamo when Cervera met his fate outside of Santiago. But fortunately for me I was no longer with the Flying Squadron. After waiting at Hampton Roads until about the 10th of May, I telegraphed Mr. Lord that, in my judgment, Schley would have no independent action; that when he left the Roads it would be to go south and join Sampson, who would be in chief command. Sampson had already taken certain newspaper men with him, and he might or might not confirm Schley's action. Then I added:

'There is still time for me to catch that Manila expedition.'

That referred to the force then being gathered in San Francisco to be sent out to support Dewey in Manila Bay. A couple of days later Mr. Lord wired me to 'go to Washington with all haste, get army passes and passports, and hurry to San Francisco to join Philippines expedition.' So I missed Santiago and all that business along the south coast of Cuba, Las Guasimas, San Juan Hill, and the rest. But by way of compensation I was in on the capture of Guam, when the Governor apologized for not being able to respond to Captain Glass's salute, and I met Aguinaldo and the Filipinos, and was there when Dewey was engaged in 'the German incident,' as well as at his capture of the city of Manila on August 13th. I was there through the first year and more of the Filipino insurrection, and concluded that period of Far Eastern experience by going to Tien-tsin at the outbreak of the Boxer rebellion in 1900 and making the march to Peking with the column of heterogeneous allies that relieved the besieged Legations on August 14th. There were sixteen breeds of fighting men in that column, and I saw, during that terrible hike, the evidence which led me to predict, in several published articles, Japanese victory over Russia whenever they should fight.

II

'THE German incident' in Manila Bay is a story by itself. Admiral Dewey once told me, in Washington, a few years before his death, that he had written a complete account of it after the fullest consultation with all the commanding officers of his squadron. He said his narrative was given in minute detail and was supported by the official records at every point. He described it as completed, and said the manuscript had been put away for safe-keeping, to be published only after his death.

Subsequently, however, the Admiral permitted the publication, in a magazine, of what purported to be his autobiography. This was written, as a matter of fact, by a very well-known correspondent, who discussed it chapter by chapter with the Admiral. It happened that at the time of this publication the international situation was such that it would have been decidedly indiscreet to put into a book under Admiral Dewey's signature any such story of the Manila Bay incident as he had told me he had written.

The correspondent who actually wrote the Dewey 'Autobiography' is a discreet man, who had himself spent a good deal of time in the Philippines, although not there during the German incident. He was fairly familiar, however, with what had occurred then. Under all the circumstances the story as given in the Dewey 'Autobiography' was no doubt the best that could have been done at the time. It has always seemed to me, however, that its publication was unfortunate, because, being published while Dewey was still alive, and as his autobiography, it was bound to have a certain undetachable authority. And as, owing to the international situation of the time, it could not be in accord with the story actually written by the Admiral himself, the fact that it had been published would tend to prevent the publication of the real story. That may, in fact, be the reason why the authentic Dewey account has never been brought out.

My attention was first attracted to the German incident on the afternoon of June 28, 1898, when the First Expedition sailed into Manila Bay. I was on the transport Australia, on which General Thomas H. Anderson, in command of the expedition, had his headquarters. We followed the cruiser Charleston, Captain Glass, which had convoyed the expedition from Honolulu. As we steamed slowly past Corregidor Island, the big German cruiser Kaiserin Augusta, which had been lying in Mariveles Bay, directly across the Boca Chica from the island, got under way and headed in toward the foreign warship anchorage off the mouth of the Pasig River. Everybody on the Australia who could get on deck was there, crowding the rails to make the most of the first view of the new country. The Kaiserin swung in on the port side of the Australia, and came so close that we could read the names on her small boats without using glasses. Her officers were all, apparently, on deck, and watching us very attentively. Several of them had their glasses up.

Lieutenant John H. Lee Holcombe, of our Navy, was on the Australia. The disregard of naval etiquette by the Kaiserin Augusta made him furious.

'By God, they're counting us!' he exclaimed. 'They ought to be shot!'

But nobody did anything, and the Kaiserin kept on her way, close to the Australia, right up to the time when we were asking Dewey for directions as to anchoring. Then she turned and steamed on across to her anchorage with the other Germans off the mouth of the Pasig. That night everybody in the fleet was talking about the German insolence, and we newcomers heard a lot about the way in which Admiral von Diederichs and his men had been carrying on.

The navy men said that it began with a dinner which Prince Henry had given on his flagship in Hong Kong, before Admiral Dewey sailed for Manila Bay. It happened that Vice-Admiral Seymour, the British commander, did not attend that dinner, and so Dewey was the senior in rank of all Prince Henry's guests. But instead of giving the toast to President McKinley first, as conventionality required, in respect of Dewey's rank, Prince Henry proposed the President last. Dewey resented that breach of etiquette very thoroughly. The next day there was a reception on the German flagship for all the officers of the other fleets then in Hong Kong roads. Dewey kept his senior officers on board their ships, and sent his juniors. His action was so pronounced that even the Germans did not need to be told in so many words that he was very angry. Prince Henry was reported to have consulted Vice-Admiral Seymour as to what he ought to do, and to have been advised to call on Dewey and apologize. But apparently he could not bring himself to do that, and the incident grew greater instead of less.

Then the Germans violated the proprieties very seriously by sending a squadron of observation to Manila Bay that was stronger, in some respects, than Dewey's blockading fleet. They had the armored battleship Kaiser, with eight ten-inch guns. There was not an inch of armor in Dewey's fleet, and only a few eight-inch guns, scattered among several ships. They played fast and loose with Dewey's blockade regulations, particularly with the one prohibiting any movement of boats on the Bay after dark. One of their methods of violating that regulation was especially annoying. They would send a boat from their flagship to convey a message to Dewey, and get it away so late in the afternoon that it could not possibly get back before dark. One evening the Olympia held up the German boat with her searchlight, and kept it bobbing about idly for some time before the searchlight was lifted and the boat permitted to go on. The German ships were frequently moved out to Mariveles Bay or elsewhere, and there were constant reports to Dewey that the Germans were in regular communication with the Spaniards in Manila.

These annoyances kept up so steadily that they compelled Dewey to regard them as studied and deliberate. Then, when the Germans interfered with the Filipinos, the lid very nearly blew off. The Filipinos were fighting the Spaniards, having renewed their old insurrection when Dewey went to Manila Bay. They captured a Spanish merchantman and fitted her out as a sort of warship, naming her the Filipinas. The Spaniards had a small garrison at Subig Bay, and the Filipinos attacked it with such success that they drove the Spaniards into the fortifications on Isla Grande, where they had some six-inch guns. The Filipinas went to Subig Bay with reinforcements for the attackers. The German cruiser Irene was there, apparently in communication with the Spaniards. She halted the Filipinas, which was flying a Filipino flag by agreement with Admiral Dewey. The Germans wanted to know what flag that was, and, when told, replied that they did not recognize it and it must be hauled down. The Filipino commander had to comply, for he was no match for the Irene and he knew it. So he turned around and headed for Manila Bay as fast as he could go.

There he reported to Dewey what had happened. The Admiral sent for Captains Coghlan of the Raleigh and Walker of the Concord, and ordered them to go to Subig Bay at top speed and cleared for action. If the Irene said anything to them, they were to sink her.

But when the Irene saw the Raleigh and Concord coming into Subig Bay cleared for action, she very promptly started out of the bay and headed for Manila. Dewey was watching, and when he saw the smoke in the Boca Chica, which denoted there the presence of a ship, he sent the McCulloch to see what it was. Captain Hooper, of the McCulloch, took his orders with thorough seriousness. When he drew near the Irene, he sent a small boat across her bows, and after that had brought her to a stop Lieutenant White went aboard, just as if he were boarding a perfectly strange merchantman.

That night there was plenty of anxious talk about Dewey's ships in Cavite Bay. It looked very much as if things were coming to a head, and no one was at all sure that we should not be at war with the Germans very soon. The next afternoon a boat came from the German flagship to the Olympia, with von Diederichs's flag lieutenant, Hintze, aboard. He had a message from the German Admiral to Admiral Dewey.

Dewey was in his usual place on the quarter-deck of the Olympia. Lieutenant Strite had the deck watch. The wardroom skylights which gave onto the quarter-deck were open, and in the wardroom several officers were sitting, some writing and some in conversation. Strite convoyed Hintze back to the Admiral and returned to his post on the superstructure. He had hardly got there when he heard Dewey say to the German:

'I want you to tell your Admiral that I want to know

whether his country and mine are at peace or at war. If
they are at war, the way to make war is to clear ship and go
into action. If they are at peace, I want him to stop breaking my blockade regulations.'

Hintze saluted and left the Olympia. The men in the
wardroom had heard what the Admiral said, and there
was hardly one of them who would have risked two cents
on the prospect for peace. But the next day, and the next,
there was no sign from the Germans.

While that situation was on I called on the Admiral one
afternoon and found him on the quarter-deck of the
Olympia scanning the entrance of the Bay. Two monitors,
the Monadnock and the Monterey, had been ordered out
to reinforce Dewey, and the first of them was about due.
It was not difficult to guess that the Admiral was anxiously
looking for her.

The second and third expeditions of troops from San
Francisco had arrived by this time, and we were all eager
to learn how soon the surrender of Manila would be
demanded. Some of the newspapermen, who were on
confidential terms with Admiral Dewey, knew that he had
been negotiating, through M. André, the Belgian Consul
in Manila, with the Spanish commander-in-chief for the
surrender of the city. We had received strong intima-
tions that there was a very good prospect that the surrender would be arranged so that there would not have to
be any fighting. Dewey had not lost a man in the May Day
fight, and he was very keen to take the city also without
loss of life.

So, when opportunity offered that afternoon, I asked the
Admiral if he was going to move on the city soon. In reply
he swept his right arm around toward the German warships, anchored in front of Manila, and said:

'Suppose I were to say to those fellows over there that I wanted that water, as I was going to move on the city. And suppose they were to reply that they would not permit me to bombard the city. I should have to say, "I'll sink you first and then I'll take the city," and I want the monitors here when I talk like that.'

III

THUS the evidence accumulated that the German incident was really a serious matter. A morning or two later I called again on the Admiral. He was sitting on the quarter-deck with Captain Coghlan, of the Raleigh. Coghlan was on his right and a vacant chair was at his left. As I came up he motioned to me to take that chair, then turned and went on with his conversation with Coghlan. It continued, uninterrupted, for about fifteen minutes, and had to do entirely with the disposition and handling of the American ships if we should fight the Germans. The problem was to dispose of the battleship Kaiser, with her armor and her ten-inch guns. The Olympia and the Raleigh both had greater speed than the Kaiser, and both were equipped with rapid-fire five-inch guns. Dewey and Coghlan talked about the possibility of ranging the Kaiser with those two ships at top speed, and pouring in such a fire from the rapid-fire guns as to overwhelm her. The German guns were mounted in sponsons, not in turrets or barbettes, on an open gun deck, and the question the Admiral and the captain were considering was the likelihood of getting some five-inch shells in on that gun deck and putting those ten-inch rifles out of service. At length Dewey said:

'Well, think it over Coghlan, think it over.'

Captain Coghlan rose at once and went back to the Raleigh, and Admiral Dewey turned to me and began to talk about other phases of the situation. Naturally it would not have surprised me to see action with the Germans begun almost any minute.

Still nothing happened, and then one morning I got word from the Olympia that the demand on Manila was about to be made. I had already secured permission from the Admiral to be on board the Concord when the move on the city took place, and as soon as I got this word from the flagship I went aboard the gunboat. The Concord was a little fellow, only about a thousand tons, carrying six six-inch guns. Her job was to take care of a 9.6-inch rifle which the Spaniards had mounted at the north end of the Male-con Drive, near the Anda Monument. Dewey had learned that this rifle could be swung only through a very small arc, and as the Concord was a light-draft vessel it was possible for her to get rather close inshore, to the north of this rifle and so out of its range.

Notice was served on the foreign squadrons of observation that the attack on Manila would be made on Thursday, August 11th. They at once got under way, so as to let the Americans have free use of the water they had been occupying right in front of the entrance to the Pasig River. Then a thing occurred which raised a big cheer from our fleet. The British squadron and the Japanese cruiser came right across the Bay to Cavite and asked permission from Dewey to anchor there. The Germans and two Frenchmen, went out toward Mariveles Bay. The British squadron was commanded by Captain Chichester. The flagship was the cruiser Immortalité, and he had also the Iphigenia, Swift, and Linnet, and four small gunboats, of the Partridge and Pheasant class. Chichester was a big, round, red-faced beef-eater, who looked like the model for the cartoons of John Bull.

Something happened that postponed the submission of the demand for the surrender until the morning of Saturday, August 13th. Meantime the Concord had taken up her position and was waiting for the word to get into action. Captain Walker had orders not to fire unless the Spaniards opened with their Luneta guns. Dewey's negotiations with the Spanish Captain-General had proceeded so successfully that he was confident there would be no real action, and that a little demonstration of force was all that would be necessary. He had submitted a colored drawing to General Jaudenes, the Spanish commander, showing the flag hoist that would be sent up on the Olympia demanding the surrender, and Jaudenes had replied with a map of the city, on which a cross had been marked to show the place where the white flag would be raised. But the Spaniards had a pleasant way of court-martialing and shooting a general who surrendered, and Jaudenes felt that he needed the protection of a show of fighting before he capitulated.

Early on the morning of the 13th we got word on the Concord that that was to be the day. No word had reached Manila Bay of the doings in Cuba and we had no hint that the war was really over. We thought we were going to help to end it that day. The day came dark and overcast, with frequent heavy rain squalls of the kind common in the tropics. The Concord got under way promptly on receipt of the signal from the Olympia and stood off and on over a line close inshore and perhaps a thousand yards long. She was cleared for action, the guns were shotted and the crews standing by for the order to fire. The ship moved very slowly up and down the line, Captain Walker keeping careful watch not to get out where that big Spanish rifle might possibly be trained on him.

Across at Cavite we saw the other ships of the squadron get under way, with the Raleigh in the lead. They steamed close in toward the old fort San Antonio Abad, which stood just below Malate, the southern suburb of Manila. The flag hoist went up on the Olympia, the battle-flags were broken out, and over the Bay rang the cheer of the American sailormen, that nerve-tingling cheer which booms out only when they are going into action.

Then the Raleigh opened fire with her forward eight-inch gun. Straining through the glasses, we on the Concord saw the shell go high above the old fort, sail clear across the southern suburbs of Manila and fall far away in the Morong hills. Afterward, we learned that Captain Coghlan, himself, had given the range as seven thousand yards, and, when Lieutenant Casey Morgan, who was in charge of the forward eight-inch gun, protested that it didn't look half that, Coghlan replied:

'Never mind what it looks. I am giving the ranges.'

It was part of the play agreed on between Dewey and Jaudenes, by which lives of attackers and defenders were to be saved. But Riley, the gun-pointer of the after five-inch gun, in the port battery, of the Raleigh, was the best shot in the fleet.

'Seven thousand hells!' he exclaimed, when he heard the range from the bridge. He dropped his sight-bar to twenty-seven hundred yards, and fired over. In two more shots he found the fort, and the port battery knew the range. Thereupon Coghlan saw that his gunners could get a range for themselves, regardless of official play-acting. So he sounded 'cease firing' and took the Raleigh out of action.

Our fellows on the Concord had hardly stopped cheering over the opening of the action, when some one called, 'Look there!' and pointed down toward the entrance of the Bay. Three German warships were coming up from Mariveles, with the big Kaiserin Augusta in the lead. Instantly all eyes on the Concord were focussed on them, for they were headed right at us, and we began to wonder what was going to happen. They did not leave us long in doubt, but came straight on, until they were less than half a mile away, and then straightened out in line, abreast of us. Thereafter, as we stood off and on, over our course, the three Germans followed suit, keeping the same distance away, but apparently watching every move we made.

They had made about one turn when we suddenly observed a new movement over Cavite way. The British were getting under way. For a few moments we watched them with absorbing interest, and then, as we saw the big Immortalité, followed by two of the gunboats, swing and head over toward us — great Lord, how our fellows cheered! Straight toward us came the three British ships, and it seemed to us that, although they had not broken out the huge number 1 ensigns, which are the sign and proclamation of battle purpose, they were flying flags considerably larger than the little fellows usually shown in such weather.

As they came on, we caught the strains of music from the flagship, and knew that her band was in action if her guns were not. Presently we got the tune. It was a Sousa march, which carried two or three bars of the 'Star-Spangled Banner.' They couldn't play our national anthem, for that would have been a violation of neutrality. But they did the next best thing, and I warrant those British bandmen can still hear the American cheers that rewarded them. I know I can.

On came Chichester, right in between the Germans and the Concord, swung, and took position abreast of us. And there he stayed all day. From the moment he arrived, there was never an instant when a German ship could have fired a shot at the Concord without crossing a British deck.

There the German incident at Manila Bay came to a
bloodless end. It was in keeping with their caution all
through that, at the close of that day, after Jaudenes had
signed the capitulation, the Kaiserin Augusta took him on
board and steamed away for Hong Kong, without even
notification to Dewey that she was going, much less his
permission to go. She was gone before he knew anything
about it or had any word as to the passengers she was
taking.

In January, 1899, a number of the officers who had
served with Dewey in Manila Bay came home, on the
expiration of their tours of sea duty. They sailed from
Hong Kong on the Coptic, for San Francisco. Captain
Chichester was then at Hong Kong, and he came aboard
the Coptic, the morning she left, to say good-bye to
Dewey's men. Leaning against the rail of the liner, with a
group of Dewey's officers around him, he told this story
of a call he had received from the German admiral the
day after Dewey sent that message by Hintze, demanding to know whether it was peace or war between them.

Von Diederichs had come aboard the Immortalité and
talked for a few minutes with Chichester about nothing
in particular, and the big Englishman could not make out
what the German wanted. But just as von Diederichs rose
to go he turned to Chichester and said:

'By the way, suppose the Americans were to serve notice
on us that they intended to bombard the city.'

'Yes,' replied Chichester.

'And suppose we were to reply that we could not permit
the bombardment of the city.'

'Yes,' said Chichester.

'What do you suppose would be likely to be the attitude
of the British in that case?' asked von Diederichs.

'Suppose you ask Admiral Dewey,' replied the British captain.

'Ah, exactly,' said von Diederichs, and started for the gangway.

'And you know,' said Chichester, telling the story, 'the Government gave me the C.M.G. for that'; and he screwed up the whole side of his big red face in one prodigious wink.

Which may, or may not, but most probably does, explain why we at Cavite heard nothing from the Germans in those anxious days after that message went from Dewey to von Diederichs.

IV

Soon after the capture of Manila, a big, bluff Scotchman, with snow-white hair and florid face, came to me with a letter of introduction from William M. Laffan, then the publisher of the 'Sun.' He was John Weir, a mining engineer in the employ of the Guggenheims. They had sent him to the Philippines to investigate some of the numerous reports of rich gold deposits, especially in the northern part of Luzon Island. Mr. Laffan's letter was practically commanding, and caused me to credit, fully, Colonel Weir's statement that they were very good friends.

As soon as Colonel Weir told me what he wanted to do, I said that it would be impossible, because the Filipinos held all the country north of Malolos, where Aguinaldo had his capital, and would not permit any white men to travel through it. Nevertheless, on Weir's insistence, I did my best to secure him a pass. I knew Aguinaldo, and most of the members of his government, several of them very well. But it was a useless effort. When I reported my failure, Colonel Weir demanded to know what was the matter with them.

'It is only another evidence,' I replied, 'that they are preparing to fight us. They don't want any Americans behind their lines.'

Weir exploded at that. 'We've got to stop it!' he exclaimed. 'There can't be any fighting. 'We've got to be able to get about this country, and there's got to be peace.'

I laughed. 'How are you going to stop it?' I asked. 'If you know a sure way, General Otis will rise up and call you blessed for the rest of your life.'

'We've got to go and talk to them,' responded Weir. 'You take me to Aguinaldo, and we'll show him how foolish all this business is. We'll stop it.'

So Weir and I went up to Malolos and saw Aguinaldo. But he was extremely busy with the affairs of his government, the collection of money and the purchase of arms with which to fight us, and Colonel Weir could not interest him in the new proposition. In fact, he hardly got started on its presentation before the Filipino leader turned us over to Araneta, who held the title of Minister of Justice in President Aguinaldo's cabinet.

Araneta was an able man, probably the best-educated and most intelligent of the whole group around Aguinaldo. After the insurrection he was made Chief Justice of the Supreme Court, by American appointment. He was a grave, silent man, who listened intently to what we had to say, but gave no indication of what impression it made upon him. In Marti Burgos, one of the minor leaders, we had an excellent interpreter, and through him Colonel Weir presented our case with all the force he could command. This was his argument:

'I am going to tell you something of the greatest importance, both to you and to me, to the Filipino people and to the Americans. You do not know me, but I know you. I am telling you the truth. You have no way of corroborating or disproving what I say, without taking a long time and making a study in the United States. So I tell you that you must believe what I say because I am telling it to you. I want your welfare, just as much as you do, because, in this case, your welfare will also be mine.

'You Filipinos are preparing to make war against the United States. Stop it! It is foolish and terrible. Moreover, it is the wrong way to go at your problem, or to try to get what you want. There is a much better way, and I am going to show it to you. You have to believe it, because I am the only one here who can show it to you, and I tell you it is the solemn truth.

'You must know that it is foolish for you to try to fight the United States. Do you know how big, and strong, and rich they are? You cannot win. I know you think that, because one of our regiments did not make a good showing the other day against the Spaniards, while your men came right on, you can whip the American soldiers as you whipped the Spaniards. Do not make that mistake. The Americans will fight. The United States has had many wars, and never lost one of them.

'Remember this, and do not lose sight of it for a moment. If you start a war with the Americans, they will keep it up until they have whipped you. However many men it requires, however many ships they have to send out here, however much money it costs, they will give and send all. They will never count the cost in men, or time, or money. They will only fight until they have beaten you into submission.

'Remember, too, that while they are fighting, they will not stop to talk anything over with you. Once the war begins, discussion will end, and it will stay ended until the war is over. They will never treat with men in arms. Not until you have surrendered absolutely will you have another chance to present your case for consideration, and then you will have to come into that discussion as the defeated enemy, not as a friend, as you might do now, on something like equal terms.

'This is the course for you to take. Listen to me, and believe what I am telling you, for this is the truth, and if all the Americans in the United States were here this morning, they would say the same thing.

'Stop this foolish spending of money to buy old, worn-out rifles from the cheap John filibusters on the China coast. Stop taking the time of your men to drill and form regiments of soldiers. Put them back at work, to earn more money that you can spend in a sensible way, a way that will get you somewhere with the American people, and help you to obtain the recognition from them that you want.

'Instead of spending your money in this foolish way for arms, use it to send delegations of your people to the United States. You are good people to meet. Many of you have cultivation and charm. You make friends quickly. You can present your case well, and with appealing force. That's what you want to do in the United States.

'Send delegations of from four to six men and women over there, eight or ten such parties. Give them money enough to make a good showing. Put a first-rate American publicity man with each delegation, and follow his lead. He will show them how to work. He will have those delegations traveling around the United States, and being received by mayors and governors and prominent men in every city where they stop. There will be great receptions for them, and banquets, and public meetings. The newspapers, all over the country, will print columns and columns about them. You will educate the American people about the Philippines and the Filipinos. And, at the same time, your delegations will educate themselves about the United States and the American people.

'Go to Washington and see the President, and the members of his Cabinet, and the Senators and Congressmen. Make politics for yourselves, American politics, in the American way. You will absolutely divide public opinion, at the very least. You might get it all on your side. You will either get what you want from the United States, or you will make the Philippines a great political question, out of which you are bound to get a great deal more than you can ever hope to win by fighting. All you can get from war is disaster, death, suffering, and loss. But out of politics you may get all you want, and are sure to get, at least, a good part of it.

Colonel Weir argued like a man pleading for his life. It seemed to me that the sheer earnestness and sincerity of it must appeal to Araneta and the Filipinos. But the interview ended without the least sign from Aguinaldo's Minister of Justice that he had been at all impressed by what he had heard.

Weir was not through, however. As long as there was any Filipino in Malolos who was in position to have any influence with Aguinaldo, Weir wanted to argue the proposition out with him. So I took him to Buencamino, the Minister for Public Works, and most of the afternoon was spent in fervent repetition of what had been said to Araneta in the morning.

It was, of course, all the truth, and the soundest advice that was ever given, by any one, to the Filipinos. But, equally of course, it was all useless, and wasted. Matters between the Filipinos and the Americans went rapidly from bad to worse, until the insurrection began and the Americans started in on exactly the course that Colonel Weir had predicted that day at Malolos.

Seventeen years, and more, later, I went back to Manila, and had another talk with Buencamino. I asked him why our fervent argument that afternoon had had no effect on the Filipinos.

'Oh,' he replied, 'our heads were so full of another idea that there was no room for yours. You were right, but we could not see it.'

V

In the early fall of 1900, after the Boxer siege of the foreign
legations at Peking had been raised by the arrival of the
allied relief column, I brought a first-class case of Asiatic
fever all the way home from Tien-tsin to Binghamton,
New York, where my family then were. The presidential
campaign was drawing to its end, and Colonel Roosevelt,
McKinley's running mate, was vigorously charging Mr.
Bryan with prolonging the Filipino insurrection at the cost
of many lives. I knew that that charge was well founded,
because I had been in numerous fights in the Philippines,
when, after we had beaten the Filipinos, we had found in
the places they abandoned copies of circulars and letters
from Aguinaldo, or members of his group, urging the
Filipinos to hold on because Bryan was sure to be elected
President of the United States and he would give them immediate independence. I had a good many copies of such
documents in the pile of papers that I brought home from
Manila.

Colonel Roosevelt was to speak in Binghamton on the
last Saturday night but one of the campaign. I told some
of my friends about the papers I had, saying that some of
them should be shown at that meeting as practical evidence
of the accuracy of what Colonel Roosevelt was charging.
The Republican chairman heard about my having these
papers and asked me to bring some of them to the meeting
and tell the circumstances under which I got them. I
agreed to do so, but when the day of the meeting came I
had a relapse of the fever and couldn't get out of bed. So
my papers were not shown.

Colonel Roosevelt spent Sunday in Binghamton, and that afternoon Lindsay Denison, who was covering the Roosevelt tour for the 'Sun,' came to see me. We talked about the Philippine situation and the campaign that Colonel Roosevelt was making.

One of the first assignments I received from the 'Sun,' after recovering from Asiatic fever, was to go up to Buffalo and report the opening of the Pan-American Exposition, which took place about the first of May, 1901. Mr. Roosevelt, then Vice-President, was to make the opening address. It happened that I took the same train for Buffalo that Mr. Roosevelt did, and had a seat in the same car. I had not seen him since he gave me the letters to Schley, more than three years before. Along in the afternoon I interrupted his reading, and asked if he remembered Davis, of the 'Sun.'

'By George! Of course I do,' he replied. 'You know, I wanted to go and see you last fall, in Binghamton, when you were sick, but they kept me occupied all that day, and I couldn't. But Denison went.'

That was just one evidence of Colonel Roosevelt's astonishing memory, that could call back even so trivial an incident at the time when it was wanted.

Then we talked about the Philippines. He had a hundred questions to ask, first about general conditions there, and next about friends in the service, army and navy. Several men who had been with him in the Rough Riders had come out to the Philippines in one or other of the volunteer regiments, and he was keen to know how they had borne themselves. It was very interesting to me to see how closely he followed his friends, and how he enjoyed any good report I could give of any of them. Later, I found him just as quick to grasp and act upon the other kind of report.

One story I told him, that afternoon, was about George Curry, a Rough Rider who later joined the Eleventh Volunteer Cavalry for service in the Philippines. I had been in a hike across Cavite Province, with a column composed of four troops of the Fourth Cavalry — regulars — under the famous Indian fighter, Colonel 'Jack' Hayes, and five troops of the Eleventh — volunteers — under Major Dennis E. Nolan. Each squadron had a pack-train, and that of the volunteers was commanded by Curry. In that crazy all-day scramble, through brush and jungle, and across deep ravines and gorges, whenever we halted we soon heard the jingle of the bells on Curry's pack-mules. But we lost the regular pack-train, and it didn't catch up for two or three days.

Colonel Roosevelt enjoyed, and remembered, that evidence of Rough Rider efficiency. Later, as President, he appointed Curry Governor of the Territory of New Mexico. That story may have helped in the decision.

VI

AFTER a hectic and thoroughly unsatisfactory experience
with Kuroki's army, in the first part of the war between
Japan and Russia, I returned to the United States in time
to see the last of the presidential campaign of 1904, when
Mr. Roosevelt was the Republican nominee. In the course
of a visit at Binghamton, New York, I talked with a
number of friends about the political situation, and it
developed that there was a very strong bolt against Frank
Higgins, the Republican nominee for the governorship of
New York. In one afternoon I met thirteen Republicans,
all of whom said they were going to vote for Roosevelt for
President, but twelve of them added that they would vote
for Herrick, the Democratic nominee, for Governor. There
was no question as to the very great popularity of Roosevelt, and it was freely predicted that he would carry New
York State by more than 200,000. The only question was
as to whether the bolt against Higgins could be made
strong enough to overcome the immense strength of Roosevelt. The election showed that it was Roosevelt's strength
which carried Higgins through. The Governor ran more
than a hundred thousand behind Roosevelt, and it was
apparent that if it had not been a presidential year the
Republican State ticket would have been defeated.

Two years later, when I was in the Washington bureau
of the New York 'Times,' the celebrated controversy
between Mr. Roosevelt and E. H. Harriman came out into
the open. As I recall it, James S. Sherman, then a member
of the House of Representatives, and either chairman, or

some other official, of the Republican Congressional Committee, asked Mr. Harriman for a campaign contribution,
which was refused. Sherman took the case to the President
and that led to the giving-out, at the White House, of some
correspondence between Roosevelt and Harriman which
had taken place in the fall of 1904, before the election.
Roosevelt had invited Harriman to meet him at the White
House, and Harriman had replied that he could not do so
before the election. That was the correspondence in which
Roosevelt had used the sentence, 'You and I are practical
men.'

The publication of this correspondence aroused a storm
of criticism of Roosevelt. The newspapers opposed to him
gleefully asserted that it proved the charge made by Alton
B. Parker, the Democratic nominee for the presidency
whom Roosevelt defeated so badly in 1904. Mr. Parker
had accused the Republicans of accepting campaign
contributions from corporations with the understanding
that the contributors were to receive special consideration
from the President if Roosevelt should be elected. Mr.
Roosevelt had replied that undoubtedly both parties had
received campaign contributions from corporations; but
that if any one had made a contribution to the Republican
fund on the theory or in the hope of receiving special
consideration from the party on that account, he was most
grievously mistaken, for if he (Roosevelt) were elected,
particular pains would be taken to prevent special consideration for any one on any account. Roosevelt added
that any one who charged that campaign contributions had
been made or received on assurance of favoritism from him
was a liar.

In the course of the controversy in the fall of 1906, the
fact came out that Harriman had either contributed him-

self or had been responsible for raising $250,000 for the Republican campaign fund in New York State in 1904, and this, with the further fact disclosed by the correspondence, that there had been at least negotiations for a meeting of Roosevelt and Harriman before the election, was taken by the Roosevelt opponents as positive proof of the substantial accuracy of the Parker charges. The New York 'Times,' one of the most consistent opponents of Roosevelt, rung the changes editorially on this, as did many other Democratic newspapers, despite the fact that their editors knew very well what the political situation in New York State had been in the fall of 1904, and that it was Harriman, or his nominee Higgins, who needed help, not Roosevelt. It was plainly apparent, to any man willing to look the facts honestly in the face, that in any meeting between Roosevelt and Harriman that fall, if either asked for help, it would be Harriman and not Roosevelt. The election proved beyond the possibility of a question on which side the need for help lay.

Only a little while after the controversy aroused by the publication of this correspondence had begun to die away, 'Big Bill' Haywood was arrested in Denver for the murder of former Governor Steunenberg of Idaho. He was then secretary of the Western Federation of Miners, which had conducted open warfare with the mine operators of Colorado and other Western States for several years, a warfare that had been marked by repeated brutal murders and assassinations, culminating with the blowing-up of a railroad station platform at Victor, Colorado, in 1904, when a score or more of non-union miners were killed. Moyer, the president, and Pettibone, another official of the Western Federation, were arrested about the same time, accused jointly with Haywood of the Steunenberg murder.

A tremendous outcry was raised by organized labor because Haywood and the others were rushed to Idaho so rapidly that their attorneys were unable to invoke habeas corpus or other legal process in their behalf. Mr. Roosevelt made a public comment on this case one afternoon, at the White House, which promptly evoked a new storm against him, at the same time reviving some of the old bitterness. In the course of his remarks he described Moyer, Haywood, and Pettibone as just 'as undesirable citizens as E. H. Harriman.' His linking of the railroad magnate with a group of organized labor leaders charged with murder furiously angered the friends of Harriman; and his description of the Federation officials as 'undesirable citizens' just as furiously angered the rank and file of organized labor all over the country.

This episode served, naturally, to attract a great deal of attention to the trial of Haywood, which was set for the May, 1907, term of court at Boise, Idaho. On the afternoon of the 2d or 3d of May when I entered my office in the New York 'Times' Bureau, in Washington, the telephone bell was ringing. I answered and found that Mr. Van Anda, the managing editor of the 'Times,' was calling me from New York.

'Do you want to go to Idaho?' he asked, without any preliminaries.

'Sure,' I replied.

'When can you start — this afternoon?'

'No. Not till to-morrow,' I answered.

'Why can't you go this afternoon?'

'There are several reasons. The first is that I haven't any money and the others don't count.'

'What do you do with all the money you win at Benning's?' (The Washington race track.)

'I have to work so hard I never get a chance to go out there and so don't win anything.'

'How much do you want?'

'Two hundred and fifty dollars.'

'All right. I'll have a check there for you in the morning. What train will you take?'

'The fast one that leaves at 1.10. Then I'll catch the one at Chicago that will get me there quickest.'

'All right. Wire me when you leave Chicago what train you are on, so I can communicate with you. Good-bye.'

That was my assignment to report the Haywood trial. I give the instructions verbatim and entire, because, subsequently, both at Boise and elsewhere, some of the supporters of Haywood, who didn't like the dispatches I sent from Boise during the trial, asserted rather loudly that I was writing under instructions, and some of the Socialist newspapers, which have a practical understanding of venality, could think of no other reasons for my views at that trial than that they were paid for. When I told one Socialist at Boise exactly what occurred when I got my assignment, he was utterly stumped. He could not conceive of a newspaper being sufficiently independent and honest to be willing to print the news as it was, regardless of its own editorial views, and of having a correspondent whom it trusted enough to get the news absolutely without special instructions.

But that was, and is, the New York 'Times.' In thirty-five years of active newspaper work, which has taken me around the world and into four wars, and has given me an acquaintance with scores of newspaper men, Carr Van Anda, of the New York 'Times,' is the greatest managing editor I have ever met. He knows the news, and how to get it, and how to print it. And he will print it as it comes, whether the 'after-breakfast' men, who write the editorials, like it or not. They can say what they please in their editorial columns. But editorial news and editorial views keep out of the news columns under his jurisdiction.

VII

WILLIAM E. BORAH, one of the ablest young lawyers of
Idaho, who had just been elected to the United States
Senate, had been retained by the State to assist in the prosecution of Haywood. At that time the Federal Government was making a hard drive against land frauds in the
Western States, and only a short time before Haywood was
to come to trial at Boise, it was announced there that the
Federal grand jury had indicted a number of men for land
frauds, and that Senator Borah, who had been attorney
for a lumber company for some time, was among them.
Governor Gooding, through whose astuteness the Steunenberg murder had been solved, and who was fearlessly determined that Haywood, Moyer, and Pettibone should be
vigorously prosecuted, at once declared that the Borah indictment was part of a scheme of the Western Federation of
Miners to keep Borah out of the prosecution of Haywood.
Borah had won reputation all through the Western country
by his handling of the case against some men connected
with the crimes in the great Cœur d'Alène strike of a few
years earlier, and the Federation men did not like his connection with the Haywood case.

Governor Gooding promptly asked President Roosevelt
to have the trial of Senator Borah postponed until after
the Haywood case had been tried. The Federal district attorney at Boise objected vigorously to any postponement,
and was loud in his assertion that if he could only get
Borah into court he would soon convict him. The district
attorney said to me one day, during the Haywood trial,

WILLIAM E. BORAH

that if it had not been for the interference of Washington
he would have had Borah in the penitentiary at that
minute. Mr. Roosevelt did act as Governor Gooding had
requested, and that delay had an important effect upon
the subsequent proceedings. For it enabled me, and a
couple of the other newspaper men who were in Boise for
the Haywood trial, to make a deliberate and very thorough
investigation of the Borah case, and to establish, beyond
the possibility of a doubt, that the indictment was an almost unbelievable outrage, without the least color of foundation, and that it was brought about either for wholly
corrupt reasons or on account of the personal vindictive-
ness of the district attorney toward Borah.

Before the Haywood trial ended, I submitted to President Roosevelt a detailed report of the circumstances at-
tending the Borah indictment. It showed that the grand
jury which found the indictment had been deliberately
packed for that purpose. The marshal had reported that
he had been unable to find a dozen or thirteen men on the
original venire, and thereupon got a special venire for ten
men, whom he selected from Borah's known enemies in
Boise. But I had found that all those men whom the
marshal said he could not locate could have been reached
by him, by telephone, in one afternoon. They were all
farmers of that county, and easily communicated with.
Moreover, they were all at home when the marshal said he
couldn't find them. Summonses from him would have
found them all in one day.

The twenty-two men named with Borah in the indictment all demurred. But Borah, although he felt that the
indictment should have been dismissed by the Department
of Justice simply because it was such a flagrant act of injustice, made the altogether sound decision that, in view

of his political career, he would answer it with the verdict of a Jury.

The Haywood verdict was rendered early on a Sunday morning, toward the end of July. Borah, Governor Gooding, and I walked together from the court-house back to the hotel where I was stopping, and I wrote a telegram to President Roosevelt, which Governor Gooding signed, asking the President to see that the Borah case was set for trial immediately, so that it could be disposed of, and out of the way, before the trial of Pettibone came on.

The President had replied to my report on the Borah case indicating a reluctance to act because of the possible effect on the murder cases.

'I could do no worse thing for the cause of justice in this particular Moyer and Haywood case,' he wrote, 'than to seem to shield a United States Senator who was concerned in the prosecution.'

He intimated that he would have a special agent sent out to investigate the Borah indictment, and, if my report were substantiated, he would dismiss District Attorney Ruick.

Naturally that position did not satisfy Borah, or Gooding, or any one connected with either the Borah case or the defendants in the murder cases. Borah and Gooding wanted a prompt trial. The miners wanted anything that would put Borah out of the murder cases, but least of all did they want an independent investigation of his indictment. I got the impression that they knew enough about the way the indictment had been obtained to realize that an honest investigation of it would react badly on those who had brought it about.

Ruick, the district attorney, protested vigorously against immediate trial of Borah. He called such a proceeding rank injustice to him. His witnesses were scattered, he said, to the four winds of heaven. It would take months to get them together again, and there were all kinds of other difficulties in the way. Attorney-General Bonaparte sided with Ruick. He had no independent report, except mine to the President, and he not unnaturally supported his organization.

But pretty much all Boise knew that the indictment of Borah was crooked, and the growing public sentiment there in his support made itself felt at Washington. President Roosevelt soon decided to accede to Governor Gooding's request and have the case brought to trial. Thereupon he took a line of action that immensely surprised and displeased the crowd that had procured the indictment. He set aside the entire court machinery at Boise — judge, district attorney, marshal, and all. He had a judge come in from Seattle and other court officers from different districts, all outside of Idaho. He set the stage for a square, honest, and disinterested trial of the case.

The judge from Seattle heard first the demurrers of the twenty-two men who had been indicted with Borah, and dismissed the indictments in a decision that simply flayed the district attorney, and left him raw, red, and gasping. Incidentally that decision cost Ruick his place, for soon afterward President Roosevelt based upon it his action in removing Ruick from office.

When Borah's case came on, he let the prosecution carry matters practically as it pleased, declining to cross-examine witnesses, making no objections on direct examination, and omitting the motion to dismiss which the judge evidently expected and was apparently ready to grant. When the case had been running on for three or four days, the judge leaned over the bench and said to the prosecuting attorney:

'When are you going to connect the defendant with any of this?'

But the prosecutor could not connect Borah, and it took the jury only four minutes to bring in its verdict of 'not guilty.'

VIII

THE Haywood verdict of 'not guilty' was as great a miscarriage of justice as the Borah verdict was an act of justice. I do not believe any open-minded, honest man could have listened to all the testimony in that case, as I did, without becoming convinced that the story elicited by the prosecution was the truth. The chief witness, Harry Orchard, went through an ordeal which could have been sustained only by a man who was relying solely on his memory of events in which he had taken part, and who was relating them exactly as his memory brought them back to him. For six solid days he underwent an extraordinary cross-examination. It was conducted at such speed that frequently the official stenographer had to request that it be slowed down. Never once did Orchard slip, or contradict himself, or involve himself in the least apparent deviation from the truth as he remembered it.

He had been the official murderer for Haywood and the Western Federation. He was the agent who had committed numerous ghastly crimes and attempted numerous others. There was no abyss of infamy which he did not readily admit having plumbed, if it was in fact a part of his experience. At the same time there was no trivial peccadillo which he would admit, if he had not in fact committed it.

His only explanation, for both his crimes and his confession, was religion. He said that when, as a young man and a devout member of a church, he had made the first false step, he felt that he was utterly damned, and it made no difference then what he did. The result could be no worse

for him. But after he had been arrested for the Steunenberg murder, and was in the penitentiary at Boise, he had
come to believe that after all he might obtain divine for
giveness if from that time on he stuck rigidly to the truth,
and did all in his power to atone for his crimes.

It was a plausible explanation, and he consistently stuck
to it, and to the course in which it involved him. Without
the slightest discernible divergence he followed the line
which that explanation marked out for him. The last time
I heard anything about him it was that he was still sticking
literally to the same course.

Because I was thus convinced that Orchard was telling
the truth, it has always seemed very strange to me that
none of the lawyers for the prosecution in the Haywood
case spent any time in arguing Orchard's credibility to the
jury. They took up all sorts of other points in the case, and
Senator Borah dwelt for hours on the matter of corrobora-
tion, which, under the law of Idaho, it was necessary to
establish by independent testimony. Borah argued ably
and powerfully, but it never seemed to me that any of the
argument was as convincing to the jury as it might have
been if there had been a painstaking examination of
Orchard's story from the sole point of its reliability and
truth.

One burst of eloquence from Borah will always remain in
my memory. Darrow, the eminent Socialist and criminal
lawyer from Chicago, who was chief of Haywood's counsel,
had given vent, throughout the trial, to one prolonged
sneer, not only at Orchard and his explanation, but at all
religion, in general as well as in particular. When Borah,
who had been speaking for some time, and had been
rather vigorous in his delivery, reached that point in his
argument, he stepped up close to the jury box, and turning

halfway around, so as to see Darrow, who sat behind him, he said, in an easy, conversational tone:

'When I heard the eloquent gentleman from Chicago uttering his sneers at your religion, and at mine, there came back to me, as there must inevitably have come back to each one of you, gentlemen of the jury, the recollection of the time when, as a little boy, I stood at my mother's knee and heard her read from our Bible.'

Then, with a swift, sweeping gesture at Darrow, his voice rang out through the courtroom:

'Too late, after two thousand years, to cry "fraud!" to the man of Calvary! Too late, in the dawn of the twentieth century, to write "impostor" on the brow of the figure on the Cross!'

IX

OF course there was talk at Boise after Haywood had been
set free that the jury had been bought. Whether there was
ever any foundation for any such talk or not, I never
knew. But I did know that if I had been on the jury I
should have felt that the judge had charged for a verdict
of 'not guilty.' It has always seemed to me that the chief
responsibility for Haywood's acquittal rested with Judge
Woods. Yet I know that he believed Haywood was guilty
and that a proper case for conviction had been made out.

The judge was a great fisherman, and the streams of
Idaho were full of trout. We went together on three or four
little week-end fishing excursions during the trial. I was
always very particular on such occasions never to bring the
Haywood case into the conversation, and, in fact, it was
never mentioned by either of us except once. Then Judge
Woods brought it up himself. We were almost at the end,
he said, and he would be glad when it was over. I replied
that it had been hard work for me, with court sitting from
nine o'clock in the morning until four or later in the afternoon, with only an hour for noon recess, especially as New
York time was two hours against us, and it was always
after six o'clock in New York before I could begin to write
my dispatch.

'Well,' he said, 'it will soon be over. It ought to go to
the jury next week. Haywood is guilty and has been
convicted. I believe he will be hanged, for I don't see how
it can be upset.'

I, too, believed Haywood guilty, and I thought he ought
to be convicted. Not being a lawyer, I was oppressed with

the notion that there might be something in our conversation that could be made use of on appeal if any word
of it ever got out, and so I switched the line of talk to trout
fishing on the instant, and kept mighty still about what the
judge had said for a long time.

But in view of that talk I was greatly puzzled when I
listened to his charge to the jury. Under the Idaho law
each side has the right to submit 'requests to charge' to
the judge who hears a case. He has the right to accept or
reject any or all of these requests; but rejected requests
may be held to be error on appeal. Haywood's lawyers
made the utmost of this legal situation, and I have always
felt that it was that which got him off. Richardson,
Darrow's principal associate, took the subject of reasonable doubt and wrote about twenty paragraphs, in each of
which he gave, in varying phraseology, a definition of what
constitutes the reasonable doubt beyond which the jury
must be convinced in order to bring in a verdict of guilty.

The prosecution also submitted several different versions
of the same point. Then Judge Woods had some of his own.
So that altogether there were about forty of them. The
judge included them all in his charge. He rejected none of
them.

The result was that out of sixty-four paragraphs, as I
recall it, in the charge, forty or forty-two dealt with the
subject of reasonable doubt. Under those circumstances it
has always seemed to me that it would have been a super-
human jury that would not have said that the judge had
charged it that there was a reasonable doubt in that case,
and so the verdict must be not guilty.

Now the queer thing about all this is that the Supreme
Court of Idaho, which would have heard an appeal, if
there had been one, in the Haywood case, had passed upon

a case only a short time before in which it had itself defined reasonable doubt. Why Judge Woods did not reject all the requests, from both the prosecution and the defense, to charge on this point, and take into his charge only the language of the Supreme Court on the subject, has always been a mystery to me. Surely that course could not have been held by that same Supreme Court to have been error. Sometimes I have thought that in his belief that Haywood was guilty the judge made up his mind to be so fair in his charge as to prevent the possibility of reversal on that account, and with that in mind took in all the requests to charge from both sides. But if that was his reason, it is clear that he overreached himself. Boise and that part of the State held him responsible for the failure of justice, and after the expiration of that term of office the administration of justice from the bench did not interfere with his going trout fishing.

X

INTEREST at Boise naturally centered chiefly in the Haywood case, but outside the courtroom there was a great deal of talk about politics. The question of the Republican presidential nomination for 1908 was attracting wide attention, and there was much discussion about the statement President Roosevelt had issued on election night, 1904, in which he declared that he would regard the unfinished term of President McKinley and the one to which he had just been elected as making, in substance, the usual two terms to which custom limited the presidency, and would not be a candidate in 1908. Despite that statement there were many friends of Roosevelt who eagerly desired him to take the nomination again and there was no doubt that he could have it if he would accept it.

When it came to the question of some one else, in case Roosevelt stuck to his refusal to run, there was much divergence of opinion. Mr. Taft, then Secretary of War in the Roosevelt Cabinet, was popularly supposed to be the President's personal choice as his successor. Taft was an open, and sometimes almost extreme, supporter of the Roosevelt policies, and it was not unknown among Washington correspondents who were on terms of confidence at the White House that the President sometimes wished the Secretary of War were not quite so unrestrained in his utterances.

Charles E. Hughes, who was then serving his first term as Governor of New York, had caught the public imagination strongly throughout the country, especially by his conflict with the Old Guard Republican organization of the State. Insurgency against machine domination, particularly in the Republican Party, was waxing rapidly throughout the country, and many men were ready to declare for Hughes who knew nothing more about him than that he was 'fighting the bosses' at home.

During the three months that I was at Boise in the early part of 1907 I met a good many men from all the intermountain and Pacific Coast States, and found about all of them greatly interested in the possibility that Hughes might be the Republican nominee the next year. Most of them were quite ready to support him, if nominated, and many of them were eager to go to work to see that he was chosen. I heard enough Hughes talk in those three months to satisfy me that, if the New York Governor should be the Republican nominee, he would start with a first-class chance of carrying all that part of the country.

Hughes, as a matter of fact, ought to have been the nominee that year, and Taft should have gone on the Supreme Court bench, where he really desired to be. Hughes, I think, would have been the nominee if it had not been that he held views regarding participation in politics which most men regard as peculiar. In my judgment nobody but Hughes himself prevented his election to the presidency in 1916 when he was the Republican nominee. The inability of Hughes to 'play the game' was, I think, the main cause of the disaster that began to bear down upon the Republican Party in 1908 and which overwhelmed it in 1912.

Mr. Hughes is a very strong-willed, forceful character. He is a peculiar combination of practicality and idealism, which, working against themselves in him, sometimes defeat each other. He is extremely dogmatic, and, when he has reached a conclusion for himself, is impatient of argument on the other side. He had been selected as the Re-

CHARLES EVANS HUGHES

publican nominee for the governorship in New York in 1906 largely at the instance of President Roosevelt. The administration of Governor Higgins had done nothing to overcome the slant against him which would have beaten him in 1904 but for the popularity of Roosevelt, and it was evident that 1906 was exceptionally promising from the Democratic point of view.

Charles F. Murphy, the new leader of Tammany Hall, apparently took that view of it, for he chose that year to dictate the nomination of William Randolph Hearst as the Democratic candidate against Hughes. It was a red-hot campaign, in which the whole strength of President Roosevelt was exerted to help Hughes. The President went so far as to send Elihu Root, the Secretary of State, to speak at Utica, just before the close of the campaign, and to make the bitter charge that articles printed in the Hearst newspapers had inflamed, to the point of murder, the mind of the anarchist who assassinated President Mc-Kinley. Even with all that the National Administration could do, Hughes was the only man on his ticket who was elected, and Hearst the only Democrat defeated. The indications that it was a Democratic year were well borne out, and it was said among observers of politics that Hearst had been beaten, rather than that Hughes had been elected.

Most men, under such circumstances, would have felt and displayed something of gratitude toward Mr. Roosevelt. Most men would have been willing and glad to take him more or less into their confidence, and to consult with him somewhat regarding party affairs in New York. After all, Roosevelt was a New York man, and had at least the interest of a citizen in his home State. Moreover, New York has the largest vote in the National Electoral College, and political conditions in New York are bound to be of interest and moment to the National Administration, whichever party is in power. And, to the ordinary man, there does not seem to be anything essentially incompatible with righteousness or honor or decency, in a consultation between the Governor of New York and the President of the United States, when they happen to be of the same party, regarding the political situation within the State.

But that was not the Hughes way. He chose to go it very strictly alone, and he let the President know it by unmistakable evidence. Mr. Roosevelt gave an indication of his readiness to bring political pressure to the assistance of Governor Hughes, in one of his contests with the machine, by cutting off the head of a federal office-holder who held his place on the recommendation, and with the support, of the leader who was opposing the Governor. Hughes promptly let the President know that he didn't want that kind of help, and Mr. Roosevelt, just as promptly, backed off, and stayed backed off, as far as any direct aid to Hughes was concerned, to the end of his term in the White House. He did, however, exert his influence strongly in the Republican State Convention of 1908 to have Hughes renominated. He knew that Hughes had made a good record as Governor, and had brought the party into better shape than it had been two years before. Taft had already been named for the presidency, and Roosevelt was eager to have the party make the best possible showing at the election.

The particular peculiarity of the Hughes view manifested itself in his refusal to do himself, or consent to the doing for him by his friends, anything that would help toward getting the Republican presidential nomination. He took the high ground, which most men also take, that the office should seek the man, but unlike most other men he construed that to mean that he should not lift a finger, either directly or indirectly, to bring about the selection of Hughes delegates to the National Convention. He refused to seek the nomination. He was willing to be a candidate for the election, after the party had nominated him. That was what he had done in the case of the governorship.

That is an easily understandable and wholly justifiable position. It is in accord with the highest traditions of American politics. It is the position taken to-day by many men who would be able public officials, and who would render fine service to the State and Nation. But since the general adoption of the primary system for the nomination of candidates such men cannot be induced to run. They balk at seeking the nomination.

Hughes carried his views to a great extreme. The result was that, although it would have been comparatively easy for his friends to capitalize the popular feeling toward him, in the shape of delegates to the National Convention, they were obliged by his course to hold off until it was too late.

It is the general belief throughout the country that President Roosevelt brought about the nomination of Mr. Taft, in 1908, because he preferred to have his Secretary of War succeed him in the White House. But that is not the fact; at least, it is not the whole of the truth. Mr. Roosevelt did prefer Taft under the circumstances. But Hughes could very easily have altered the circumstances so that Roosevelt would have preferred him and would have exerted his influence to secure the nomination of Hughes, just as he did to secure that of Taft.

The fact is that during the fall and winter of 1907–08 Mr. Roosevelt was seeking eagerly for an available man who would carry on the policies to which he was devoted and which had made his administration conspicuous. He had a very large and militantly enthusiastic following, earnestly committed to those policies. Mr. Taft had endorsed them publicly and fervently — too fervently, at times, for the entire satisfaction of the President. Mr. Roosevelt made no secret of his own hesitation regarding the nomination of Mr. Taft. He talked to numerous callers at the White House, who were on terms of intimacy with him with that frank openness which was characteristic where his confidence was given, but which sometimes bordered closely on indiscretion. In such confidences he let it be known that the man he would most like to have succeed him would be Elihu Root, then Secretary of State. He believed then that Root was thoroughly in accord with the policies of his administration, and if elected to the presidency would carry them on loyally and effectively. But he recognized the political unavailability of Mr. Root, and knew it would be useless to endeavor to nominate him. Mr. Root, during his distinguished career at the bar, had won wealth, as well as fame, in the representation of great corporations. In the temper of those times that, in itself, was sufficient to make him unavailable for an elective office. No one knew it better than Mr. Root himself, as he proved when, after six years of conspicuous service as Senator from New York, he refused to run for reëlection, the constitutional amendment providing for direct election of Senators having been put into force.

XI

In the fall of 1907 the Roosevelt wing of the Republican Party, as distinguished from the Old Guard, or the Regulars, was making every effort to induce the President to disregard his election night statement of 1904, and take the nomination himself in 1908. It was plain to everybody that he could have it if he would take it. Men on the other side were just as eager to get him to declare that he intended to stick to his statement.

The newspapers, of course, paid close attention to this situation, and among the Washington correspondents there was no small effort to extract some kind of word from the President that could be construed either as an expression of willingness to run again or as a renewal of his refusal. It was always amusing to be at a White House session of newspaper men with the President in those days, and to see the ingenuity with which the correspondents framed questions, and with which the President evaded them. One afternoon a group of fifteen or twenty correspondents were making the usual effort, and, to their great joy, the President seemed, at last, willing to permit some discussion of the matter. But just as he uttered the sentence that gave most of the crowd the feeling that the next thing would be what most of us were after, a chap who represented one of the smaller Pittsburgh papers, and was consequently mostly interested in purely local news, cut in with:

'Mr. President, has any action been decided on in the Allegheny Bank case?'

Instantly Mr. Roosevelt went into a full discussion of that, and the great chance of the afternoon, for most of us,

was lost. If looks could have killed, it would have been a
dead Pittsburgh man who left the White House that day.
He is still doing newspaper work in Washington, and I
don't believe he has heard the last of the Allegheny Bank
case yet.

I was one of those who wanted Mr. Roosevelt to take
another term, and one afternoon, when I had an opportunity to talk with him alone, I brought the matter up. It
seemed to me that there was no longer any real difference
of principle between the Republican and Democratic
Parties. The essential difference was mostly one of partisanship. The real cleavage of the voters was along the
line between what, for convenience' sake, may be called
liberal and conservative. The Democrats had clearly
swung away from their original constitutional principles,
and the Republicans were not much better.

To my surprise the President discussed the matter most
freely. He began with a reference to the effort that was
going on to get him to renew or disavow his 1904 statement. It disgusted him that the people generally, and the
newspapers particularly, did not at once see and explain
his position.

'They want me to keep repeating myself,' he exclaimed,
'and they don't see that it would make people think I
didn't believe myself. If what I say isn't worth believing
when I say it, what additional value would it have from
being repeated? If I were to repeat that statement this
afternoon, in two weeks the newspapers would all be
clamoring to have me say it again. Then pretty soon I
should have to say it every day, and then nobody would
believe it, and no one would have a right to believe it.'

That struck me as an eminently common-sense view to
take of the thing, and it was so obvious that it was no

wonder the President thought it strange the newspapers, especially those friendly to him, had not seen it.

Mr. Roosevelt went on to say that the demand for something further from him might become so urgent that it would be advisable to make some additional statement. But if he did, he would make it clear that he did not intend to keep on repeating himself, and in any event he would not say anything for some time. It could not possibly do any good to say anything until just before the convention, in any case, and it would be time to determine as to that when the convention was about to meet.

In response to my suggestion that he ought to take the leadership himself the next year, and to endeavor to bring about the realignment of parties which was commonly thought to be due, Mr. Roosevelt was equally prompt and explicit. He said that that suggestion had been made to him many times, and he, of course, recognized the condition in the two parties which led to it. But he did not think the time had come when the proposed realignment was possible. Partisanship was still too strong. The Republican Party was standing as strongly as ever by its policy in the South, and as long as that continued there could be no hope of bringing about a division of the white vote in those States. If the Republican Party could ever be brought to face the negro question in the South fairly and honestly, there would be hope for an attempt at a general reorganization. But just as long as the race question continued to be the dominant factor in Southern politics, there was no chance at all for dividing the white vote there, and that was vital to the success of the proposed plan.

This talk about the negro question did not at the time give me the suggestion that I should have received from it.

My mind was so much taken up with the immediate political question as to the possibility of Roosevelt for 1908,
that the real bearing of what he said that was not directly
on that point did not strike me until long afterward. But
when I sat in the Progressive National Convention, in
Chicago, in August, 1912, and heard him deliver his famous reply to a question from the gallery as to how he
would handle the negro voters, that White House talk of
nearly five years before flashed upon me, and I understood
what he had meant. He tried it in the Progressive Party,
and distinguished Southern men followed him into that
party on that account. They believed with him that it
would be better for both whites and blacks in the South if
two white parties could be built up there, and that in the
building-up of two white parties lies the real hope of the
negro for recognition of his political rights. Many negro
leaders, North and South, came into the Progressive Party
with that belief and solely on that account. So far as I
know, Mr. Roosevelt is the only political leader who has
had the courage and the vision to meet that question
honestly and squarely in the face.

Naturally when the President declared so emphatically
that he would not consider the nomination in 1908 for himself, I wanted to know whom he preferred, and I asked him,
directly. His reply was just as direct.

'I would rather see Elihu Root in the White House than
any other man now possible,' he said. 'I have told several
men recently that I would walk on my hands and knees
from the White House to the Capitol to see Root made
President. But I know it cannot be done. He couldn't be
elected. There is too much opposition to him on account
of his corporation connections.

'But the people don't know Root. I do. I knew him

ELIHU ROOT

when I was Governor of New York, and I have known him here, very intimately, during the years he has been in my Cabinet. The very thing on account of which there is so much objection to him would make him an ideal President. He is a great lawyer. He has always given all that he had to his clients. He has great intelligence, wonderful industry, and complete fidelity to his clients.

'What the people do not understand about him is that if he were President they would be his clients. He would be serving the Nation with absolute singleness of purpose, and with all that intelligence, industry, and fidelity. Nothing would be, or could be, paramount with him to the interests of his clients. I know that, for I have seen him repeatedly take that attitude as a Cabinet officer.

'Root is really for the public programme that you boys call the "Roosevelt policies." If he were to succeed me there would be no question about their being carried out. But it can't be done. In the first place, he couldn't be elected because of the ignorant opposition to him, and in the next place wild horses couldn't drag him into making a public campaign. I have had awful trouble with him to get him to make a few public speeches. He simply would not campaign for himself.'

XII

THIS presentation of Mr. Root as a great lawyer who in the presidency would regard the Nation as his only client, was new and very interesting to me. My opinion had quite coincided with that of the opposition, but it could not be denied that the President had given a keen analysis of Root's character.

Subsequently, at the Republican National Convention in 1912, we saw Mr. Root give an exhibition of fidelity to his clients that bore out, in many particulars, Mr. Roosevelt's analysis. Then Mr. Root was chosen as chairman of the convention for the purpose of preventing the nomination of Roosevelt and obtaining the renomination of Taft. When, on the roll-call for nomination, three distinguished delegates from Massachusetts, who had been elected at the primaries as Roosevelt men, followed Mr. Roosevelt's request and declined to vote, Mr. Root, as chairman of the convention, had the names of their alternates called, and directed the recording of their votes for Taft, despite the fact that the delegates themselves were present and protesting with all their might. How an alternate, with the delegate for whom he is a substitute present in person, can have any right to vote in any convention, it takes a lawyer with the astuteness and fidelity to his clients of Elihu Root to determine. In so strongly celebrating Mr. Root's fidelity to his clients, Mr. Roosevelt had assumed that understanding of the principle of right and wrong, and a willingness to apply it, were included in that fidelity.

After discussing Root, the President talked of the general situation, and the reasons why he was inclined to support

the nomination of Taft. No one had a keener appreciation
than he of the opposition to himself, especially on the part
of what is generally described as 'Wall Street.' The panic
of 1907 was a recent and bitter memory; in fact not yet
wholly a memory. He believed that it had been brought
on by the folly of the very men who were most vigorously
denouncing him for causing it, and he was pretty sharp
about their efforts to shift the responsibility to his shoul-
ders. At the same time he had a lot of fun over the attempt,
already showing its head in several States, to hold the opposition together by means of the 'favorite son' game, with
the idea that if the Old Guard could get enough State
delegations by this means they would get together at the
convention and determine whom to nominate.

His interest, first and last, he said, was in insuring the
permanence of the policies which had marked his administration. His own popularity around the country was
due to the fact that the people believed in those policies.
If his successor would stand straight for them, he, too,
would be popular and there would be every probability of
his reëlection in 1912. If those policies were firmly carried
out for two more administrations, he believed they would
so prove themselves as to be practically beyond successful
attack. He was thoroughly convinced, moreover, that
faithful adherence to those policies for another administration or two would head off the growing trend toward
Socialism in the country.

Of course, none of the favorite sons would admit taking
stock in the Roosevelt policies, despite the fact that he
knew some, at least, of them agreed with him as to a substantial part of the programme he favored. That was particularly true of Senator Knox, who was being brought
forward as the favorite son of Pennsylvania. Taft was the

only man it might be possible to nominate who had declared unreservedly for the Roosevelt policies. Hughes was apparently for most of them, but, at the same time, he seemed to feel that it was necessary for him, in some way, to differentiate himself from them, and to make it clear that he was wholly free from Roosevelt influence. Taft was an able, upright man, a hard worker and a good administrator. He was not a fighter, and the President feared he would have a good deal of trouble with the Old Guard over his legislative programme. But he had courage, as he had shown while on the bench and in the Philippines. If anything, he was inclined to go too far with some parts of the programme. The President seemed to think it not impossible that Taft might develop into almost a radical.

The controlling factor, however, it was clear, was that Taft was the only man who had made himself available, from the Roosevelt point of view, by public endorsement of the Roosevelt policies. Roosevelt's leadership in the Republican Party was undeniable. There was no question that he could have the nomination for himself if he would take it. His supporters all over the country looked insistently to him for guidance as to the make-up of the convention, and he could not avoid that responsibility, even if he had wanted to do so, which he did not.

It was very plain to me, from this talk, that the 1908 situation was still open in the President's mind, and that if Hughes, or any other available man, were to declare publicly for the Roosevelt policies, it would immediately become a close question whether Taft could be nominated or not.

That was the opportunity for Hughes, which he himself rejected. I knew from the talks I had had at Boise the preceding spring that there was a feeling for Hughes in the

Western country that would have made itself emphatically felt very quickly if it had received the least encouragement from Hughes, and probably would have done so without direct encouragement if it had not felt that it was actually repressed. A simple statement by Hughes, a letter to some friend, saying that he would, of course, accept the nomination, if rightly used could have produced the result. But Hughes did not come out. Whether or not he was deliberately playing with the situation, I have never had any means of knowing. But if he was, he played too long. When he finally brought himself to the point of admitting that he was a receptive candidate, it was too late. Mr. Roosevelt was then publicly committed to the nomination of Taft. The organization of the Taft candidacy had made substantial progress with the hearty support of the White House. Roosevelt had to stand or fall by Taft, and the result was a foregone conclusion.

XIII

THE first story I sent to the New York 'Times' after I had been appointed chief of its Washington Bureau was written on material furnished by President Roosevelt, and drew a $500,000 libel suit from William Randolph Hearst. I had been in the bureau for a year and a half, when, in the spring of 1907, Charles Willis Thompson, then the chief, resigned from the 'Times' to take charge of the Washington Bureau of the 'World.' My appointment as chief of the 'Times' Bureau did not come until in the fall, some time after my return from Boise. The afternoon after I received the definite word from Mr. Van Anda which entitled me to sign myself, 'Washington Correspondent of the New York Times,' there was a gathering of newspaper men at the White House for a talk with the President. The word had gone around that the President would see us at four o'clock, and just at that time I reached the executive offices, with two other correspondents who were among those who had ready entrance there, and who enjoyed the confidence of the President.

To our great surprise and dismay we were told by Secretary Loeb that we could not go in. The President had completed his afternoon work a little earlier than he had expected, and had admitted the newspaper men at a quarter of four. Among those who were waiting to see him was Mr. Tighe, one of the Hearst Washington staff. The President barred Tighe from the meeting and gave instructions that no one who came later was to be admitted.

So the three or four of us who came about four o'clock, waited until the 'séance' as such meetings were called, was ended, and then began canvassing the men who had been in the conference for the story. It came to me, in minute detail, from four different friends, one of whom had taken stenographic notes of what the President said. Mr. Roosevelt had opened up on Hearst right at the start, and had declared that in California Hearst was working with Harriman, despite the fact that in his Eastern papers he was constantly assailing Harriman.

There was a lot of detail to the story, but that was the nub of it. I was as sure of my ground as if I had heard every word the President had said, and had not the least hesitation in sending the story to the 'Times.' Of course, no Washington correspondent ever attributes any story directly to the President, even if it is written at his personal instigation, as this one was. No one ever quotes the President, unless there is very specific authorization for it. Consequently all the stories from Washington that night merely used phraseology of one kind or another intended to assure the reader that what was said was based upon the best authority. My story was just like all the others. But it happened that Hearst and the 'Times' were having some kind of a controversy at the time, and Hearst seemed to think it would help his side of the case to bring a whacking suit for libel against the 'Times.'

The first I heard of it was the arrival in Washington of one of the 'Times' lawyers. He was a young man, and the size of the damages demanded by Hearst seemed to have him pretty much what the boys call 'buffaloed.' He certainly impressed me as convinced that the matter was extremely serious, and that we had to have the best preparation of our case possible. I went up to the White House at once and saw the President, who promptly gave permission to bring the lawyer in too. As soon as the lawyer had a chance to say a word, he asked the President if he would be willing to testify at the trial.

Mr. Roosevelt laughed at that, and replied with some instruction in law that seemed to me rather elementary. In the first place, he said, the President never goes into court as a witness, and is not obliged to respond to a subpœna. But he did not base his refusal to testify personally on that ground. He gave it a better legal basis, which was that all his information was only hearsay, so that if he were willing to take the witness stand the lawyers for the other side would object to his testimony and the judge would surely sustain the objection.

Then he went on to say that all his information in the case, and everything he had said at the conference which led to the publication of the story, had come to him from a Californian who was very closely in touch with affairs in that State, and who knew exactly what he was talking about. Mr. Roosevelt said that his informant was then in Washington, and he volunteered to get in touch with him and ask him if he would be willing to see us and give us the facts, as well as any information he could as to how we could substantiate the facts in court.

The lawyer and I went back to the 'Times' Bureau, where we had waited only a few minutes when there was a telephone call from the White House, and I was told that if we would come back there we could see Mr. Roosevelt's informant. Of course, we lost no time at all getting there, and found that the President had been as good as his word. To my surprise I learned that the man who had given him the information was Franklin K. Lane, then a member of the Interstate Commerce Commission. Mr. Lane had been the Democratic candidate for the governorship of California only a few years before, and we soon saw that he had kept extremely well informed as to political doings and developments in that State during all the time that he had been serving on the Interstate Commerce Commission in Washington.

The President made it plain that he was keen to have the 'Times' beat the Hearst suit, if possible, and Mr. Lane readily agreed to give us all the help he could. He and the lawyer left the White House together, and I went on about my regular newspaper work. That afternoon the lawyer came in to see me, very happy about the state of the case, and enthusiastic about the way in which the President had helped. At the same time he admitted he had been fearful that Mr. Roosevelt would not take that attitude. The 'Times' was constantly assailing the President editorially, never losing an opportunity to pound him, and the lawyer thought it would be only natural for Mr. Roosevelt to show some resentment about it. But that wasn't the Roosevelt way. He was a fighting man, and he fought in the open. When he went after the editor of the 'Times,' he did it by putting the editor publicly in the Ananias Club, not by taking technical advantage of his position as President to evade responsibility for a story which he himself had instigated.

The libel suit never came to trial. Whether it was started merely as a bluff, or whether Mr. Hearst, for some other reason, reached the conclusion that it would be better not to force the issue, I never knew.

XIV

THERE was a good deal of talk among politicians in Washington in the fall of 1907 about Hughes, and the newspaper men were constantly confronted by the question why he and Roosevelt didn't get together. There was no public answer. Those who were really on confidential terms at the White House understood the situation pretty well, but their information was such that they could make only the most guarded use of it, and that is far from satisfactory to either side of a news story, the writer or the reader.

The campaign for the nomination of Mr. Taft went along very steadily, and the line-up of an imposing array of favorite sons of different States only furnished amusement to those who were in a position to know even a little of what was actually going on. By the time that the Republican National Committee met in Washington, about the middle of December, to fix the time and place for the National Convention of 1908, it would have taken some vigorous and practical moves on the part of Hughes himself to obtain the nomination, and he was the only man who could possibly have beaten Taft. Hughes could have done it, if he had known how, or had been willing to make the necessary moves.

New York politicians were frequently seen in Washington that fall, and they never had any open reason for coming down. Their stock reply to questions was that they had come 'to pay their respects to the President.' That, of course, was a joke to the Washington correspondents of New York newspapers, and to the political writers of other papers as well. For the average New York 'leader' had almost any feeling but respect for the President. They had found it exceedingly difficult to get him to go their way, and he had a habit, that was very unpleasant to them, of doing and saying pretty much as he pleased. He always listened to their advice, whenever they offered it, and often asked for it of his own accord. Then he decided on his own judgment and forthwith took corresponding action.

One question was particularly puzzling to the New Yorkers that fall. It was as to the proper time at which to give Hughes the New York delegation to the National Convention. It was the plan of the Taft forces, all along, to give Hughes the delegation from his own State. The Taft men were making a point of not contesting with any of the favorite sons in their own States, and Hughes was tacitly admitted to be the favorite son of New York. But they took mighty good care not to let any favorite son get any delegates outside his own State if they could help it. Also they meant as far as possible to keep the States with favorite sons from declaring their preference too early. The Taft men did not want any other candidate to get enough delegates so that by any possibility he might become embarrassing to the Taft campaign. The favorite sons, under the apparent leadership of Senator Murray Crane, of Massachusetts, were doing a lot of amusing maneuvering in the effort to find out if there was not some one of them, or possibly some one else, acceptable to the Old Guard, upon whom they could all unite in the hope of defeating Taft for the nomination. They were well aware of the old political maxim that 'you can't beat somebody with nobody,' but their trouble was that they couldn't find the man.

They didn't like Hughes at all. He was plainly not their kind of man. He was already in a hot fight with the Old Guard in New York, and it was that fact which was mak-

ing him a presidential possibility. If Hughes were to win
the nomination, it was obvious that he would have to get
it from the forces that constituted the bulk of the Roosevelt support, and which were rapidly lining up behind Taft.
To do that Hughes himself had to come out into the open
and play the game the way everybody else played it. He
couldn't sit alone in the Executive Chamber at Albany and
wish the nomination into his lap.

The Taft men understood the Hughes peculiarity, and
played skillful politics with it. They let the word go
around quietly that 'at the proper time' the New York
delegation would declare for Hughes, but they always
meant to keep for themselves the decision as to when that
'proper time' had arrived. Then something entirely unexpected happened that gave them a terrible jump. It
occurred at the regular monthly meeting of the New York
County Republican Committee, in December, and took
the shape of a resolution, offered by one of the few real
Hughes men in the committee, endorsing the Governor for
the presidency.

That was not on the programme for the meeting, and
immediately it threw the Old Guard into some confusion.
They didn't know just what to do about it, except that
they must not permit it to come to a vote. They couldn't
afford either to pass or defeat it. One would put Hughes
into a dangerous position, as far as Taft's nomination was
concerned. The other would be an unnecessary and
trouble-making affront to the Governor.

Herbert Parsons was chairman of the committee at that
time. He solved the difficulty in the good old way by ad-
journing the meeting. Then the whole troupe of Republican leaders throughout the State swarmed down to Washington to try to find out from the White House just where

they were at. I had never seen such a collection of Republican leaders from New York in the capital. They were there from the northern part, the southern tier, the western end, the middle of the State, and from New York City. Greiner, Franchot, Aldridge, Hendricks, Merritt, Barnes, Dunn, and a score or more others, gathered with the Republican Congressional delegation from New York State in the lobby of the Willard Hotel and sat around looking as foolish as two boys caught in a melon-patch. Their only answer to questions as to the purpose of their visit was that they had come down 'to pay their respects to the President.' Plainly they had more respect for him just then than they had had in a long time.

Then, one afternoon, when they were all in consultation at the White House, none of them having been able to propose any practical solution of the matter, William Loeb, secretary to the President, told them how to do it.

'Pass the Hughes resolution,' he said, while the New York leaders gasped and wondered whether they had heard correctly or not. 'Only add another paragraph endorsing the President in the strongest terms you can write.'

Then there *was* excitement. One of the Congressmen, from the southern tier, who told me about it, said that several of those who heard Mr. Loeb's advice jumped up in prompt protest.

'Why don't you see, Billy, what that would do?' one of them exclaimed. 'That would put Hughes on the Roosevelt platform.'

'Yes,' replied Loeb, 'it would if he would get on.'

'But that would nominate him,' cried the New York leader.

'Well, why not?' queried Loeb. 'If he stood on the Roosevelt policies that would be all right. We could elect him, and he'd make a good President. But he won't get on.

They talked it over for some time, and at length decided that Loeb's analysis of Hughes was correct. The Governor felt that he must differentiate himself in some way from the President, and although he was for the principle of the Roosevelt policies he considered it necessary to frame the declaration of them in his own way. He would rather be Hughes than President, and that, of course, is a perfectly understandable attitude. But a great many men in a similar situation would feel entirely confident of being able to be themselves and President as well. Roosevelt had felt that way and had proved his ability to meet the test.

So when the January meeting of the New York County Committee came on, the Old Guard were ready with their amendment to the Hughes resolution. Some inkling of what was brewing had evidently reached the Hughes camp, probably with Old Guard connivance, for just as soon as the resolution came up and the amendment was proposed, the man who had offered it at the December meeting arose and withdrew it. Thus Loeb was proved to have been right in his judgment as to what would occur if his suggestion were adopted. Hughes declined to get on the Roosevelt platform, even though it might mean the presidential nomination.

XV

SOON after this Hughes apparently concluded that the time had come to act for himself, and the word went around that the Governor would accept an invitation to speak before the Republican Club. It was understood immediately that this announcement meant that the Governor was a receptive candidate for the Republican nomination. Those who paid attention to national politics expected the Governor to discuss that field in his address before the Republican Club, and to make a speech that would, in effect, lay down the platform on which he would be willing to run for the presidency. That, surely, was the interpretation which the White House put on the announcement.

The date fixed for the Governor's Republican Club speech was the evening of January 30, 1908. There was a great anticipation among the Hughes men about the effect this speech would have, and there was corresponding anxiety among the Taft men. As the time for the Governor's address drew near, the Washington correspondents learned at the White House that the President was contemplating sending a special message to Congress, dealing with several matters of great importance, especially with the so-called 'money trust' about which Senator La Follette and some others were making a good deal of talk just then. We learned from inquiries at the White House that the message had been completed and delivered to the Press Associations 'under release.' That is, it was given them in confidence for advance distribution to their members, with the understanding that no part of it was to be published until

it had actually been delivered to Congress and read in one
house or the other.

The day for the Governor's Republican Club speech
finally came, and not a word of the President's message
had leaked out. There were all sorts of rumors about it,
but the very few men who really knew anything of its contents kept what they knew very closely to themselves. I
spent a good part of that afternoon in the Senate press
gallery, waiting for the special message. The day wore on
and the Senate droned along on routine and extremely un-
interesting business. There was hardly a paragraph of
news in the whole session, to say nothing of any thrills or
excitement. It got to be after five o'clock, so late in the
day that no afternoon paper in the East could possibly
print any of the message. It was winter and there were no
late sporting editions. The last edition of all the evening
papers in the Eastern time zone had gone to press when the
White House messenger appeared and the Sergeant-at-
Arms of the Senate announced:

'A message from the President of the United States.'

The envelope was received and taken up to the desk.
There it lay for several minutes more, while the Senate
droned on with its routine. Then, about six o'clock, when
several Senators who were not aware of what was going on
had been wondering for some time why they did not adjourn and get home to dinner, the reading of the special
message began. It had not proceeded long before there
were plenty of signs of interest and attention in the Senate.
For that was the celebrated 'Wall Street message' in
which Mr. Roosevelt paid his compliments to his opponents among the 'malefactors of great wealth,' and spoke
of them as 'men with hard faces and soft bodies,' as well as
in other ways which some of them seemed to relish even
less than that.

It was a blistering message, a genuinely sensational news event. Every newspaper in the country carried all it possibly could of that message the next morning, and many of them, even in New York City, found it necessary to curtail the space held for the Governor's Republican Club speech in order to run the message.

Of course, Mr. Roosevelt's opponents promptly accused him of prostituting his high office and the machinery of government in order to play petty and mean politics against Hughes for the benefit of Taft. It was asserted that the message was never meant to accomplish anything more than the blanketing of the Hughes speech in the newspapers. That it did, very thoroughly, and it is a fact that Congress took no action in line with the President's recommendations. But there was nothing especially significant in that. Mr. Roosevelt was in the last year of his presidency. He had driven Congress very hard and aroused much bitter hostility and opposition among its members. There was determination among the leaders in each House to prevent the enactment of any legislation that he particularly recommended, and when, as in this case, his recommendations hit so savagely many of the men who were the closest friends of numerous Senators and Representatives, not even Mr. Roosevelt himself could really have looked for favorable action on them. If it had been the first year of his term, or if he had been willing to take the nomination himself that year, the situation would have been very different. It is not inconceivable that under such circumstances there would have been no such special message.

But in any event that wound up the Hughes candidacy for the Republican nomination. In due time the New York delegation solemnly declared for him, and actually voted

for him on the one ballot taken at the convention. But
that was all. Hughes came out in support of Taft promptly
after the convention, and opened the campaign that fall
with a speech at Youngstown, Ohio, that was one of the
ablest campaign speeches ever delivered. It was a master-
ful and merciless analysis of Bryan, who was making his
third losing campaign as the Democratic nominee. It was
the high-water mark of political effort for Hughes. Nothing he did in his own behalf, when he was the Republican
nominee in 1916, even approached that Youngstown speech
in behalf of Taft.

That fall the New York State Republican Convention,
at the vigorous insistence of President Roosevelt, renominated Hughes for the governorship, and he was re-
elected — this time with his whole ticket — on the same
day that Taft was chosen President. Then, in 1910, President Taft appointed Governor Hughes a member of the
United States Supreme Court, and thus, by eliminating the
most promising possible contender with himself in 1912,
completed the setting of the political stage for the disaster
that ultimately overwhelmed the Republican Party. Most
persons speak of this disaster as occurring in 1912. But
that was only its climax. The preparation had been going
on for several years, and in 1910 the country gave a thoroughly convincing demonstration of what was its own
feeling. It needed only eyes just a little open to see that
demonstration and read its lesson. There were not a few
men who saw it coming. One of them was Mr. Van Anda,
the managing editor of the New York 'Times.'

XVI

WITH his nomination practically assured, Mr. Taft did what few, if any, other candidates have done in a like situation — he had a complete platform drafted in advance for adoption by the convention. Thereby he gave me the opportunity to obtain what was probably the greatest single newspaper 'beat' that it was ever my good fortune to get for any newspaper. I telegraphed that platform in full to the New York 'Times' from Chicago — the convention city — on the Monday night before the convention met. It was printed in the 'Times' on Tuesday morning, about ten hours before the convention assembled.

When I took charge of the Washington Bureau of the 'Times' in the fall of 1907, I had as my chief assistant Mr. Jackson Elliott, who had worked for some years for the Associated Press, and in that capacity had attended several national political conventions. We used to talk about the 1908 convention, and he was very strong in his belief that the only possible 'beat' that could come out of such an occasion, and that was really worth while, would be some part of the platform. Predictions as to the nomination of this or that candidate were always largely in the nature of guesses, and even if events happened to prove them correct they were sure to be quickly forgotten, and never to make any lasting impression even 'on the office' where 'beats' are always likely to be remembered long after they have passed out of the public mind. It has to be something pretty important that a man reads in one newspaper these days, and cannot find in the others, to make him remember it very long.

Elliott's talk about this impressed me a good deal, for I had never worked at a national convention, and that at Chicago was to be my first such experience. But I had had enough of newspaper work to know that if there was any chance of success whatever it would be ruined completely by talking about it. So I said nothing, even to Mr. Elliott, but went ahead with my own plans. I was on very good terms with Senator Borah, who controlled the Republican organization in Idaho. I went to him and told him what was in my mind. I asked him to see that some man capable of doing good reporting was named on the Idaho delegation to the convention. I wanted that man appointed to the Committee on Resolutions, which always writes the platform, and, if possible, named also on the sub-committee which does the actual drafting. If such an arrangement could be made I was sure that from that source I could secure advance and reliable information as to the different planks of the platform. At that time I had no notion whatever of being able to get the whole platform, and was pinning my hopes entirely to this scheme for getting two or three of the most important planks.

But then Mr. Taft concluded to have his platform drafted completely in advance. He got his friends, Wade Ellis, of Ohio, and Senator Chester Long, of Kansas, both experienced platform writers, to work at it. It was no secret among the Washington correspondents what was going on, and I suppose that several of them considered the possibility of getting a copy in advance. I went to Senator Borah and modestly told him that, instead of the scheme I had proposed for actually reporting the proceedings of the committee, I wanted to get a copy of the Taft platform. We had quite a bit of talk about it. It was not so easy as it might sound, for there was hardly any chance

that it would be shown to Borah except under the strictest
confidence, and that a copy of it should come into his possession under such circumstances that he would feel free to
give it to me for publication was well-nigh inconceivable.
However, Borah felt that he wanted to do anything he
could for me in return for the efforts I had put forth the
year before in his behalf, and he agreed to see what could
be done.

We had no further talk about it until we met in Chicago,
on the Sunday before the convention. I had been there
two or three days, watching the work of the National Committee in preparing the temporary roll of delegates, and
trying, through newspaper reports, to keep track of
Borah's whereabouts. He had left Washington, ostensibly
for the convention, but had disappeared somewhere on the
way to Chicago on some very mysterious political errand,
the purpose of which I never did learn.

Some time before noon on Sunday I heard from another
correspondent that Borah was in Chicago. He had quarters at a hotel about two blocks from the one where the
convention crowd gathered. I got there as quickly as I
could, but he was out. Then began that hunt for a man in
a great crowd, the weariness of which every newspaper
man well knows. I did nothing else all that day but run
from hotel to hotel, looking for Borah. I had to be careful
not to make my search for him so obvious that other
newspaper men would notice it, for if I got my 'beat' it
was going to be decidedly important to keep everybody
guessing as to the source of it, and any 'hell hound of the
opposition' who remembered my anxious search for Borah
that day would promptly put two and two together and
get the answer.

It was a quarter past eleven o'clock that Sunday night

when I at length found the Senator and accompanied him
to his room. I didn't know, even then, whether or not he
had been able to get the document, and it was not until we
were in his room, with the door closed, that he relieved my
anxiety. Then he did not tell me in words what he had. He
simply opened a small gripsack that stood on the dresser
and indicated a folded document that lay on top. A minute
later I was hurrying up Michigan Boulevard to the hotel
where the 'Times' staff was quartered. I didn't stop long
enough to read the first word on the first page. It was
twenty minutes past eleven, Chicago time, when I dropped
that document on the desk before Arthur Greaves, city
editor of the 'Times,' who was in charge of the convention
staff. That was twenty minutes past twelve in New York,
and the first edition of the 'Times' was already on the
presses.

'What's this?' demanded Greaves, with a note almost of
resentment in his voice, for I had interrupted him in some
work he was doing.

'The Taft platform,' I replied.

With an exclamation that is not repeatable, he grabbed
up the folded sheets and began to scan them.

'Somebody get a machine,' he called, and two or three
jumped for a typewriter.

In a moment Greaves was dictating the language of the
tariff plank. He finished that and had some one rush it
downstairs to the telegraph office while he turned to the
platform again and picked out one or two more planks.
That was the limit of what we could do for that night.
These planks were printed in the later editions of the
'Times' on Monday morning, with a line or two of introduction stating what they were.

We sat around the hotel rooms for some time after that

discussing what we should and could do with the whole platform. None of the other 'Times' men, not even Greaves, knew where I got it, and none of them asked me. They all knew that it was a matter of the highest confidence. I told Greaves that I wanted to give a copy of it to Dick Lindsay, the Washington correspondent of the Kansas City 'Star' and 'Times.' Greaves naturally wanted to know why, but when I explained he said it was a good thing to do.

It was well known in Washington that Chester Long had been working with Wade Ellis in the preparation of the Taft platform. Mr. Long was also known to be on very friendly terms with the Kansas City 'Times' and 'Star.' Colonel Nelson, the owner of those papers, was a stanch supporter of Senator Long, and Dick Lindsay was one of the closest friends Mr. Long had in Washington. It struck me that if the platform were printed in the Kansas City 'Times,' suspicion would be cast first of all on Senator Long as the source from which the 'Times' got it. That would protect me and my source, for by the time Long got through explaining his own innocence the hue and cry would have died down a good deal, the campaign would be opening up, and there would be a good prospect of getting away without further inquiry.

On Monday there was a lot of buzzing among the newspaper men in Chicago about the planks that we had printed that morning. They were promptly handled by the Associated Press, credited to the New York 'Times,' and sent broadcast over the country. Several of my Washington colleagues asked me directly whether or not I had obtained them, and one of them, the late Sumner Curtis, then Washington correspondent of the Chicago 'Record-Herald,' went farther and wanted to know whether

I had the whole platform or not. I did the best I could to put him off, without a flat and false denial, by telling him, which was the truth, that he had all three parts of Gaul to ask me such a question.

The 'Times' telegraphed us from New York that Mr. Loeb, at the White House, had issued a formal denial of the accuracy of the planks as we had sent them, and that gave us a good laugh. We wondered what he would say when we printed the whole document the next morning.

Sumner Curtis was a good newspaper man. He wasted no time that day trying to get a copy of the platform himself. But he posted his office, and they took advantage of the hour difference in time between New York and Chicago to get it from the 'Times.' They had six wires set up and ready, and the moment their New York men got a copy of the 'Times' — and it was one of the first ones off the press — they started that platform. It took thirty-two minutes to telegraph the whole thing and the 'Record-Herald' printed it in full on Tuesday morning, just as we did in the 'Times.' But they credited it to the New York 'Times,' and we had our 'beat' duly recognized.

There was a lively buzzing about it when the convention met that morning. Mr. Loeb had repeated his denial of the day before, and extended it to cover the whole thing. As I took my seat at the press table in the convention hall, Dick Lindsay passed a note to me warning me to get my 'forgettery' into first-class condition at once, and not to know anything or anybody for some time. He was sure there was going to be 'a big fog' about it.

When the Committee on Resolutions reported the platform the next day, there were only half a dozen alterations in it, and most of them merely the change of a word or two. Nowhere was sense or meaning altered. Mr. Ochs, the owner of the 'Times,' directed that the page of the Tuesday paper on which the platform had been printed should be photographed and the changes made on it in proof-reader's corrections. In that way it was printed in Thursday morning's paper, with the Loeb denials under it. It was a wholly convincing demonstration of the accuracy of the Tuesday publication.

On Tuesday Mr. Greaves had a message from the office asking who had secured the platform, and he replied that I had. I was then under instructions to go to Cincinnati after the convention, and to stay with Mr. Taft until it was time to go to Denver to the Democratic Convention. But the day before the Republican Convention adjourned, I received a message from the office directing me to return to New York from Chicago as soon as the convention was over. So I went back, wondering what was up, and promptly reported at the office. But beyond pleasant congratulations on the 'beat' and a lot of newspaper talk about it, nothing developed, and I was left in a quandary. It was mighty interesting to see how keen they all were in the office to know how it was done, and yet not one of them would ask a question about it. After hanging around a day or two and getting no instructions, I went up into the country over the week-end to be with my family.

When I got back to the office the early part of the following week, Mr. Van Anda said that Mr. Ochs wanted to see me. So I went up to his office. He was alone at his desk. I told him Mr. Van Anda had sent me to see him, and he replied that he wanted to congratulate me on the platform 'beat.' Then he talked pleasantly about it for a moment or two, and I thought that was all. But as I turned to go he picked up a little box that was lying on his desk and said he wanted to give me that as a little indication of the way they felt about it in the office. The box contained a beautiful gold watch, with an inscription saying that it was presented to me by the New York 'Times' 'for services of exceptional merit.'

XVII

In the early part of 1908, William Bayard Hale, who was then on the staff of the New York 'Sunday Times,' came to Washington and spent the best part of a week with President Roosevelt in the executive offices. He saw and heard everything that went on there during that time. Mr. Hale wrote a four-page article about the Roosevelt way of conducting the Nation's business which made a great hit. The success of that article suggested to Mr. William C. Reick, who was, at that time, one of the owners of the 'Times,' the idea of having Hale go to Germany to endeavor to do something of the same kind about the Kaiser. There was a good deal of talk about Mr. Roosevelt being very like the Kaiser in a good many ways, and Mr. Reick thought that if Hale could succeed in getting such an article it would duplicate the hit made by the one about the President.

I had come back from the Democratic Convention at Denver, and was preparing to go to Hot Springs, Virginia, to be with Mr. Taft during the first part of the campaign, when Hale's first report reached the office. It was in the shape of a short letter to Mr. Reick, announcing that he had had an interview with the Kaiser and giving some details of the German Emperor's talk. It was obvious at a glance that nothing of that kind of talk could be printed in any responsible newspaper. It was so extremely provocative that it might very easily lead to war between Germany and England, and any publication of it would be decidedly dangerous.

Mr. Van Anda, the managing editor of the "Times,"

thought that President Roosevelt should be informed at once of what the Kaiser had said to Hale, and Mr. Ochs and Mr. Reick agreed with him. So I was instructed to take Hale's letter down to the President, who was then at Sagamore Hill for the summer. I arranged an appointment by telephone and went out to Oyster Bay. The letter from Hale was written at Bergen, Norway, and dated July 19th. It said:

After many tribulations and much very hard traveling by coasting steamers, I found the Hohenzollern [the Kaiser's yacht] here and was invited aboard last evening. The Emperor talked to me eagerly for nearly two hours. He is exceedingly bitter against England, and full of the yellow peril idea. Among the things he said were: 'England is a traitor to the white man's cause. She will lose her colonies through her treaty with Japan.' The invitation to our fleet [the American battleship fleet, which was then on a cruise around the world] to go to New Zealand and Australia was to serve notice on Britain that those colonies were with the white man and not with a renegade mother country. To his positive knowledge Japan is fomenting insurrection in India. It will break out in about six months. The solution of the Eastern question is about to be made by Germany and the United States. It has been agreed between himself and Mr. Roosevelt to divide the East against itself by becoming the recognized friends of China. In a few months a high Chinese official will visit the United States and Germany and the terms will be made known. They will guarantee the integrity of China and the Open Door. The world now realizes that Russia was fighting the white man's fight — fighting it miserably. Pity *his* battalions could not have had a chance at the Japanese. If Japan be suffered to get control of China, Europe will suffer attack first. He is keeping friends with the Mohammedan world, yes, he is supplying them with rifles — because they are devils in a fight and stand there between the East and the West, where they can break the first force of attack. Japan and America will fight within ten years.

Germany is expecting to fight England, and, in my [Hale's] judgment, the Emperor does not care how quickly. He poured a steady stream of insult upon the English for two hours. He is bitter against the Catholics. Ireland is the worst enemy (I mean Archbishop Ireland) America has. He is (literally) a Jesuit. Watch out for Ireland. He made a victim of Taft at Rome.

Dr. Hale fully understood, of course, the highly provocative and dangerous character of this interview, and that any publication of it would be simply setting a match to powder. He gave merely an outline of it to Mr. Reick, and spent most of that night setting down notes of all the Kaiser had said. It was as important to have a full record of the Kaiser's conversation as it was not to publish it.

Immediately upon mailing his preliminary report to Mr. Reick, as quoted, Hale set out for Berlin to consult with the German Foreign Office. There he met the same man who was Under-Secretary for Foreign Affairs when the Great War came on, Baron von dem Bussche-Haddenhausen, who had been Counsellor of the German Embassy at Washington for several years, and was supposed to be well acquainted with America and American affairs. It was through Baron Bussche that Dr. Hale's interview with the Kaiser had been arranged, but neither of them expected the Emperor to explode a powder magazine as he had done. Writing to Mr. Reick from Berlin on July 24th, Dr. Hale said:

The officials absolutely forbid any publication regarding the audience with the Emperor. They are, in fact, horror-stricken at the idea of what he said to me being repeated, even in private, and declare that the worst results would follow. Dr. Hill [David Jayne Hill, then United States Ambassador at Berlin], to whom I have given a full account of the audience, is of my opinion that the Emperor was perfectly willing to be quoted, but thinks that, apart from the attitude of the officials here, it would be most unwise to repeat his words.

Baron Bussche confirms what His Majesty said with regard to the arrangements progressing between the Emperor and the

President with regard to China. Tang-Shao-yi, the Chinaman now on his way to Washington, is really on that mission. But Bussche declares the treaty would be made impossible, and the largest possible plans upset, by any hint of all this by the 'Times.'

I took these two letters to the President on the morning of August 7th. Mr. Roosevelt received me in his library at Sagamore Hill, and I at once gave the letters to him, with the remark that the editors of the 'Times' thought he ought to see them.

Mr. Roosevelt sat down at his desk and opened the letters. He had hardly more than glanced at the first one when he jumped out of his chair and strode toward me, waving the letter in front of him and exclaiming:

'You must not print this!'

'We have no intention of printing it, Mr. President,' I replied. 'I have brought the letters to you merely for your information, because the editors of the "Times" thought they would interest you and felt that you ought to see them.'

That at once satisfied the President. He sat down at his desk again and finished reading the letters. When the reading was ended, he turned to me and began to talk, first about their contents, then about the Kaiser, and finally about the Emperor and himself. He talked about an hour, referring chiefly to the alleged arrangement between Germany and the United States regarding Far Eastern affairs. He also told me in detail about a Venezuelan incident, to which he ascribed the Kaiser's seeming friendliness to him. When the interview closed, the President said that all he had told me was to be kept strictly confidential between himself and me. I was not at liberty to repeat it even to my superiors in the 'Times' office, with the one exception of the facts about the Venezuelan incident. The

President particularly desired me to explain that incident to Mr. Charles R. Miller, who was then editor-in-chief of the 'Times.' Mr. Roosevelt had noticed some editorials about that incident in the 'Times,' which, he thought, might have been written by Mr. Miller, and he wanted the editor to have the full information.

On my return to New York I went immediately to my room at the hotel and made certain notes of the President's conversation. I also made copies of Hale's two letters to Mr. Reick. Then I went to the 'Times' office and reported to Mr. Van Anda that I had delivered the letters to the President, who returned his hearty thanks to the 'Times' for permitting him to see them. I explained that I was not at liberty to repeat what the President had said about them, except that he felt they should not be printed, with which, of course, Mr. Van Anda agreed.

Then I went up to Mr. Miller's office and gave him the President's message about the Venezuelan incident. Mr. Miller was very much interested, and remarked that this information explained what had always been a puzzle to him.

XVIII

AFTER that I took the earliest opportunity to put my
notes of the President's talk and the copies of the letters
from Dr. Hale in my safety deposit box, where they have
remained most of the time since. At the beginning of our
own war with Germany, in the spring of 1917, several
newspapers made considerable effort to get the story of the
Hale interview. They tried first to get it from Mr. Roosevelt, who referred them to me, with the remark that all he
knew about it had come from me. When the newspaper
men came to me about it, I said that I had had the story as
a member of the staff of the New York 'Times,' and
considered that it belonged to the 'Times.' I called Mr.
Van Anda privately on the telephone and asked him
whether the 'Times' was willing to have me give the story
to other newspapers for publication. I assumed, of course,
that the original letters from Hale to Reick were still in the
possession of the 'Times,' and it could have published
them, at any time, if it so desired. Mr. Van Anda declined
to say, in his telephone conversation with me, whether the
'Times' would oppose my publishing the letters or not. He
simply took a complete 'hands-off' attitude, and I could
not get even an expression of opinion from him as to
whether I had any right to use the letters or not. It seemed
to me that, as a general principle, when a newspaper reporter brings a story into his office and his editors do not
use it, it remains his property, and he is at liberty to use it
thereafter as he sees fit. It is in accordance with that
principle that I have given the letters here. The notes of
the conversation with Mr. Roosevelt were always mine. By

Mr. Roosevelt's express direction they never did belong to the 'Times.'

When the effort by other papers to get the story was made in the spring of 1917, I met Mr. Roosevelt one afternoon, at the Harvard Club, and showed him the notes I had made of his talk at Sagamore when he read the letters. He read the notes with keen interest, and ejaculated, with a laugh:

'By George! I did say that. You have got it right.'

He then gave me his permission to publish the notes, with the request, however, that I should eliminate one sentence. He agreed that he had used that sentence, but he thought then (in 1917) that it would be better not to print it. That was because the sentence referred, not to anything the Kaiser had said to Hale, but to a man who had made a viciously anti-Japanese speech at the Democratic National Convention, and whom Mr. Roosevelt characterized as 'either a lunatic or a liar.'

Following is an exact copy, save for that one sentence, of my notes of the President's talk:

This is the funniest thing I have ever known. That Jack of an Emperor talks just as if what he happens to want is already an accomplished fact. He has been at me for over a year to make this kind of an agreement about China, but every time I have replied, 'That means a treaty, to which the Senate must consent.' It is true the invitation to the fleet to go to New Zealand and Australia was to show England — I cannot say a 'renegade mother country' — that those colonies are white men's country — and that is why the fleet was sent there. This is the first time I have ever heard the name of Tang-Shao-yi. For at least nine months he — that Jack — has been telling me that a distinguished Chinese official was 'on his way' to this country and Germany to settle affairs, but he has never come. I do not know whether this is the man or not, or whether he is really on his way or not. But the policy, as I have always told the Emperor, is ours. It has been our policy for seven or eight years, ever since Hay first enunciated it

I can't believe he talked for publication. He is, of course, very jumpy and nervous, very jumpy, and often does things which seem jumpy. But people say that about me, whereas I never act except upon the most careful deliberation. Then, too, I seem particularly susceptible to being misinterpreted or misunderstood, and when that happens, and the thing doesn't come out as was expected, people are likely to say that I have changed my mind, when I haven't changed it at all, but only others have been mistaken.

They say the Emperor and I are alike, and have a great admiration for each other on that account. I do admire him, very much as I do a grizzly bear. For several years he has been profuse in his expressions of admiration and friendship for me. It goes back to the time when I warned him that I would fight. I never make a bluff, either in public or in private life. I never bluff in politics. When he was going into Venezuela, several years ago, the question with me was what to do about it. I didn't want to repeat Cleveland's bluff, which would be bound to have a bad effect. So I told the Ambassador (Baron von Holleben) that if he took any customs houses there, I should have to take them back. He backed up, then, and the trouble was settled without any difficulty. Ever since then he has been profuse in his expressions toward me.

There will be no war with Japan just as long as we keep our navy built up. It is not necessary for the fleet to stay in the Pacific. It must be brought back to be kept efficient. I can delay matters in negotiation long enough to get the fleet back there if it becomes necessary.

Those are my notes of the interview, exactly as they were written on August 7, 1908. When I showed them to Mr. Roosevelt, in 1917, he suggested with regard to the last sentence, that he had probably said: 'Matters can always be delayed in negotiation,' instead of 'I can always delay matters in negotiation.' He thought he probably had used that phraseology, because, at the time of the interview, he was nearing the end of his presidency, and there was no indication that there would be negotiations of any kind with Japan. Therefore, in speaking of the possibility of delay in negotiating, he was referring to what might occur in a subsequent administration.

In making these notes I purposely minimized the reference to Mr. Roosevelt's objection to printing the Hale letters, because that was obvious, and omitted most of his comment on the Kaiser's indiscretion in talking in such a manner to Mr. Hale. My notes were confined largely to matters of direct interest to the United States, and were skeletonized a great deal.

The President had talked for about an hour, and had gone into detail especially regarding the Venezuelan matter. He told me, for instance, how he had warned Admiral Dewey to be ready for action. Dewey had gone to the Southern training waters for maneuvers, and was in position to strike quickly if the order came. The incident occurred not many months after Mr. Roosevelt had succeeded to the presidency upon the assassination of President McKinley. There was much talk, in certain quarters, to the effect that he was a quarrelsome, danger-ous man, who was not merely liable, but likely, to get the country into war. He knew, of course, of this talk, and was naturally anxious to avoid any action that would seem to give color of justification to it. But what the German Emperor was proposing to do in Venezuela was a far more serious disregard of the Monroe Doctrine than the action of Great Britain which had evoked Mr. Cleveland's famous message to Congress, in December, 1895.

While the German preparations for a move against Venezuela were going on, Baron von Holleben called on the President. Mr. Roosevelt talked the matter over with him, and told the Ambassador very frankly that he did not intend to permit Germany to seize a lodgment in Venezuela. He informed von Holleben that Admiral Dewey, with his fleet, was in position to move very promptly and intimated that, if he were not informed by a certain time that the German plans had been changed, he would order Dewey to Venezuela. He indicated a certain Tuesday as the day on which such orders would be given.

Baron von Holleben did not seem to grasp the seriousness of the situation. At least, he permitted several days to elapse, apparently without communicating to Berlin the import of what the President had said to him. Mr. Roosevelt at length began to feel that Berlin might actually mean to force the issue. So he sent for von Holleben and asked him directly whether or not he had heard anything from Berlin. The Ambassador seemed then for the first time to realize that he was dealing with an extremely important and critical matter. He told the President that he had received no instructions, which was no doubt scrupulously true, and which, also, was probably due to his own failure to report the matter to Berlin.

'In that case,' President Roosevelt said to him, 'I shall not wait until Tuesday, but will send instructions to Dewey on Monday.'

Von Holleben left the White House in a perspiring hurry, and this time he made no delay in cabling to Berlin. Monday morning he was back at the White House all smiles, with instructions from his Government to inform the President that Germany had not the least intention of carrying out any such plan as had been reported to Mr. Roosevelt. From that moment the Venezuelan incident began to fade into insignificance.

When Mr. Roosevelt talked to me that August morning in 1908, he had never met the Kaiser, whom he discussed so freely and likened to a grizzly bear. A little less than two years later, however, when he was on his way home from his hunting trip in Africa, he went to Berlin and was the guest of the Emperor, who had some special army maneuvers conducted for him. During the 1912 campaign I saw Mr. Roosevelt several times at Sagamore Hill, and on one of these occasions he discussed, with great frankness, a number of events of his return from Africa, and gave his impressions of several different courts and monarchs whom he had visited. His talk then about the Kaiser was of particular interest to me because of that previous talk, when I had taken the Hale letters to him.

Mr. Roosevelt was a full man. Whatever any one may think about his politics or political actions, no one will deny that he was a man of extraordinary cultivation, with distinguished attainment in numerous different lines. He was an indefatigable and omnivorous reader, whose remarkable memory caught and held the vast bulk of what he read. He had so developed the habit of concentration on what he read that all sorts of things could go on in the room about him without in the least disturbing him, or distracting his attention from his book or magazine. He was a highly competent judge, therefore, of the cultivation of other men. He was aware, of course, of the many claims to attainment, in different lines, put forward on behalf of the Kaiser. The Emperor was reputed to be an artist of no mean ability; a musician of exceptional talent; a writer of unusual skill. He was said to be a great diplomatist; a qualified historian; remarkably well versed in the literature and poetry of half a dozen languages, and not a bad poet himself. And of course he knew the science of government and the military art. It was a comment on the justification for this many-sided reputation of the Kaiser that I sought from Mr. Roosevelt, and this was his reply:

'I tried him with everything I knew, but the only subject on which I could strike fire was war. He knows military history and technique. He knows armies, and that is all. I couldn't get a spark from him on anything else.'

That was Theodore Roosevelt's final judgment of Emperor William II. It was the opinion of a man thoroughly qualified to make the test, and highly competent to form a judgment. How amply subsequent events have borne it out!

XIX

THE campaign of 1908 materially aggravated the illness which was already affecting the Republican Party. The G.O.P. was seriously stricken, and it is doubtful whether any political doctor, even Mr. Roosevelt himself, could have brought it back to reasonably good health again. One class of Republicans, by whatever name they might be called, regulars, reactionaries, stand-patters, or Old Guard, with their all-absorbing passion for high tariffs and special privilege, regarded the other class, who called themselves 'Progressives,' and whom the Old Guard denounced as 'Radicals,' or 'Insurgents,' with a hatred sharper than they felt toward any group of Democrats. The great ground of Old Guard opposition to Mr. Roosevelt had been his tendency to be 'Progressive.' He had proved to the Old Guard that he was absolutely independent, always his own man, making up his mind for himself and acting on his own decision. It is true he was always ready to confer with them, and was so punctilious about doing so that sometimes the Progressives were inclined to resent the influence that the Old Guard seemed to have with him. But always after such conferences, the decision was his own.

The Progressives had no particular liking for Mr. Taft. They knew him to be a genial, pleasant personality, a lovable man to meet, but they took him as their candidate with a good deal of mental reservation. Not a few of them were frankly suspicious of him, and Mr. Taft did not hesitate to express, in private, an opinion about some of them that was far from commendatory. He had a faculty for saying sharp things, despite his reputation for good nature, and he showed it by describing one of the Progressive Senators as 'so narrow that he can see through a keyhole with both eyes at once without squinting.'

The nomination of Hughes, instead of Taft, would probably have postponed the disaster to the Republican Party for some years if it had not wholly averted it. But it was only a few weeks after the Chicago Convention had adjourned, after naming Taft and Sherman for its ticket, on a platform pledging tariff revision downward, and several measures of Progressive legislation, that it became apparent to close observers that things were not well with the party, and that they were likely to be worse before they were better.

Mr. Taft was immensely popular with the newspaper men in Washington. As Secretary of War he was always a 'good scout.' It was a favorite occupation for the correspondents to 'go Tafting,' and almost every afternoon about four o'clock a large group of them would seek him out in his office. Then there was always a half-hour or so of very pleasant conversation which often furnished a good deal of news. Mr. Taft exerted himself to get, and keep, on good terms with the newspapermen. He talked frankly about affairs in his own department, was much more communicative, as a rule, than other Cabinet officers, and at times would even 'take assignments' for the boys. When they had struck difficulties in other departments, it was by no means unusual to appeal to Mr. Taft, and not infrequently he dug out the desired information. He seemed to accept the argument which the correspondents at Washington are constantly advancing to Government officials, that the Government business is public business, knowledge of which, in all but a few special cases, belongs of right to the public.

WILLIAM HOWARD TAFT

There is sharp differentiation between newspaper work in Washington and elsewhere by reason of this fact, for the correspondents there very rarely are obliged to pry into private, personal affairs. They are dealing most of the time with business that is wholly public, or should be. Of course, diplomatic affairs are in a class by themselves, because that is the habit and rule of all the world, and no one country can break it down, despite Mr. Wilson's passionate plea for 'open covenants, openly arrived at.' The preparation of cases for enforcement of the law must also be closely guarded lest there be premature publication that helps to a miscarriage of justice. But outside of those two classes there is very little Government business about which any Government official has a right to maintain secrecy. Yet a great many officials habitually treat the work that goes over their desks as if it were their own private affair, and seem to resent the simplest inquiry about the most trivial matter.

Mr. Taft's attitude of friendliness and coöperation with the correspondents naturally helped his popularity with them. No man has ever been a candidate for the presidential nomination who had such a great body of voluntary newspaper support as Mr. Taft had. It was a going as well as a coming support, and, many a time, a story that might have been printed has been let alone simply because the correspondent thought it might do Taft some harm. They were just about as quick that way as they were to print the things that would do him good.

I first met Mr. Taft on a sunny Sunday afternoon in June, 1900, when he sailed into Manila Bay on the transport Hancock, as head of the Philippine Commission. The newspaper correspondents out there, and the army and navy officers, were all very anxious about the situation.

The reports from home had given us the impression that the Taft Commission would proceed to install civil government in the Philippines promptly upon its arrival in Manila, and none of us thought the time was ripe for that. Those of us who had been shot at up, down, across, and around the islands for a couple of years, had decided opinions about what ought to be accomplished before civil government was undertaken, and it made us all mighty happy to hear Mr. Taft's first announcement, that Sunday afternoon, that he would not deal with men in arms, and there must be a complete surrender by the Filipinos before he would begin negotiations with them. So my own first impression of Mr. Taft was very pleasant, and that feeling grew with me during the short time that I remained in the Philippines after he arrived. But he had been there only a few days when I was sent up to North China to the Boxer campaign, and the next time I saw him was in Washington, when he was Secretary of War and I was in the New York 'Times' Bureau there.

Gradually I came to be on what I regarded as intimate terms with Mr. Taft. I saw him often about my newspaper work, and he was extremely kindly and helpful. We came to be on the telephone basis, and not infrequently, when I had tried to reach him at night at home, but he was out, he called me up at my office, when he had returned, with a hearty 'Hello, Old Man, what is it?' I was interested to see him get the Republican nomination in 1908, partly because I liked him personally, partly because I regarded him as a strong executive and thought he would make a good President, and largely because I was very heartily for the Roosevelt policies, and he was the only candidate for the nomination who stood on that platform.

In the pre-convention work I took as large a part as I

could, and helped somewhat in the publicity for Taft. I wrote several magazine articles about his record, some of which appeared over more widely known and authoritative signatures than mine, and did what I could in other ways. I wrote one of the campaign 'lives' of Taft, he himself having suggested me as the author to a publisher who wanted to bring out such a book and had applied to him for material. In preparation for this book Mr. Taft let me examine his personal correspondence running over a number of years, and for several weeks I had sixteen or eighteen thick volumes of it in my house. I give all this detail here not for any purpose of self-boosting whatever, but simply because, on account of some things that happened later, it seems to me important to do so.

XX

AFTER Mr. Taft had cleared up his work as Secretary of War, in the summer of 1908, he went to Hot Springs, Virginia, and about the 1st of August I was sent down there by the 'Times' to be with him during that month. A number of other newspaper men were there also, among them Dick Lindsay, the Washington correspondent of the Kansas City 'Star.' Lindsay and I worked together, closely, throughout that campaign. Dick was as keenly interested in the Taft campaign as I was, and he was a mighty good politician. Naturally, we talked the campaign most of the time, and, also naturally, we saw Mr. Taft frequently, several times a day as a rule, and had numerous long discussions of campaign matters with him. Mr. Taft usually played golf at least once a day, and often made two rounds of the course there, morning and afternoon. Lindsay and I frequently played around just ahead of or just behind Mr. Taft and his partners.

Mr. Taft, having been nominated for the presidency, was now the titular leader of the Republican Party, and Mr. Roosevelt retired to Sagamore Hill with the intention and purpose of giving Taft a free swing, without interference in the campaign. There were a number of knotty and troublesome problems to deal with. One of them was the bitter fight on Roosevelt himself. As far as the Old Guard were concerned, they were appeased, on the surface at least, by the nomination of James S. Sherman, one of their high priests, for the vice-presidency. But there was a local row in Ohio that had all sorts of unpleasant possibilities, and Roosevelt had warned Taft repeatedly to keep

entirely clear of that. It would not have been difficult, in
the least, for Taft to develop a bitter fight on himself in his
own State. He had been on the edge of it in 1905, when he
spoke at Akron on behalf of Governor Myron T. Herrick,
who was running for reëlection, and assailed the régime of
George B. Coxe in Cincinnati. That had its influence in the
defeat of Herrick that year, but it had been largely smoothed
over by 1908, although it would have been easy to revive.

The chief trouble in Ohio was made by Senator Foraker,
who was violently against Roosevelt. Foraker had taken
up the President's dismissal of a battalion of the Twenty-
Fourth regular infantry, on account of the Brownsville,
Texas, affair, and was doing the best he could to excite the
negroes all over the country against Roosevelt. But despite the fact that Foraker, and his colleague, Senator
Dick, as inheritors of the old Hanna machine in Ohio, had
control of the regular organization, the organization set up
by Mr. Roosevelt's friends in behalf of Taft had been able
to take most of the Ohio delegates to the Chicago Convention away from Foraker and give them to Taft.

With two or three situations like that scattered about
the country, it was an anxious time for an astute politician
like Roosevelt at which to turn over the leadership of the
party to Mr. Taft. For Mr. Taft, although one of the most
lovable men ever in American public life, has absolutely no
genius for politics whatever. His bump of politics is a deep
hole. The political sense was just left out of his make-up.
His is an easy-going good nature that takes much for
granted, and is slow to suspect the machinations of the
wily. The most obvious political moves pass right under
his nose unnoticed. For instance, Frank Hitchcock, the
chairman of the Republican National Committee, who was
in charge of the campaign, called a meeting of State Chair-

men and National Committeemen from the inter-mountain States at Colorado Springs soon after the convention. They interrupted business for a trip to the top of Pike's Peak, and from the mountain-top telegraph office Hitchcock sent a message to Taft saying:

'We are on top and intend to stay there.'

'Humph!' said Mr. Taft, when he read it. 'What does he send me a message like that for?' And he tossed it into his waste-basket.

But one of his newspaper friends who happened to be in his office just then said:

'Why, Mr. Secretary, that's only a publicity stunt. Hitchcock expects you to answer with a message expressing confidence in your election. That message he will give out and every newspaper in the country will print it.'

'Oh,' replied Mr. Taft, 'I see.'

Then he dug the Hitchcock telegram out of the waste-basket and sent the kind of reply his friend had indicated, with exactly the result that had been predicted.

Mr. Taft had hardly gone to Hot Springs when there began to be signs of trouble. There was a row in the making between the Old Guard and Chairman Hitchcock, and the Old Guard had placed a representative with Mr. Taft, who was completely in his confidence, and who saw and commented on most, if not all, of Mr. Hitchcock's personal communications with his candidate. The Old Guard, under the leadership of Senator Crane, of Massachusetts, was carrying on a steady subsoiling campaign to undermine Hitchcock with Taft, but thus far had not done much more than make underhand trouble. Things at length got to such a pass, however, that Mr. Hitchcock found it important to go down to Hot Springs and have a frank talk with Mr. Taft about the situation. He took with him a young newspaper man who had been closely associated with him in the pre-convention campaign, which he had managed for Taft, and when he left Hot Springs this representative remained there to keep close watch on the activities of the other crowd. Mr. Taft gave out a statement, in which he praised very highly the management of his campaign by Mr. Hitchcock, and expressed the highest and most complete satisfaction with the chairman of the National Committee. Then Hitchcock went to Chicago to complete the organization of Western headquarters, and the subsoiling at Hot Springs continued, but under considerably less advantageous conditions than before.

XXI

Lindsay and I had not been long at Hot Springs before we began to feel that the leadership which Mr. Roosevelt had turned over to Mr. Taft was not being exercised to anything like its fullest possibilities. Bryan, who had been nominated for the third time at the Denver Convention, was stirring up the Western country with a whirlwind campaign, but no response to him was coming from the Republican candidate. Lindsay and I spoke to Mr. Taft about it several times, without getting any satisfactory response. At length we began rather strongly to urge a definite line of action. But Mr. Taft only laughed, and went on playing golf.

We thought it was time for him to begin making his personal preparations for the speaking campaign that he kept saying he intended to make, and that it was the general expectation he would make. Both of us knew, and liked, the Roosevelt method of preparing speeches sufficiently ahead of time to permit their distribution in full by mail to all newspapers before the date of public delivery. No press association will, or can, carry a political speech, except one of the greatest importance, in full by wire. But many newspapers, especially those supporting a candidate, will print his speeches very fully, if not entire, when they can get them by mail in time to have them set up and in type when they are delivered.

So Lindsay and I kept at Mr. Taft to prepare some speeches. He countered by asking us what we wanted him to say. We pointed out several issues that he might well discuss, and he replied that he had handled them all in his speech of acceptance. But that speech had been so long, and had gone into detail on so many issues, that no one but newspaper men, and the most active politicians, would ever read it. For any purpose, except to make a record, it was practically useless, and, so far as campaign effectiveness was concerned, might just about as well not have been delivered. So when Mr. Taft said he had done, in his Cincinnati speech, all we were asking him to do, Dick and I took that speech and spent most of one night going over it very carefully, and separating it into various parts, each one of which would make a subject for an admirable campaign speech by itself.

With this analysis all prepared, I went to see Mr. Taft when he got back from his round of golf the next morning. He was lying on a sofa in his sitting-room, and greeted me with the customary demand to know what I wanted. I said it was the same old subject, and he replied, as before, that he had done it in his acceptance speech.

Then I produced the analysis of that speech which Lindsay and I had made the night before, and I pointed out how many good campaign speeches there were in it. I said the acceptance speech, by itself, was too long for good campaign effect, and that each of the speeches we had outlined, being shorter and confined to a single issue, would have much better effect. Mr. Taft heard me, all through, good-naturedly. Then he got up from the sofa and came over to the chair where I was sitting.

'That's a long, hard work,' he said.

Lindsay's feeling about that answer was expressed unprintably, and mine did not differ. We both felt that we had received an accurate line on the character the campaign would take, and it was decidedly depressing. But we made another effort to get something like vigor injected into the candidate and the campaign. We pointed out that, having accepted the nomination for the presidency, he had obligated himself to make a fight for it on behalf of the party, whether he wanted to do so on his own account or not. He might be willing to subordinate his personal interests, but he had no right to subordinate the interests of the party, or its members. We put that argument up as hard as we could to several of Mr. Taft's close friends who were there at Hot Springs, for transmission to him, in the hope that he would consider it more seriously if it came from them than if it were merely the suggestion of some of his newspaper friends. I went over this argument, myself, with John Hays Hammond, who promised to use it, as his own, with Mr. Taft. He told me, afterward, that he had done so with all the vigor he could command. But it did no good, and the campaign continued to be marked by list-lessness, except for Mr. Hughes's speeches, until Mr. Roosevelt was, at length, forced to take a part in it.

The depression which Mr. Taft's apparent indifference caused both Lindsay and me was aggravated by a certain kind of indiscreet talk that began, about that time, to be heard occasionally in the corridors of the hotel where the Taft family were stopping. It was talk gratuitously critical of Mr. Roosevelt, and it seemed to proceed from, if not to originate with, those very close to Mr. Taft.

We began to feel then, what afterward came to be con-siderably clearer, that there was a certain resentment against Mr. Roosevelt among members of Mr. Taft's family. It had long been understood that Mr. Taft himself really preferred appointment to the Supreme Court in-stead of the presidency. He was admirably qualified for that post, and it may be that he had some personal reservation as to his own success in case he should be elected President. His ambition for the bench was widely known, and the question of his choice was so much in his own mind that he had endeavored to obtain Mr. Roosevelt's specific advice on that point. I myself was responsible for the publication that summer of two long letters, one from Mr. Taft to Mr. Roosevelt seeking this advice, and the other from Mr. Roosevelt to Mr. Taft declining to give it. Mr. Roosevelt summed up all the advantages and disadvantages on both sides, and having, very clearly, stated the case, said that it was one in which Mr. Taft must make the decision for himself — that no man could make it for him.

It has always been my feeling that the presidential ambition was much more a family matter than a personal one with Mr. Taft, and that family influence was the factor which determined him to make the race for the presidency instead of taking the place on the Supreme Court to which President Roosevelt stood ready to appoint him.

Then, when he had set out to get the Republican nomination for the presidency, Mr. Taft and his family found, I believe, to the chagrin of the family, if not of Mr. Taft himself, that the great public popularity of which the family were so convinced was not of the kind that demands a presidential candidacy for its favorite, and produces delegates at a national political convention. It was not of the kind that had been displayed toward Hughes in the talks I had had with men from the inter-mountain and coast States at Boise the year before.

Under those circumstances it became necessary to take effective measures to secure Taft delegates at the Republican Convention. And there Mr. Roosevelt did yeoman service to Taft. But that very service, it has always seemed to me, increased the feeling of the members of the Taft family to which I have referred. They resented the failure of Mr. Taft's personal popularity to produce delegates. They naturally wanted the nomination to come to him for his own sake, and not for that of Mr. Roosevelt or of anybody else. And when they saw it requiring the very strenuous efforts of the Administration and Mr. Roosevelt to obtain the necessary Taft delegates, their disappointment took the form, that is not infrequently observed in human affairs, of a resentment which subsequently came pretty close to being ingratitude toward Mr. Roosevelt.

That is my understanding of the causes of the so-called 'break' between Roosevelt and Taft, which subsequently led to the disruption of the Republican Party, its smashing defeat in 1912, and the election of Woodrow Wilson to the presidency, with all that that involved for this country.

XXII

ABOUT the 1st of September Mr. Taft left Hot Springs and
went up to Middle Bass Island in Lake Erie for a little more
rest before he began the strenuous labor of his speaking
campaign. Two things which occurred while he was at
Middle Bass illustrate his extraordinary lack of political
intuition. At that time there was a good deal of question
as to the attitude of organized labor toward Mr. Taft. His
decision in the famous Addystone Pipe case had been used
against him very vigorously, and it had attracted no little
attention among organized labor leaders. A big labor
parade had been organized for Labor Day at Sandusky.
Two friends of Mr. Taft in Ohio, General J. Warren Keifer
and General Henry C. Corbin, two as fine political dodo
birds as ever lived, neither of whom had any connection
with organized labor, took it upon themselves to invite Mr.
Taft, as the Republican candidate, to go down to Sandusky
and review that parade. Apparently Mr. Taft never asked
either of them what authority they had to issue such an
invitation. No such question seems ever to have occurred
to him. He merely accepted the invitation without
examining it, and announcement of his acceptance was
issued by his publicity service at Middle Bass.

That filled the labor leaders with amazement. They
promptly got together and formally resolved that Mr. Taft
was not invited to review their parade and would not be
permitted to do so. They did not even take the trouble to
be polite about it. They indicated with unmistakable
plainness that they thought Mr. Taft was 'butting in' to

their affair, and they notified the newspapers that he was
to be kept out.

Of course the result was extremely unpleasant for all
those interested in bringing about the election of Mr. Taft.
It was a slap in the face from organized labor, just at a
time when the Republican managers were making every
effort to secure some measure of Taft support from that
quarter. It made their task all the more difficult, and the
fact that it had all been a wholly gratuitous and unnecessary performance added to their vexation.

The other incident was somewhat similar. Senator
Foraker had an engagement to address a Grand Army
meeting at Fort Meigs. Mr. Roosevelt had repeatedly and
most earnestly warned Mr. Taft to keep absolutely clear
of any entanglement in the row between himself and
Foraker, and thus far Taft had done so. But again Corbin
and Keifer bobbed up with an invitation to Taft to go
to Fort Meigs and speak from the same platform with
Foraker. Both were honestly friendly to Taft, but the
trouble was that neither of them seemed to have any more
political sense than Taft had. This time there did seem to
be a little more color of authority for their invitation, for
both were Grand Army men.

There was a lot of curiosity among the newspaper men
at Middle Bass as to what Mr. Taft would do about this
invitation. The decision hung fire for some time, but they
had grown accustomed to that kind of delay and did not
attach much importance to it. One morning Mr. Taft
strolled over from his cottage to that where the newspaper
men were staying, and remarked, casually:

'Well, boys, we're going to Fort Meigs to-morrow.'

Some little discussion followed, confined by the correspondents to questions of detail as to transportation and

time, and that kind of thing. Then Mr. Taft turned and started back toward his own cottage.

When he had gone a few yards, George Hill, of the Washington Bureau of the New York 'Tribune,' slipped off the porch where the newspaper men had been sitting, and followed him. Hill was very much concerned about the Fort Meigs business. He was genuinely attached to Mr. Taft's cause, and he sensed all kinds of trouble if Taft should really appear at that meeting with Foraker. When he caught up with Mr. Taft he said:

'Mr. Secretary, I was in hopes you were not going to Fort Meigs.'

'Why, George,' said Mr. Taft, 'what's the matter?'

'Well,' replied Hill, 'you know Foraker is going to be there.'

'Yes,' responded Mr. Taft, 'that's why I am going.'

'Oh,' said Hill, very much relieved, 'then you know what Foraker is going to say.'

'Why, no,' replied Mr. Taft, 'I don't know anything about it.'

Instantly Hill was filled with consternation. 'Well, suppose he sails into the President,' he said. 'With you right there on the same platform you will have to defend Mr. Roosevelt, and the fat will all be in the fire.'

Mr. Taft paused a moment in his walk and stood looking down at Hill quizzically. He took off his cap and scratched the top of his head.

'George,' he said, 'go back and tell the boys I am not going to Fort Meigs, after all.'

Apparently Hill's suggestion of the perfectly obvious outcome of a meeting of Taft and Foraker on the same platform was the first thing that had ever brought it into Mr. Taft's consciousness. His bump of politics is surely a deep hole.

Meanwhile, with things like this going on, and the efforts of the Old Guard to make trouble between Taft and Chairman Hitchcock continuing unabated, Bryan was keeping up his whirlwind campaign, and meeting with the old-time enthusiasm on the part of his audiences. Of course there was nothing like the cause for alarm in those enthusiastic meetings that there had been when they first occurred in the campaign of 1896, and the fact that cheers do not necessarily mean votes had long been an established maxim of politics. But there was more than enough to cause uneasiness among the real leaders of the Republican campaign, and signs were not lacking that Mr. Roosevelt, at Sagamore Hill, was becoming rather fidgety about the situation.

Those indications received vigorous Rooseveltian confirmation when the President took a direct, personal hand in the campaign through the medium of a challenge to Bryan. His open letter examining the Bryan position instantly injected life into the Republican campaign and promptly put it on a fighting basis where nothing that Taft then seemed likely to do gave any promise of putting it. But this resurgence of Mr. Roosevelt into the campaign certainly did not tend to diminish the resentment against him among members of the Taft family. It was added evidence to them that Mr. Taft not only could not get the nomination for himself, but needed the Roosevelt help to secure the election after being nominated.

By this time, I believe, the feeling involved Mr. Taft himself, to some extent. Moreover, I think it grew on him during the campaign. Of course, long before election day it had become quite clear, to close observers, that Bryan was not really arousing any great measure of support by his whirlwinding. Taft was known to be gaining everywhere. The Hughes speeches were powerful factors in this, with their keen and merciless analysis of Bryan's position and arguments. Mr. Taft also helped himself somewhat, especially in the Progressive Western States, by his forceful repetition of his endorsement of the Roosevelt policies. His declaration in a speech at Omaha in favor of legislation that would control the issue of railroad securities, so as to prevent a repetition of such a thing as the Alton scandal, was especially helpful to him then, although, subsequently, it became a matter of extreme embarrassment to him, when, as President, he accepted a plan that was very far from measuring up to his Omaha promise.

In the second week of October I reported to the New York 'Times' that Taft was certain of election. I had then traveled extensively throughout the Middle West, and had done nothing for several weeks but talk politics and the situation with every man and woman whom I could get into conversation on the subject anywhere. I had made a particular point of talking with local managers of the Democratic side, and it was plain to me, despite all their efforts to hide their real feeling, that they foresaw the outcome. One of them, the State Chairman in Ohio, was especially amusing. I used to drop into Columbus every once in a while just for the fun of hearing him say:

'I tell you we're going to carry Ohio for Bryan.'

He always wound up our talk with that statement. He never could make it at the beginning. He always had to work himself up to it, and when it did come, it was always in a shout. He simply could not utter those words in a low voice. He had to have a full head of steam to get them out.

The morning of election day, 1908, we printed in the 'Times' a table of States that Taft would carry. With one exception it was completely accurate. I had not been personally in Colorado since immediately after the Democratic Convention, and so did not have real first-hand information. But a number of reports had come to me from that State which indicated that it was safe for Taft, and so I included it in my Republican column. But it went for Bryan. Our statement gave Taft 331 electoral votes. He actually received 325.

Mr. Taft received the election returns at the home of his brother Charles in Cincinnati. Long before midnight he knew that he had been elected. Coincidentally with the receipt of that information occurred, in my judgment, the break between him and Roosevelt. For that was the exact moment when he learned that he was no longer dependent upon the President, and from that instant he felt himself free to go his own way as he pleased. He had made the campaign for nomination and election on the Roosevelt policies. Now he proceeded at once to differentiate himself, in numerous ways, from Mr. Roosevelt. It was not long before the very large Roosevelt following throughout the country, which had made Mr. Taft's election to the presidency possible, began to feel the new development, and we began to hear talk about the possibility of a break between the two men. Most persons even yet talk of that break as having occurred much later than the fall of 1908. There are even those who think that it did not occur until the announcement by Mr. Roosevelt, in February, 1912, of his own candidacy for the Republican nomination of that year.

But it is my belief that it occurred, as I have said, on the night of Mr. Taft's election, and at the very moment when he received the definite news that he had won. Subsequent developments were only details.

XXIII

Soon after I returned to Washington, following the election of 1908, a newspaper story 'broke' that became of very great importance to me. During the campaign the New York 'World' and the Indianapolis 'News' had attacked Mr. Roosevelt on account of the purchase of the Panama Canal property from the French company. Both papers intimated that Mr. Roosevelt had manipulated the purchase in such a way as to permit his brother-in-law, Douglas Robinson, and Mr. Taft's brother, Charles P. Taft, to make a lot of money by speculating in the stock. Mr. Roosevelt not only vigorously denied this yarn and reëlected its authors to front-rank membership in the Ananias Club; he promptly undertook to have both newspapers and their editors prosecuted for criminal libel.

As usual where Mr. Roosevelt was involved under any such circumstances, there was a hot controversy. The opposition to him was becoming noticeably more bitter, as the end of his term in the White House approached, and in Congress there was pretty nearly flat refusal even to undertake any legislation that he specially recommended. While this controversy over the Canal purchase was running strong, I picked up a copy of the Washington 'Post' one morning at my breakfast, and read on its first page a letter from the President to his old friend William Dudley Foulke, of Richmond, Indiana, in which Mr. Roosevelt bitterly denounced the slander against himself. Among other things he said that all the papers in the case were on file, in one or other of the Government departments, and were open to the examination of any reputable citizen. I put down the newspaper, went to the telephone, and called up the White House. I got Rudolph Forster, the Executive Secretary, and said that I saw by the 'Post' that all the Canal papers were open to any reputable citizen.

'They are,' replied Mr. Forster.

'Well,' said I, 'I am a reputable citizen, and I want to see 'em.'

'Come right down and take a look,' was Forster's response, and, as soon as I had finished my breakfast, I started. I stopped at my office on the way, and told Reginald Schroeder what was in my mind. He was the Washington correspondent of the New York 'Staats-Zeitung,' and had office room with me. We talked the matter over a little, and then went up to the offices of the Canal Commission. Neither of us had any idea what we were going to look for, but both of us thought there ought to be something among the Canal papers that would give a line on the question of whether or not the purchase had been conducted in such a way as to enable, or permit, any speculation in the stock.

The officials at the Canal Commission received us with the cordiality of an iceberg, and were not in the least disposed to show us any of the Canal papers, not to mention all of them. I showed my copy of the 'Post,' with the President's letter, and suggested that we were there with Mr. Roosevelt's sanction, and it might be just as well if some signs of coöperation were exhibited. But the Commission official to whom we were talking did not seem in the least impressed by that. Then Schroeder suggested that he call up the White House and make an inquiry there on his own account. The Commission official, after cogitating that suggestion for a moment or two, apparently concluded it could do him no harm, and decided to act on it. Half a minute's conversation with the White House produced the most remarkable change in that man's manner that I ever saw in any one. He was courtesy's own sweet self when he came back to Schroeder and me, and was profuse in his offers of every kind of coöperation. It made me think the President must have spoken personally to him.

Naturally this official wanted to know what papers Schroeder and I wanted. Just as naturally we didn't know. Then the official remarked, casually, that there were four or five carloads of Canal papers, and it seemed likely that it would require some time for us to examine them all. That struck me as quite probable. Schroeder and I retired gracefully to talk it over and see if we couldn't reach a conclusion as to just what we did want.

We decided, at length, that there must have been a record of the meeting of the French Panama Canal Company at which the stock vote was taken authorizing the sale to the United States. We thought that the minutes of that meeting would include a record of the stock vote, from which we could get the list of stockholders who voted, and, although we realized that such a list might have been filled with dummies, still it did seem as if that paper would put us on the track where we could, at least, make a beginning of following the trail of any such collusion and speculation as the 'World' and Indianapolis 'News' alleged.

We returned to the Canal Commission offices and demanded the minutes of the stock vote by which the transfer to the United States was authorized. None of the Commission officials seemed to think there was anything unusual or wrong with that idea. They said they would start a search at once and see if they could find the paper.

We sat around for a while and watched them examining indices and card files, but without result. Then we concluded to go back to the office while they made further search. Also we had not detected any sign, yet, that any of the other correspondents was taking up the President's challenge for an examination of the Canal papers, and we began to suspect and hope that we might score a 'beat' out of it. If there was any prospect of that, we certainly did not want to attract any newspaper man's attention to ourselves by hanging around the Canal Commission offices. Correspondents were in and out there all day, but just as soon as any one of them stayed on unduly it would be bound to arouse the suspicion of his competitors.

We had hardly reached the office when I had a telephone call from the White House. Mr. Loeb told me that the President wanted to know how I was getting on. It was evident that he was interested.

After luncheon Schroeder and I went up to the Commission offices again, but found that no progress had been made in the search for that particular paper. I called the White House' on the telephone and told Mr. Loeb the state of the case. The Commission officials had satisfied themselves that they did not have the paper in their files. If it was in United States possession, it was in some other department. Mr. Loeb told me to come over to the White House, and as soon as I got there he sent me into the President's office.

Mr. Roosevelt at once demanded a report of progress, and was obviously disappointed when I told him that I had not been able to find what I wanted. He asked what paper I was after and when I told him, he called in Mr. Loeb and dictated this letter to General Luke Wright, who had succeeded Mr. Taft as Secretary of War:

THE WHITE HOUSE
December 7, 1908

TO THE SECRETARY OF WAR:

Mr. O. K. Davis, of the New York 'Times,' a thoroughly reputable correspondent, is looking into the papers connected with the purchase of the Panama Canal. He will, of course, have access to all papers. He has not been able to find at the War Department one paper, which, he says, he especially desires to have, namely: the minutes of the final meeting of the stockholders of the new Panama Canal Company, held in Paris, April 23, 1904. I, of course, have no knowledge whether any such paper was ever forwarded to us; but will you have the files examined, both in the War Department and at Panama? If any such paper is in existence, give it to Mr. Davis. If it is not in existence, find out if it has ever been received by any representative of the United States Government, and if so, what has become of it. Will you ask if this is in any of the public documents, or whether it is in the Department of Justice or of State?

THEODORE ROOSEVELT

I took that letter over to the War Department and gave it to General Wright, whom I had known ever since he went out to Manila with Mr. Taft in the summer of 1900. He read it through and glanced up at me with a little whistle.

'That's a tall order,' he said. 'The President seems to want you to have that paper.'

'Well,' I replied, 'it seems to me that from that, or some such paper, we are going to get on the track of any possible speculation in the new Panama Canal Company stock, because the men who held it when that vote was taken, by that vote accepted a price that had been fixed by Congress. That was a public price, and I don't see how there could have been any possible speculation after that.'

The Secretary agreed that that seemed logical, and in a few minutes, when I had told him of the hunt in the Canal Commission offices, he had a message on its way to Panama, and an inquiry to the Departments of State and Justice. There was nothing more I could do about it that day, and so I went about my regular work. But before dinner-time I had another telephone call from the White House. The President wanted to know how matters stood.

That was on a Monday. On Tuesday morning Schroeder and I made an early call at the War Department. By the middle of the forenoon, General Wright had a reply from Panama to the effect that the paper was not there, and the State and Justice Departments reported that neither had ever had it. I had had two or three telephone calls from the White House asking how I was getting on, and it was evident that none of the other correspondents was on the trail. But there was no telling how soon they would scent something doing, and it was important for Schroeder and me to get our story on the wires as promptly as possible if we were to score a 'beat' on it.

When I heard from General Wright that he could not get any trace of the paper, I went to the White House and reported personally to the President. He was very keenly interested, and asked me if there was anything else I could suggest. I said that Senator Knox, who was Attorney-General when the Canal purchase was made, might know something about it. Instantly Mr. Roosevelt summoned Secretary Loeb and directed him to call Senator Knox on the telephone and ask him to come down to the White House. The President told me to be there when the Senator came. It was about three o'clock when Senator Knox came into the President's office. Immediately Mr. Roosevelt asked him what he remembered about the Canal purchase, and particularly whether or not our Government had ever received such a paper as the one I had been seeking.

The Senator laughed. 'No, Mr. President,' he said, 'of course, we did not receive such a paper. That was the one paper we were never entitled to, because it was the authority for the transfer of the property of the New Panama Canal Company to the United States. I don't know where it is, but I assume that it is in the archives of the company, somewhere in France, like as not in Paris.'

Mr. Knox went on to say that he had personally examined the title to the property this country purchased and all the papers connected with the transaction. He knew it was all right, and he scoffed at the idea that any speculation had been possible.

The President then asked him to write out an exact statement of just what had taken place, so that I could have it for the story which I was to send to the 'Times' that evening. Mr. Knox immediately dictated a brief statement covering the whole transfer of title from the French Company to the United States, and went back to the Senate.

Then President Roosevelt asked me if I could think of anything else that might be done. I suggested that our Embassy in Paris might help the 'Times' correspondent there to find the paper. Immediately the President dictated a cable to Henry White, our Ambassador to France, directing him to help the 'Times' man there in every way to get at that paper. The President thought, as I did, that we had held off the story as long as it was safe to do so, from the point of view of a possible 'beat' and gave his consent to my writing what I had that night. The next morning the 'Times' had a story, about three columns long, giving in detail the President's explanation of his action in the Canal purchase, and recounting the efforts I had made to get at the documents in the case and the 'sky limit' order for assistance which Mr. Roosevelt had given me.

XXIV

ONE part of this story was extremely pleasing to the President. I pointed out that Congress had sent a commission to Panama, which had appraised the French property there and had reported back to Congress with a recommendation that this Government should offer $40,000,000 for it. The French Company was still trying to interest the United States in the purchase on a basis of something over a hundred million. I said in my story to the 'Times' that when Congress voted to offer $40,000,000 for the property, that act forever fixed the price, and accordingly the value of the stock of the French Company. Thereafter there was no possibility of fluctuation in the value of that stock, and consequently no possibility of any speculation in it. Moreover, Congress, having fixed the price, had then directed the President to purchase the property for that price. It had given him no discretion whatever as to the amount to be paid. In carrying out that direction of Congress, it made absolutely no difference to the President who got the forty millions, or any part of it, so long as the United States got the property, with a clean, straight title to it. It was nothing to the President whether Frenchmen, Patagonians, or heathen Chinese received the American cash.

Schroeder and I scored our 'beat,' and it was a real one. His paper being printed in German did not compete with mine, and we could both use the same story at once. But other correspondents, who had not followed the lead given by Mr. Roosevelt's letter to Mr. Foulke, heard from their offices unpleasantly about it. The managing editor of the

New York 'Tribune,' whose owner, Whitelaw Reid, was then our Ambassador at London, was so much exercised about it that he reorganized his Washington Bureau. He felt that, with Mr. Reid's relations with the President what they were, there was no excuse for the 'Tribune' being beaten on a story like that, which was really a personal explanation by Mr. Roosevelt.

The publication of the story in the 'Times' had a decided effect on the controversy, and little more was heard of the charge that the President had permitted, or helped, relatives and friends to make money out of the Canal purchase. Incidentally it helped my relations with the White House so much that within the next twelve days I had nine stories from the President, all 'beats' of more or less importance. One of them was a story about Venezuela that I had tried in vain to get out of the State Department. When I asked the President to get it for me, he said:

'I hate to do that, O. K.; Elihu always makes such a row with me when I go after the facts about anything he is handling, especially if subsequently any of those facts happen to find their way into the newspapers.'

But he got the story, and gave it to me with a laugh, asking how the 'running debate' was getting on. By that he meant the 'debate,' as he described it, between the stories he was giving me for publication in the news columns of the 'Times' and the editorials critical of himself which the editorial page of the paper carried very frequently. He enjoyed this very much. His keen understanding of publicity values made him infinitely prefer the news columns to the editorial page. He would rather have one column of news a week than a page of editorials a day. The 'Times,' on the other hand, enjoyed it also. For Mr. Van Anda, the managing editor, and the 'after breakfast'

writers for the editorial page as well, held the view that
anything the President said, or did, or that emanated from
him, was news worth printing. And the 'Times' holds very
rigidly to the principle that the news columns belong to
the news, and the editorial page to the editors, and no
interference with either by the other is permitted.

A second interesting 'beat' came out of the Canal story,
in the shape of an accurate advance publication of a special
message from the President to the Senate. 'Beats' are
very seldom scored on presidential messages, without a
betrayal of confidence, and this one counted a great deal
for me.

Ambassador White's reply to Mr. Roosevelt's cable,
directing him to help the 'Times' man in Paris, had said
that the paper in question was deposited, with the archives
of the French Canal Company, in the Crédit Lyonnais, in
Paris, by order of court, and that it would require a formal
court order to inspect it. Such an order could not be had on
a request which, like ours, had only a publicity basis.

When the President told me this, he asked, again, if I
could think of anything else that might be done. I suggested that William Nelson Cromwell, who had been the
American attorney for the French Canal Company, might
have a copy of the paper we were seeking. Immediately
the President wrote Mr. Cromwell, asking to see any such
paper if he had it. Mr. Cromwell responded by sending a
representative to Washington with several great boxes of
Panama Canal papers. I was at the White House when
Mr. Cromwell's representative reported to the President.

Since I had been the only newspaper man to take up the
President's challenge for an examination of the Canal
papers, I felt that I should have the first right to look
through those sent by Mr. Cromwell. But the President

declared that he was going to send them all, at once, to the Senate, where some very unpleasant things had been said about his course with regard to Panama and the Canal. He would let that body do what it pleased with the papers. He said that he would send a special message to the Senate, the next day, transmitting the papers.

Of course I knew, from all the talk I had had with him, just about what that message would contain. So I told Mr. Loeb, right away, that I would send a story to the 'Times,' that night, giving the substance of the special message. Loeb warned me, earnestly, to look out, or the Associated Press would fine the 'Times' heavily for premature publication of a document delivered in advance, and under confidence until released. But I knew, of course, that the 'A.P.' did not have the message yet, for it had not been written. So I called Mr. Van Anda on the telephone, and told him all about it. He, in turn, notified the 'A.P.' that the message was to come, and declined, in advance, to receive a copy of it from the Press Association. So the 'Times' was not bound by the confidence under which the Associated Press received the message, and we got our 'beat' without incurring a fine for premature publication.

Mr. Roosevelt was a great news-maker and a great news-giver. At the same time he was a stickler for the exact proprieties in handling news that came from him. When he gave his confidence to a correspondent, he gave it completely, and trusted to the correspondent's judgment and sense of propriety as to the use that was made of it. I have had many confidential talks with him, and doubt if there were half a dozen times when he uttered any word of caution as to the use to be made of what he had said.

The standing White House rule, that the President is never quoted, was, of course, enforced strictly. Any violation of that terminated a correspondent's usefulness to his paper, so far as the White House was concerned. Also, it got him immediately elected to the Ananias Club. Mr. Roosevelt trusted a confidant until something happened to cause him to think his confidence had been misplaced. Then he ceased entirely to give his confidence to the man who had not respected it. It was all or nothing with him. He either talked, with entire frankness and freedom, about anything and everything, or he didn't talk at all.

The life of a Washington correspondent who was on terms of confidence at the White House in those days was always full of interest and activity. You might have an hour with the President, and talk all around the horizon, politics, diplomatic affairs, military, naval or congressional situation, money trust, labor, undesirable citizens, or what not, and yet not get out of it all a word that you could write that day. Then, within a week, something might happen that would be trivial and unimportant to one who had not had such a talk with the President, but which furnished a good story to one who had.

There was an old guide up in New Brunswick who used to say: 'Heigh-ho! The days and nights are just as long as they used to be.' But sometimes I think the nights are longer now than they used to be when I was 'covering' the White House for the New York 'Times,' and 'T. R.' lived there.

XXV

For some time after the election, Mr. Taft did not return to Washington. The air was, naturally, full of rumors and gossip about Cabinet appointments, but there was very little that could be relied upon as authoritative. My efforts to secure reliable information through President Roosevelt were entirely fruitless. He told me right at the start, and with emphasis, that he had no knowledge as to what the President-elect would do, and he certainly would not ask. There was already too much talk to the effect that Roosevelt would attempt to dominate the new administration, and to avoid giving the least possible pretense for such gossip was one of his reasons for planning the year-long hunting trip in Africa, preparations for which were then well under way.

But Mr. Roosevelt did talk about the Taft Cabinet, a little, after all. He said that in one of his conversations with Mr. Taft — I do not now recall whether it was before the convention, or after the nomination, but before the election — Mr. Taft had volunteered the statement that it was his intention, if elected, or when elected — for he always was very sanguine about the result — to keep the entire Roosevelt Cabinet in office. Mr. Roosevelt told me that he had replied that that would, of course, be for Mr. Taft to determine, but it seemed to him much more likely that the new President would find himself obliged by circumstances to change his mind. Mr. Roosevelt thought it extremely doubtful that Mr. Taft would be able to retain many, if any, of the members of his own Cabinet. He was, however, much interested in two men who had

been close to him throughout his administration, and whom
he would like to see in the Taft Cabinet. These were
William Loeb, Jr., his Secretary, and James R. Garfield,
who had been his chief of the Bureau of Corporations, and
was then Secretary of the Interior. Mr. Roosevelt hoped
that Mr. Taft would keep Garfield in the Interior Department, and that he would appoint Mr. Loeb Secretary of
the Navy.

When that conversation ended, Mr. Roosevelt understood that he had the distinct assurance that Mr. Taft
would make those appointments. I believe there was never
any further conversation on the subject between the two
men after that. It will be recalled that Mr. Taft did not
make either appointment. Mr. Roosevelt never knew why.
His first information that Mr. Taft had chosen Richard
Ballinger, of Washington, to be Secretary of the Interior,
instead of Mr. Garfield, came through newspaper sources.
That fact was the cause of no little uneasiness on the part
of Mr. Roosevelt. It would have been quite simple for Mr.
Taft to write him or send him a message to the effect that he
had found it necessary, or better suited to his own plans, to
select Ballinger instead of Garfield, and Mr. Roosevelt, or
any other man at all experienced in politics, would have
understood the matter perfectly. There could have been
no unpleasant after effects from such a course. But there
was bound to be some feeling of resentment at being just
blankly ignored.

Some time in the winter — I think it was after Christmas
— Mr. Taft came to Washington. The announcement of
his coming was, of course, accompanied by a good deal of
newspaper speculation as to whether or not he would visit
at the White House. That was set at rest by the announcement that he and Mrs. Taft would be the guests of Miss

Mabel Boardman, who was their close friend, and who was prominent with Mr. Taft in the Red Cross.

One afternoon during this visit I went, with one or two other correspondents who had been very friendly to Mr. Taft, to call on him. Naturally, we wanted any news we could get, but our chief purpose was merely to pay our respects to the President-elect, and to offer again our congratulations on his election. In both respects the call was a good deal of a failure. We did see Mr. Taft for a few moments, but there was certainly no important news in what he told us, very little, indeed, that was worth sending, beyond the fact that he had received us and had nothing to say. And when we left the Boardman house every one of us had the same queer feeling that something had happened to 'put us in bad' with the new President. The old cordiality and friendliness which had always marked his dealings with us, in the days when he was Secretary of War and a candidate for the nomination, was wholly gone, and there was in its place a reserve that almost amounted to coldness. There was not one of those correspondents who had not done Mr. Taft substantial favors repeatedly, but there was nothing in his bearing that afternoon which would indicate the slightest realization of that fact on his part.

XXVI

DESPITE the fact that the New York 'Times' was constantly criticizing Mr. Roosevelt editorially, and steadily opposing many of his policies, it was always eager to get for its news columns anything from or about him. In the closing days of his administration, Mr. Van Anda, the managing editor of the 'Times,' exercised his ingenuity to a considerable extent in the production of questions designed to draw out from the President some kind of a good news story, usually about himself. These questions would be sent down to me over the leased wire that connected the Washington Bureau with the New York office, for transmission to Mr. Roosevelt. One such question, which came along some time in January, 1909, was as to what Mr. Roosevelt considered to be his greatest achievement.

At that time I was in the habit of seeing the President two or three times a week, for private talks, some of which had been rather extended. I had found that the evening hour, when he signed the day's mail, was by far the best time to see him. He would come back to the Executive offices directly from his exercise, clear up his desk, and then go over to 'the big house' to dress for dinner. He had amazing facility for carrying on conversation while he was going over the mail. He would glance over a letter, make an addition or alteration with his pen, and sign his name at the same time that he was keeping up a steady fire of talk about whatever subject happened to be under discussion.

The evening when I presented to him Mr. Van Anda's question as to his greatest achievement, the President had a great many letters to sign, and a huge pile of army and navy commissions, for there had recently been a lot of promotions in both services. We talked a few minutes about some of the things of immediate interest, and then I showed him the telegram from Mr. Van Anda.

Instantly the President replied: 'The Panama Canal, of course.'

Then he began to talk about that, going back to the days when an American canal across the Isthmus of Darien had first been projected, and recalling the story that one of the first questions asked of Commodore Perry by the Japanese at their first formal conference, away back in 1853, had been as to whether or not the Americans had as yet completed that canal.

'We should still be talking about it, instead of actually digging it,' said Mr. Roosevelt, 'if I had not acted as I did in the fall of 1903. As it is, we are in sight of the time when large vessels will be steaming through the Canal, and the long run around South America will be ended forever. Of course, I should have liked to see the Canal completed during my administration. But it was too great a task. You remember the tremendous amount of criticism there was when the work began because we did not "dig dirt." I had to change the organization two or three times, partly to satisfy the public clamor for digging. But it was a clamor that came chiefly from persons who didn't know anything of what they were talking about. Finally, when we put the army engineers at the head of the organization the criticism died away somewhat. They were nearly ready then for the actual digging, and they never answered back, no matter what any one said about them, so that there was less encouragement for nagging than there had been under civilian chiefs of the organization.

'It had done very little, if any, good, while this criticism was going on, to explain that a great deal of time was required, first, for the sanitation of the Isthmus, so that it could be made safe for white men to live there, and then to get together the organization and equipment necessary for a work of such magnitude. But when the preliminary work was done and we got to "making the dirt fly," it flew considerably faster than had been estimated, even by the most eager critics.

'I shall always feel that this was the greatest single accomplishment with which I have had anything to do. It is the greatest fact in my career. Don't you think so?'

I have put what he said in quotation marks, not because I mean it to imply that he actually used those particular words, but because I do mean that I have given accurately the substance and import of what he said. His talk made such an impression on me, not only this about the Canal, but the rest of what he said that evening, that I have always carried it vividly in my recollection. During all the time that he had been talking, he had also kept his pen busy, and he was still rapidly signing commissions when he asked me that direct question, as to whether I, too, did not think the Canal his greatest achievement.

'No, Mr. President,' I replied. 'I do not.'

I can see to-day the expression of puzzled surprise that came over his face as he looked up at me and laid down the pen.

'Well, if the Canal isn't, what is?' he demanded.

'I have always thought that the greatest thing about you,' I said, 'and the thing that will live longest, and have most influence, is the example you have set to youth.'

'What do you mean?' he asked.

'I mean this. As a boy you were a weakling, physically

inferior. You determined to overcome that weakness. By your own will you kept yourself everlastingly at it, with all kinds of exercise and work, until you have built that weakling boy into the great burly man that you are to-day, capable of more endurance, by far, than the average man, and of keeping up, in fact, with the exceptional man.

'That is one thing. There is another as great, and no doubt many persons will think it even greater. As a boy you fixed upon yourself the habit of application and of work. You have kept that up, until I sometimes think it has got a little the best of you, because you never seem able now to take it easy at all. You must always be at it "four bells and a jingle," as they say at sea. The habit of hard and rapid work is now so fixed upon you that it takes a great deal to keep you occupied, and you get through so much more than the average man does, or can, that you are always liable to overestimate the amount that another can accomplish.

'I think these two habits of self-reliance and hard work constitute an example to youth of far-reaching and long-continuing influence that will outweigh, in the judgment of history, any single fact accomplishment in your career, such as the Panama Canal.'

The President got up from his desk and came around to the side on which I was sitting. I had been facing him directly across the desk.

'Now, O. K.,' he said,' you have got me to talking, and you have got to listen to a lecture.'

But instead of a lecture he proceeded to give me his own analysis of himself. 'I am just an ordinary man,' he began, 'without any special ability in any direction. In most things I am just about the average; in some of them a little under, rather than over. I am only an ordinary walker. I can't run. I am not a good swimmer, although I am a strong one. I probably ride better than I do anything else, but I am certainly not a remarkably good rider. I am not a good shot. My eyesight is not strong, and I have to get close to my game in order to make any shot at all. I never could be a good boxer, although I like to box and do keep at it, whenever I can. My eyesight prevents me from ever being a good tennis player, even if otherwise I could qualify.

'So you see that from the physical point of view I am just an ordinary, or perhaps a little less than ordinary man. Now, take the things that I have done in public life or in private life either, for that matter. I am not a brilliant writer. I have written a great deal, but I always have to work and slave over everything I write. The things that I have done, in one office, or another, are all, with the possible exception of the Panama Canal, just such things as any ordinary man could have done. There is nothing brilliant or outstanding in my record, except, perhaps, this one thing. Whatever I think it is right for me to do, I do. I do the things that I believe ought to be done. And when I make up my mind to do a thing, I act.

'Having made a decision, I do not permit myself, as a rule, to reconsider it. That doesn't mean that I think my decisions are always right. I know they are not. I know that, of course, I make mistakes. But I also know that to permit yourself to be constantly reconsidering a decision you have once made, especially if you happen to be in public office where you are called upon to make a great number of decisions, is to develop yourself into a man of no decision. That promotes delay and piles up work and trouble.

'I believe that in the long run less damage is done through the mistakes resulting from sticking to decisions once made than would occur from getting into the habit of constantly worrying whether you had decided rightly or wrongly, and changing your mind all the time. No man can get ahead on two or more courses. You have to go one way at a time to get anywhere.

'I know I am criticized on this account. A good many of my "dear friends" call me impulsive and jumpy, and say that I go off half-cocked, when, as a matter of fact, I have really given full consideration to whatever it is that is to be done. But because I act when I have made my decision, and usually as vigorously as I can, it may sometimes seem to others that there has not been as much deliberation as some of them would have taken.

'The accomplishments of my record, whatever they may be, are all such as might have been accomplished by any average man who had made up his mind to decide promptly and to act on his decisions.

'There *is* a lesson to youth in that, and I'm glad you thought of it in that way. Of course, when a man becomes conspicuous, as any President of the United States is bound to be among the American people, it is natural that such a thing as building up his own body by his own work should be held up as an example to other boys to show them what they, too, can do if they will. It is a fine thing for any boy to get himself into the habit of work. Work, and hard work, is a good thing to preach, to men as well as to boys. Do what you have to do for all you are worth. It was just that which made me act as I did in the Panama case, and that is just why we are going to have that Canal so soon. When we get it, there will never again be the necessity for sending a fleet on such a cruise as that the

battleships are making now. That Canal will be a great
factor in our national defense, and a great means of pro-
motion of our commerce. After all, I think it is the greatest thing I have ever done.'

XXVII

ABOUT this time Mr. Van Anda called me by telephone one day and asked me if I would care to join him in a new enterprise and put a proposition up to President Roosevelt involving his own occupation after his return from the hunting trip in Africa, the plan for which had been announced some time before. Mr. Roosevelt had also announced his intention to take an editorial place on the staff of the 'Outlook,' on his return from Africa, and it was understood that he had entered into a formal contract with the owners of the 'Outlook' to that effect. He was to have the title of Contributing Editor.

Mr. Van Anda's proposition would have involved the cancellation of this contract with the 'Outlook,' and I told him, when he spoke to me about it, that it was more than doubtful whether we could persuade Mr. Roosevelt even to consider the new suggestion. But Mr. Van Anda's idea appealed to me very strongly, and I was glad to speak to the President about it. The proposition was that Mr. Roosevelt should take the editorship of one of the great New York City newspapers. Mr. Van Anda told me an organization had been formed and was ready to purchase the 'Sun.' It was known at that time that the 'Sun' could be purchased, and Mr. Van Anda also had reason to think that the 'Press' could be bought. The purchase of the 'Press' was deemed necessary by him in order that it might be consolidated with the 'Sun,' the latter thereby gaining the Press Association service it lacked.

The first opportunity I had to see the President was at one o'clock on the day following that on which Mr. Van Anda had telephoned me. That was the regular shaving hour for the President. Every day, at one o'clock, Delaney, a colored messenger employed at the Treasury Department, came over to the White House and shaved the President. There was a small room, between the President's private office and Mr. Loeb's office, which was always used for this purpose. There was, of course, no regular barber's chair, but Delaney did the best he could with a big arm-chair. The shaving hour was always a good one to see the President, for it gave the interviewer a better chance to say what he wanted to say in full, as the President, with his face covered with lather and Delaney's razor sweeping over it, was rather at a disadvantage as to talking.

On that particular day I had to share the time with Angus McSween, the Washington correspondent of the Philadelphia 'North American,' but he was a good friend of mine, and I did not mind letting him know what my business with the President was. I knew he would regard the confidence, just as he knew I would not reveal his own business with Mr. Roosevelt. I have forgotten what it was he wanted, but I dare say he remembers, quite well, my talk with the President.

Mr. McSween submitted his question to the President first, so that when I came to speak Mr. Roosevelt was about half shaved. Mr. Van Anda had supplemented his telephone talk with me by a telegram, and I opened proceedings by handing it to the President. He stopped Delaney's work and brought the message close to his face, as he always did when reading without his glasses. Then, as he got the purport of the message, he burst out laughing,

CARR V. VAN ANDA

and jumped up from the chair. Waving the towel in one hand and the telegram in the other, he walked about the room and continued to laugh for a moment or two.

'This is the most extraordinary thing I have ever heard of,' he said. 'Why, O. K., I couldn't edit a paper. It's preposterous!'

Then he began to laugh again. Delaney stood there, with a grin on his face, waiting for the President to get back into the shaving chair. But the President seemed to be immensely amused by the proposition, and yet apparently he recognized the fact that there was a serious side to it. For presently he went into a more extended explanation of his view of it.

'You see,' he said, 'I am not a good writer. As I have told you before, I always compose with difficulty, and I have to work over everything I write, frequently several times, to get it to suit me. I have to say exactly what I mean, and that sometimes necessitates my using a good many words. I have no style, and I never could write those short, pithy, pungent paragraphs that it is so absolutely necessary for an editor to be able to write.'

'But, Mr. President,' I said, 'we hadn't asked you to write anything.'

The President was getting back into the shaving chair when I said that. Instantly he stood up again. He was obviously surprised, and didn't get what I meant.

'What do you want, then?' he asked. 'I thought you asked me to edit a newspaper.'

'Yes, sir, exactly that,' I replied. 'Did you ever happen to consider, Mr. President, what it was that made Horace Greeley and Charles A. Dana great editors?'

'I never thought particularly about it,' he said, 'but have always supposed that it was their ability to write, especially those short, hard-hitting paragraphs. That was the chief thing that made Dana famous.'

'No, I think that was only incidental,' I said. 'Plenty of men can write that way. They can be hired for comparatively small salaries. Many of the editorials, especially the short ones and paragraphs, that were popularly credited to Mr. Dana were as a matter of fact written by other men. The famous "sting of the whiplash" editorial about Mr. Cleveland, which evoked such a bitter comment from him about Mr. Dana, was written by Edward Page Mitchell, but always popularly credited to Mr. Dana.

'What made Mr. Dana such a great editor was his keen and constant interest in everything that was going on all around the world and his determination to have something about it to print in the "Sun." It was his breadth of sympathy and his range of interest. That is the sort of thing that it is extremely difficult to find. But that is what you possess more than any other man alive to-day. I know of no one who has such catholicity of sympathy and interest as you. What we want is to have you give us the benefit of that. We don't want you as a writer, but of course we should be glad to have you write anything you wanted to. But the main thing is to have you come to the office for a few hours every morning and tell us what to get for the paper. We can get it. We can always find men expert in that sort of thing. It is inspiration that we want from you. That is what makes a great newspaper.'

'I never thought of it in that way before,' Mr. Roosevelt responded, 'but you are quite right. I do have some qualification for editorship in that respect, but it is too late now. I am under contract with the "Outlook," and of course I could not ask Mr. Howland to release me. Besides, this is not what I want to do, and writing for the

"Outlook" is. I want to preach. I have a good many sermons in me that I want to deliver, and the "Outlook" will furnish me a bully pulpit.'

The President climbed back into the chair and the shaving was finished. It was obviously no use to try to carry the argument any further, at least at that time, and I so reported to Mr. Van Anda. But two or three times later, Mr. Roosevelt brought the subject up again, and it was evident that the proposition interested him more than a little. Moreover, as I learned afterward, Mr. Loeb had been taken by the proposition. He thought it was eminently a fitting thing for Mr. Roosevelt to do, and that as editor of a great newspaper he would have a far better opportunity to 'preach,' as he said he wanted to do, than as contributing editor for the 'Outlook.' However, the factor which controlled, and which made it impossible for us to get Mr. Roosevelt to consider our proposition, was that contract with the 'Outlook.' He simply would not think of breaking it, or of asking Mr. Howland to release him.

Years afterward, when he was connected, in a contributing capacity, with the Kansas City 'Star,' we talked again of this scheme that would have made him head of a great New York City newspaper.

'It would have been great fun,' he said, 'but I should have been involved in even worse political difficulties than I have been as it was. I could not have taken any place of editorial responsibility with a daily newspaper after coming back from Africa without at once getting into trouble over Taft. I could not have kept still. I should have had either to support or to criticize. If I supported, that would have made Taft's position more difficult, for all my opponents would immediately have charged that I was running the Administration and that Taft was only a figure-head. If I criticized, that would have been just as bad. I should not have been credited with sincerity in either case. No, it is better as it is. But it would have been great fun.'

XXVIII

THERE were some men among the editors of the New York 'Times' who used to tell me that Mr. Roosevelt had no sense of humor. That was particularly the theory of Mr. Charles R. Miller, then editor-in-chief, whose principal interest was economics, and who wrote most of the editorials on tariff and financial subjects. In the winter of 1908–09 an incident happened at Washington that gave me a vivid illumination of Mr. Roosevelt's sense of humor. The battleship fleet was then on its cruise around the world. It had called at Callao, Peru, where a great reception had been given to the officers and crews of the fleet. President Pardo, of Peru, cabled to President Roosevelt a message of felicitation to the United States upon the possession of such a fleet, and in due time a reply was sent, in the name of President Roosevelt. The message from the Peruvian President was given to the newspaper men in Washington and printed widely around the country. But for some reason the reply of Mr. Roosevelt was not made public. In due time, however, it was published in Peru. There it at once caught the attention of the correspondent of the Associated Press, who cabled it back to this country, and it received wide publication. Immediately it aroused a storm of criticism of President Roosevelt because it began with the words 'I and my people thank you.' That 'I and my people' telegram furnished material for scores of editorials condemning the President, and some of them were by no means gentle in their criticism. Nor were they confined to the opposition politically. Many of them appeared in newspapers of the President's own party.

Naturally, the correspondents at Washington were interested to find out what the President had to say about it. But the President refused to say anything. He declined absolutely to comment, and there was neither explanation nor defense of the peculiarly worded message.

One morning while the criticism of this message was at its height I saw the President, for a moment, in the Cabinet room. He told me to go into his private office, for there was something he wanted to say to me. Presently George Hill, of the 'Tribune,' came in. He was followed by Sumner Curtis, of the Chicago 'Record-Herald,' and by the late Henry Beach Needham, a special writer, who was on very good terms with the President. None of us knew what it was that Mr. Roosevelt had in mind, and we watched with interest while he swept through the usual crowd in the Cabinet room, heard what each had to say and got rid of them. Then he came into his private office, and, shutting the sliding doors behind him, stood rocking back and forth obviously bursting with whatever it was that was on his mind, and ready to go into a gale of laughter.

'This thing is so good,' he said, 'that I've got to tell it. But you've got to promise not to print it.'

Of course we promised. There was no help for that, and the President went on. 'You know that "I and my people" telegram that all the newspapers are roasting me about,' he said. 'Well, I never saw that message. Old Adee did that to me. And now I can't say a word about it, for then old Pardo would know I hadn't answered his telegram to me!'

With that the President simply roared. He thought it was a huge joke on himself, to be pounded, from one end of the country to the other, for something he hadn't done, but which he couldn't explain.

'Old Adee' was a well-known character in Washington. He had been Second Assistant Secretary of State so long that most of the newspaper men used to say he was the original organizer of the Department when Washington was President. He was the great authority on style and form for all the Department. No official communication was sent out until Mr. Adee had passed upon its phraseology. Much of his work was drafting documents, of one sort or another, for the approval or signature of some of the Department officials. It had fallen to him in the usual routine to draft the President's reply to the Peruvian message, and, as it was merely a routine and formal matter, it had not been thought necessary to submit it to Mr. Roosevelt for his approval before it was sent.

'You know,' the President went on, 'I am always in correspondence with all the kings, princes, potentates, and powers around the earth. Every President is. It is not a personal correspondence, but merely the formal way in which the head of every State congratulates the head of every other State every time anything happens that calls for congratulation. I suppose I write four or five letters or telegrams every day, and old Adee does that for me. I never see them unless there is something of special importance. But I am always sending a congratulation, or a felicitation, or a message of condolence or sympathy to somebody in a palace somewhere or other, and old Adee does that for me. Every time there is an engagement or a marriage or a birth, I send the proper message, and old Adee does that for me. Every time there is an accident or other misfortune, or a death, I send the right sort of message of sympathy or condolence, and old Adee does that for me.

'Why, there isn't a kitten born in a palace anywhere on earth that I don't have to write a letter of congratulation to the peripatetic Tomcat that might have been its sire, and old Adee does that for me!

'D'you remember that "Great and Good Friend" letter that Cleveland sent to Liliuokalani? Old Adee did that to Cleveland!'

The President roared with laughter as he recounted the things of this sort that 'Old Adee' had done to different Presidents. But there was never any public explanation of the 'I and my people' telegram.

XXIX

ABOUT a month or six weeks before the end of President Roosevelt's term in the White House, I received a telegram from Mr. Van Anda directing me to ask the President for an appointment for Mr. Williams, of the 'Times' staff in New York. The message did not give any indication of the business on which Mr. Williams wanted to see the President. I went over to the White House, saw Mr. Roosevelt, and handed him the message. He read it and said:

'What does he want?'

'I haven't the slightest idea, Mr. President,' I replied. 'My only information is in that telegram.'

Mr. Roosevelt looked at me with a grin. 'Tell him I'll see him to-morrow evening at six o'clock,' he said; 'and whatever it is he wants I won't do it.'

I went back to my office and called Mr. Van Anda on the telephone. I told him just what had happened, and we had some talk as to whether it was worth while for Williams to come to Washington or not. Mr. Van Anda did not tell me what it was that Williams wanted to see the President about, which made me suspect that he had some scheme for trying to get a man in the Roosevelt party for the African trip.

The next afternoon Williams came into my office with a great suitcase. He asked what hotel he should go to, saying that he wanted to get a room where he could dress for the White House call. He had a hatbox, and it was evident that he expected to array himself in frock coat and tall hat. I said it was not necessary to dress; that the newspaper men always called on the President in their working clothes,

and no one thought of putting on a frock coat to go to the
White House on business. Moreover, I said, we should
find the President in the clothes he had worn that afternoon while taking his exercise. I didn't know whether he
had been riding, or walking, or playing tennis, or what.
But whatever it was that he had been doing, he would
come into the Executive offices at six o'clock to sign his
mail and clean up his desk before going to the 'big house'
to dress for dinner.

Williams was a good deal inclined to demur at that. He
couldn't get over his ingrained respect for what he regarded
as the proprieties of such an occasion. He was an Englishman, and it seemed to amaze him that any one should
think of calling on the head of the Government in anything
but official dress. We had an hour or more to wait before
six o'clock, and Williams kept coming back to the question
of dress at frequent intervals. His anxiety made me laugh,
and that seemed at last to convince him that I was right,
although it by no means satisfied him.

At six o'clock we were at the White House, and immediately were admitted to Mr. Roosevelt's office. He was
at his desk, in riding-clothes. The moment I had presented Williams, the President asked him bluntly what he
wanted. Williams was a good deal fussed by that direct attack, and all the carefully prepared approach in which he
had drilled himself deserted him. He wobbled about a bit,
and then remarked that he had been in that part of Africa
where the President was going to hunt, and thought Mr.
Roosevelt might be interested in talking a little about it.

The President was interested, instantly. He dashed
through the remainder of the work on his desk, left his
chair, and came around and sat on the edge of the desk, at
the end facing Williams, who was seated at the side of the

room. The President sat there swinging one foot out and in. He had his spurs on, and every time that foot swung toward the desk Williams watched it with a kind of fascination, obviously expecting that spur to rowel the highly polished mahogany. He was so charmed by the menace to the desk of that swinging spur that two or three times he lost track of the conversation and obviously did not follow what the President was saying.

Mr. Roosevelt wanted to know just where Williams had been in Africa, just how he got there, how he traveled, and what he saw. Was he hunting, or what was he doing? What guns did he have? What game did he see? and a score of other related questions. In two minutes plenty of opportunity had been given Williams for him to disclose the real purpose of his visit. That was the suggestion that he might qualify as a member of the President's party.

But although Mr. Roosevelt was very keen to get every possible fact that Williams could give him, he was not in the least impressed by the suggestion that Williams would make a good member of the party. He had already perfected all his arrangements on that score. He had men to take charge of the traveling and camping part of the journey who had hunted all kinds of big game in all parts of the country through which he was to pass. He had scientific men to take charge of all the scientific work of the expedition, and for companionship he was taking his own son Kermit. There was no place for an outsider, such as Williams was, and, moreover, Williams was a newspaper man, and Mr. Roosevelt had not the least intention of permitting any one else to do any writing about that hunt.

Williams varied the conversation by introducing another subject in which he found the President a good deal interested. He was a Mason, and, I think, a member of the

Blue Lodge in which Mr. Roosevelt had been made a Mason. He was either a member of that Lodge or had visited it several times. He was present, as I recall it, on the occasion when Mr. Roosevelt had been 'raised.' This furnished a topic of additional and friendly conversation, but without in the least affecting the main situation.

The whole thing was immensely entertaining to me. Any correspondent in Washington could have told Williams, before he left New York, that there was not the slightest possibility of his being accepted as a member of that party. Mr. Roosevelt had made arrangements with a magazine to write a series of articles about the hunt, and he certainly would not permit any other writing man to go along. Especially was he opposed to having any one send anything to a newspaper. He wanted to get away from newspapers, completely out of their range, if he could. There was a very strong special reason for that. He had made up his mind to keep entirely out of politics after leaving the presidency, and especially not to have anything to do or say about the Taft Administration. He was intent on maintaining a 'hands off' attitude. There had been plenty of talk about how he would endeavor to influence the new President, and he proposed to defeat all such talk. That was one of the strong reasons for his going to Africa. He would be so thoroughly out of the way, and out of reach, that there could not be justification for any suggestion or assertion that he was 'running' Taft.

All during the conversation, which must have lasted half an hour, the President sat there on the edge of his desk swinging that spurred foot, and constantly menacing the polished mahogany, without once touching it. Not once did it lose its fascination for Williams. I think that part of his interview will always remain most vivid in his recollection. I have not seen him for several years, but the last time I did meet him he spoke at once of that spur. He left the White House that evening, disappointed a little, but on the whole immensely pleased. Of course, he had never had any real expectation of being accepted as a member of the African party. But he had been a little hopeful, and that hope had been thoroughly dissipated. In return he had met Mr. Roosevelt most pleasantly, and had seen him for half an hour swing a big spur within a thirty-second of an inch of his desk without once even grazing it. That was something.

XXX

Mr. Taft had once remarked that 'it will be a cold day when I go into the White House,' and it was. In fact it was not only cold, but snowy, and very wet. It was a day that no newspaper man who had anything to do with reporting the inauguration ceremonies will ever forget. A heavy, damp snow began to fall early in the evening of the 3d of March, 1909. In the Washington Bureau of the New York 'Times' we were very busy. There was a lot to tell about the closing days of the old Congress, and there was the usual batch of politics to send. Besides this I had a special story, which I was sure would be a beat, about the new Cabinet, and the reasons which had actuated Mr. Taft in selecting its members. This story was based upon a long letter that Mr. Taft himself had written to Colonel William R. Nelson, the owner of the Kansas City 'Star' and 'Times.'

It was about eleven o'clock that evening when the operator on our leased wire began to send this Cabinet story. We had not completed the first paragraph when the wire 'went out.' A telephone call to the telegraph office disclosed the fact that the heavy snow had been knocking down wires all the evening, and at length it had taken ours. There was no other wire available, and so far as telegraphing was concerned our work was ended for the night.

But I had to get that Cabinet story over to the 'Times.' So I called the office on the long-distance telephone and began to dictate the story to a man in the 'Times' office. It was slow and tedious work, for the connection was not good, and there had to be a lot of repetition. I was about halfway through it when, suddenly, and without any warning, some weary telephone operator switched on to my wire a friend from New York who had come down for the inauguration and felt that that was about time to call me up and have a little gossip about the political situation. He had been dining very well, and that was a long time before the enactment of the Volstead Law. He was feeling very well, indeed, and was so good-natured that he could not understand how it could possibly be that I did not desire to talk with him.

By the time I had gone through the first pleasantries, and learned where he was stopping, I was quite ready to have him ring off and permit me to go on with my dictation to the office in New York. It was getting well on toward midnight. The storm was raging worse than ever, and there was danger that even the telephone wires, which, as a rule, are much more strongly put up than telegraph wires, would go out, too. So I suggested to my friend that he should ring off, and told him I was very busy. But he couldn't hear that, or, at least, he was so happy that it didn't register. I sent a couple of men into adjoining offices to call up central from other telephones and have my friend cut off, but everything was 'busy' and no relief was obtainable in that way. Meantime he kept up a steady stream of bibulous chatter, oblivious to everything but the fact that he had had a mighty good dinner, and was very happy.

Then I suspect that I lost my temper. 'Will you kindly get to hell out of there and let me finish my work?' I said.

Something about the language, or the tone, seemed to catch his attention. 'I say, Old Man,' he replied — and I could hear him chuckle as he said it — 'would it help you any if I should hang up?'

'You drunken imbecile,' I shouted, 'will you ring up?'

The next minute I had the New York office again, and was going on with the Cabinet story. When I had finished that, I asked for Mr. Van Anda, and told him about the storm in Washington. It had not struck New York yet, and there was no indication there of the seriousness of our situation in the capital. I suggested that Mr. Van Anda should arrange, at once, with the telephone people, for two wires from Washington to New York for the next day. We should have plenty of use for them if we could get them. Mr. Van Anda agreed to see that it was done immediately, so that we should be protected in case our telegraph wire was not restored by morning. Also it was wise to get in early, before other newspapers had taken all the telephone wires.

The morning of inauguration day found Washington under ten or twelve inches of snow, with every telegraph and telephone wire leading to other cities down, and half the telephones in the city put out of business. The Capitol was absolutely cut off from communication with the rest of the country, and it had that day the biggest newspaper story in the United States. The storm had ended, but it had done its work with complete thoroughness. In the 'Times' Bureau we had from forty to fifty thousand words to send, covering the different phases of the inaugural ceremonies, and not a wire on which to send one of them. When I got to my office about nine o'clock that morning, the first thing I did was to call the telephone company and ask about the two wires Mr. Van Anda had promised to lease for the day. The telephone people simply laughed.

'You can't telephone to Alexandria,' they said, 'say nothing of New York. There isn't a wire in service anywhere outside of the city, and only about half of those in town.'

A number of extra men had been sent down from New York to help out the Washington Bureau for the inauguration, so that we had ten or twelve reporters ready for work that day. Each had received his assignment the day before, and went directly that morning to his place of work for the day. My part was to write the 'general lead' and to see to the handling of the stories turned in by the different men and women reporters. But as soon as I found that the wires were all down, my job was turned into something very much more important. That was to devise some way of getting something about the day to New York for the next day's 'Times.'

There was what purported to be a wireless station on top of the Willard Hotel. But that was some time before the wireless had been developed to a practical commercial basis, and I had no hope of being able to get anything through by that means. My judgment was amply justified by the experience of Mr. Van Anda in trying to get something to me by wireless. He filed two or three messages that day, but none of them has been delivered yet, and that was sixteen years ago.

About ten o'clock that morning 'Jimmy' Michael, the Harrisburg correspondent of the Philadelphia 'Ledger' came into the office. Our Bureau in Washington served the 'Ledger,' as well as the New York 'Times,' and Michael came to report to me the arrival of the Pennsylvania Legislature, which had come down by special train for the inauguration.

'You won't get a word out of here to-day,' he said. 'You might as well quit and enjoy the show. I tell you every telegraph pole between here and Baltimore is flat down. There isn't one standing. It took us three hours to get here from Baltimore. They just passed the train from man to man. They have signalmen all along the track, standing close enough together so that they can see one another, and they are sending trains through by flag signal, all the way. You won't get a word out of here by wire to-day. It's going to be days before they get any wires up, and all those poles will have to be replaced.'

Michael went out to see how his Pennsylvania legislators were getting along, and I got busy on the telephone. Fortunately, the wires to the Capitol were still in service, and I was able to get the 'Times' men on duty there. I told each one to come down to the office as quickly as possible and to write everything he could. The man who was to cover the actual inaugural ceremony, which was to be held in the Senate Chamber instead of at the East Front of the Capitol, had been through other inaugurals and could write, from his knowledge of what occurs on such occasions, a fairly accurate story. Several others could do as well. When they reached the office, I told each one to write his story in triplicate. That would be one copy for the 'Ledger,' one for the wire in Philadelphia, or for the 'Times' in case no wires were available from Philadelphia, and would leave one copy for the Bureau, in case, by any chance, we should get a wire any time during the day or night.

Having given these directions, I went over to the White House to see the old and new Presidents set out for the Capitol. They came out of the front door of the 'Big House' together, all bundled up for the weather. Mr. Roosevelt was wearing 'goloshes' with his trousers tucked into their tops. He was going directly to the railroad station from the Capitol after the inaugural. That, I think, was the last time he was in the White House, except possibly once when he went there to see President Wilson, regarding his offer to raise a division of volunteers for service in the Great War.

Mr. Taft had his cold day for going into the White House, all right, and he recalled it, with a laugh, as he and Mr. Roosevelt came out to start on their way up to the Capitol.

From the White House I went back to my office and wrote a story of a column or so about the weather that day in Washington, and the isolation of the Capitol from the rest of the country. Then I wrote a little story about the departure of Mr. Roosevelt and Mr. Taft from the White House. By that time several of the other men had finished writing, or at least had written enough to warrant starting it on its way to the 'Times' and 'Ledger.' Michael had come back to the office, and I asked him to take two copies of everything that was ready and try to get to Philadelphia with it. If he reached Philadelphia before midnight, he was to file one copy of everything at once to the 'Times,' on as many wires as he could get, and then take the other copy to the 'Ledger.' Michael got away by the half past twelve train, just about the time the inaugural ceremony was going on in the Senate Chamber.

From that time on, until six o'clock that evening, every train that left Washington carried a messenger for me with copy for the 'Times' and 'Ledger.' By the six o'clock train I sent my chief telegraph operator. He is just about the best telegraph man I ever saw, fast, accurate, and steady, and absolutely dependable. He knew exactly what was to be done, and it was certain that if he could get to Philadelphia in time he would get everything from there into New York in the shortest possible order.

I do not recall now just why it was that I sent all these

men to Philadelphia. Probably we had heard from railroad
sources that wires were up between Philadelphia and New
York. At any rate, we knew that the storm was pretty
sharply localized, although it had affected the wires for
some distance north of Baltimore. One phase of the situation I did not clearly realize at the time. It was the fact
that it took so long to get a train from Washington to
Baltimore. I probably could have made time by sending
my messengers as far as Baltimore by motor car, for even
in that weather and snow they probably could have done
better than ten miles an hour, which was all the trains could
do.

With all this going on I naturally had no time to see any
part of the inauguration ceremonies. I did see a little of the
parade down Pennsylvania Avenue well along in the afternoon, but that was all. Along in the middle of the afternoon I was thrilled by a telephone message from the telegraph office to the effect that they had succeeded in getting
one wire open, but that it could be used only for bulletins.
As I had no bulletins to send, but did have better than
forty thousand words, I was not interested in that one wire.
It went all the way around Robin Hood's barn, anyway,
and took nearly as long for a bulletin as the trains were
taking to Baltimore. Louisville and Cincinnati were two
of the cities that bulletin wire touched.

That wire served, however, to bring me one message
from Mr. Van Anda. It was the only word he managed to
get through to me all that day. It said:

'For God's sake, send us something.'

It made me wonder what he thought we were trying to
do in Washington in that emergency. It certainly was no
day to play golf.

Late that afternoon a group of the Washington cor-

respondents went over to the White House to pay their
respects to the new President. There and then we got our
first, emphatic demonstration that it was not only a new
President in the White House, but, in fact, a new man, and
not at all the pleasant, genial, helpful, good-natured man
we had known as Secretary of War. If differentiation from
Roosevelt was an essential principle of the new Administration, as some of us straightway came to believe, it received
a practical enforcement that afternoon. For the President
declined to receive us. I think it was the most surprised
group of Washington correspondents that I have ever seen,
to whom Fred Carpenter, the new Secretary to the President, brought that message. This was a group of men who
had hewed wood and carried water to help make Mr. Taft
President, and to be told rather curtly by the new Secretary
that the new President could not see them was not in the
least what any of them had expected. Then, when Mr.
Carpenter added that the President did not expect to see
newspaper men as frequently as he had done when
Secretary of War, but if and when he desired to see any one
he would send for him, the climax was very fittingly capped.

For a minute or two the boys stood around, first on one
foot and then on the other, and not much of anything was
said. Then somebody had the inspiration to suggest that
we were really not after news, but only wanted to pay our
respects to the new Chief Magistrate. That seemed to re-
lieve Carpenter, who went again into the inside office.
Presently he returned and said the President would see us,
and at once Mr. Taft came out. He shook hands, gra-
ciously, all around, and some one said something at which
he laughed.

There wasn't anything in that White House call that I
could write for the New York 'Times,' and so I went back

to my office and sat around, waiting in the vain hope of getting a wire, and listening to the bitter tale of the lady who had the job of reporting the inaugural ball, and who was paid by space instead of a regular salary. There she was, with the biggest story she would have in four years, and not a wire that would carry a word of it to New York, with the added certain knowledge that, if any wire did come in, many thousands of other words would be sent before her story was reached.

We were still sitting there about half-past one o'clock the next morning, just waiting for something to happen, when all of a sudden our telegraph instrument began to click, and we knew we had a wire. The copy was ready on the desk and in a second a highly expert operator was clicking Phillips code into the New York 'Times' office at a rate that made the man at the receiving end pay mighty close attention to his business. It was then too late, by an hour, to get anything into the first edition, and we didn't take the time to ask whether or not anything had got through by way of Philadelphia. We just fired what we had as fast as we could shoot. The next day could report the results.

But after all we didn't have to wait for the next day. After we had had the wire for two hours, the telegraph company telephoned that it would have to be taken away for somebody else. We had had our share for that night. But just before we lost the wire, it brought us this message from Mr. Van Anda:

'We had five columns in the first edition and more in every other edition. "Sun" had one column in first edition, the others nothing. Oh, they are a frost-bitten lot.'

That was good enough to go home on.

XXXI

On the day after his inauguration President Taft issued his call for the special session of Congress that had been determined upon some time before. The first thought had been to have Congress meet on March 5th, but then somebody had raised the question of the authority of the outgoing President to call the new Congress, and it was found that ten days would be required after the issuance of the call before Congress could assemble. So March 15th was settled on as the date, and Mr. Taft's proclamation was made accordingly.

This special session of Congress was to revise the Dingley tariff law, in accordance with the promise of the Republican platform, and Mr. Taft's campaign speeches. These promises had been made in such a way as to give the country the definite understanding that there was to be a general lowering of the rates of the Dingley schedules, and there was no question, except among the stand-pat Old Guard crowd, that such a revision was urgently demanded and would be decidedly popular.

During his seven and a half years in the White House Mr. Roosevelt had avoided the tariff issue. When he came into the presidency there was no special demand for tariff action, except from the Democrats, who always want lower rates than the Republicans. Afterward, when he was serving the term to which he had been so triumphantly elected, Mr. Roosevelt had several other issues in which he was much more interested than the tariff. In fact he was never interested in tariff matters. He used to say quite frankly that he didn't know anything about the tariff and couldn't make himself take any interest in it. He was in accord with the Republican theory that a protective tariff enables the payment of higher wages to workingmen, and he was heartily in favor of that. But as a general rule economic questions did not interest him nearly as much as those of a sociological or humanitarian character. So, when, during his second term, there began to be a demand for tariff revision, he was quite ready to agree with the leaders of the Republican organization in both Senate and House to postpone tariff action until after the next election.

So that was the first important matter of legislation to come up in the Taft Administration. But there was a tremendously important political question that had to be settled before there could be any tariff action. The settlement was bound to affect the entire Administration of Mr. Taft, and, perhaps, even the question of his reëlection. Mr. Taft had gone into his campaign in the summer and fall of 1908 confident of his election and looking forward with no small confidence to his reëlection. Repeatedly on the golf course at Hot Springs I heard him speak of it, always, of course, in a semi-jocular way, but with a good deal of real seriousness evident, nevertheless.

This political question was as to whether he would support the 'Regular Organization,' as the Old Guard called itself, in the Senate and House, or would side with the Progressives, or 'Insurgents,' as the Old Guard called them. The insurgents were the Roosevelt men. They were the ones who had followed 'T. R.' in bringing about the nomination of Mr. Taft, and they had accepted Taft for exactly the same reason that Mr. Roosevelt did, namely, his public endorsement of the Roosevelt policies, and his open and repeated pledge to carry them out faithfully if elected to the presidency.

The meeting of Congress on March 15th was certain to bring this political question to a sharp decision. For 'Uncle Joe' Cannon would surely be a candidate for reëlection to the speakership in the House of Representatives, and he would certainly be opposed by the Progressives. The House organization, under the dominant leadership of Mr. Cannon, was anathema to the Insurgent faction of the Republican Party, and, although there was only a small group of Insurgents in the House, they represented the preponderant element of the Republican vote of the country. They were especially strong in the Middle West.

About a month after Mr. Taft's election, it began to be occasionally whispered around, in most confidential manner, in Washington, that he was considering making a fight on Cannon when Congress met. It was intimated to me that Frank Hitchcock, who, it was understood, was to go into the Taft Cabinet as Postmaster-General, and have charge of politics for the Administration, had been commissioned by Mr. Taft to take special soundings with a view to finding out what the chances were of beating 'Uncle Joe' for the speakership. It was known that Mr. Hitchcock was carrying on some kind of special activity, but he was successful in clothing it with his usual mystery, and it was put down generally as having some connection with the formation of the Cabinet. A month or two before the inauguration, this whispering about a fight on Cannon ceased, and Congress met with no definite indication of what the developments would be.

The press gallery of the House of Representatives was jammed at noon on March 15th, when the clerk of the old House called the new one to order. Very little time was required for the regular formalities, and in a few minutes the voting on the speakership was under way. Immediately the answer to the big political question of the hour was apparent. Taft was supporting Cannon, not opposing him. The new Administration was lined up with the Old Guard for the organization of the House, and not with the Insurgents.

I watched that roll call just long enough to be convinced of the situation, and then hurried down to the White House as fast as I could go. I wanted the President's side of that. There must be an explanation of this apparent change of sides since the election, and it was of supreme importance to Mr. Taft and his political fortunes to have that explanation go to the public along with the presentation of the fact that the change had been made.

At the White House I explained very briefly to Fred Carpenter, the President's Secretary, what I wanted, and he went in to see Mr. Taft. When he came back he said that the President could not see me then, and he doubted if I could get in that afternoon, but I might wait. I did wait. There was no story going out of Washington that day or night as important as the one I was after. I sat there all the afternoon. Other newspaper men came in and asked to see the President. They got the same answer I had received. Some of them waited awhile, and others, particularly if they happened to represent opposition newspapers, accepted the situation at once and went about their other work. I stayed there until seven o'clock, when Carpenter told me that the President had gone over to the 'Big House' for dinner, and would not be back at the Executive offices that evening. Then I went to my office to see to the preparation of the story of the day.

Before ten o'clock the next morning I was back at the White House. The answer to my request to see the President was just what it had been the day before, and again I

sat down to wait. I didn't even go to my office, but talked
with the other 'Times' men by telephone from the White
House. I meant to see the President if possible, and to
make it very thoroughly clear that it was impossible to see
him before I gave it up. When he went to luncheon, I
began to think the effort was useless. But Carpenter told
me Mr. Taft would be coming back to the Executive offices
that afternoon, so I kept on waiting.

At length, about half-past three o'clock, the President
came suddenly into the little room where I was sitting. He
had not come to see me, but was on his hurried way to
another room. When he saw me sitting there, he stopped,
as if surprised.

'Hello,' he said, 'what do you want?'

'I want to see you, Mr. President,' I replied.

'Come in here,' he said, turning back to his private office.

I followed him in, and he closed the door. Then he said:

'Now, what is it?'

'Mr. President,' I said, 'do you know what the country
is saying about you to-day?'

'What do you mean?' he demanded.

'I mean,' I replied, 'that the country is saying that Taft
is lined up with Cannon.'

He shook one fist at me and exclaimed, angrily: 'By
God, you can't bluff me by talking that way.'

'Oh, Mr. President, I'm not trying to bluff you,' I retorted. 'I only want the answer. Your friends are entitled
to that. They are entitled to some explanation. There must
be an explanation. You are entitled to have it go out on
your own account. It ought to have gone out before. It
should have been made before Congress met. Now it is
pretty late, but it ought to go yet, and will still do some
good.'

Mr. Taft looked at me as if that were the very first time any such idea had occurred to him. Then, with something almost like a return of his old friendliness, he said: '

'There's something in that, Oscar. I don't know but you are right. The explanation is simply this. I have a big and important legislative programme to put through. I have looked over the situation in the House very carefully. "Uncle Joe" is the leader of the regular organization, on which I must depend for most of my legislative programme. There is a much better chance for me to get that programme through, by working with the organization, than there would be if I were to start things off by fighting it. If I did that, I should have nothing but a fight on my hands all the session. I could probably win it, but it would be at the expense of a bad split and a lot of hard feeling. Roosevelt always worked with the leaders. He found that was the best way to get legislation. He has insisted on working with Aldrich when I wanted to fight him. Now I find myself in pretty much the same situation. That's all there is to it.'

That was an exact statement of the facts of the case, and the reasoning was good enough. But the management of the situation disclosed again Mr. Taft's peculiar lack of the political sense. Mr. Roosevelt had, as Mr. Taft said, worked with Senator Aldrich and Speaker Cannon, at times, just as, at other times, he had fought them vigorously and tenaciously. On one occasion he had singled out one of the Cannon men, and opposed his reëlection so effectively as to defeat him. The Roosevelt method and reasoning were clearly set forth in a letter he had written to Mr. Taft, several years before, in reply to a criticism of Senator Aldrich by Taft. That was probably what President Taft had in mind when he said to me that Roosevelt had worked with

Aldrich when he (Taft) wanted to fight him. The Roosevelt letter, dated March 19, 1903 said:

You are unjust to Senator Aldrich. My experience for the last
year and a half, including two sessions of the last Congress, and
the special session of the Senate, which has just closed, has made
me feel respect and regard for Aldrich, as one of that group of
Senators, including Allison, Hanna, Spooner, Platt, of Con-
necticut, Lodge, and one or two others, who, together with men
like the next Speaker of the House, Joe Cannon, are the most
powerful factors in Congress. With every one of these men, I,
at times, differ radically on important questions. But they are
the leaders, and their great intelligence and power, and their
desire, in the last resort, to do what is best for the Government,
make them not only essential to work with, but desirable to work
with.

Several of the leaders have special friends whom they desire
to favor, or special interests with which they are connected, and
which they hope to serve. But, taken as a body, they are broad-
minded and patriotic, as well as sagacious, skillful, and resolute.
Each of them is set in his ways on certain points. Thus, with
both Hanna and Aldrich, I had to have a regular stand-up fight
before I could get them to accept any trust legislation; but, when
I once got them to say they would give in, they kept their
promise in good faith, and it was far more satisfactory to work
with them than to try to work with the radical 'reformers' like
Littlefield. Aldrich, for instance, has shied off from a number of
propositions in which I was interested, but, if I thought the
matter vital, and brought it before him fair and square, I have
always found him a reasonable man, open to conviction, and a
tower of strength when thus convinced.

If Mr. Roosevelt, under circumstances similar to those
confronting Mr. Taft, had decided to support Cannon for
reëlection to the speakership, the first the country would
have heard about it would have been from Roosevelt
himself, and not in any such way as Mr. Taft permitted it
to develop. Roosevelt would have written a letter to Conrad Kohrs, or Seth Bullock, or some other friend, telling

all about how he had managed to take 'Uncle Joe' and his organization into camp, and putting his own stamp on the whole transaction. Then it would have been up to the opposition to explain and overcome that impression, if it could. Roosevelt would have got the jump with the public, and the other side would have had hard work to catch up.

Long afterward, when I was talking with President Taft at the White House about an entirely different matter, he recalled this incident.

'You were right about that,' he said. 'It could have been handled in a way that would have prevented a lot of the trouble it did make.'

XXXII

THE special session of Congress which enacted the Payne-Aldrich tariff, produced one of the most spectacular fights seen in Washington in many years. It is not essential to the purpose of this book to go into any particular detail as to that fight. I am more concerned with its results. Very early in the progress of the bill in the House, it became apparent that the Cannon organization did not intend to carry out the promises, made by the party platform and candidates in the campaign of the year before, to effect a genuine reduction of rates. They talked 'revision downward,' but they acted in quite another way.

The course of the Republican leaders in the House and Senate recalled very vividly to me a conversation I had had at Youngstown, Ohio, in the fall of 1908, with James S. Kennedy, who was at that time the Representative from that district in the House. Kennedy was a wheel horse of the Cannon organization. He was an 'Old Guard' stand-patter, who had no sympathy with the downward revision pledges of the platform. I went out to Youngstown to report a Bryan meeting, and took advantage of the opportunity to call on Kennedy and talk over the political situation with him. He discussed the tariff and the promised revision with the cynical frankness of an old-school politician, and seemed to think the plan he described for hoodwinking the public was very smart. He talked as if he were really proud of it.

That plan was simply this: they would actually reduce the rates of duty, but at the same time would so change the classification of merchandise as to increase the total

amount of duty to be paid. The 'joker' was to be concealed in the administrative part of the tariff bill. Kennedy illustrated this plan by describing how it would work
in the pottery schedule. Youngstown is in the great pottery district of Ohio, and is as much interested in that
schedule as in any part of a tariff bill.

'You take a set of dishes, for instance,' said Kennedy,
'that under the present law pays sixty per cent duty, and
is so classed under the administrative clauses as to be
valued at ten dollars. That would be six dollars duty. We
will reduce the rate to forty per cent, and if the classification were not changed that would make the duty only four
dollars. But we'll fix it so that it will be valued at from
fifteen to twenty dollars. Then, with a forty per cent duty,
it will pay at least as much as it does now, and perhaps a
couple of dollars more.'

Of course, such barefaced trickery as that could not
escape the attention of the press gallery in either the
House or the Senate, and all but the extreme stand-pat
newspapers of the country printed columns, from day to
day, describing what was going on, and denouncing it in
unmeasured terms. The Progressive Republicans fought it
at every step. They were denounced as 'Insurgents' by
the Old Guard, and there was a good deal of talk about
reading them out of the party. Cannon, for the House
organization, and Aldrich, the Republican leader of the
Senate, demanded that President Taft should take that
course, and should emphasize it by denying any presidential patronage to the Insurgents.

But the President was not for that kind of a fight. In
point of fact he is not the kind of fighting man who takes
on such a struggle. He kept on trying to work with the
organization leaders in both houses, with the inevitable re-

ALDRICH—"Aw, Hang the Consumer!"

CARTOON IN THE PHILADELPHIA 'NORTH AMERICAN,' JULY 24, 1909

sult of coming more and more under their influence, and
less and less sure of his own position and leadership. And
all the time the temper of the country was rising, and his
own popularity was waning.

The President seemed utterly unable to discern the
effect upon himself. He developed a strong disinclination to hear adverse reports, and it soon became apparent
that he was receiving his information about the political
situation chiefly, if not solely, from those who were most
concerned in putting through the piece of legislative
chicanery that was going on at the Capitol. Mr. Taft's
private comments on the Insurgent leaders began to be
more and more bitter, and their public remarks about him
became more and more provocative. Such men as Dolliver,
of Iowa, Beveridge, of Indiana, and Bristow, of Kansas,
made the debate in the Senate extremely lively and entertaining. Dolliver's handling of the cotton schedule was
especially able. It was during this debate that Senator
Dolliver made that terribly cutting comment on the
President:

'He is an amiable gentleman, entirely surrounded by
men who know exactly what they want.'

Mr. Taft did make a little show of fight while the bill
was in the House. But it was a fight on details, and not on
principle. I suspected at the time, and have never had any
reason to change my feeling, that it was a well-staged fight
which very successfully tore to pieces a man made entirely
of straw. The President demanded free lumber and free
hides. One was a sop to the farmers, and the other, while
it possessed an element of general appeal, since everybody
wears shoes, was heartily desired by the shoemakers of New
England, and in that Congress New England influence was
just about paramount. The farmers were opposed to free

hides, because they still fondly imagine that in some way a duty on hides increases the price they get for their cattle, although none of them has ever been able to figure out just how much it amounts to. Free lumber was to be the special grant to the farmers to compensate them for the loss of the duty on hides.

The fight in the Senate, maintained for several weeks by the seven Insurgents, was made on principle, and went to every part of the bill. It was a fight for full redemption of the party pledge, and it came very near success. I am satisfied that but for some very effective Democratic assistance rendered to the Old Guard, the Insurgent fight would have been successful. Watching the battle daily, from the Senate press gallery, I was impressed by the fact that the Democratic opposition was not as steady and constant as I had thought it would be. There was a curiously interesting variation in the votes by which different items were passed upon. Searching for the explanation of this variation, I received from one of the floor officials of the Senate the surprising information that, very frequently, an arrangement was made with certain Democrats which enabled the Old Guard to put through an item in which it was especially concerned, and on which the Insurgent fight seemed likely otherwise to succeed.

The Senate official who told me this said that he himself had been the messenger who carried the word from Senator Crane, the Republican whip, to the chief Democratic ally in this game. Senator Crane was the right-hand man of Senator Aldrich, of Rhode Island, the powerful leader of the Old Guard, who, as chairman of the Finance Committee, was in charge of the tariff bill on the floor. My informant said that every once in a while, when a vote became imminent, and Senator Crane found that the Old Guard did not have quite enough strength to pass an item in which they were particularly interested, he would be sent to tell a certain Democratic Senator just how matters stood and how many votes were needed. Thereafter, it usually, although not always, happened, that when the vote came enough Democrats would be out of the chamber and unpaired to permit the item to go through despite the Insurgent opposition. Sometimes, he said, some of the absent Democrats would not even take the trouble to go away from the Capitol, but would merely remain in the cloakroom.

This information was confidential, and I was not permitted to use it in my reports to the New York 'Times.' I did, of course, make use of such deductions as I was justified in drawing from it. I used it in one way which evoked from that Democratic Senator a two-hour speech, one afternoon, in which he delivered a furious denunciation of me, electing me to all the Ananias Clubs that had ever been organized. The story which called forth this outburst was an analysis of the Senate, showing how each individual Senator stood in the tariff fight. I gave this man a class all by himself, as the chief Democratic assistant to Aldrich. It happened that on the afternoon when he denounced me and the 'Times' for this article, I was not at the Capitol, being on track of a story elsewhere. My assistant, who was covering the Senate and the tariff bill fight, was the late W. Sinkler Manning, son of Governor Richard I. Manning, of South Carolina, who, while serving as Major of the 316th Infantry in the Great War, was killed gallantly leading his men into action on Hill 378.

Manning was a Democrat, of course, being from South Carolina. But he was also a Democrat on principle. He knew very well what was going on in the Senate and he had no use whatever for this particular Senator. So that afternoon, after the speech, when Manning met the Senator in one of the corridors, there was a collision. Manning was a slender youngster and the Senator a great burly fellow, who carried, and used, a big umbrella. But the Capitol policemen, who stopped the row, were of the opinion that it was lucky for the Senator that they were on hand to end hostilities.

XXXIII

PRESIDENT TAFT signed the Payne-Aldrich tariff bill on August 5, 1909, and Congress promptly adjourned. There followed immediately a storm of public denunciation of the new law and of the Republican Party for violation of its platform pledges. Mr. Taft came in for his share of the condemnation, and it was plain that, in his own party, a very large faction held him chiefly to blame. The Insurgents everywhere took him to task for failing to make the kind of fight for an honest bill that they were all sure Mr. Roosevelt would have made. They earnestly believed that if Mr. Taft had made such a fight he could have obtained a greatly improved law, and one for which the claim could have been made sincerely that it was a 'revision downward' and did fulfill the pledge made by the platform of the year before and by Mr. Taft himself in repeated campaign speeches.

The situation became such that Mr. Taft's political advisers deemed it wise for him to make a swing around the country, going particularly into some of the strongly Insurgent States, and delivering a series of speeches. They thought that Mr. Taft's personal popularity could be called into play to help stop the very apparent swing against the Republican Party. They were frightened about the outcry against the Payne-Aldrich Law, and were fearful that it would cost the party the congressional elections of 1910.

So Mr. Taft made the swing, and one of the first speeches he delivered was at Winona, Minnesota, the home of Congressman James A. Tawney, chairman of the House

Committee on Appropriations, and one of the wheel horses of the Cannon organization. Tawney had once been an Insurgent himself, but Cannon annexed him, in the fall of 1905, by making him chairman of the powerful Appropriations Committee out of his regular turn. That incident brought down on Tawney a speech of denunciation in the House that was about the most effective single speech I ever heard in either branch of Congress.

That speech was less than a minute long and was confined entirely to the quotation of less than two verses from the Bible. The bill under consideration at the time was the one proposed and favored by the Cannon organization for the forcible joinder of the Territories of Arizona and New Mexico and their admission into the Union as one State. Tawney had opposed this proposition when it had first come up in the preceding Congress. He had spent a considerable part of the summer of 1905 in the Territories, pledging himself to continue his opposition to that proposition. He had headed a Republican insurrection against the bill and had some eighty Republican Congressmen signed up to help him. But the Congress elected in 1904, the year of Mr. Roosevelt's election, had such an overwhelming Republican majority in the House that it took more than eighty Republican Insurgents to defeat a measure favored by the 'organization.'

However, the extremely able and astute 'Uncle Joe' did not want that issue to come to a decision with Tawney as leader of the opposition. So he traded the appropriations chairmanship for Tawney's support of the forcible joinder bill. When the measure came up for debate on its passage, Speaker Cannon was not content to let Tawney sit quiet and merely vote for the bill that he had promised Arizona and New Mexico should pass only over his dead body; he compelled the gentleman from Minnesota to stand up and actually attempt to argue for the proposition.

That was a little too much, even for Tawney, and that voice, which usually was able, with conspicuous ease, to dominate every nook and corner of the House Chamber, was scarcely audible in the press gallery, directly above where Tawney was standing. When Tawney ceased mumbling into his bosom whatever it was he was saying, John Sharp Williams, leader of the Democrats, who controlled the time of those opposing the bill, arose and said:

'Mr. Speaker, I yield two minutes to the gentleman from Arizona, Mr. Smith.'

At that up rose Mark Smith, the delegate from Arizona. He sat next the aisle in the outer row, clear at the back of the House. He was a powerful bulk of a man, with a huge head surmounted by a shock of white hair that fairly bristled as he started down the aisle toward the seat where Tawney was huddled down, with his face as much concealed as it could be by one hand. Smith's usually florid face was flame-red with anger. Shaking one finger at Tawney, he strode along until he stood directly over his victim, and then, in a voice that filled the whole Chamber, he said:

'And Joab said to Amasa, "Art thou in health, my brother?" and Joab took Amasa by the right hand to kiss him, but Amasa took no heed to the sword that was in Joab's hand: So he smote him therewith in the fifth rib, and shed out his bowels to the ground.'

That was all. With a final shake of his big finger, Smith turned and strode back up the aisle to his seat. For an instant the House was breathlessly quiet. Then, with a shout and a roar the galleries swung into action, and the whole great chamber rang with applause, in which the Democrats and the Republican Insurgents liberally joined.

That was the Tawney for whom Mr. Taft went to Winona to speak in the early fall of 1909. Tawney needed not only such help as Mr. Taft might be able to give him, but a lot more, for his district was full of Insurgents who clamored their disapproval of the course of their representative on the tariff bill. Tawney had managed to survive his conduct in the forcible joinder case, because that was only treachery to Arizona and New Mexico, and did not directly affect the people of his district. But this tariff bill came right home to them, and from all corners of it they were calling aloud to tell 'Jim' Tawney what they thought about the tariff law and him.

Mr. Taft did, at Winona, the thing that unfortunately was not uncommon with him; in fact, it was so common as almost to justify describing it as characteristic. He made a clumsy, ill-thought-out speech, that did Tawney and himself far more damage than good. He praised the tariff law as one of the best ever made. Long afterward he confessed that he had not prepared the speech until he was on the train that was taking him to Winona. He had not received any special information as to the situation in Tawney's district, nor, in fact, did he want any. In this respect he was wholly unlike Mr. Roosevelt. The things that Mr. Roosevelt usually wanted to hear first were of the kind that Mr. Taft always regarded as unpleasant and to be kept in the background. Mr. Roosevelt wanted always to know what the opposition was, and what it was doing. Mr. Taft liked to be told that everything was well. But that is absolutely fatal in politics, as it is in war.

A little while after Mr. Taft started on his swing, Mr. Van Anda called me over to New York, and gave me in-

structions for a trip over the same country covered by the
President. I was to take my time and to find out political
sentiment in those States. Particularly I was to ascertain
the effect of the President's swing and the result of his
speeches. Mr. Van Anda was a good deal stirred up over
the situation.

'You can't fool the people of this country and get away
with it,' he said. 'Our people have made up their minds
that they want a lower tariff, and they will beat any party
that doesn't give it to them.'

I spent seventeen days on that trip, and sent only five
dispatches to the 'Times.' Each one was very thoroughly
prepared and carefully written. I put in my entire time
talking politics, getting into conversation with complete
strangers, keeping at it on trains and in the hotels where I
stopped, as well as seeing party leaders of all factions
wherever I went. There was not the least doubt in my
mind as to the situation. Everywhere there was rage
against Taft and the Republican Party. Republicans were
even more outspoken in their criticism and wrath than the
Democrats were. The Democrats took it for granted that
they would get what they had received. They were neither
surprised nor disappointed. In fact, they were inclined to
be gleeful, for they argued that it meant success for them
in the 1910 elections. In my dispatches to the 'Times' I
told the cold truth as I had found it. It certainly was not
pleasant reading for Mr. Taft and his friends, and I knew it.
But I really thought they would be glad to know the truth.
Certainly the way to meet an adverse situation is first to
learn exactly what it is.

When I got back to Washington, I went at once to the
White House. It was the coldest reception I had ever had
there. I asked to see the President, and was promptly

informed that an appointment could not be arranged. It was very plain that I was no longer in even the little favor that I had enjoyed during the summer. So I went straight at the matter:

'What's the matter with you, Fred?' I said to Mr. Carpenter, the Secretary to the President. 'You act as if you were in the middle of an ice house.'

Carpenter fidgeted a little with a pencil on his desk, and then apparently made up his mind to be as frank in his reply as I had been in my question.

'We don't like your stuff,' he said.

'Naturally,' I replied. 'I don't like it myself. But it's the truth, and the best thing a man in politics can do for himself is to find out the truth, if he can.'

'But we don't think it's the truth,' said Carpenter.

'For the love of Mike, Fred,' I said, 'where have you been? Who has been talking to you? Where have you got your information? I spent seventeen days on those five dispatches, and went very thoroughly through every State I wrote about. I didn't do a thing all that time but talk politics. What have you got that makes you think my stuff isn't true?'

Carpenter was a Minnesota man himself, but he wasn't a politician. He was a shy, reserved, quiet chap, who had been private secretary to Mr. Taft in the War Department, after serving with him in the Philippines. There had been nothing in his experience to develop any political instinct he might have had, and, if there had been, Mr. Taft was not the man to permit the same sort of relations between himself and his secretary that Mr. Roosevelt had fostered between himself and Mr. Loeb.

It finally came out that the information on which the President and Carpenter were relying about Mr. Taft's

Western trip, and the whole situation in the country he had covered, had come chiefly from Tawney, and, of course, it was rose-colored. Tawney knew Taft, if he didn't know some other things.

'Fred,' I said, 'did you ever hear the story of what Ben Butler did when the Democratic Convention of 1884 nominated Cleveland? He got up and walked out saying, "Gentlemen, may God help you, for I can't." If you're going to rely on Jim Tawney for your political information, God is the only one who can help you, and He won't.'

XXXIV

TROUBLE piled up for President Taft in 1910. Hard on the trail of the Payne Aldrich Tariff Law came the Ballinger-Pinchot controversy. The Old Guard, reluctantly recognizing the fact that its tariff trickery had produced a tremendous outburst of anger throughout the country, had been assuring the President that the popular wrath would soon die away. All that was needed was a little time for the marvelous new tariff to begin to show its effects, and then it would become even more popular than the Dingley Law had been. But the Payne-Aldrich Law was not permitted to gain the sorely needed time. Before its unpopularity could begin to subside, the Ballinger-Pinchot row came along to add a new stimulus to the anger of the Insurgent Republicans, and instead of their opposition to the President relaxing it was increased and made stronger.

Mr. Taft's selection of Richard A. Ballinger instead of James R. Garfield, to be Secretary of the Interior had been a bitter pill for the Progressives in his party to take. They wanted a man who would follow out the conservation policy of Roosevelt, and they suspected from the start that Ballinger's sympathies were on the other side. The retention of Gifford Pinchot, as Chief of the Forestry Service, did not offset the antipathy to Ballinger. Pinchot was popularly credited with being the originator of the conservation policy adopted by President Roosevelt. He was a member of the famous 'Tennis Cabinet' along with Garfield, and a most enthusiastic supporter of Mr. Roosevelt.

Pinchot, as head of the National Conservation Organization, made it his business to keep a very close watch on the actions of the new Secretary of the Interior in everything that concerned the conservation policy. It was not long before he received information which led him to believe that Mr. Ballinger was facilitating a Morgan-Guggenheim combination in the acquisition of large tracts of coal lands in Alaska, by what were practically, if not actually, fraudulent means. The charge was that entries of coal lands by dummies had been permitted, and that some lands had been patented to these dummies, although they were under contract or agreement, either being illegal, to sell the lands to the Morgan-Guggenheim combination. It was asserted that Mr. Ballinger had not made proper effort to protect the Government in these cases, and that as a result very large acreage of valuable coal lands was in danger of coming into possession of a combination that would have a practical monopoly of the vast coal supplies of Alaska.

Mr. Taft met this situation in a characteristic way. He had an investigation of the accusation by the accused, with the inevitable result of a fine coat of whitewash. The President's disinclination to tackle trouble was well displayed in this case. Two or three of the hard-headed and cynical newspaper men, who had seen many such a case run its regular course to disaster, volunteered advice, right at the start, that, if followed, would have saved Mr. Taft and his Administration from the heavy political burden that the Ballinger-Pinchot controversy soon became. This advice was to crack the heads of both Ballinger and Pinchot together on the spot, and throw them both out of the Government service.

But that called for vigorous and prompt action, and was incompatible with the Taft way of doing things. That was

the Roosevelt way. There was no better indication that
the Roosevelt influence was wholly removed from the Taft
Administration than the manner in which this controversy
between the Chief Forester and the Secretary of the
Interior was permitted to run along piling up trouble for
all concerned. It even developed into a congressional
investigation, which, in those days, was neither so easy nor
so common as in 1924.

This congressional investigation brought out some
testimony that directly involved President Taft in a
curious fashion, and even set up a question as to his
veracity. It concerned a certain memorandum that one of
Ballinger's subordinates testified had come to him from
the President. Mr. Taft was playing golf at Chevy Chase
when that testimony was given. His Secretary undertook
to reach him by telephone. The President sent General
Edwards, one of his golf partners, in from the course to the
club-house to answer the telephone call and see what was
wanted. When General Edwards brought him the word,
Mr. Taft declared at once, and with emphasis, that he
didn't know anything about it. Then he went on and
finished his game. The President's denial went out over
newspaper wires very soon after the original statement of
the Department of the Interior official.

But it soon came out that the President had in fact
prepared such a memorandum, and that the testimony of
Mr. Ballinger's subordinate had been substantially true.

Some time afterward the President volunteered to me an
explanation of this incident, which is, no doubt, the exact
truth. It simply illustrates the rather easy way in which
he sometimes took matters that were liable to be of great
importance. His explanation was that he had just plain
forgotten all about the memorandum, and that when the

word came to him on the golf course he did not recall it.
Nor did it recur to him, in fact, until that evening when he
returned to the White House. He found there, waiting for
him, the lawyer who was handling the Ballinger side of the
case before the congressional committee. The lawyer was
looking rather solemn, and the President, who was feeling
very well and happy said:

'Well, Old Man, what can I do for you?'

'Nothing, Mr. President. I thought that perhaps I
might be able to help you.'

That rather startled Mr. Taft, and he demanded to know
what the lawyer meant. The reply was that the facts, as to
the preparation of that memorandum, did not seem to
comport with the statement made by the President that
afternoon at Chevy Chase. The lawyer wanted to know
what was to be done next, for if the President stuck to his
complete denial he was certainly going to have to face an
ugly situation.

Mr. Taft told me that even under such circumstances it
was fully half an hour before he recalled what had happened
about that memorandum. He had to go back over the
events of the time when it was written, step by step, before
he got it, it had passed so thoroughly out of his mind.

The result of this interview between the President and
the lawyer was a revision of Mr. Taft's statement which
took most of the sting out of the hasty denial. The
memorandum itself was of minor importance, and that
phase of the matter did not contribute much to the
sensation.

The occasion on which Mr. Taft gave me this explanation
of the memorandum incident was an interview with
Charles Willis Thompson, then a special writer on the staff
of the New York 'Times.' I had arranged the appointment

on instructions from Mr. Van Anda, and was present at the
interview. The late Charles D. Norton was then Secretary
to the President, having succeeded Fred Carpenter some
time before.

Mr. Norton was an Assistant Secretary of the Treasury
when the post of Secretary to the President was offered to
him. He was uncertain whether to take it or not, and asked
me to come over to his office in the Treasury and talk it
over with him. He wanted to get a newspaper man's ideas
as to what the secretaryship to the President should be,
and as to how he was going to get along with the correspondents and the President as well. There had been a
great deal of criticism of Mr. Carpenter, some of it public,
and I had written an article, that had been printed in the
'Times,' saying that the trouble was not so much with
Carpenter as it was with the President himself. There had
been much talk that the Secretary should be a man like
Mr. Loeb, or Mr. Cortelyou, capable of holding a place
more nearly on a level with that of the President. It was
not a place for a mere stenographer and clerk, but for an
assistant to the President. But I had pointed out in my
article that, unless the President were willing to have his
Secretary serve him as his assistant, it was no place for a
man of the assistant caliber. It was bound to develop an
incompatibility that would make only trouble all the
time.

When Mr. Norton went into the White House, he
evidently had talked this situation out pretty thoroughly
with the President, for there was an immediate and distinct
improvement in the relations between the President and
the newspaper men. We began to get back into something
of our old status with Mr. Taft, and it was no longer such a
rare thing to get an appointment with him, even on very

short notice. I had sometimes succeeded, in emergencies, in seeing him immediately on submitting the request.

Mr. Thompson came down to Washington from New York for that interview, and we saw the President in the 'Big House' one evening after dinner. Mr. Norton was with him. Mr. Taft was feeling very well, and was as jovial and good-natured as he is generally reputed to be. The interview went along very well, indeed. The President talked a great deal about the Ballinger-Pinchot case, besides giving that explanation of the memorandum incident. He also talked about the tariff law and its effects, and about the general legislative situation. He voluntarily brought up my talk with him about the election of Speaker Cannon, and said I had been quite right about it.

XXXV

A NEWSPAPER man's recollection of dates is often uncertain, and mine is no exception to that rule. It must have been about this time — that is, in the fall or winter of 1910–11 that an incident occurred which led the New York 'Times' to print a story that it knew would be denied on every hand as soon as it was printed, and which was yet absolutely true, at least up to the moment of its publication. This was the story of Secretary Knox's contemplated resignation from the Taft Cabinet. It was printed for the purpose of preventing that resignation, and of course it had the desired effect.

Just after I had finished my dinner one evening, Senator Borah came to my house and asked if I would walk downtown with him. Of course I did so. As soon as we had started, he began to tell me about trouble in the Cabinet. It seemed that Senator Knox had accepted the post of Secretary of State with the understanding that he was to be the chief political and legal adviser of the President. In fact, he was to be the administration premier. But he had found by experience that he had been mistaken. It had developed that Mr. Wickersham, the Attorney-General, was the chief consultant of the President, and Mr. Knox, although left with a free hand in the State Department, began to find that he was comparatively out of it so far as other matters of importance to the Administration were concerned.

The Secretary was hurt and chagrined. Naturally, he brooded over the situation, and more and more it came to seem to him that others must be noticing the way in which he was being overshadowed by Mr. Wickersham. Mr. Knox was a great lawyer. He had served with distinguished success as Attorney-General in Mr. Roosevelt's Cabinet, and had been one of the outstanding figures in the Senate, at a time when men of distinction and attainment were not a rarity in that body.

On the day on which Senator Borah came to me, Senator Crane had come to Borah, in the Senate Chamber, and talked with him a long time about Secretary Knox and this situation in the Cabinet. Crane urged Borah to go up to the State Department and see Knox and endeavor to dissuade him from resigning. Senator Crane thought it would be a great mistake for Mr. Knox to permit his personal feeling, even though he had been slighted by the President, to lead him to resign. It would not only have bad political effects, but Mr. Knox himself could probably never recover from it. It would be absolutely impossible to conceal the real reason for the resignation, for there was no other cause that could possibly be assigned. There was nothing in the diplomatic situation that would warrant it, and the Secretary's health and that of the members of his family was very good.

Senator Borah was a great admirer and friend of Mr. Knox. He held the Pennsylvanian in the highest esteem, as a constitutional lawyer and an executive of unusual ability. Moreover, he felt, for party reasons, that it would be a bad thing for Mr. Knox to quit. So he went to the State Department and saw the Secretary. He was there for a long time, and the two men had a very frank discussion of the situation. But no argument that the Senator could make seemed to produce any impression upon the Secretary. Mr. Knox was determined to resign, and did not seem to care what the effect might be upon himself. He was outspoken in his resentment of his treatment by the President, and declared that he had endured it just as long as he could.

Senator Borah left the State Department in a great quandary. He felt that it was urgently necessary to prevent Mr. Knox from resigning, but he didn't see how it could be done. At length it occurred to him to talk it over with me. He knew that I would protect the confidence, if that were desired, and he thought I might possibly have some suggestion that neither he nor Senator Crane had thought of.

When the Senator concluded his account of the situation I said:

'I can stop his resignation.'

'How?' asked the Senator.

'By printing the story, just as you have told it,' I replied. 'No man can afford to leave the Cabinet for a reason like that. I don't know whether Knox has any further political ambition or not, but, if he has, such a resignation would kill him. The printing of the story won't affect him very much, for it will be denied very promptly by everybody connected with the Administration, including Knox himself. He and the President will be the first to get out their denials, and Wickersham will come along with a vigorous description of the nonsense of such a tale. You and Crane will deny it, and I shall be left without a leg to stand on. All the other correspondents will have the laugh on me, and their papers will rig the 'Times' about it. But Knox will stay in the Cabinet.'

Senator Borah and I talked this scheme over for some time, and it was at length agreed that I should try it on. I pointed out to the Senator that I could not assure the publication of the story in the 'Times.' I could only send it to the office and abide their judgment there. I said that

I should have to call up Mr. Van Anda and explain the whole matter to him, so that they could know in the New York office exactly what the situation was, before determining what to do with the story. Borah said all right, and to go ahead on that basis.

So I wrote the story, pretty fully, but, as I recall it now, without mentioning the name of either Senator Crane or Senator Borah. I felt, when it came to the actual writing of the story, that it would be better, for the purpose I had in mind, not to go into such minute detail as to carry inherent evidence of its accuracy. It seemed better to leave the door open to a charge of willful and complete imagination, although that was very far from the character of the New York 'Times,' then or now.

When the story was finished and ready for the wire, I called Mr. Van Anda on the telephone and told him what I had. I said that the story was literally true at that moment, but would be wholly untrue the moment it was printed, and predicted that everybody in official position in Washington, who could by any means have any knowledge of the Cabinet situation, would hurry up the next day to deny it if it were printed.

Mr. Van Anda laughed and said: 'Send it along, and we'll see what we can do about it.'

So I put it on the wire, and went home wondering what the outcome would be. Next morning when I picked up my 'Times' there was my story in the most prominent place, outside column front page, with a big black headline of several banks. Mr. Van Anda had decided to give it all the force he could.

My predictions to Senator Borah and Mr. Van Anda proved to be absolutely accurate. I had hardly got to my office that morning before some of the other correspondents

began to call me up and 'ride' me about that story. They
wanted to know where in the world I had got hold of such
stuff. Of course, it was denied. The White House led off
and the State Department followed, with the Department
of Justice coming along well in line. There wasn't a shred
left of the story by noon. Along in the afternoon a group of
correspondents went up to the State Department to see
Secretary Knox, and I went with them. As we entered the
Secretary's office, I was in the lead. Mr. Knox was sitting
at his desk. He looked up, and, as he saw me, a broad grin
came over his face. He got up from his desk and came
toward me with outstretched hand. He knew exactly what
had happened to him, although whether or not he ever
learned just how it happened, I do not know. I do know
that the incident did not alter in the least the very pleasant
relations I had long had with him.

XXXVI

Colonel Roosevelt returned to New York, from his hunting trip in Africa, in the early summer of 1910, after having spent some time in Europe, during which he had visited the various capitals, and been the guest of a number of monarchs. The enthusiasm with which he was received in the United States surpassed anything that had been shown for him, even at the height of his popularity as President. While he was in Africa he had been out of touch, of course, with details of political happenings in the United States, but, before he left Europe, he had seen a number of his close friends, including Gifford Pinchot, who had given him full information as to the situation at home.

Mr. Roosevelt landed in New York silent on the subject of politics, and with the announcement that he intended to maintain that silence, as he was out of politics, with no intention of getting in again. By this time the dissatisfaction of the Progressive, or Insurgent faction, of the Republicans with President Taft was complete. From all parts of the Middle West, especially, they were crying aloud that they would have none of him or his works. They were openly accusing him of apostasy to his pledges to carry out the Roosevelt policies, and were saying sarcastically that the only way in which he had ever intended to carry them out was on a shutter, for burial.

Naturally, there was prompt and emphatic appeal to Colonel Roosevelt to resume his leadership of the Progressives, and he was urged by some of his closest friends to put himself in position to be a candidate for the Republican nomination in 1912 to succeed Mr. Taft. But to all such suggestions and appeals Colonel Roosevelt responded with a decided refusal to reenter politics.

It remained for Governor Hughes to persuade Mr. Roosevelt to depart from this resolution. Mr. Roosevelt was an Overseer of Harvard College, and in that capacity attended the commencement exercises of that year. Governor Hughes was also there, as the recipient of an honorary degree. The Governor was at that time engaged in a sharp fight with the Old Guard Republican machine in New York, under the leadership of William Barnes, of Albany. The particular measure about which this fight centered, for the moment, was a bill pending in the legislature to establish a system of direct primaries for New York State. It was known as the Hinman-Greene Bill, being sponsored in the Senate by Senator Harvey D. Hinman, of Binghamton, and in the Assembly by Assemblyman Greene.

When Governor Hughes and Colonel Roosevelt met at the Harvard commencement, the Governor asked the Colonel to help out in the fight for this bill. He pointed out that the men who were supporting the bill at Albany had been among Mr. Roosevelt's steady supporters when he was the leader of the Republican Party. This was a measure in accord with the principles which Mr. Roosevelt held. These men, who had always responded when he called upon them, were now carrying on the same old fight for progressivism in which they had served faithfully under his direction. They felt that they were entitled to have his support now, as they had given him their support in other times.

'And, by George, they'll get it,' responded Colonel Roosevelt.

Thus he made the one answer that he could always be

expected to make to such a plea. No man who had ever done anything for Theodore Roosevelt, which could be held to have put Mr. Roosevelt under a personal obligation, ever called on him in vain for the redemption of that obligation. In such a case he did not consider the result generally, or the effect upon himself or his political or other fortunes. He simply paid the debt. Before my political connection with him came to an end, with the demise of the Progressive Party, I saw him make payment on many an obligation of that sort, some of them no doubt real enough, but most of them, it seemed to me, only fancied. Nevertheless, they were represented to him as real, and he responded as though he believed them to be such.

His response to the appeal of Governor Hughes was thoroughly characteristic. That day he sent a telegram to Senator Frederick M. Davenport, who was leading the fight for the Hinman-Greene Bill, promising his hearty support of the measure. From that moment Colonel Roosevelt was back in politics, and the way was opened for all the amazing events of the next four years.

Thus, singularly enough, it fell to the lot of Governor Hughes to take another effective step toward the downfall of the Republican Party. If he had been in the White House, instead of Taft, at that time, as he might very well have been, if he had been willing, or had known how, to play the game in 1907 and 1908, the particular situation which was used to bring Colonel Roosevelt out of his political retirement would not have arisen. Nor is it likely that there would have developed in the party generally anything like the revolt against Hughes that had grown up against Taft. For Hughes showed, throughout his four years in the governorship, both a willingness

and an ability to fight the Old Guard which never characterized Mr. Taft's administration of the presidency. And
it was that lack of political aggressiveness, particularly in
behalf of a considerable number of definite measures to
which he was pledged by his platform and his own campaign speeches, that chiefly led to the undoing of President
Taft.

Mr. Roosevelt's promise of support for the primary bill
immediately brought him a flood of requests and demands
from old political supporters for help in their personal
campaigns all over the country. It was a country-wide
secret that the Republican campaign for the congressional
elections was in a very bad way. The Old Guard, in control of the Republican Congressional Committee, were
openly refusing assistance to the Insurgents, and everywhere the Insurgents were denouncing the Old Guard.
If the Insurgents could not secure help from Colonel
Roosevelt, there seemed no place where they could get it.

In New York State, the Progressive faction in the Republican Party came forward with a demand that Colonel
Roosevelt should be a candidate for the temporary chairmanship of the State Convention that was to be held at
Saratoga in September. The Old Guard had picked James
S. Sherman, of Utica, for this post. Mr. Sherman was then
Vice-President of the United States, having been elected
with Mr. Taft in 1908. He had served previously for
several terms in the House of Representatives, where he
was one of the stanchest supporters of 'Uncle Joe' Cannon and the 'regular' House organization. That 'regular
organization,' by the way, was nothing more than a little
group of strong men who appointed themselves to leadership and enforced their appointment by their own skill and
ability. It was absolutely dominated by Mr. Cannon, who,

whatever else might be said about him, was a fighting man
from the headwaters of Fight Creek. There was never any
doubt about where 'Uncle Joe' stood, or that he would
contend to the utmost of his strength for his position.

Everybody in the country understood perfectly that, if
Colonel Roosevelt accepted the appeal of the Progressives
to stand for the temporary chairmanship of the Saratoga
Convention, it meant his resumption of the leadership of
that part of the Republican Party in New York State, with
all sorts of possibilities so far as the national situation was
concerned. Everybody understood, also, that it meant a
first-class, bitter fight at Saratoga, and that it probably
foretold the defeat of the Republican candidate for the
governorship of New York that fall.

For some time Colonel Roosevelt held the matter under
advisement, and during that time he consulted freely with
men in all walks of life and all degrees of influence and
authority in Republican Party affairs. Meantime he went
ahead with preparations for a trip out through the Middle
West, on which he was to make a number of speeches. In-
vitations to deliver these speeches had been sent to him
even before he returned to the United States, and one, at
least, of them had been accepted, although with the distinct understanding that there was to be no political flavor
to the occasion. That was an invitation forwarded through
Senator Warren, of Wyoming, to attend the annual stock
men's celebration in Cheyenne. There was a peculiar appeal to Colonel Roosevelt in such an invitation, because of
both his fondness for the West and his previous ranching
experience.

It was finally arranged that the trip should be made
under the auspices of the 'Outlook,' on which Colonel
Roosevelt had assumed his place as contributing editor.

It was to include stops in many of the States of the Middle
West, and the Colonel was to make eight or ten formal addresses, on different non-political subjects, with, of course,
an unestimatable number of rear-platform, five-minute
appearances, at the more important places where his train
stopped. The trip was to begin on August 23d, and there
were to be formal speeches at Cheyenne; Denver; Ossawa-
tamie, Kansas; Kansas City; Omaha; Sioux Falls, South
Dakota; Sioux City, Iowa; Fargo, North Dakota; and
some other places.

So many newspapers wanted to send reporters with
Colonel Roosevelt that they joined in chartering a private
car for their men, and it was arranged that this car should
be coupled in ahead of that of Colonel Roosevelt on whatever train he took. I represented the New York 'Times'
with the party, and was with Colonel Roosevelt throughout that fall until the election, with the single exception of
a trip that he made from New York to Des Moines, Iowa,
in October.

Having been in Washington all the summer, I had not
had opportunity to see Colonel Roosevelt, or have any
talk with him, since his return from Africa. I knew from
others, however, of some of the reports of the political
situation that had been made to him, and was aware, of
course, of the proposition that had been put up to him regarding the Saratoga Convention. It was not until the
morning of August 23d that he announced his decision in
that matter. Then, when he came to the Grand Central
Station to take his train for the long trip West, he told the
twenty-odd newspaper men who were going with him that
he had decided to make the run for the temporary chairmanship.

The big fight was on.

XXXVII

ALL of the formal speeches for the trip had been prepared well in advance and distributed through the press associations for release as delivered. The job of the correspondents with the Roosevelt party was to report the incidents of the trip rather than the speeches. There was no politics in any of the prepared speeches, and, despite the announcement of his intention to make the fight for the temporary chairmanship at Saratoga, the Colonel insisted that he would not be drawn into any political discussion before that time.

His first speech was delivered that afternoon, at a farmers' picnic, at Oriskany, New York. Mr. Roosevelt had always been very greatly interested in rural life, and as President he had appointed a commission to make a special study of it, with a view to suggesting means of improving the conditions of farm life. He had a great deal to say on that subject, and his speech at Oriskany was correspondingly long.

It was delivered in a wooded natural amphitheater, with a great crowd of farmers and their wives and children seated among the trees in front of him. He stuck religiously to his text, and it was not many minutes, after the first enthusiasm at seeing him had worn off, before it began to be perfectly plain that his audience was not particularly interested in what he was saying. Those farmers seemed to think that they knew a great deal more about the subject than Colonel Roosevelt did. They were plainly bored. They wanted him to talk politics, in which they were just then very much concerned.

Mr. Roosevelt was always very quick to sense the feeling of his audience, and he saw plainly that the Oriskany crowd was not with him in what he was telling it. At length, when he was about halfway through his printed speech, half a dozen men in one of the back rows got up to leave. In order to get out of the place they had to come right down the middle aisle, directly in front of, and toward, Colonel Roosevelt. He could not help seeing them, or understanding what was the trouble. So, with characteristic readiness, he injected a single remark on the political situation.

Instantly those farmers, who were so bored with his farm talk that they were quitting the meeting, caught the new slant and changed their minds. They sat right down on the grass in that middle aisle, just where they were, and there they remained during the rest of Mr. Roosevelt's talk, obviously hoping that he would get on to their favorite topic again before quitting. But he had nothing more to say on that subject, and they were disappointed. It was a very clear indication, however, of the situation in that part of the State. And before that trip was ended there were plenty of other similar indications as to the feeling in other States.

Our train went back to Utica from Oriskany, and Colonel Roosevelt motored out to Henderson Farm, the home of his brother-in-law, Douglas Robinson, to spend the night and the next day. He told us that he planned to have some fun the next morning doing some cross-country riding.

On the afternoon of August 24th about a dozen of the newspaper men motored out to Henderson Farm for a talk with the Colonel. It was then that I had my first private conversation with him after his return from the African trip. We sat out on the porch of the Robinson home, and for quite a while discussed the general political situation in the country. The colonel was very blue about the prospects for Republican success that fall, and did not see how anything could be done to forestall defeat. He admitted a great disappointment in Taft as President, and talked for some time about how he had been mistaken in his estimate of Mr. Taft's character. He said that when he began to receive letters in Africa telling him of the way things were going at home, and of Mr. Taft's increasing tendency to ally himself with the Old Guard, there had come back to him the recollection of incidents that had occurred while he was President and Mr. Taft was Secretary of War, and he had realized that at the time of the incidents he had misinterpreted their meaning. He spoke particularly of the way in which Mr. Taft would bring a case to him, as if for report on a decision made by the Secretary, but would really report it in such a manner as to lead him — the President — to make the decision. Mr. Taft was a master hand at summing up each side of a case, and presenting it in such a way that a man so prompt in decision as Mr. Roosevelt would almost inevitably be ready with his judgment by the time the Secretary was through his summary.

Recalling these things, Colonel Roosevelt said he began to see how Mr. Taft, as President, coming more and more into contact with those men whom Senator Dolliver had described as 'knowing exactly what they wanted,' would fall, insensibly, but in increasing degree, into the habit of turning to them for decision and relying upon it when it had been given.

Turning to the question of his own course, Colonel Roosevelt said it was clear to him that he must continue to support Taft, at least for the present. He did not relish in the least the prospect that was ahead of him for that fall, for he foresaw the party defeat, and did not believe that any good could come out of his own participation in the campaign. But he could not help going in, for he had to meet his obligations to the men who demanded his support in return for support they had given him when he was the party leader.

When the talk had proceeded in this way for some time, I said:

'Well, Colonel, how about the White House again for yourself?'

'I don't care that for it,' he replied instantly, and with a little gesture that was characteristic of him. He snapped his thumb and forefinger together with a motion as if tossing something very light over his right shoulder.

'I don't care that for it,' he repeated. 'I've been there for seven and a half years. I've had all the work and all the fun, all the honor and all the glory, of it, and I wouldn't give that [repeating his gesture] for any more of it.

'I am the only man in the United States who can speak of the presidency without the thrill that always comes to the man who has never been in the White House. To go to the White House again simply for the sake of being President doesn't interest me in the least. There are so many things that I haven't yet done and that I want so much to do. I want to take some time now, in the next few years, to do some of those things. I have done something in geography and something in ornithology, and something in other lines. I want to put myself in position where I can be rightfully recognized as a scientist in one or two of these lines.

'Most men in this country think of the presidency

as the supreme thing, and that is natural and all right. But I've had that, and another term could not add anything to what I have had there. Of course, if there were a big job of work to be done, which the people of the country wanted me to handle, that would be a different thing. But then it would be going back in order to do a particular thing, and one that I had not done before. It would not be going back simply for the sake of being President again. There is a far greater probability that another term in the White House, unless under the exceptional conditions I spoke about, would detract from my record, than there is that it would add to the record.'

Continuing his talk a little, and turning again to some of the things he wanted to do, the Colonel indicated his desire to travel and to do some scientific work in geography. He said he wanted to go to South America, now that he had been in Africa. Of course, his work in Africa had been essentially scientific, but it had not been of a character to qualify him as a scientist. He thought he could qualify in geography, if he had the opportunity. He spoke also of wanting to go to China, but conditions there were not so favorable as they were for a trip to South America.

XXXVIII

THIS private talk with the Colonel lasted probably more than half an hour. When it was ended, we went into the house, and at once the Colonel was surrounded by the newspaper men who had come out from Utica, and went into a discussion of the general political situation in the country as well as in New York State. I probably do not recall all the men who were there and heard his talk, but I remember Angus McSween, of the Philadelphia 'North American'; John Snure, of the Des Moines 'Register'; Charlie Kern and Lucius Curtis, of the Associated Press; Arthur Samuels of the 'Sun,' and Griffin, of the 'Evening Sun.' I think George Hill, of the New York 'Tribune,' was there, but am not sure. There were probably five or six others also.

Colonel Roosevelt began by expressing the opinion that the Republican Party was in for a 'licking,' and said that nothing Taft could do would prevent it. Nor could anything that he could do prevent it. The country was displeased with the tariff law, and the Progressive Republicans were displeased with the way President Taft had associated himself with the reactionary element in the party. It did not seem likely that anything could be done to improve either phase of that situation. As for the tariff law, that was probably as good as any. He himself was not a tariff expert and frankly did not know. He meant to steer, as nearly as possible, clear of tariff discussion during his campaigning, but, if he had to say anything, it probably would be that the Payne-Aldrich Law was a pretty good one, and, anyway, it was entitled to a chance to show how it would work. It was not fair to condemn it out of hand, before it had had an opportunity to prove or disprove itself. That was merely what the Democrats were doing, and that was just what they had done before any part of it had been settled by Congress.

As for Taft's association with the Old Guard, that was frankly disappointing, but he thought he could understand pretty well how it had come about. He himself had always been ready to work with the organization in Congress to get through legislation that he wanted. That had to be done sometimes. Take the Meat Inspection Law, for instance, and the Railroad Rate Bill of 1906, the so-called Dolliver-Hepburn Law. Neither was all he had wanted, but each was all he could get, and if he hadn't been willing to work with the organization leaders, in both House and Senate, he couldn't have had either. In the case of the Rate Bill, he had even worked with Senator Tillman, when the opposition to the bill in committee had tried to put up a job on him by placing the bill in Tillman's charge during its discussion on the floor.

The Colonel spoke particularly of Senator Aldrich, leader of the reactionary faction of Republicans in the Senate. He described the Rhode Island Senator as a very strong man, with whom he had frequently worked in order to get some legislation that he was after. But he always took care to get Aldrich on his side before he would work with him. Once Aldrich agreed to do anything, he could be very sure that it would be done, for Aldrich always kept his word.

'Now there's another thing about this situation,' the Colonel said. 'I am going into this campaign. You will see that at once all those who are opposed to me, for any reason, will try to make me the sole issue. I shall be

pounded from one end of the country to the other. They
will ignore all the real issues and concentrate all their fire
on me.

'In the end we shall be beaten. Then they will all shout
"Roosevelt was the cause of it." And then they will cheer
and shout that Roosevelt is dead

'On the other hand, if I were to keep out of it, we should
be beaten just the same, but the campaign would have to
be made on other lines, and the real issues might have a
chance for some consideration. But the Republican Party
is due for a licking, and nothing that any or all of us can do
will stop it. If I were to keep out, then, after the defeat,
there is a probability that some portion of the party would
turn again to me for leadership. Some of the Progressives
are urging that on me right now.'

'But, Colonel,' said one of the boys, 'under those circumstances why don't you stay out? Why do you go in now?'

'Because I couldn't live with myself if I didn't go in,'
replied the Colonel. 'These men who are asking me for
support now were always ready to do all they could whenever I, as President, or Governor of this State, called on
them for support. They say to me now, in effect, that they
want my help in return. I am under obligation to them,
and when they call on me I must respond.'

That was the real explanation of the action of Colonel
Roosevelt, in politics, during the last few years of his life.
He saw, as clearly as any one could, the effect of this action
upon himself and his own fortunes. He indicated, that
afternoon at Henderson Farm, how clearly he understood
that if he really did want to go back to the White House
again, the way to get there was just to sit tight, keep quiet
in that campaign, and let events take their natural course.

Already more attention was being paid to him through-

out the country than to President Taft, and from all parts
of the Nation there were coming insistent calls for him to
renew his leadership of the party. These calls were by no
means confined to the Progressive element. In fact a considerable number of those who were acting together in
getting him into the fight in New York State that fall were
distinctly of the Old Guard stripe, and in subsequent years
lined up against him. But with Colonel Roosevelt it was
just a case of obligation to others who had done favors
for him. As long as that case could be made out, he would
make the same response. In the end he paid every such
debt. Then he did get out of politics and kept out, to the
extent of letting no demand from others for support interfere with his own ideas as to what he should or should not
do.

'Just one thing more,' said the Colonel, in closing that
general interview. 'Win or lose in this fight, I am going to
Sagamore for ten days or two weeks after election, and I
shall not see any one. I want to rest. There is every probability now that we shall be defeated. But win or lose, I
am going to take that rest. I shall not see any one, and I
tell you this now, so that you will not be coming out and
asking to see me, for I should have to disappoint you, and
I do not want to seem discourteous. I do not want to have
to put the bars up at the Sagamore gates, and I am telling
you this now, so that you will know just why you must not
come out there then.

'That is what I am going to do whether we win or
whether we lose. If we win, I shall probably be accused of
plotting some deep schemes of personal political advantage. If we lose, I shall certainly be accused of being a
sorehead and a bad loser. But you boys will know the
truth.'

It is worth remembering that this conversation with Colonel Roosevelt took place on August 24th, more than nine weeks before the election. I do not know what the other newspaper men did about it, but I took pains to let my office know that Colonel Roosevelt intended to stay quietly at home for ten days or two weeks after election, no matter what its result, and would not see any one. The event proved him to be an absolutely accurate prophet. The Republican Party met an overwhelming defeat, and Colonel Roosevelt, in his retirement at Sagamore, was roundly denounced, from one end of the country to the other, as a sorehead and a very poor loser. He was so denounced by some newspapers whose representatives had been present that afternoon at Henderson Farm and heard what he said about his post-election plans. I call that dishonest journalism.

But it made no great difference, at that time, what Mr. Roosevelt did, or did not do, whether he spoke, or was silent, criticism of him flourished. There were always some newspapers pounding him. He illustrated the situation, perfectly, one afternoon in conversation with me in his room at the 'Outlook' offices. It was on the sixth floor.

'There are only two elevators in this building,' he said, 'and I must use one or other of them. If I go down by the side elevator, that is evidence of furtiveness. If I go down in front, that is proof of ostentation.'

XXXIX

THE Roosevelt party left Utica on the night of August 24th, headed toward Cheyenne and Denver. Wherever the train stopped, a crowd was gathered in the hope of catching a glimpse of the Colonel, or receiving even a short greeting from him. At Cleveland there was a great throng around the station. They could not get down to the car, and so Colonel Roosevelt left it, climbed over an iron fence and up a steep embankment, and talked for a few minutes. He always had a message for such a crowd, and throughout this trip his message was received with an enthusiasm even greater than any he had enjoyed while President.

Even at night, the crowds kept appearing at stations where the train was scheduled for a stop, and often, even when the train was not due to stop, the crowd would be there just the same. They waited until midnight and after, and not a few times, when the train stopped in the small hours, the crowd would gather about the Colonel's car and shout: 'Teddy! Teddy!' Sometimes they added the plea, 'Stick out your head. We want to see you.' Occasionally the Colonel responded to these demands, and when he did there was always a wild cheering and jamming to get into better position just to see him.

As the train was coming east from Denver, after his stop there, it ran for a long time through the very sparsely settled section of western Kansas. It was a dark afternoon, with a rather hard rain falling. I was sitting in the Colonel's car talking with him about the events at Denver when I noticed a woman standing at the wire fence that ran along-side the track. She had a baby in her arms, and had protected him from the rain by throwing a part of her shawl over his head. About half a mile away was a small ranch house, where evidently she lived. It seemed that she had walked all that way in the rain, carrying the child, just on the chance of getting a glimpse of Colonel Roosevelt as his train swept by. The Colonel was facing the other side of the track and did not see her. I touched him on the knee and pointed out the window. Instantly he took in the situation. He jumped to the rear platform and waved his hand to the woman. She saw him, and with both hands lifted the baby up toward the Colonel. There she held him until the train had rolled far down the track and was almost out of sight. Then she turned and started trudging back through the rain toward her house.

'By George!' said the Colonel, as he came back into the car and resumed his seat. 'A thing like that gives you a lump in the throat. It makes me feel like a great calf. These people have such trust and confidence, and so often they think a man can do all sorts of things that no one can do.'

There were no incidents about the trip, as far as Denver, which I recall especially, but a thing happened at Denver which gave a new opportunity to the Roosevelt opposition all over the country to raise an outcry against him. This was a speech which he delivered before the legislature of Colorado. That speech was not in the programme that had been arranged before he left New York, and consequently had not been prepared in advance. The press associations, therefore, had not been able to make distribution of it to their members, and the newspaper men with the Colonel expected to report it themselves, as they heard it. But on the way down from Cheyenne to Denver that morning, the representatives of the Associated Press and United Press

ROOSEVELT IN ACTION
AT ASHEVILLE, NORTH CAROLINA, 1904

went to the Colonel and urged him to give them something
about his speech before the legislature that they could send
out at once. They told him that, unless that were done,
there would be no probability of getting the publicity for
that speech to which it would be entitled. The Colonel
was to deliver the speech that he had prepared for Denver
in the afternoon at the great convention hall, and was to
go from there directly to the State Capitol to address the
legislature. The association men told him that, unless they
had something of the second speech which they could send
out ahead, the first one would absorb all the space the
newspapers could give to his Denver meetings.

Colonel Roosevelt understood very well the force of that
argument. He was never lacking in appreciation of publicity, or in skill in getting it. But he told the newspaper
men that he had not prepared anything for the legislature,
and was going to speak entirely extemporaneously. Thereupon they urged him to dictate something that they could
use. At that Colonel Roosevelt took from his pocket two
typewritten sheets. He said that that was the only part of
his speech before the legislature that he had ready. But he
did not want to give that to the association men because it
needed both an introduction and a few paragraphs to
follow it, in order to make the application that he intended
to make in his talk.

The boys immediately promised to send his introduction
and his application if he would outline it for them, and he
did so. He told them the substance of what he meant to
say in leading up to the two pages, which, he said, were a
quotation, having been written for him. Then he outlined
to them the manner in which he intended to apply what
he had quoted.

The association men took the two typewritten pages and

hurried into the newspaper car to copy them. Then they wrote out their 'leads,' giving the Colonel's introduction and close, and, immediately on arrival at Denver, put this all on the wires. But I doubt if a single newspaper in the country printed either the opening or the closing part of that talk, whereas every one of them printed the two typewritten pages. Every paper I saw gave only that, and carried for introduction of it a single line, saying, 'In his speech before the Colorado legislature this afternoon Colonel Roosevelt said.'

If any newspapers did do more than that, they were so few that they were lost in the general run. At any rate, it was immediately apparent that the whole country had received the impression that the quoted part was all the Colonel had said to the legislature that was worth considering.

That quoted part—those two typewritten pages—contained the famous attack on the Supreme Court of the United States, for which Colonel Roosevelt was so roundly denounced in all parts of the country. It may be recalled, but probably by few, if any, that Colonel Roosevelt never replied to any of this criticism. He never, so far as I am aware, made any public explanation of this incident.

But the fact was that those two typewritten pages had been prepared for him by a friend, who was at that time an Associate Justice of the Supreme Court, and who had been on that bench for some years. The Colonel had told me, in confidence, at the time he made the speech, where that part of it came from. But, when he found that the use he had made of it had produced such a sensation and evoked such criticism of himself, he simply took his medicine and never said a word about it.

The Justice of the Supreme Court who had prepared

those pages also maintained absolute silence. It did seem
to me that he might have come forward with a statement
that would have thrown a different light on the matter.
But, as long as he did not, the Colonel felt that it was in-
cumbent upon him not to say anything.

There would have been nothing inappropriate in an ex-
planantion by the Justice of his authorship of that criticism
of the Court. Justices on the bench not infrequently say
things about the Court more severe than anything contained in what Colonel Roosevelt used. I once heard
Justice Peckham deliver from the bench a criticism of the
Court in language that always seemed to me most extraordinary. He was reading his dissenting opinion in the
famous Shipp contempt of court case. Sheriff Shipp, of
Chattanooga, had been served with an injunction, issued
by Associate Justice Harlan, intended to prevent the
lynching of a negro, who was at that time confined in the
Chattanooga jail, in the custody of Sheriff Shipp. Nevertheless, the sheriff did not prevent a mob from getting the
prisoner and the negro was lynched. Thereupon the sheriff
and some others were brought before the full Court, and,
after extended hearings, were adjudged guilty of contempt
and punished. The Court divided, five to four, as I recall
it, and when Justice Peckham delivered his dissenting
opinion he gave every appearance of being much wrought
up. His naturally florid face was very red, his eyes flashed,
and he did the unheard-of thing of making gestures while
reading his opinion. At one point he actually pounded the
bench in front of him, and exclaimed:

'There isn't a scintilla of evidence in this case upon
which to found the judgment of the Court.'

It has always been a source of wonderment to me what
would happen to anybody but an Associate Justice of the

Court who ventured to make in public such a remark about one of its decisions. That remark seemed to need only applause from the audience to make its contempt of the Court complete.

XL

THE pressure on Colonel Roosevelt to talk politics on this trip was tremendous. There was no variation in the enthusiasm with which he was received, and the stops of one day were much like those of another. No person has ever received greater evidences of popularity in this country, and if Mr. Roosevelt had been smitten by the personal ambition, of which he was so often accused, this trip could not have failed to set him thinking about ways and means of capitalizing the feeling for him so generously demonstrated every day.

At Kansas City his speech was delivered in the convention hall, a huge building that was estimated to accommodate sixteen thousand persons. However many it would hold, it was full. I doubt if a single additional adult or child could have squeezed in. There was a tumult when the Colonel entered, like that which greets the formal naming of the favorite at a national political convention. And when the prepared speech had been delivered, the crowd rose and cheered, and demanded more. Colonel Roosevelt was not often eloquent. He had a style that did not lend itself to moving oratory. He always felt it necessary to balance his statements in a way to make his meaning perfectly explicit, and, although he was a master at coining phrases that would stick in the memory, he rarely built up oratorical periods.

But this Kansas City reception stirred him to impromptu eloquence. He added an appeal that reached that vast crowd and moved it to an unusual demonstration. He had turned away from the audience to resume his seat when the cheers and applause and cries for more gave him a new inspiration. Turning back to face the audience he said, in substance:

'My friends, I have just come back from Africa, and I had a good time there. On my way home I visited a number of the different courts of Europe. I saw how they lived there. I heard what they said. Everywhere I had the the same experience. The things they knew and thought about America were of the scandals and crime and the low, unpleasant side of life. There seemed to run through all of them a feeling of cynicism, a kind of half-concealed scorn of America and American life.

'And then, too, everywhere I went, I met the common people. And among them I found a different feeling about this country. Everywhere among those people there was a wistfulness about America. They thought of this country as a place of relief for the things in their own life that oppress and dismay them. Here was escape. Here was freedom to live their own lives and make the most of themselves.

'Oh, my friends, I beg of you so to live and so to see that your country is governed that this Nation may always be in very truth the door of golden hope to the oppressed and downtrodden of all the world!'

It is quite probable that not many of the sixteen thousand or more persons who heard that Kansas City speech remember much more of it than what it was about, if they recall that much. But it is safe to say that pretty much all of them remember clearly that final appeal. Their response was an outburst of cheers and applause that eclipsed all that had gone before, and it lingered in the recollection of Colonel Roosevelt vividly down to the last time I saw him, only a little while before his death.

It was at this Kansas City meeting that an incident occurred which showed how prompt Colonel Roosevelt was to keep himself and his own position exactly straight before the public. Some of the newspaper men were up in the gallery. They had made a parody of a popular song and applied it to the Colonel, and while they were waiting for him to make his speech they interrupted the proceedings by singing:

> Has anybody here seen Teddy?
>   T E double D Y.
> Has anybody here seen Teddy,
>   Did you meet him passing by?
> Oh, his head is clear and his heart is true,
>   He is an Insurgent through and through,
> Has anybody here seen Teddy,
>   Teddy from Oyster Bay?

The crowd cheered tumultuously at that, and very evidently shared the sentiment. But instantly Colonel Roosevelt was on his feet, and waving his hand toward the boys in the gallery he cried out, as soon as he could make himself heard:

'Just change that word "Insurgent" to "Progressive," and it's all right.'

From Kansas City Colonel Roosevelt went up to Omaha, and thence to Sioux City, where he interjected into his prepared speech a brief reference to the tariff. What he said was of no special importance, as I recall it, and followed pretty much the lines he had indicated in his talk with us that day at Henderson Farm. But afterward the opposition to him, especially among the Old Guard, attempted to make a great deal of it. They tried to use it to show that he had really supported the Payne-Aldrich Bill, and therefore the Taft position. Consequently, according to their line of reasoning, he was himself guilty of treachery and apostasy in opposing Mr. Taft in 1912. It was pretty thin, but they made the most they could out of it.

At Sioux Falls, South Dakota, the next stop, there was a remarkable demonstration. The meeting was held in a great tent, in the afternoon. Colonel Roosevelt did not like to speak in the open air, for it put too much of a strain on his voice. But in several of the towns where he stopped there was no hall that would begin to accommodate the crowd that always wanted to see and hear him. So many came to the Sioux Falls meeting that those in charge there realized the impossibility of providing seats for them. So they stood under that tent, and the sides were raised so that hundreds who could not get under the canvas might stand around the outside and catch an occasional word. John Snure, of the Des Moines 'Register,' sat beside me on the little platform that had been prepared for the speakers. We counted several sections of the crowd and made the most careful estimate we could of the number present. We agreed that there were something more than ten thousand under the canvas.

While the Colonel was delivering that speech, some one interrupted with a cry of approbation.

'That's the stuff,' he shouted; 'you know how we feel up here.'

'Of course I know how you feel,' instantly retorted the Colonel, 'for that's the way I feel myself.'

The most amazing reception I ever knew to be given to any man was given to Colonel Roosevelt on this trip at Fargo, North Dakota. We arrived there in the evening, and the meeting took place the next afternoon in the public park. There was an open space among the trees in the park, which would accommodate several thousand persons. A little platform had been erected there, as a speaker's stand,

and the crowd gathered on all sides of it. Just before
Colonel Roosevelt arrived at the stand, a small dark cloud
appeared off at one side. It grew steadily and moved
toward the park. Those in the crowd saw it, and the word
went around that it was going to rain. It was in September,
and several persons remarked that the rain would be cold.
But nobody seemed to go away. There were ten or twelve
thousand persons gathered around that stand. They had
come from all over the State. Special trains had brought
them in by the hundreds, and every kind of individual
conveyance — automobiles, wagons, buggies, and horses,
even Shanks' mares — had brought their quotas.

By the time Colonel Roosevelt reached the stand, the
cloud had grown so large as to cover the place. The sun had
been shut out, and it was obvious that the rain was nearly
due. But still no one went away. The chairman of the
meeting made a few remarks, and introduced some one who
was to introduce the Colonel. The introducer went ahead
with his own speech, and the crowd stood there and waited.

At length the introducer finished, and Colonel Roosevelt
stood up. There was a wild shout and a burst of cheering.
The Colonel waved his hand to the crowd, and then the
rain came. It fell in great drops, and it was cold. It came
in sheets, and the crowd simply stood there in the open,
and took it. Hardly a person went away. Everybody —
men, women, and children — was drenched to the skin. No
one could stand two minutes in that downpour without
being soaked as thoroughly as if dropped overboard from a
boat. But they all knew that it was only a shower. They
could see that cloud slowly drifting on over them, and it
was merely a question of endurance. They had come to
hear Colonel Roosevelt. He was right there before them,
waiting to speak, and no rain was going to keep them from

hearing him. He was sheltered by the roof of the stand, but there was no shelter for them.

For forty minutes that rain fell, and still the crowd stood there. Then the cloud passed on, the rain ceased, and the sun came out. In a moment Colonel Roosevelt was speaking. The crowd listened with rapt attention. He spoke for about an hour, and I did not see a single person go away. They even stayed a few moments to give him a hearty cheer when he finished. But then they broke and ran in every direction.

Colonel Roosevelt was rather wet, too, for the roof of the stand had not been, by any means, water-tight, and every one in his party had been more or less soaked. We newspaper men had gathered under the floor of the stand, but the water had penetrated even there. The Colonel was quite ready to get back to the hotel and dry clothing, but as he started to leave the stand a man came running toward him, waving his right hand, and shouting out something that was unintelligible to any of those who heard it. It seemed a question, but might have been almost anything, even a curse.

Two or three men started toward this man, but the Colonel reached him first. With his left hand the Colonel caught the right wrist of the other and swung his arm quickly and sharply across in front of his own face, so that the man was partly turned around and did not directly face the Colonel. At the same time his right hand was rendered wholly useless for any attack, if he had wanted to make one.

'Now, what is it you want?' said the Colonel.

It was only a simple question, after all, that the man had wanted to ask, and he had hurried because he saw the Colonel preparing to leave. But it served to illustrate the

Colonel's quickness and readiness to act in his own behalf in case of emergency. The man laughed at the way he had been handled, and admitted that he had been careless in his approach. And that ended the matter.

XLI

From Fargo Colonel Roosevelt went over to St. Paul. It was at the time of the State Fair, and he spoke at the Fair Grounds on an afternoon when the management reported that there were more than eighty thousand paid admissions. Of course nothing like that number could get anywhere within range of any human voice, for this was long before the days of amplifiers, loud speakers, and the radio devices of to-day. But it seemed as if all Minnesota was there, crowding to get a chance just to see the Colonel, if they couldn't get within hearing distance. It seemed quite natural to me that Colonel Roosevelt should speak to that throng, even though it was in the open air, and there was no possibility of making more than a fraction of them hear what he said. And there was no hint of objection on the Colonel's part about the arrangements. But a couple of years later, when I was in charge of the speaking trips of Governor Johnson, of California, who had been nominated by the Progressive Party for the vice-presidency on the same ticket with Colonel Roosevelt, I found out that there is at least one public man who has decided objection to speaking at State fairs.

We went to Milwaukee from St. Paul, and there the arrangements seemed to be wholly in the hands of Colonel Roosevelt's German friends. There was a special entertainment for him at a club, which, I think, was called Germania. No question was raised then of hyphenated Americanism.

Nor was there anything during the stay in Wisconsin about Senator La Follette, who was running in the pri-

maries that year for renomination. The Colonel's silence
on the subject of La Follette was all the more striking because he had gone out of his way, on other occasions, to put
in a stroke for one man or another who had been with him
in the days of his leadership of the party. In Nebraska he
had spoken strongly in praise of Senator Burkett, who was
also a candidate that year for reëlection, and in Iowa he had
praised Colonel Hepburn, the old war horse from that
State who had given his name, with that of Senator
Dolliver, to the Rate Bill of 1906.

But La Follette had never been a Roosevelt man, and
Roosevelt was not a La Follette man. La Follette claimed
to be a Progressive, but he, like Hughes, always felt that it
was necessary, for the preservation of his own independence to differentiate himself, in some way, from Roosevelt.
Moreover, La Follette had already disclosed some of those
qualities that have since made him break with a good many
men who started out to support him. Colonel Roosevelt
had appraised him correctly from the very first, and, although he never opposed the Wisconsin man, neither did
he ever support him. That attitude of the two men became
one of the very important factors of the situation in the
early part of 1912. Senator La Follette won the 1910
primaries, as he won those of 1916 and 1922, largely by the
aid of Democrats, who voted freely in the Republican
primaries, so freely, in fact, as to lose the right in several
counties to nominate county tickets under the party
emblem. In such cases, if the Democrats wanted to put up
a county ticket, they had to do it by petition. That was because the State law prohibited a party that did not cast,
at the primaries, a certain percentage of its vote at the last
election from putting its county ticket on the official ballot
except by petition. It was designed to prevent cross-voting

in the primaries, but it does not seem to have worked very well in Wisconsin.

The morning we left Milwaukee for Chicago, Colonel Roosevelt told the newspaper men that he had just learned that Senator Lorimer, of Illinois, had been invited to be present at the dinner of the Hamilton Club, in Chicago, at which he was to speak that evening. He said that he had at once notified those in charge of the dinner that if Senator Lorimer was to be present he could not be, and he wanted an assurance before his train reached Chicago that the invitation to Lorimer had been withdrawn, or he would withdraw his acceptance.

Our train stopped about halfway down to Chicago, and there a committee from the Hamilton Club met Colonel Roosevelt. They had been astonished by his message and were obviously distressed by the situation. But Colonel Roosevelt evidently felt that the occasion for surprise was all on his side, and that any one who knew him must have known that he would not sit down to dinner with Lorimer, who was under open charges of having bought his seat in the Senate. Of course, the Colonel had his way, and there was one prominent Chicago Republican who was not at the speaker's table that night.

The next morning the Chicago 'Tribune' published a cartoon by McCutcheon, one of the very few hard-hitting pictures that genial artist has drawn. It showed a banquet table with one vacant place, and Colonel Roosevelt speaking. It bore the legend, 'One seat Lorimer couldn't buy.'

XLII

THE Republican State Convention at Saratoga occurred soon after Colonel Roosevelt's return from this Western trip. From reports of the doings in New York that had reached us, all during the Western trip, it was evident that there was to be a first-class fight at Saratoga, but I doubt if any member of the party had visualized just what took place. The air of Saratoga was highly charged with political electricity even before the convention met, and, when the assemblage was called to order, the tension was as keen as it ever is even at a national convention.

Sherman and Roosevelt were both placed in nomination for the temporary chairmanship, but before the voting Colonel Roosevelt was recognized to address the convention. I thought I had seen him in all kinds of moods, but never had I seen the real 'Roosevelt fighting face' until then. He strode out on the platform, with his pugnacious lower jaw thrust belligerently forward, and his eyes narrowed until they could hardly be seen except for the way they flashed. When he began to speak, it was with a vehemence I had never heard him employ. His hands were clenched, and he strode back and forth on the platform, uttering his thoughts in short, jerky sentences, and pounding them home with one doubled-up fist struck violently into the palm of the other hand.

The delegates and spectators sat absolutely breathless before such an exhibition of tremendous energy and determination. Irresistibly there came to me the suggestion of the cave man, with his club on his shoulder, going forth to seek and seize his woman.

Seated beside me at the press table was a reporter for a Canadian paper. Being an English newspaper man, he was, of course, a stenographer, and he took verbatim what the Colonel said.

'It's the most tremendous thing I ever heard,' he said when the speech was ended. He felt the spell of it just as I did, and evidently as many of the delegates did, for the result of the voting was the election of the Colonel by a substantial majority.

My Canadian friend and I did not stay to see any further proceedings. We hurried to my room in the hotel and there, while he dictated from his notes, I wrote out the speech in full. By that time the session was ended, and the other two 'Times' men, who were with me on that job, came in. They agreed that this speech should be sent to the 'Times' verbatim, and we promptly put it on the wire. The Canadian reporter also sent it in full to his paper.

All that evening, even while we were all keenly engaged in watching the maneuvering that was going on in preparation for the nomination, next day, of a candidate for the governorship, we were still under the spell of that speech. Next morning, when I got my New York 'Times,' the first thing I looked for was the report of Colonel Roosevelt's address of the day before. But not a line of it was printed. I was dumbfounded. I sought out the other 'Times' men and asked them what they made of that. Neither could explain it. Then we looked at the other New York papers. Not one of them printed the speech. There was hardly more than a stickful of it in any of them.

Thereupon I went back to my room and re-read my copy of the speech. Then I saw that after all there was nothing sensational in it, nothing that would really justify any paper in printing it, to the exclusion of news about the

evening's events, and the planning and scheming that were
going on over the governorship. It had not been what
Colonel Roosevelt said, but the manner of his saying it,
that had affected that convention. In the cold gray light
of the morning after the speech itself was dull and prosaic.
It had been the living, vivid personality of the speaker
that had been so gripping. And that I had failed entirely
to transmit to my paper, just as every other newspaper
man there had failed. Perhaps it could not be done. But
as for me, I shall always feel the thrill of that contact with
a great fighting personality, always see that vivid picture of
the cave man, setting out on his conquest.

The Roosevelt mastery of the convention continued to
its end, and the defeat of the Old Guard was complete.
Henry L. Stimson was named for the governorship, on a
platform framed by friends and adherents of the Colonel,
and the fight was on.

Colonel Roosevelt was not deceived for an instant as to
the effect of the fight on the party prospects, or as to the
probability that the Old Guard would knife the ticket
wherever it could. After the convention had adjourned, I
saw him for a few minutes in his room at the hotel, and
asked him what he thought of the chances in the campaign.

'We have about one in five,' he replied. 'We have the
general dissatisfaction with the National Administration
to face, and on top of that we have to overcome the effects
of the fight here. My judgment is that there is about one
chance in five that we can do it. Perhaps we can lift that a
little in the campaign, but not much. Stimson is a good
man, and he will make a good campaign. And then the
Democrats may do something to help us. But I do not
think we can win. However, the fight was worth the

making. We have beaten the reactionary machine, and the Progressives are in charge of the party organization. We ought to be able to get the party in line for another year.'

XLIII

THE Saratoga Convention was followed by a brief trip into New England, where Colonel Roosevelt spoke in behalf of some of his friends. He delivered one address in Boston, where he urged the reëlection of Senator Lodge, and he spoke for Governor Bass in New Hampshire. I do not recall that trip very distinctly, but think he spoke in all the New England States, although some of them may have been omitted.

After the New England trip there was a long swing through the South, at the close of which Colonel Roosevelt came up into Indiana and then turned into New York State on an active campaign tour in behalf of Mr. Stimson and the whole Republican State ticket.

The Southern trip opened with a speech at Briceville, on the Virginia-Tennessee line, in behalf of C. Bascom Slemp, who had succeeded his father as the Representative in Congress from the Ninth Virginia District. This district was usually solidly Republican, the Slemps, father and son, ordinarily carrying it by from 5000 to 9000 majority. But Bascom Slemp was feeling the effects in his district of the general swing against the Republican Party, and he very much wanted the help of Colonel Roosevelt. The Colonel's speech at Briceville was devoted mainly to the question of the control of large capital. It was a thorough handling of the so-called trust question, in my judgment the ablest ever delivered by Colonel Roosevelt. I telegraphed it in full to the 'Times,' which printed it all the next morning.

Having completed his discussion of this subject, Colonel Roosevelt devoted a few minutes to an appeal for Mr.

Slemp. Whether that had any effect or not, I do not know. But Slemp was one of the very few men, for whom the Colonel spoke that fall, who managed to squeeze through at the election. His majority was cut from thousands to hundreds, but he was elected. Senator Lodge barely made it in Massachusetts. So far as I now recall, those two were the only men supported by the Colonel that fall who made their reëlection. Mr. Roosevelt campaigned, from first to last, in pretty nearly every State north of the Ohio and east of the Rocky Mountains. Wherever he went he urged the voters to support the Republican ticket. He did his utmost in behalf of the party. He called on his own personal following everywhere to stay in line. He did that with a complete understanding of the national situation, as he had demonstrated in his talk to the newspaper men at Henderson Farm on August 24th. But the utmost he could accomplish was to save two of his friends from defeat.

That is the cold-blooded fact of the 1910 campaign. It is well worth while, for those who contend that Colonel Roosevelt should have supported Taft in 1912, and who hold him responsible for the Republican defeat of that year, to remember these facts about 1910. Unquestionably they have a distinct bearing upon the question of what was right, as well as of what was wise, for the Republican Party, in 1912.

The trip through the South was just a repetition of that through the West, so far as enthusiasm for Colonel Roosevelt was concerned. Plenty of men, along the way, told him they wished he was to be the candidate again in 1912, and assured him of their belief that he could break the Solid South. But Colonel Roosevelt was too old and too wise a bird to be caught by such chaff. He knew very well that, until there is some definite settlement of the negro problem in the South, there is no possibility of breaking it by a Republican victory in any of its States.

The Republican Party is distinctly aligned with the 'nigger-driving' element of the white population there; that is, with the element that professes adherence to the Republican Party chiefly for the sake of the spoils available during a Republican national administration. The great majority of the whites of the South will never openly align themselves with that party, although many of them would vote for its national ticket if they could do so secretly. The protectionist sentiment has been growing rapidly in the South, with the development of its industry, and on principle there is surely room for two parties. But it will have to be some other party than the Republican which takes its place with the Democratic Party there, and the new party cannot be tied up with the negro issue as the Republican Party is. It was recognition of this fact, and a clear understanding of this whole situation, that led Colonel Roosevelt in 1912 to take the position he did with regard to the negro question, North as well as South. The intelligent negro leaders of the South approved his stand and followed him in it.

In answer to a question from the gallery at the Progressive National Convention in Chicago, Colonel Roosevelt declared that he would treat the negro as the people of his State treated him. In the North, where he was accepted as a political equal, he should have his vote. In the South, he should be treated as the people of the South determined. Colonel Roosevelt pointed out that, by the building-up of another political party in the South, acting toward the negro on the same principles on which the Democratic Party acted, there would be developed a demand all through those States for the negro vote, and that both parties would be contending for it, just as they do in the North. In that way, he predicted, the negro would come into his political rights.

An incident occurred at Knoxville, on this Southern trip, which showed again Colonel Roosevelt's remarkable memory for names and faces. His party was taken for an automobile drive around the city, which included a trip through some exposition grounds. A Wild West show was performing there at the time, and its members paraded for the entertainment of the Roosevelt party. As the cowboys were riding by on their bronchos, one of them turned in his saddle and shouted:

'Hello, Teddy! Remember the Lazy Y?'

I am not sure that that was the name of the ranch that the cowboy gave, but it was a ranch that the Colonel did remember. He looked sharply at the cowboy for an instant and then shouted a response, naming the man and the ranch where they had met, nearly thirty years before. The Colonel's quick response, and his accurate and immediate placing of the man who had greeted him, brought a wild whoop from all the cowboys of the show that greatly pleased the Colonel.

One of the stops of this Southern trip was at Roswell, Georgia, the home of Colonel Roosevelt's mother. The whole town turned out to greet its distinguished visitor, whom it proudly described as one of its own sons, and the Colonel was taken to the old Bullock place, and to several others connected with incidents in his mother's childhood. The Roswell people had located some pieces of furniture of the old Bullock household, including, as I recall it, a mahogany cradle, all of which they wanted to give the Colonel. There was plenty of assurance here that, if he should run for the presidency again, he would certainly carry Georgia.

XLIV

AFTER making stops in Mississippi, Arkansas, Missouri, and Illinois, Colonel Roosevelt headed for Indianapolis, where he was to deliver a speech in behalf of Senator Beveridge, who was running for reëlection. Beveridge was one of the seven Insurgents of the Senate who had fought the Payne-Aldrich Tariff Bill. He had been a steady supporter of Mr. Roosevelt during his presidency, and had made two or three especially effective efforts in behalf of some measures particularly favored by the President. One of these was the Meat Inspection Bill, and another, which counted even more with Mr. Roosevelt, was his fight for more battleships. The President urged a four battleship a year programme, and Beveridge supported this in the Senate with great vigor. So now the Colonel went into Indiana to do all he could for Beveridge.

There was a great meeting at Indianapolis. It was attended by a huge crowd, and there was so much delay, because of the press to see and speak to Colonel Roosevelt, that his train was several hours late in getting away. He was due to stop at Richmond, where there was another Beveridge meeting that evening, but he was also due to open his New York campaign for Stimson at Dunkirk the following morning. On the way over from Indianapolis, Charley McCullough, the Pennsylvania passenger agent who was in charge of the train, told the Colonel that, unless they ran at about top speed all the way to Columbus, they would miss the connection there, which they had to make in order to reach Dunkirk next morning. Thereupon the Colonel decided that, inasmuch as he had to cut out

one meeting or the other, and had put in the day for
Beveridge, anyway, it would be better to out out the
Richmond meeting and keep his Dunkirk appointment
than to delay opening the New York campaign and throw
all arrangements in that State out of schedule.

Senator Beveridge was on the train, and he pleaded
very earnestly with the Colonel to make the Richmond
meeting, if he only stopped long enough just to show himself and say he was for Beveridge. Telegrams had come
from Richmond saying that an enormous crowd had turned
out and was waiting very eagerly to greet the Colonel. Mr.
Roosevelt would have liked greatly to make the stop, and
several times asked McCullough if it could not be managed
in some way. But McCullough's answer was always the
same. It was nothing to him whether the Colonel stopped
or did not. But if he did stop, he couldn't make the Dunkirk connection. It was going to be a mighty close shave to
make it at all, even without stopping at Richmond.

So, reluctantly, the Colonel cut out the Richmond stop.
His old friend William Dudley Foulke was waiting there
to see him, and added his appeal by wire. But our stop at
Richmond was only long enough to let Senator Beveridge,
and a few friends who were with him get off, and then the
train raced for Columbus. It made the fastest time ever
recorded between those two points, and just barely caught
the eastward connection there, which put us into Dunkirk
the next morning.

Some time after that I heard a story about Senator
Beveridge that illustrated thoroughly the way in which
absolutely groundless scandals, especially of a political
nature, will spread. It was to the effect that he was so
drunk that night that he was unable to appear at his great
Richmond meeting until about eleven o'clock, when the

crowd was thoroughly disgusted with him and would not stay to hear him. Of course, I knew that there wasn't a word of truth in such a yarn, and I promptly said so. But I had a hard time convincing the man who repeated the tale to me of its utter falsity. I had been with Beveridge at short intervals nearly all that day, and during the evening, on the run from Indianapolis to Richmond, had seen him constantly. He could hardly have taken a single drink without my knowing it, and it was certainly impossible for him to be drunk without my knowledge. But I saw and heard a good deal more of the same sort of thing about Colonel Roosevelt later, with similar total lack of justification.

XLV

Beginning at Dunkirk Colonel Roosevelt went through the western part of New York State making from a dozen to fifteen speeches a day, at meetings everywhere attended by great crowds. There was always the same tremendous enthusiasm for him that had been shown throughout all his travel that fall, and now that he had discarded all camouflage and was openly talking politics and nothing but politics, of the straightest and most vigorous Roosevelt kind, at every opportunity, it was more than ever plain that the people were with him and would welcome him back as their leader. But it began also to be more and more plain that, while they were for, and with, him, they were not so sure about being for somebody else at his urging. His own leadership they would be glad to follow, but they were not so keen about another man of his selection. Sometimes it came out, quite frankly, that they had trusted him in the selection of Taft and had been fooled. They were sure he could handle things himself all right, but they were not so sure that he was a good chooser of other men.

By this time the Democratic State Convention had been held in Rochester, and John A. Dix had been nominated for the governorship. This nomination had been made at the dictation of Charles Murphy, the leader of Tammany Hall, who had occupied room 212 at his hotel. Colonel Roosevelt rung the changes on that fact all through his State campaigning:

'You're wanted in Room 212,' became his slogan, and he pounded Murphy and Tammany with all his might wherever he went. As the campaign went on, it began to seem as if he were making some headway, even against all the very great odds that he was facing. He felt so, himself, but was by no means sanguine as to the result of the election. On the day on which this trip ended, and we returned to New York City, he talked with the newspaper men about the situation, and said he thought a little headway had been made.

'I think we have about two chances in five,' he said. 'When we began I estimated our chance at about one in five. I think perhaps we have doubled it. But that's about all. Maybe, if we had a couple or three weeks more, we could do something. But as it is, I'm afraid not.'

Of course, that frank talk was only his confidential opinion, given to the newspaper men with him whom he knew he could trust. For publication he was doing the regular thing and claiming everything in sight. He was altogether too good a politician ever to admit defeat publicly before election.

It was on this trip that Colonel Roosevelt took the only hard liquor I ever saw him take or knew of his taking. The day began at Penn Yann, at seven in the morning, and after getting around as far as Auburn in the afternoon, he went back to Rochester for three big evening meetings. It made some fifteen speeches, in all, for that day, and even Colonel Roosevelt was about worked out when he got back to his private car after eleven o'clock that night. A distinguished Catholic prelate of that district was waiting in the car to see him when he arrived.

As the Colonel came in, he said to the car steward: 'Make me a milk punch.' Then, when he saw his visitor, he offered one to him. The milk punch consisted of a huge glass of milk with a tablespoonful of brandy in it.

The election brought the defeat that Colonel Roosevelt

had predicted nine weeks before, and despite all he had done, in so many States, and all the evidence he had had of his own popularity, it was overwhelming. The voters repudiated the Payne-Aldrich Tariff Law with tremendous emphasis, and overthrew the strong Republican majority in the House, putting the Democrats in power there for the first time in several years. Dix was elected Governor in New York State, and in numerous other States there was a similar overthrow. It was just about a complete Democratic triumph. Lodge and Slemp were the only two men for whom Roosevelt had campaigned who were reëlected.

Then, as he had told us at Henderson Farm he intended to do, Colonel Roosevelt went to Sagamore Hill for a ten days' complete rest. He saw no one, and had nothing to say to any one about the election. Still they said he was a sorehead.

XLVI

ELECTION day of 1910 should have given both Mr. Taft and the organization leaders of the Republican Party, with whom he was now working in rather close harmony practically all of the time, a very clear perception of just where they stood in the estimation of the voters of the country. But it seems to be a peculiar characteristic of organization leaders, of the Old Guard type, that they cannot make plain and obvious deductions from open events. They seem to develop an extraordinary fondness for the 'ostrich game' in which they think that they conceal their motives by not declaring them, and if they keep still about their plans, no one else is ever able to fathom what they intend to do.

The Republican Old Guard apparently believed very firmly that possession of power in the organization was the chief desideratum in politics, and they preferred to retain their leadership, such as it was, to winning an election, whenever the situation necessitated a choice between those results. They were quite content, in 1911, to 'go along' with Mr. Taft on his legislative programme, for they were convinced that their influence with him would enable them to shape whatever measures were passed in such a way as to protect the interests which they had most at heart. An illustration of this was their attitude on the proposition to control the issue of securities by the railroads. That had been specially stressed by Mr. Taft in his pre-election campaign, and it was one of the pledges of the party platform in 1908.

But, when the bill was brought in, it was of such a character that the Progressives, in both houses, immediately attacked it as a device to favor the railroads rather than to protect investors in railroad securities. The late Franklin K. Lane was, at that time, a member of the Interstate Commerce Commission, where he had rendered very able service for some years Mr. Lane was thoroughly committed to Government control of the issue of such securities, and believed he could draw a bill, in a few sentences and in very simple terms, that would effect all that was desired, without in the least interfering with the railroads' need for obtaining capital through the public flotation of securities.

Mr. Lane was not at all in favor of the plan brought forward by the Taft Administration. I had talked with him several times about that bill, in the hope of getting help from him that would enable me to understand just what its effect would be. I had read the bill several times, in fact had studied it very carefully, but had not been able to understand it. At length I went to the President about it. His reply was that the bill had been drawn by Mr. Wickersham, the Attorney-General, who had had a great deal of experience in the reorganization of railroad companies, and that one had to have experience in such matters before he could understand, thoroughly, just what the effect of the proposed bill would be.

The action of the House Insurgents, however, saved me the necessity of going through a railroad reorganization in order to gain an understanding of that bill. They struck out the Administration provisions and inserted three or four paragraphs of their own. They were enabled to do this by reason of the fact that most of the regular Republicans in the House, and the Democrats as well, were as unable as I had been to understand what the effect of the Wickersham Bill would have been.

If the whole truth must be told, the provisions of the Insurgent bill were little more intelligible to the layman than those of the Wickersham measure. The bill passed the House, with some sort of provision ostensibly aimed at control of security issues. But in the Senate it struck a different kind of snag. There the Old Guard was still in fairly secure control, with the Administration openly with Aldrich, its leader, and the Insurgents wholly on the outs with the President. The Old Guard had not the least intention of doing anything that would interfere with railroad freedom in security issues, and the mere fact that Mr. Taft was wholly committed to such legislation, and that the party, of which they claimed to be the leaders, was similarly pledged, did not disturb them in the slightest degree.

It began to be apparent, before the bill had been long in the Senate, that there was no hope whatever for this legislation, unless the Administration took the matter up with unusual vigor, and made a real fight for it. It seemed to me that an exceptional opportunity was thus offered to the President to regain some of the support of the Insurgents that he had been throwing away during the time he had been in the White House. I talked a good deal about it with Mr. Norton, the Secretary to the President, who took the same view of the matter. The Old Guard, in both the House and the Senate, had insisted to Mr. Taft that, by their opposition to the Payne-Aldrich Tariff Bill, the Insurgents had voluntarily left the Republican Party, and there had been a great deal of talk about formally reading them out of the organization. During all of this insistence by the Old Guard, they had based their case upon the fact that the Insurgents were opposing an 'Administration measure.' Yet it was a measure that, under the Constitution, had to originate in the House. The railroad bill, how-

ever, was distinctly an Administration measure, and
nothing else.

Application of their own test of party regularity, therefore, to the Old Guard on the railroad bill, must either force
them to support it or admit that they should be turned out
of the party. Mr. Norton agreed that this was a club which
would enable the President to force through this legislation,
if he could be persuaded to use it. But it very soon became
evident that the President was so thoroughly committed to
the Aldrich-Cannon leadership that he could not be induced
to make a fight against it. He was not a fighting man, anyway, and he greatly enjoyed the ease and luxury of the
presidency. He hated trouble, and habitually put it as far
away from him as he could. He disliked the disagreeable
features of his presidential duty, and frequently they were
the last items of the day's routine that he would take up for
consideration. Consequently, they often found themselves
put over until the next day or the next, and sometimes to
the next week, or even the next month.

When the railroad measure had been in the Senate for
some time I had a talk with the President about it. It was
greatly disappointing, for it disclosed at once the fact that
there would be no real attempt to deal with the question.
Instead of insisting on a measure that would comply with
his campaign pledges, Mr. Taft had agreed, and he told me
as much, with the Senate leaders — which meant Mr.
Aldrich — that the bill as passed should contain, not a
provision seeking to control the issue of securities by railroads, but authority for the President to appoint a commission that should study the whole question and report
at some later date. And this report was not to be a
recommendation of legislation to cover the matter, but
merely the judgment of the commission as to whether it

was or was not a subject for legislation; that is, whether or not the Government had the power to control security issues. Thus that particular Roosevelt policy was carried out — no, it did not achieve the dignity of being removed on a shutter; it was unceremoniously kicked out of the window. Yet, when somewhat earlier in the history of that bill I had talked with the President about it, he had thumped the table in front of him, with his doubled-up fist, and exclaimed:

'By God, the people of this country will find out whether I'm for the Roosevelt policies or not.'

The only deduction the people could make from his action on the railroad bill was that he was not.

Naturally, this did not tend to diminish the effect of the 1910 elections. Those elections had made it clear that the Republican Party was trying to carry a heavier load than it could handle, at least under its existing leadership. But the events of 1911 increased rather than diminished that load. It was in that year that Mr. Taft brought forward his great conception of reciprocity with Canada. He had a Democratic House to deal with, and Mr. Underwood, of Alabama, was chairman of the Ways and Means Committee, while Champ Clark had succeeded 'Uncle Joe' Cannon as Speaker. The Republican leadership had been weakened a good deal, in the closing session of the preceding Congress, by the great Insurgent victory which sheared a considerable part of the Speaker's authority from him, and provided for the election of committees instead of their appointment by the Speaker. The Canadian Reciprocity Bill was put through in a shape acceptable to the President. On this measure he did show some signs of willingness to make a fight, but it was in a cause that was as unpopular with a large part of the voters, especially of the farming sections of the Middle West, as a fight for a real tariff reduction would have been popular.

It seemed to be Mr. Taft's fate that, whether he fought or was acquiescent, he diminished his strength and increased his unpopularity. The rejection of this measure by Canada may have saved him somewhat in his own country, but his advocacy of it unquestionably cost him dearly among the very elements he would have liked to attract to his support.

The net result was the almost complete alienation of the Progressive or Insurgent element of the party. It was obvious, to any one who was watching the political situation at all closely, and who was able to view it with the detachment necessary to prevent the view from being obscured by personal interest, that Mr. Taft's hopes of re-election to the presidency had been completely shattered. Clearly, if the Republican Party desired to win in the 1912 campaign, it must choose for its candidate some one else than the President, and it was very far from certain that it could win under such circumstances, even if Mr. Roosevelt were to be the nominee. There was no one else in sight whose nomination would offer nearly as much hope of bringing the two factions fairly well together again.

It was also obvious that Mr. Taft, and his Old Guard support in the House and Senate, were bent on renominating him. This was one of the most perplexing political situations that I ever saw, because I was wholly unable to get the point of view of the Old Guard, especially in the Senate. Take, for illustration, a man like Senator Penrose, of Pennsylvania, who, on the retirement of Senator Aldrich, had succeeded to the chairmanship of the Committee on Finance, the most powerful and desirable committee assignment in Congress. It seemed only natural that Mr.

Penrose, who was reputed to be a very skillful politician, and who had done much to deserve that reputation, should desire to maintain himself in that chairmanship. Yet the defeat of the party nominee for the presidency was certain to carry with it Democratic control of the Senate, and the loss, not only of that chairmanship to Penrose, but of other highly desirable chairmanships to all the other Senate members of the Old Guard. It was certainly a plausible view that these Senators would seek, by every means in their power, for purely personal, selfish reasons, to keep their party in power, if they were no longer actuated by genuine party loyalty. It did seem to be a time for real honest and disinterested consideration of the party's welfare and of the thing to do that would be for its best interests. But that seemed to be, in fact, the very last thing that these Old Guard leaders were considering.

XLVII

WHILE these things were going on at Washington, Mr. Roosevelt kept himself busy with his work on the 'Outlook,' and in other ways, and fairly free from politics. I saw but little of him that year, although in correspondence with him more or less throughout the year. I had been so steadily with him, during the campaign of 1910, that I had not met Mr. Stimson, the Republican nominee for the governorship in New York, except quite casually. Consequently when, in the spring of 1911, Mr. Stimson became Secretary of War in the Taft Cabinet, I wrote the Colonel and asked him to give me a line of introduction to the new Secretary. He complied very promptly, and when I had presented his note to Mr. Stimson I asked the Secretary if I might have it back, saying that I should like to keep it.

'I should think you would,' replied the Secretary, and handed me the letter.

Naturally, I am proud to have this letter, but I give it here, not so much because of what it says about me, as for the light it throws upon the relationship which it was my good fortune to have established with Colonel Roosevelt. It seems, to me, to be an authoritative testimonial to the reliability of some of the things narrated in this volume. Here it is:

THE OUTLOOK
287 FOURTH AVENUE
NEW YORK

May 31st, 1911

OFFICE OF
THEODORE ROOSEVELT

MY DEAR MR. SECRETARY:

This will introduce to you Mr. O. K. Davis, of the New York 'Times.' It is rather difficult for me to write just what I feel about

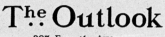

T^{he} Outlook

287 Fourth Avenue
New York

Office of
Theodore Roosevelt

May 31st 1911.

My dear Mr Secretary:

This will introduce to you Mr O. K. Davis of The New York Times. It is rather difficult for me to write just what I feel about Mr Davis without seeming to make it fulsome. You probably know something of his career, of his services as war correspondent and the like. He is one of the very best newspaper men in this country, with that combination of efficiency and of high sense of honor which when we find it in the newspaper world makes the profession of a newspaper man on the whole the highest that our country has. You can trust him implicitly not only as to good faith, but as to judgment. There is literally nothing that I have hesitated to tell him and to consult with him about.

Faithfully yours,

Theodore Roosevelt

The Hon. Henry L. Stimson,
Secretary of War,
Washington, D. C.

Mr. Davis without seeming to make it fulsome. You probably know something of his career, of his services as war correspondent and the like. He is one of the very best newspaper men in this country, with that combination of efficiency and of high sense of honor which, when we find it in the newspaper world, makes the profession of a newspaper man, on the whole, the highest that our country has. You can trust him implicitly, not only as to good faith, but as to judgment. There is literally nothing that I have hesitated to tell him and to consult with him about.   Faithfully yours   THEODORE ROOSEVELT

In conversation with the editor of 'Hampton's Magazine' that spring, I had told him something of what Colonel Roosevelt had said to me about the political situation the year before, and about his own position regarding another term in the White House. Mr. Hampton was much interested, and asked me to write an article for publication in the June, 1911, number of his magazine, under the title 'The Battle of 1912.' I did so, but, as the talk with Colonel Roosevelt had been confidential, I did not refer to it. Mr. Hampton, however, insisted that I should add a little to the article discussing the possibility of a Roosevelt candidacy in 1912.

Thereupon I wrote a few paragraphs, summing up what had happened in New York State in 1910, and said that if, in 1912, the same call were made upon Mr. Roosevelt from the Nation that had been made upon him in 1910 from New York State, he would make the same response, because he did not count the effect upon himself, and if he were the admiral in command of the fleet, he would never hesitate to go into a harbor after the enemy simply because it was mined. If he were the general in command of an army, he would never hesitate to give battle simply because he might himself be shot. That was not at all the kind of man he was. I sent a copy of this article to Colonel

Roosevelt, when it appeared, and under date of June 30th he wrote me:

The article was all right, and I really like and appreciate everything you said of me — except that I am by no means certain that I would not refuse the nomination, even if it came to me unanimously. Certainly that is my feeling now. However, the question is academic, for I won't have to decide it.

To this I replied in a letter, of which, unfortunately, I find I have no copy. The purport of it was that my article had merely given my estimate of how he would act under certain circumstances. It was a question of individual psychology, and would have to abide the event for determination. My judgment has always been that the explanation of Colonel Roosevelt's action in 1912 was to be found in this consideration of his actions in 1910. Again, in 1914, I saw him several times act in precisely the same way under similar circumstances. I came naturally to the conclusion that it was practically a settled rule of his life. He paid his debts. It was a fixed habit with him. Whenever it was represented to him convincingly that he owed a political debt, he paid it, without consideration of the effect upon himself or his own fortunes. That is hardly accurate either, for he did give consideration to such effects, at least to the extent of taking cognizance of them, and not infrequently of foreseeing what they would be. But I never knew that consideration to alter his determination in the matter, or to prevent him from paying the debt. No doubt many men endeavored to persuade him, first and last, that he was under political obligation to them, and were unsuccessful in convincing him. No doubt such men will say that he did not always pay his political debts. But I never knew a fairer man, or one more capable of absolutely honest determination of such a question. Mr.

Taft is a generously fair man by habit. I have known him to weigh both sides of a case with the utmost care even when his own feelings were distinctly engaged on one side or the other. His is preëminently the judicial temperament. Mr. Roosevelt, on the other hand, was of a very different temperament. He was action and prompt decision. Again and again I have seen him follow the statement of a case as it was being presented to him and be ready with his decision almost before the speaker had finished his presentation.

My letters to Colonel Roosevelt, at this time, were usually written in my office at the New York 'Times' Bureau, in Washington, and there seem to have been some of which I did not retain copies, or of which the copies have been lost. At least I have some letters from Colonel Roosevelt, evidently in reply to something I had written to him, but am without the record of what I had written. There is one letter from him, in the fall of 1911, which I give here, for very much the same reason as that in the case of his introduction of me to Secretary Stimson. But I do not recall what it was that I had written which evoked this response from him:

THE OUTLOOK
287 FOURTH AVENUE
NEW YORK

OFFICE OF   *September 5th, 1911*
THEODORE ROOSEVELT

DEAR O. K.:

You are one of the men in whom I most believe, and you do not owe me any gratitude — I owe you gratitude for existing! I only wish there were more men like you in the newspaper business.

This Fall, if you are in New York, I wish you would come and lunch with us at the Outlook on some Tuesday or Friday.

Sincerely yours
THEODORE ROOSEVELT

XLVIII

IT was in the fall of 1911, I think, that in collaboration
with Reginald Schroeder, the Washington correspondent
of the New York 'Staats-Zeitung,' who had offices with
me in the New York 'Times' Bureau, and with Ernest G.
Walker, the Washington correspondent of the Boston
'Herald,' I secured a 'beat' that made some sensation in
the newspaper world, and which was about a matter that
I have always regarded as showing pretty well just about
the true valuation, from the political point of view, which
is placed on the anti-Japanese sentiment of the Pacific
Coast States by the politicians of those States. I was
walking up Fifteenth Street, opposite the Treasury Building, one afternoon, when I met a man whom I had known
rather well in the Far East. We stopped and talked for
some time, and in the course of our conversation he asked
me what was going on then in Washington with reference
to Far-Eastern matters. I had been busy with other things,
and had rather neglected this side of the newspaper possibilities. So I couldn't tell him. But, as soon as our talk
ended, I started for the State Department to try what a
little questioning might develop.

In the course of the afternoon, I got into a discussion
with the man who was at that time chief of the division of
Far-Eastern affairs. It was not about anything in particular, but in some way the subject of the power of Congress
to control immigration came up. In the course of our talk
about that, the division chief made a statement which I
rather questioned. Thereupon he replied: 'You are forgetting your international law,' and he gave me a citation

to a particular page of Moore's Digest. Still it did not impress me that I received any particular 'tip,' and it was some time before I went back to my office, thinking that the afternoon had not been very profitable. Moore's Digest occupied most of the space on top of my desk. I casually picked up the volume to which I had been cited, and looked at the designated page. It contained a decision of the Supreme Court affirming the right of Congress to limit or prohibit immigration, even in contravention of a specific treaty provision. This was on the ground that the treaty, although the law of the land by specific provision of the Constitution, must yield to subsequent legislative enactment by Congress.

I had told Schroeder about the matter, and we read this citation together and began racking our brains to discover what was then going on in diplomatic circles to which it could possibly refer. Presently it occurred to one or other of us that the treaty of commerce and navigation with Japan was to expire, by limitation, the next year, and it might be that the Department of State was, at that time, busy negotiating a new treaty to succeed it. That seemed, on consideration, to be a very good lead. So we sat down and began to 'dope out' the new treaty.

That process involved, of course, a careful consideration of the existing treaty, in the light of any developments known to us since it had been in force, which might cause either nation to desire to make changes in the new treaty. Reading the existing treaty with that in view, we very promptly came across a provision which it was certain that Japan would be very anxious to drop out of the new treaty, or, at least, replace with something less objectionable. This was a paragraph at the conclusion, as I recall it, of Article II, in which Japan recognized, in terms, the right of Congress to prohibit immigration into the United States.

At that time I was the American correspondent of the 'Jiji Shimpo,' one of the leading newspapers of Japan. In that capacity I went frequently to the Japanese Embassy, and was on fairly good terms there, especially with Mr. Matsui, who was then Counsellor of the Embassy. Accordingly I called at the Embassy, the next morning, and saw Mr. Matsui. I told him that I understood that the Embassy and the State Department were negotiating a new treaty to replace the one that would expire the next year, and he promptly confirmed that. The conversation naturally turned to the terms of the new treaty, and I found that several of the surmises that Schroeder and I had worked out the preceding evening were correct. Particularly I was confirmed in the belief that Japan would seek to omit that provision in Article II of the existing treaty which was so objectionable to her. Of course, omission of it from the new treaty would not in any manner affect or limit the power of Congress to prohibit Japanese immigration, but every Japanese felt that the inclusion of that provision in that treaty had been a public disparagement of Japan.

Mr. Matsui's talk gave me the distinct information that the State Department had definitely agreed to the elimination of this objectionable provision in the new treaty. That fact alone was enough for a substantial 'beat' for Schroeder and me, but we naturally wanted all we could get besides, and so I kept at Mr. Matsui for some time. When I left the Japanese Embassy, I felt that we had a fairly good outline of the new treaty.

But there was still another lead that might be followed up. Both Schroeder and I knew Senator Lodge, then chairman of the Senate Committee on Foreign Relations, fairly well, but neither of us was on such confidential terms with him as to warrant going to him with this treaty business. We were both afraid that he might muzzle us, by telling us all about it in confidence, and then all we had done would be lost, and we should have to wait until there was a release that would give the story to all our competitors as well. But Ernest Walker, of the Boston 'Herald,' was on such confidential terms with Senator Lodge that we thought it would be safe to take him into partnership on the story, and have him see what he could add to what we had in that way. His paper, being published in Boston, did not compete with our New York papers in a way that would impair our 'beat.'

Walker, of course, agreed to this very promptly, and he soon saw the Senator. As a result he was able to add several items that we had not obtained otherwise, and that night all three of us had a first-class 'beat.' But it was not until well along in the afternoon that one of the most important phases of it occurred to us, and that was the phase which throws light on the political valuation which the Pacific Coast puts on the Japanese question. That phase was, How is the Administration going to get this new treaty ratified by the Senate? At first thought, it seemed certain that every Pacific Coast Senator could be counted on to vote against ratification. Japanese opposition was a considerable part of their political capital, and they could hardly be expected to do anything that would diminish that.

But then one of us hit upon the solution. The location of the Panama-Pacific Exposition, which was to be held in 1915, was then up for determination by Congress. New Orleans and San Francisco were lively competitors for it, and advocates of each were doing everything in their power

to gain support in Congress. Here was a first-class opportunity for a trade. The Administration could say to the
Pacific Coast Senators that, if they would vote for the
ratification of the new treaty with Japan, it would lend its
influence to San Francisco's side of the Panama Exposition question. But, if they did not vote for the treaty, New
Orleans would get the 1915 show.

Well, that was the exact situation. The treaty was
ratified and San Francisco had the Panama-Pacific Exposition in 1915. Which demonstrates that an international
exposition is the exact political value of the anti-Japanese
issue on the Pacific Coast.

XLIX

FORMAL preparation for the campaign of 1912 began with the meeting of the Republican National Committee in Washington about the middle of December, 1911. From that meeting issued the call for the National Convention, which fixed the time when, and the place where, that convention should be held. It was to meet in Chicago, in the first part of the next June.

That meeting of the National Committee brought out sharply the fact that the Progressive or Insurgent faction in it was in a distinct minority, although it was able to muster a number of votes that should have given the Old Guard majority ample warning that it could not ride rough-shod over the Insurgents without producing a very dangerous situation. But then, perhaps the Old Guard had concluded that the dangerous situation already existed and could not be cured, so that the best thing to do, from its point of view, would be to drive the Insurgents openly clear out of the party.

The division between the two factions came to a head over a question raised by Senator Borah, who was the National Committeeman from Idaho. He proposed that the delegates from the different States should all be chosen at primaries. At that time a few States had presidential preference primaries, but most of the States were without laws on that subject, and lacked the formal legal machinery for holding such primaries. The Old Guard at once objected that this was an insuperable obstacle, and that the attempt to select delegates to the Republican National Convention in such a manner would, in many States,

actually result in throwing the choice into the hands of the
Democrats, who would be wholly free to vote in the Republican primaries. As a matter of fact, that was already
possible in some States where laws had been enacted
governing the primaries, notably in Wisconsin. Only the
year before, Senator La Follette had palpably secured his
renomination in the Republican primaries through the aid
of Democrats. It takes a primary law, so rigorous as practically to enforce a decided reduction of the party vote, to
prevent the members of one party from voting in the
primaries of the other. In New York State a voter must
be enrolled with a party in order to secure a primary ballot,
and the only ballot which the election officers will give him
will be that of the party in which he is enrolled. But in
California, where Governor Hiram Johnson, one of the
most enthusiastic advocates of primary nominations, secured the enactment by a friendly legislature of just the
kind of primary law he desired, it permits this cross-voting.
When Mr. Johnson, who had been elected to the United
States Senate, ran for the Republican presidential nomination in 1920, and Herbert Hoover contested California with
him, newspapers in San Francisco, that were supporting
Senator Johnson, openly urged the Democrats to vote in
the Republican primaries and to support Johnson. Every
day one of the largest San Francisco papers published in
thirty or forty different places a paragraph telling the
Democrats that it was perfectly legal for them to vote in
the Republican primaries and begging them to vote for
Johnson.

In the National Committee meeting, in December, 1911,
the argument that this sort of thing could be done, especially in the informal primaries that, under the Borah
proposition would have to be held in those States where

there was no primary law, was used effectively by the Old Guard, whether that was the real reason for its opposition to primaries or not. Senator Borah argued very forcibly for the primary method of selecting the delegates, urging the right of the voters to express themselves as to candidates, and declaring bluntly that only by some such method could it be hoped to avoid a split that would render defeat of the ticket at the election certain.

But the Old Guard was in no mood for compromise or conciliation. It was bent on enforcing its own absolute control, and the fact that the Borah proposition was supported by nearly a third of the committee did not give the reactionary faction the least pause.

At the time of that meeting, the Old Guard did have the justification that there was very small, if any, indication of the possibility that Colonel Roosevelt would be a contender with Mr. Taft for the Republican nomination in 1912. The Colonel had steadily maintained the attitude disclosed in his letter to me about my article in 'Hampton's Magazine,' and in his talk with me in the fall of 1910. There was no particular big job of work in sight that was causing any special popular demand for him in the White House. The popular call for him was very large and vociferous, it is true, but it was of a general and not of a specific character. It came from his enthusiastic followers, all over the country, who eagerly desired a renewal of his leadership. It came from Progressives, who had been thoroughly angered by what they declared to be the apostasy of Mr. Taft to all the Progressive principles, and by his recusancy toward the pledges of the platform, on which he had been elected, and which he himself had made in his campaign speeches.

This kind of demand for him did not greatly affect

Colonel Roosevelt, and had no power to shake his determination to keep out of the fight. He was naturally pleased by the evidences of personal popularity, but his attitude toward another presidential term had been well reasoned out, and nothing had occurred to change the grounds on which his conclusion had been reached. There was nothing, for instance, like the situation in 1916, when, with the Great War in progress, and this country standing by on the outside, endeavoring to maintain a policy of neutrality that was extremely hateful to him, he saw in the presidency an opportunity for great work, and the highest call that could come to any man.

Colonel Roosevelt was insistent, however, that the Progressive fight within the Republican Party should go on. He detested the turn matters had taken under the Taft Administration, and the way in which the Old Guard had swung back, through the complacency of the President, into complete domination of the party machinery, policy, and programme. But he did not regard this situation as sufficient reason for him to abandon the position he had taken and endeavor to regain the party leadership.

With the Colonel thus refusing to reassume the leadership of the Progressives, there was only one other man in sight on whom there was any chance of Progressive agreement. This was Senator La Follette. Nothing had occurred to change Colonel Roosevelt's feeling about La Follette, and he could not bring himself to offer open and active support of the Wisconsin Senator. But, as long as La Follette was maintaining the Progressive fight, Mr. Roosevelt was satisfied to permit matters to go on as they would, and to stand aside himself.

The Progressive demand for Roosevelt, despite the fact that La Follette was in the position of titular leadership, was gall and wormwood to the Wisconsin man. It made him more than usually bitter, and when, occasionally, he forgot his customary caution, and made remarks about Roosevelt of an expressive if uncomplimentary character, that did not help him with the Roosevelt Progressives. Nevertheless, La Follette managed to carry on his own campaign with a certain measure of success, for some time. He was an open candidate for the Republican nomination, and his friends were seeking delegates to the Chicago Convention everywhere.

But it was the Senator himself who defeated his own campaign and brought about the reëntrance of Colonel Roosevelt into the political arena. Mr. La Follette was making a number of speeches about the country in furtherance of his campaign for the nomination. He accepted an invitation to address a banquet of publishers in Philadelphia in February, 1912. He did speak there, spoke, in fact, so long and in such a manner as to carry to those who heard him the impression that he had suffered a nervous breakdown. The public effect upon his candidacy was instantaneous and calamitous. The newspapers everywhere the next day carried the word that La Follette was out of it.

.The Senator himself, at first, recognized this situation. He returned to his home in Washington and summoned some of his most effective supporters, including his Wisconsin manager. He at first told his supporters that he released them from their obligations to him, and that he could not go on with his campaign. But within a very short time he endeavored to recall this release. He seemed to recover from the nervous strain under which he had been laboring at Philadelphia, and evidently considered himself in fit physical condition to go on with the fight.

But it was too late. Some of those whom he had released,

at that first conference in Washington, had gone at once
to Oyster Bay and called on Colonel Roosevelt. Included
in their number was Gifford Pinchot, long one of the most
active and enthusiastic of the real Roosevelt men in all the
country. The argument that these men made to Colonel
Roosevelt was exactly the same, in principle, that Governor
Hughes had made to him at the Harvard commencement
in 1910, and that his friends in New York State had made
to him that fall, in their successful effort to get him into
the New York fight. They told him that the Progressive
contest, under La Follette, had gone to pieces with the
breakdown of the leader, and that unless Roosevelt took
the leadership at once, it must be abandoned. The flag-
staff had been shot away. Unless he caught up the flag
there was no one else to do so, and it would fall.

That was precisely the one plea that would gain Colonel
Roosevelt's consent. I do not believe anything else could
have been offered that would have moved him. But that
plea would and did move him. He accepted at once, for he
saw, as clearly as anybody else, that unless immediate
action were taken the result would be disastrous to the
Progressive cause. He accepted absolutely without regard
to the effect upon himself. He saw, just as clearly then as
he had seen in 1910, what that effect would be. He knew
that there was very little, if any, hope of defeating President Taft for the nomination at the Chicago Convention,
and he knew perfectly well that, if by some miracle, he did
succeed in that, the result at the election would almost
certainly be defeat. His nomination would surely mean
such a split in the party that the election of the Democratic nominee would be assured.

But the effect upon himself was not at all what he was
considering. What he wanted was to prevent the dis-

PURSUED!

STOP FOLLOWING ME!!

CANDIDACY RUMOR

CARTOON IN THE 'BROOKLYN DAILY EAGLE,' NOVEMBER 27, 1911

astrous overthrow of the whole Progressive movement and the disruption of the Progressive forces. He felt that the Progressive fight within the Republican Party must go on, and, when the only other man who had seemed at all able to carry it on had fallen out, he promptly took it up, let what might happen to him.

The motive which actuated him, therefore, was quite different from that which the public generally attributed to him. He was accused, of course, of personal ambition. The popular thought was that he had responded to the wide public appeal for his leadership. The governors of seven States had written him a strong letter, urging him to become a candidate for the nomination. This letter did, in fact, furnish the pretext upon which his announcement was made. But it had nothing to do with furnishing the motive on which that pretext was used.

Colonel Roosevelt was often accused of being a casuist and a Jesuit. He described himself, in his famous letter to Mr. Harriman, as a 'practical man.' When he had made up his mind to do a thing, he usually took the best means at hand for accomplishing his purpose. That was exactly what he did in February, 1912, with regard to this announcement of his candidacy for the Republican presidential nomination. Having determined to go after that nomination, he would not have been Theodore Roosevelt if he had not instantly devoted himself to the contest with every ounce of his energy and ability.

He had the reputation of being a skillful politician, and he deserved it. But his action in 1912, if based upon personal ambition, must forever belie that reputation. Because he knew perfectly well, and he had made it incontestably clear to a dozen or more newspaper men many months before that he knew, that the way for him to get back into the White House — if that was his ambition — was to keep out of the 1910 and 1912 fights; to let the situation take its natural course and produce its natural results. He knew as well as any one — and there were plenty of others who knew it, too — that the first of the natural results of a course of reticence on his part would be an overwhelming and enforcing demand for him again, to enable the party to recover from the defeat that was inevitable under Taft.

Granted the skill in politics with which Colonel Roosevelt is popularly credited, and which he unquestionably possessed in very marked degree, it must also be admitted that his actions after his return from Africa were absolutely incompatible with the theory that he was motivated by personal political ambition. Some other and entirely different explanation of his course is imperatively necessary. That explanation, I believe, is to be found only in his habit of responding to his political obligations. It seems to me that the events of 1912–14 absolutely confirm the analysis of his psychology presented in my article in 'Hampton's Magazine' of June, 1911.

L

COLONEL ROOSEVELT formally 'threw his hat in the ring' in a speech at Columbus, Ohio, on Washington's Birthday. That speech produced a tremendous sensation, for it disclosed an advance toward radicalism on the part of Mr. Roosevelt that dismayed some of his very good friends, and gave his adversaries material for opposition to him which was extremely acceptable to them.

It was in the Columbus speech that Colonel Roosevelt declared for what came to be known during that campaign as the 'recall of judicial decisions.' His advocacy of it undoubtedly kept away from him, that year, men who had been his good friends, and who would have preferred to support him for the presidency instead of Mr. Taft if they had not felt that in this doctrine he had gone altogether too far.

As the Colonel stated his position at Columbus, he made the new proposition just about as offensive to the conservative, old-line Republicans as it could well have been made. It was in effect that decisions of the Supreme Court should be submitted to vote of the people, and if ratified they should stand, but if not supported by popular vote they should not become effective. In other words, the people were to have the power to recall a decision by the highest court.

Mr. Roosevelt's opponents — and even some of his friends — declared that this was nothing more or less than appeal to mob rule. They argued the impossibility of maintaining enduring institutions in the United States under such a system. Popular sentiment is altogether too shifting and unstable, they said, to permit it, at frequent intervals, such as would be the result in this case, to wield such authority as that. Moreover, it is, as a rule, beyond the capacity of the electorate, as a whole, to make sound and accurate interpretation of the Constitution.

This speech at once became the subject of violent controversy. The stanch Roosevelt men, all over the country, accepted it with open eagerness, or, if they could not do that, did not permit their disappointment about it to become evident or to affect their course. Their action proved again that it was not for the performance of any specific task that they desired to have Colonel Roosevelt return to the White House, but only because of their general wish to follow his leadership.

One of the stoutest supporters of Colonel Roosevelt in the country was Colonel William R. Nelson, owner and editor of the Kansas City 'Star' and 'Times.' Through those newspapers he had preached the Roosevelt doctrines at all times, and with the greatest energy and conviction. Colonel Nelson was in Washington either at the time of the Columbus speech or very soon afterward. The Washington Bureau of his newspapers was next to that of the New York 'Times,' and the men of the two staffs were in the habit of visiting back and forth during the evening. When Colonel Nelson was there, he almost always came into my office for a chat with me. On this occasion I was in the 'Star' Bureau one evening when he came in, and he immediately asked what I thought of the Columbus speech. I replied that I liked part of it very much, but could not stand the recall of judicial decisions. I felt that that was the overthrow of the whole constitutional system, and I was not for it. It had to be recognized, of course, that the power did lie in the people to alter their government to suit themselves, but it must be done in an orderly and constitutional manner, and not by mob edict.

Colonel Nelson became very much excited. 'My boy,' he exclaimed, 'I'm for Roosevelt, first, last, and all the time. I'm for him right or wrong. I won't admit, even to myself, that I don't like anything he does. The way to fight is to fight, and, by God, we're in a fight now. This is going to be a fight to the finish, and every man in this country has got to get on one side or the other. My side is with Roosevelt. Where are you going to stand?'

There was only one answer to that question for me. I saw, of course, the force of Colonel Nelson's position. No man can make a real fight with only half his heart in it. In his political battles in Kansas City, Colonel Nelson had demonstrated his quality as a fighting man, and I knew he meant what he said when he declared himself in this fashion. But while that argument could and did silence me, so far as open opposition to the recall of decisions was concerned, it could not, and did not, satisfy me as to the soundness of that position. I was eager to talk with Colonel Roosevelt about it, and to learn the origin of the theory with him. I was certain it had not sprung out of his own thought, and before very long I learned that my belief was correct.

In fact I had already received some very good evidence that the doctrine did not originate with Colonel Roosevelt. During that winter I had done several interviews with prominent public men for the 'Outlook.' One of these interviews had been with Senator La Follette. In the course of that interview the Senator had talked, at considerable length, about this very subject, and had declared himself as much taken with the idea. That interview was in type at the time Colonel Roosevelt delivered his Co-

lumbus speech, and the proofs had been submitted to
Senator La Follette for his approval. Immediately after
the Columbus speech, one of the Senator's close friends
asked me, very pointedly, when I had seen Colonel Roosevelt last, and what I had been writing to him. It was plain
La Follette suspected that I had told Mr. Roosevelt about
this new doctrine, and that the Colonel had promptly
appropriated it to his own use, hastening to make it public
before La Follette could do so.

But the Senator's talk with me on this point had been
confidential, and there was no reference to the subject in
the interview I had prepared. Nor had I seen Colonel
Roosevelt or written to him. There had been no communication whatever between us, on any subject, so that it was
impossible for him to have received this suggestion in that
way from La Follette. I think it illustrative of La Follette's
suspicious mind, however, that he never returned the
'Outlook' proofs, and, in consequence, the interview was
not published.

The truth soon came out. It was that Colonel Roosevelt
had received the suggestion from the same source which had
given it to Senator La Follette. It was not the Senator's
original idea any more than it was Colonel Roosevelt's. It
originated, in fact, with Dr. Van Hise, then president of
the University of Wisconsin. It happened that Dr. Van
Hise had called on Colonel Roosevelt at Sagamore Hill
only a short time before the Columbus speech was delivered. I believe, indeed, that the speech was, at that
time, in course of preparation. The two men naturally
talked about that speech. It was Colonel Roosevelt's
habit to discuss his speeches with any and all comers in
whom he happened to have confidence, or who, he thought,
might have knowledge of the subject about which he in-

tended to speak. I remember well one occasion when he was going out West to deliver a speech on a railroad question. He had it prepared, and it had been put into proof for advance distribution to the newspapers. On the train he fell into conversation with one of the brakemen, whom he found to be intelligently interested in the subject of his speech. Thereupon he asked the brakeman to read what he had prepared. The brakeman did so, and very strongly disagreed with the Colonel on one point. They talked it over for some time, and the brakeman convinced the Colonel. The result was that, there and then, the Colonel altered his speech so as to include the points made by the brakeman, and in that form the speech was delivered.

Dr. Van Hise thought much about his recall of decisions proposition, and he had a way of stating it that was very attractive instead of being positively repulsive, as was the blunt fashion in which the Colonel phrased it. Dr. Van Hise, starting with the fact that all power resides in the people, proceeded to argue that the people had set up two agencies for the execution of this power. One was the legislature, charged with the duty of giving form and direction to the manner in which any part of the power of the people is to be exercised. The other was the judiciary, charged with the duty of interpreting the action of the legislature and determining whether or not it conformed to the intent, purpose, and actual rule of procedure laid down by the organic law itself, which the people had adopted for their own government. Now, it happens sometimes, argued Dr. Van Hise, and not infrequently, that the courts hold the action of the legislature to have been unconstitutional; that is, not in conformity with the rule and intent of the organic law. But the legislature has acted honestly, and in the sincere belief that it was proceeding exactly as laid down in the Constitution. Thus, there arises an honest difference of opinion, between two of the servants of the people, as to the meaning and effect of an act of one of them. Dr. Van Hise argued that, in such cases, the power and the right to decide between their two servants must reside in the people themselves. Therefore, in his view, it was entirely appropriate for the people to pass upon such a question, after the court had rendered its decision, and to determine, by popular vote, whether the legislature or the court had expressed the popular will.

Colonel Roosevelt had been very much interested in this presentation of the matter by Dr. Van Hise. He forthwith incorporated the idea in his Columbus speech. But its transformation, from the smooth and studied phraseology of the University president to the blunt and almost brusque language of Colonel Roosevelt, resulted most unfortunately for the Colonel. It is, in fact, very doubtful whether that speech alone was not responsible for the determination of the Republican National Committee that Colonel Roosevelt should not be the nominee of the Chicago Convention. Several men contributed to the outcome of the June Convention that year, who, in all probability, would either have had nothing to do in the way of helping forward the renomination of President Taft or would have been actually in the Roosevelt column. I have been told that men like Senator Lodge and Mr. Meyer, Secretary of the Navy, who kept aloof from that convention, would have been glad to support the Colonel but for the Columbus speech, and I have also been told that even Elihu Root, who was one of the most active and efficient opponents of the Colonel at Chicago, would not have taken any steps against him but for that speech.

LI

WITH Colonel Roosevelt's hat definitely in the ring, it was a matter of first importance immediately to organize a committee to manage the campaign for the election of Roosevelt delegates to the Republican National Convention. Some of his closest friends met in New York City and discussed this matter within a few days after the Columbus speech had been delivered. There was plenty of expert material available among the Roosevelt men in various parts of the country, but it was natural that the committee headquarters should be somewhere in the East, preferably in New York or Washington. The seven governors who had joined in the appeal to Colonel Roosevelt to become a candidate against Mr. Taft were, of course, relied upon to conduct activities in their own States. But that left forty-one other States in which the campaign would have to be managed by the central committee, and it would also have an active interest in the States of the seven governors.

Among the men in the United Stated Senate who were supporters of Colonel Roosevelt, none had more native political genius than Senator Joseph M. Dixon, of Montana. Dixon was a North Carolinian by birth, but had spent most of his life in the State he represented in the Senate. He was a young man, being still considerably under fifty, with a good deal of energy and capacity for hard work. Also he was gifted with political inspiration in a degree seldom possessed by even those of long experience in politics. He had a very pleasant and winning personality, easy manners, and attractive address. He knew the value of attention to detail in politics, and he had a sureness in reading the intention and purpose of the opposition that I have never seen exceeded. In addition, or perhaps it would be more accurate to say in subtraction, he had a carelessness of office routine, particularly with regard to important papers, that made it worth while to keep several secretaries around who could be relied upon to see that every letter was promptly acknowledged or answered, and that all papers and documents were duly filed and preserved, so that they could be found when wanted. I used to tell him that, if he had a sight draft on the Federal Treasury, payable to bearer, he would leave it lying on his desk or anywhere else he happened to lay it down, handy for the first person who wanted it to pick up.

Dixon had served in the House for several terms, and was then in the close of his first term in the Senate. He had been in Washington during all the Roosevelt presidency, and knew the Colonel very well. He was the choice of the New York meeting for the chairmanship of the Roosevelt National Committee which it was proposed to organize for the campaign, and he accepted the task. As soon as he had agreed to that, he asked me to take the secretaryship of the committee. This request was seconded by several of the New York men, especially by the late George W. Perkins, who was one of the most active and influential of the Roosevelt men in New York, and one of the chief financial contributors to that campaign and to the Progressive Party.

At that stage of the fight, none of us thought the organization would be for longer than the three, or three and a half, months before the National Convention met in Chicago. I therefore asked the New York 'Times' for a leave of absence of three months to enable me to take the

JOSEPH M. DIXON

secretaryship of the Roosevelt Committee. Of course, I knew that the 'Times' was editorially opposed to Mr. Roosevelt, and never lost an opportunity of pounding him on any and every subject. But my predecessor as chief of the Washington Bureau was then on the 'Times' staff in New York, and could fill the place while I was away. So I hoped the leave would be granted. But it was not, and thereupon I resigned from the 'Times,' and at once took hold, with Dixon, in the Roosevelt Committee.

President Taft had appointed Congressman William B. McKinley, of Illinois, to conduct the campaign for his renomination, and headquarters had been opened in Washington. Dixon also opened headquarters in the capital, and the two camps were located only a block or two from each other. A day or two after I joined the committee, Senator Dixon told me that he intended to challenge McKinley to a settlement of the whole issue between Taft and Roosevelt at a general primary. He meant to propose that the delegates to the National Convention from every State, those without primary laws as well as those having such laws, should be chosen at public primaries.

There were two great points in this idea. One was that the primary suggestion was bound to be extremely popular, and the other was that only by some such means as this were we going to be able to get adequate publicity for what we were doing on the Roosevelt side. The primary idea was then well into the great swing of its development. Everywhere the conservative in politics was being denounced as 'reactionary' and 'stand-pat.' The 'machine' and the 'organization' were becoming increasingly unpopular. 'Boss rule' was anathema to the voters in general, and 'bi-partisan combinations' were especially execrated. Such combinations were possible, of course, only as a product of boss rule and the domination of the party, through hidebound organization methods, by stand-pat or reactionary leaders. In the popular mind Taft clearly represented the reactionary, or Old Guard, side of this situation, and Roosevelt the other, or Progressive side. A challenge from our side to the other, therefore, to settle the issue at primaries in every State was bound to wake up our own supporters and to be generally popular throughout the country.

At the same time we were tremendously handicapped in the matter of publicity. Very few newspapers throughout the country were for Roosevelt. The chief of them were the 'Star' and 'Times' in Kansas City, owned by Colonel Nelson; the 'North American,' in Philadelphia, owned by E. A. Van Valkenberg; the Chicago 'Tribune'; and, in New York, the 'Evening Mail,' edited by Henry L. Stoddard, a stout friend of the Colonel, in which George Perkins was interested. The smaller papers, generally, were in the hands of the opposition. This was especially true of the little county weeklies. That was perfectly natural, and will always happen under such circumstances. It arises from the fact that the editor of a county paper is usually active in county politics, and is recognized as a leader and a man of influence. He is either in office himself or has supported the man who was elected. Very often the office-holder owes his place to the support of his newspaper friend, who, as likely as not, was the one who first suggested him for the office. That almost invariably ties the newspaper to the office-holder, and the office-holder, being tied to the National Administration, takes the newspaper along with him.

That was the exact situation in the Taft-Roosevelt fight. The Roosevelt Committee found, at once, that it had very few agencies of publicity, and, of course, wide and effective publicity was absolutely essential to our campaign. The question was how to get it. To do so we must devise something that would be carried in the papers of the op-position. That was exactly where Dixon's challenge to a general primary came in. The newspapers supporting Taft would be almost certain to carry that, and, having started it, would have to go on to the end with it. So we should be in the Taft papers, in some fashion, even if not favorably, and that was bound to be helpful.

Dixon and I invited two other Roosevelt men to help us frame up the challenge to McKinley. They were J. C. O'Loughlin, Washington correspondent of the Chicago 'Tribune,' and Fred Bullene, Washington correspondent of the Kansas City 'Star.' We four met in our headquarters one afternoon, and spent several hours writing notes to McKinley on the subject. Each man had his own ideas of how the challenge should be worded, and it seemed as if each idea had some points of merit. At length, however, we got them all into one note, and sent it by messenger down to the Raleigh Hotel, where Mr. McKinley had his headquarters. Then we four sat around the rest of the afternoon wondering what was going to happen, and inventing answers to the different replies that we imagined McKinley might make to the challenge.

It was an amusing and exciting afternoon. We found that we could make an effective answer to any reply that Mr. McKinley might send us, except one. There was one reply from him to which we could not frame a suitable answer. As the afternoon wore along, we began to be pretty nervous about it. For we were more and more convinced that, if McKinley should happen to hit on that reply, our challenge would be largely a failure, and we didn't see, then, just what we could do to serve the same purpose.

The one reply with which McKinley would have scored heavily against us was merely a laugh at our challenge, and a refusal to regard it as anything that called for answer. If he refused to dignify it by responding to it, we were absolutely defeated in our effort to obtain publicity through the medium of the Taft newspapers. If he simply said, to the newspaper men who were swarming about his headquarters, demanding to know what he was going to do with the challenge, that he was busy renominating Taft and had no time to waste on frivolities like that, it would have been by far the most effective thing he could have done.

But, very fortunately for us, that course did not occur to Mr. McKinley, or, if it did, he rejected it. He chose, instead, to reply to the challenge. And then he sent the least effective reply he could have invented, the one that, in fact, gave us the best opportunity, and that was bound to obtain for us the greatest publicity. He merely said that he had been appointed by Mr. Taft to conduct the campaign for the renomination of the President, and inquired whom Senator Dixon represented. We learned afterward that this brilliant idea was suggested to Mr. McKinley by Congressman Tawney, or rather ex-Congressman, for he had fallen by the wayside in the 1910 elections, despite, or perhaps partly because of, Mr. Taft's Winona speech in his favor. At any rate, this suggestion was another sorry favor from Tawney to Taft.

It gave Dixon the best opening for publicity that we had in the whole campaign. He immediately got Colonel Roosevelt on the telephone and explained the situation to him. The result was a humming telegram from Roosevelt directly to Taft, endorsing the Dixon suggestion for settlement of the case at primaries, and asking the President to agree. Immediately the Taft side was on the defensive. It was forced to argue against primaries, well knowing all the time that the primary idea was intensely popular throughout the country. And, of course, all the Taft newspapers in the country had to carry the whole story, because their side was so thoroughly involved. Moreover, they couldn't carry just the Taft side and omit our side, for that would not have made their presentation of the case intelligible to their readers. Decidedly we got all the best of that.

This gave us, also, another advantage that we had not thought of in our first afternoon meeting. It was a tremendous incentive to the Roosevelt people everywhere to demand primaries, and there promptly resulted, in several States, efforts to get special legislation providing for the election of delegates to national conventions in that manner. The Chicago 'Tribune' took the matter up with the utmost energy, and made a hot campaign for a primary law. It went after the Governor of Illinois so effectively that he promised to call the legislature in special session to pass such a law, if he were assured that enough members of that body were in favor of it to insure its passage if the special session were called. Thereupon the 'Tribune' canvassed the members of the legislature and obtained signatures from more than enough, in each house, to put through the primary bill. The Governor then called the session, and the law was enacted. The presidential primary was set for April 9th, and the real campaign was on.

LII

BEFORE Senator Dixon had had time to get his headquarters anything like thoroughly organized, we were plunged into the middle of the fight for delegates. It was, already, much too late to do anything effective toward obtaining Roosevelt delegates from the South when T. R. threw his hat in the ring at Columbus. Public sentiment plays a very small and unimportant part in the selection of delegates to Republican National Conventions from the States of the Solid South. The party organization in those States is maintained, very largely, for the sake of its influence in securing patronage from Republican administrations, and it was only natural that the Taft Administration should be able to exert an influence in this case that, in many districts, was strong enough to overcome the personal preference of the party members for Roosevelt.

There were certain parts of the South where we were entitled to hope for some delegates. Dixon had maintained his relationships with his old State of North Carolina, was widely and well acquainted there, and had a great deal of personal influence with which to back up the strong Roosevelt sentiment among the Tar Heel voters. Cecil Lyon, who had been for years the leader of the Texas Republicans, was an enthusiastic Roosevelt man, a warm personal friend of the Colonel. Bascom Slemp, in the Ninth Virginia district, we naturally counted on to remember, with some show of gratitude, the vigorous support Colonel Roosevelt had given him in 1910. There was plenty of Roosevelt sentiment in Georgia, and more than a little in Louisiana.

But, in most of the States of the South, the delegates had been selected, or actually chosen, before Mr. Roosevelt announced his candidacy. We knew many tales, from previous conventions, of the outright purchase of delegates from some of the Southern States, and we promptly heard many more. Prices, we were told, ran from two hundred dollars to one thousand dollars a delegate, and the yarn most frequently heard was that a bill, of the agreed-on size, would be cut diagonally in two pieces, one being given to the delegate in advance, the other to be handed to him after he had voted, always provided that he voted as he promised.

I heard much talk of this kind of corruption, during the months before the Republican Convention met, but it was all about the doings of the other side, and I never had confirmation of any of it. On our side I never heard or saw anything that would indicate the least effort to obtain a single vote by such means. Money was not lacking with us for legitimate purposes, although we had a very careful and conscientious treasurer at Washington, and strict account was kept of every expenditure. But the whole Roosevelt campaign was keyed on opposition to corruption in any form, and it is certain that, if anything of the sort was attempted, whoever did it was mighty careful to keep the knowledge of it from Colonel Roosevelt, and all those at either the Washington or New York headquarters.

Not only had many of the Southern districts chosen their delegates by the time we were getting fairly organized at Washington; several of the Northern States, which had presidential preference primaries, or selected their delegates to national conventions by the primary system, were swinging into action. North Dakota led off, with a State-wide presidential preference primary, early in March, and

New York followed with district primaries in the same month. Our debate with the McKinley headquarters in Washington had hardly begun to fade away when the North Dakota primaries came on, and they promptly revived this discussion, with much emphasis on the part of the Taft organization.

As a matter of fact, we were practically unprepared for the North Dakota primaries. In the first place, that was really a La Follette State, and it was a tactical mistake for us to go into it at all. But the Roosevelt men, everywhere, were so tremendously enthusiastic that their insistence in North Dakota as to the certainty of carrying the State led us to make the attempt, although against the better judgment of pretty much everybody in the East. Gifford Pinchot went out there to make a few speeches, and a man from Chicago was sent to try to help the State organization, which was headed by a man who had distinguished himself in politics only through association with the stand-pat faction. We had some pretty good politicians in our organization, but we were children when it came to the gentle art of blanketing the other side by professing to be for it and then doing absolutely nothing to support the profession. The Old Guard worked that game on us from start to finish, and we never did seem to learn how to meet it.

We backed and filled about the North Dakota primaries almost up to the day they were held. Only two or three nights before primary day, there was a long discussion in our office at Washington about the advisability of withdrawing. It was decided on the strength of telegrams from the State to the effect that there was a good chance of carrying it for Roosevelt. But it went for La Follette, and then our Chicago man issued a statement in which he said that the Democrats had voted freely in the primaries and it was their votes which had carried the State for La Follette.

That was exactly the argument which the McKinley managers had been using to bolster up their refusal of Senator Dixon's challenge. They picked up our Chicago man's statement and sent it broadcast, with a statement of their own showing how absolutely it justified the position they had taken. There was just nothing we could say publicly in answer to that. All we could do was to take it out in private on our own man, who had certainly 'spilled the beans.'

But about this time something else happened that gave us the laugh on the other side, although the amusement we got out of it did not offset the North Dakota reverse. The district primaries were held in New York City. One of our district leaders had been associated for a long time with the regular organization in the city, but he was against it, that year, in deadly earnest, and had accepted the Roosevelt leadership in his district with the intention of winning it if he could, and not for the purpose of blanketing us. The regulars had a lot of money for several of the city districts, and this man, although he had some, felt that he did not have nearly enough to offset the regulars. He had done a good deal of circularization of the district and other publicity work, but he wanted, in addition, to hire a number of poll-workers for primary day, and he didn't have the money to do that. The evening before primary day he was walking uptown, when he saw a man, whom he recognized as belonging to the other camp, walking ahead of him and carrying a gripsack.

'There,' he said to himself, 'is the dough I ought to have for to-morrow and they've got it.'

Just then the man ahead of him stepped into a restaurant, and this district leader saw him speak to the cashier, who took the gripsack and put it down behind his desk. Then the man who had been carrying it came out of the restaurant, and jumped aboard a street car bound uptown. Our leader waited a few minutes, then hurried breathlessly into the restaurant and told the cashier that the other man, whom he named, had sent him for that gripsack. Without a word the cashier handed it over, and the dough for that district changed hands right then and there. Next day the regulars were without the poll-workers they had planned to have, and the other side had several it had not expected to have.

The employment of poll-workers for election day is regarded everywhere as a legitimate political expense, and so it is, up to a certain point. But when the workers hired are so numerous that their own votes, if they cast them according to their own employment, become a factor in the result, it is only another way of buying an election. In districts that are intensely 'practical,' such as several of those in New York City, that is a well-recognized method of 'influencing' an election. It is essentially corrupt, although perhaps technically legal. The duty of the poll-worker is to help get out the vote, call on voters of the district who have not cast their ballots, and get them to come to the polls, as well as to talk to those who come voluntarily and seek to secure their support. In such a task it is easy, of course, to overstep the line between legitimacy and corruption.

LIII

Up to this time the Roosevelt movement had not carried enough delegates to begin to assume 'band-wagon' proportions, and those who were in the anti-Taft camp were pretty sure to be thoroughly in earnest and sincere. In every State we had a more or less numerous group of greenhorns and enthusiasts, filled with energy and ideas, with a maximum of optimism and a minimum of experience. We had, also, radicals of every degree, some of them coming from the regular Socialist organization, and more of them from the class described by Colonel Roosevelt as 'parlor Socialists.' There was a good representation from that other group classified by the Colonel as 'the lunatic fringe.' They might count, somewhat, at the polls on election day, but otherwise they were likely to be a liability rather than an asset, for they were always saying or doing something that furnished campaign material to the Taft men.

The enthusiastic greenhorn was probably the worst of the lot, from the point of view of efficiency, or rather of lack of it. We had one such as chairman of our organization in a Middle Western State that was overwhelmingly Roosevelt in sentiment. He was so happy in his enthusiasm, and so certain of winning all the delegates from his State, that he paid little or no attention to organization work at home, but traveled around the country sending in the most optimistic reports from all the places where he stopped. He wired Dixon repeatedly from Colorado, for instance, where we thought we had a very small chance, and was so cock-sure in his assertions that he induced the Senator to take on some activity there. Not only was this effort entirely wasted, but the chairman's own State was so badly neglected that we lost half of the delegates from it, although Roosevelt carried the State overwhelmingly in November.

Illinois really started the Roosevelt movement, and gave it an element of practicality which warned the Taft men and the Old Guard that they were facing a situation of extreme danger. The campaign in that State was very well managed, and with the powerful support of the Chicago 'Tribune,' the Roosevelt forces simply ran away with the April 9th primaries, carrying every district in the State but one, and electing fifty-six of the fifty-eight delegates. That was the day on which the Roosevelt 'band-wagon' got its real start, and from then on there was a rush to get aboard it. This was so marked that, at the Washington and New York headquarters, we formed a little inside organization of our own, composed entirely of 'Before April 9th' men; that is, of those who had been so genuinely for Roosevelt that they had not waited to see whether or not the movement was going to enlist popular support before they joined it.

It was a time of tremendous labor and extreme excitement from the day of the Illinois primaries until the adjournment of the Chicago Convention. There was at least one State primary every week, and several in some weeks. In order to assure a majority of the convention for Roosevelt, we had to win or make a substantial showing in every one of them. We could not afford to lose a single important State. The Taft forces had obtained so long a lead through the South, where no Republican electoral votes are ever cast, that the Roosevelt side had to carry the North almost solidly. We saw, of course, that the Old Guard was ready to make any sort of a fight at a primary or State convention, in order to obtain delegates, but we had not yet realized that the Republican National Committee would go to anything like the lengths to which it did go in making up the temporary roll of the convention.

The fight had already become extremely bitter, however. Colonel Roosevelt went on the stump in several of the primary States, and, the moment he began to discuss the record Mr. Taft had made as President, he was assailed with extraordinary vituperation as having started 'personalities.' He retorted, of course, that examination and consideration of the record of a man in public life was wholly legitimate in a political campaign, and could not be classed as 'personality.' But that reply only increased the vehemence of the denunciation of the other side. Thereupon the Colonel went into the Taft record with a characteristic thoroughness, and delivered some speeches, of great vigor, setting forth the manner in which the President had abandoned the policies on which he had been elected.

Both headquarters were busily following the lead given by their chiefs, and the publicity material issued from each took on a tone of the utmost bitterness. Such words as 'liar,' 'crook,' and 'thief' were in common use, and the day when some such excess of vituperation was not employed was worthy to be marked with a large red letter in our calendars. It remained for Mr. Taft, himself, however, to say the worst thing that was said about him. Driven beyond the limit of his patience by some of the attacks upon him, he cried out in one of his speeches that 'even a rat will fight when cornered.' I look back now with amazement on the readiness with which, after that, we rang the changes on that unhappy sentence, and almost daily quoted the President's description of himself as a cornered rat.

Massachusetts, Indiana, and Maryland represented the climax of our struggle. In the first we divided evenly with the Taft forces, each side getting eighteen of the thirty-six delegates. In Indiana, there was the most flagrant crookedness at the primaries, which were carried for Taft by methods that would have put Tammany Hall and the notorious Philadelphia and Chicago gangs to the blush. The Maryland primaries came just about at the close of the campaign, when we were straining every nerve to get every possible delegate.

Our organization in Baltimore numbered among its members a man who had been eminent among the practical politicians of that city for some years. He knew Baltimore very thoroughly, and he understood completely the value of careful organization work. The State organization seemed to rely entirely upon our prospects of carrying Baltimore. The law in Maryland was peculiar. The result did not hinge on the popular majority in the State, but was determined, county by county, in the State Convention.

There was one small county, having only three votes in the State Convention, in which negro voters were predominant. Our Maryland chairman did not seem to think this county was worth while, or that there was any prospect of carrying it. But Senator Dixon thought otherwise. Two young colored men, who lived in that county, came to see him in Washington, and he talked over with them a suggestion that one of them made, for the nomination of a ticket composed of colored men. The Senator gave them a little money, to pay for some printing and some other expenses, and they started in. From time to time, before primary day, they reported directly to Dixon. The Maryland chairman scoffed at it all, and declared that it was wasted effort.

On the night of primary day, we got the first returns, of course, from Baltimore, and they were all our way. We carried the whole city, and the Maryland organization was very happy, claiming the entire State by a large majority. But as the evening wore on, one county after another kept reporting for Taft, and before midnight we saw that it was an extremely tight race. We carried western Maryland, as had been expected, but lost in some other counties where we had been fairly sure of winning.

At midnight the returns showed a tie, with only one county yet to be heard from. That was this little three-vote county, where Dixon's negro boys had set up their own ticket. It was one o'clock in the morning before we got word from there. Then one of the boys called on the telephone and reported, in a jubilant voice, that all three of his delegates had won. He only knew that he had carried his county, but we knew that that meant that we had carried the State, and it made a mighty difference in the tension in our office.

That night was the only time, during all that long and grueling fight, that I ever saw Senator Dixon lose his confidence. But that night, after having been so sure of victory on the early returns, the constant reports of Taft victories later on seemed to get his nerve. He went into his private office and lay down, refusing to see any one, or to hear anything further. No one was permitted to interrupt him until we got that word from his negro boys. Then the shout that rose made special notification unnecessary. Dixon came out of his room all smiles again, and from then until the morning after election day in November the smile never left his face.

The Indiana primaries, especially in Indianapolis, showed us the lengths to which, by this time, the other side were willing to go. In Indianapolis, the polling-places were arranged so that a voter had to pass his ballot through a small wicket in a wooden partition, and could not see who received it or what was done with it. Two judges of the Superior Court of Indiana, who went to the polls in Indianapolis, protested against such an arrangement, and each offered to remain at his polling-place and serve as a watcher. But both were ungently requested to move on. It was made perfectly evident to them that no honest man was wanted around that day. Nevertheless, despite the fact that we had the affidavits of these two judges, and some hundreds of others, to submit to the National Committee, when it met at Chicago, that committee held that there had been no fraud at Indianapolis, and that the Taft delegates had been regularly elected.

In California, Governor Johnson had secured the enactment of a primary law under which all the delegates from the whole State ran on one ticket, instead of making the campaign district by district, which would have been in strict accord with the call for the convention issued by the Republican National Committee. The Roosevelt delegates carried the State by a majority of more than 76,000, but two of them were unseated by the National Committee on the ground that, in the district which they represented, the Taft vote had been heavier than the Roosevelt vote. The Secretary of State of California certified that there had been a change in the boundaries of some districts which made it impossible to tell just how many votes had been polled in the district these two delegates represented. But that made no difference with the National Committee.

I have referred very briefly to only a few of the outstanding incidents of that long and bitter struggle. Every day was full of action, and, before we came to the end, the strain had begun to have a sort of numbing effect. But, after all, it was really mild in comparison with what we were to meet at Chicago, when the National Committee came to handle the various contests and to make up the temporary roll of the convention.

LIV

No good can be done, now, by rehashing in any detail the action of the Republican National Committee in making up the 1912 Convention roll. It became apparent, almost as soon as the committee met, that the Old Guard members who controlled it had determined to seat enough Taft men, on any pretext or on no pretext, to give them a majority. They were 'out to beat Roosevelt' at all costs and hazards, and it made no difference to them what else happened, or what means were employed to accomplish that purpose. They threw out Roosevelt delegates without a shadow of right, and cynically announced that, if necessary, they would throw out more. To our protest about the action in the California case, their reply was that we were lucky to lose only two, and that if they needed the rest they would take them.

The star performance of the Committee was in the case of the Fifth Louisiana District. There the so-called 'Republican Convention,' for the election of delegates to the National Convention, had been composed of eight white men. One was chairman and one secretary. One of the others made a motion naming two men for delegates and two for alternates. That motion was declared carried, and the other formalities having been disposed of the 'convention' adjourned. Some time subsequently the Taft chairman in Louisiana sent blank affidavits to the two delegates from the Fifth District, requesting them to swear to their intention to vote for Taft at Chicago. One executed the affidavit and the other refused. The National Committee threw out the one who refused, although he had exactly the same credentials as the other one, having been chosen on the same motion and by exactly the same vote. Political robbery can go no further.

The Roosevelt men on the National Committee started in to make a fight for some of these cases, and, for the first day or two of the committee meeting, there were some lively times. But they were outnumbered so greatly, and the determination of the committee majority to steal the convention, if necessary to the achievement of its purpose, became so apparent, that the Roosevelt men let down in their opposition. Their own fight weakened, and presently they were letting good cases go almost by default. The climax came when that happened in the Indiana case. This had been prepared for the Roosevelt delegates by Senator Beveridge, assisted by several of the best lawyers in the State. But the National Committee paid no attention to it, and even the Roosevelt men on the committee, under the leadership of Senator Borah and Frank B. Kellogg, of Minnesota, did not insist on going into it.

That brought an explosion. A meeting of the Roosevelt members of the National Committee was called for that evening at the Blackstone Hotel, where they were met by Senator Dixon and a number of other members of the Roosevelt National Committee, including Bainbridge Colby, of New York City. Dixon is a great smoother, and can stroke the ruffled feelings of an angry man with a more delicate touch than any other man I ever saw. Colby, on the other hand, is the possessor of a perfectly vitriolic tongue, along with the manners of a gentleman. He has also the ability to say as nice things in as pleasant a way as any one could wish.

Colby and Dixon went at the National Committeemen who had failed to make a stand for the Roosevelt side in the Indiana case, and for a couple of hours there was one of the most interesting performances I ever saw. First Colby would talk to them, saying the most extremely irritating things, often brutal in their frankness, but always with a smile and the pleasantest manner. He would keep at them until he had them just about ready to resort to blows. Then Dixon would come in, and in his soft voice and Southern drawl, which he could affect to perfection on occasion, would smooth them down and get them good-natured again.

After that Colby would go after them again, and the whole performance would be repeated. So it went on, until nearly midnight. Not much, if any, good was accomplished by it, but the Roosevelt managers hoped that there would be some stiffening of the Roosevelt men in the National Committee on the cases that remained to be heard. It did have that effect, but that was all. Nothing, at that stage of the proceedings, could have made any difference in the final outcome. The Old Guard had determined to steal the convention, and it had the votes in the committee to carry out its purpose. It looked for no result beyond that to be obtained then at Chicago. November and the election had ceased to exert any influence with that group. Consideration of personal fortunes, and the certainty of the loss of important and influential committee places in the Senate and House, were all forgotten. 'Beat Roosevelt' was the battle-cry, and they acted as if they actually believed that winning that battle would be bound to win the war.

Bitter as the contest was, it was not without its amusing features. One of them was furnished by George Henry Payne, of New York. He was at that time a reporter on the 'Evening Mail,' Henry Stoddard's paper. Stoddard

BAINBRIDGE COLBY

was a sure-enough Roosevelt man, a 'before April 9th-er,' and he had been very active in the pre-convention campaign. The morning that the New York delegation, which was nearly solid for Taft, arrived in Chicago, Payne went to George W. Perkins and suggested that it would be a good scheme to have a band go down to the station and meet the New-Yorkers. The delegation was going to march up to the hotel, and, with a Roosevelt band heading it, the parade might add a little to the Roosevelt enthusiasm with which Chicago was already running over. Perkins thought that was an amusing idea, and told Payne to go ahead.

Immediately Payne went out and engaged a band. He told it what to do, and the Old Guard in the New York delegation was scandalized and angered at having a Roosevelt band head its parade up to the Congress Hotel. The result pleased Payne so much that he kept on hiring bands. He told all the leaders to look to George W. Perkins for their pay. All they were to do was to deck themselves with Roosevelt banners and play all the time all around the convention hall and in the hotels where the delegates were stopping.

Everybody connected with the Roosevelt Committee, except, apparently, George Henry Payne, was extremely busy with work bearing directly on the convention fight, and nobody paid any attention to these bands. Nobody in any position of official responsibility ever gave them a thought. But they were there every day and all day, and there was Roosevelt music in Chicago, if nothing else.

Then, when the convention ended, and George Henry Payne had gone back to New York City, the bills came in. They amounted to something over ten thousand dollars. If you ever saw a man really thunderstruck, it was George W. Perkins the morning he received the information that

those bands had been playing by his directions and he was
expected to pay for them. Mr. Payne's exquisite sense of
humor had taken him out of the neighborhood just in time,
or he would have heard things that would have minimized
his enjoyment of that convention.

Of course Mr. Perkins refused to pay. He insisted that
he had given instructions to Payne covering the employment of only one band, and that for only one brief occasion.
For that he was quite ready to pay at once, but as for all
the rest they could go find Payne and get the money out of
him if they could. The band leaders, however, stood their
ground. They had their labor organization behind them,
and this was a case of politics, with the ever-ready threat of
the displeasure of organized labor as a lever. But they had
met a Tartar in Mr. Perkins, and we went away from
Chicago, to get ready for the Progressive Convention, with
that ten-thousand-dollar band bill unpaid.

Then Perkins made the mistake of forgetting all about it,
and of agreeing to the holding of the Progressive National
Convention in Chicago and in the same hotels and convention hall where the Republican show had been held.
We were all ready for the opening of that great semi-
religious gathering called the Progressive Convention, on
the morning of August 5, 1912, when a delegation of band
leaders called on Mr. Perkins and informed him that, unless
he handed over that ten thousand and odd dollars right on
the spot, there would be no music, except howls, at the
Progressive Convention, and that no other labor would be
done in the convention hall, or on behalf of the convention,
in Chicago.

Some of the howls were heard right then and there, for
this was a hold-up, pure and simple. But then, what was
ten thousand dollars compared to that convention? The

bands got their money — I think the matter of interest for six weeks was waived — and George Henry Payne was not connected with the Progressive campaign of that summer.

When the National Committee had finished its work on the temporary roll, we issued a statement from the headquarters of the Roosevelt Committee describing the 'saturnalia of crime' in which the Old Guard reveled. This statement was written with a vigor and vehemence that caught the attention of every newspaper in Chicago. Their editors sent to me at once to find out who had written it, and to say that there was a job waiting for him at their offices any time he wanted to come around. But we didn't tell who was the author. Any one of the men on our publicity staff would have been glad to have the credit for it, but it had been prepared for us by a man who was not regularly in the writing business, and who did not want his name used in that connection. Unless he has himself told about it afterward, I think the authorship of that scathing denunciation of the Republican National Committee never has been revealed. Only a little while ago one of my newspaper friends recalled it and asked me who wrote it. He was much surprised when I told him that Bainbridge Colby was the author.

LV

It was Colonel Roosevelt's intention, up to a short time before the Republican Convention met, not to go to Chicago. Means of immediate and private communication with him, by those in charge at Chicago, had been established by the installation of a direct telegraph wire between the headquarters in the Congress Hotel and his house at Sagamore Hill. Mr. Perkins had favored, at first, the setting-up of a private telephone wire, but experience had taught me that such a wire could be tapped very easily and without detection by those using it, whereas that cannot be done on a telegraph wire when expert operators are in charge. I had seen Edward W. Libbey and William Lee, the operators, in my office in the 'Times' Bureau at Washington, several times detect, by the action of their instruments, the fact that some one else had been cut in on our wire. Some operators have such a delicate touch that they can tell, instantly, when such a thing has happened, by the difference in the working of their sender. When this was explained to Mr. Perkins, he decided in favor of a telegraph wire, and I arranged with Mr. Libbey to take charge of it. I knew him to be an absolutely trustworthy man, who could be depended on under all circumstances, and was certain that, with him in charge, we should be protected completely against any wire-tapping or leaks.

Mr. Libbey was at that time employed in the Department of Commerce during the day, and worked the 'Times' wire at night. He arranged to take part of his vacation during the convention, and secured the services of three other expert operators from Washington, all of whom he knew intimately, and whom he certified to us as thoroughly reliable and trustworthy. My recollection is that one of them was on the White House wire staff. One came to Chicago with Libbey, and the other two went to Oyster Bay and were quartered at Sagamore Hill. The wire operated perfectly, and at all times conversation between Chicago and Sagamore Hill could be carried on almost as readily as by telephone, and with much greater certainty of avoiding misunderstanding. With two operators at each end of the wire we maintained a day and night service, the wire being always open.

Through our reports over this private wire, Colonel Roosevelt was kept minutely informed of developments at Chicago. As the situation there became more critical, Senator Dixon and Mr. Perkins began to consider the advisability of asking the Colonel to come out. After that evening conference with National Committeemen at the Blackstone Hotel, they decided that it would be better to have Mr. Roosevelt on the ground, and told him so. He agreed to come, and from the time of his arrival, a day or two later, the fight was under his personal direction.

It being perfectly clear to all of us at Chicago that the National Committee had determined to steal the convention, it was a matter of supreme importance to make the record so plain that the theft would be entirely obvious to all the country. The Taft vote in the National Committee was 37; the Roosevelt vote, 15. The Taft forces were made up largely of men either from Southern States that never cast a Republican electoral vote, or of men who had been repudiated in their own States and would not be continued as National Committeemen after that convention. This group of patronage peddlers and 'had beens' was the body that arranged the temporary roll of the convention so as to insure the renomination of President Taft, despite the fact that the very great majority of the primary votes in the States which cast Republican electoral votes and elect Republican Presidents had been against him.

Immediately upon his arrival Colonel Roosevelt went to the Congress Hotel, where a great throng had gathered to greet him. We had reserved a suite on the second floor, with a large parlor, for the Colonel's conference rooms, and another suite in a different part of the hotel for him and Mrs. Roosevelt. The crowd waiting to see and hear him was so great that there was no possibility of receiving it in the conference rooms, and so the Colonel stepped out on the balcony and made a speech, in which he described, in the bluntest kind of language, exactly what was going on in the National Committee. He was received with wild enthusiasm, and his declaration that he 'would not take it lying down' was cheered to the echo. That crowd was obviously ready and anxious for the fight.

Colonel Roosevelt and the managers of the Roosevelt Committee at once went into conference as to the tactics to be followed when the convention met. Governor Herbert E. Hadley, of Missouri, was chosen as floor leader, and it was determined that, at the first opportunity, he should offer a motion to amend the temporary roll prepared by the National Committee so as to substitute the names of seventy-two men, all of whom had been clearly and honestly elected as delegates from their respective districts and States, but who had been unseated by the Old Guard majority in the National Committee.

The Wisconsin delegation was expected naturally to support La Follette for the presidency, but there was a good deal of Roosevelt sentiment in it, and it was felt by the conference that this sentiment might be made effective in the struggle bound to come over the organization of the convention. Governor Francis E. McGovern, of Wisconsin, was therefore chosen as the Roosevelt nominee for temporary chairman, and he consented to make the fight against Elihu Root, who had been named by the National Committee.

Colonel Roosevelt had an extremely difficult situation to handle in these preliminary conferences, because a considerable part of his followers, led by Governor Johnson, of California, wanted to bolt the convention even before it assembled. They declared, stoutly, that the whole thing had been framed up; that it was so obvious a steal that all the country would recognize it; and that it would add strength to the Roosevelt movement if the Progressive forces refused to enter the convention at all, basing their course upon the action of the National Committee.

Colonel Roosevelt felt, however, that it was of the utmost importance to make the record perfectly clear, all the way up to the point where the theft of the seventy-two delegates had been irrevocably confirmed. In this he was supported by most of those in the conference, including some of the men most experienced in political leadership. But Governor Johnson and some of his friends were eager for fight, and it couldn't begin too soon for them. They argued for it vigorously, not only in the conferences, but elsewhere, and did not conceal their disappointment when the decision to go through on the lines suggested by Colonel Roosevelt was made.

We had reserved, for the duration of the convention, the Florentine Room, one of the small banquet rooms of the hotel, on the second floor right at the head of the main stairway. It was in the most conspicuous place in the hotel. There we organized a continuous open meeting, and from

early morning until late at night Progressive oratory, some
of it an extremely fiery and vehement type, was in full flow.
As soon as one speaker wore out, another took his place.
Chairmen served in relays. There was always a crowd, although the audience constantly shifted as men came and
went. But, without cessation, even at meal-times, the unending harangue kept up, and everybody in Chicago had
opportunity repeatedly to hear just exactly what the
Progressives thought of the National Committee and its
action. The details of our cause were set forth in vivid
phrases, and, while the Old Guard was plotting behind
closed doors, our side was really beginning its national
campaign.

LVI

VICTOR ROSEWATER, of Omaha, was chairman of the National Committee, having succeeded to that place on the resignation of Frank Hitchcock, who had become Postmaster-General in the Taft Cabinet. Mr. Rosewater was not a man of great force, and by no means one of the leaders in the group that was engaged in the theft of the convention. But he mustered up sufficient courage to go through publicly with the scheme laid down for him.

The convention was called to order by Mr. Rosewater at noon on Tuesday, June 18th. There was a very brief prayer, followed by the reading of the call of the convention, and then the two sides came to grips. Governor Hadley offered his motion to substitute the names of the seventy-two men unseated by the National Committee, and Mr. Rosewater ruled it out of order. He declined to entertain an appeal from that decision, on the ground that the only business that could properly come before the meeting was that of effecting a temporary organization.

The speeches nominating and seconding Governor McGovern and Mr. Root opened the door for a presentation of the whole situation, and produced a red-hot and brutally frank debate. The Roosevelt men did not mince words. They charged the Old Guard with deliberate fraud, and with deliberate intention to maintain that fraud. They set forth the consequences of the fraud with unmistakable clarity. Taunts and jeers, crimination and recrimination, punctuated the oratory, and frequently there was such disorder that the sergeant-at-arms had to threaten to clear the hall.

But at length the roll was called, and in State after State that involved the polling of the delegation. Chairman Rosewater did not hesitate, in such cases, about carrying through the instructions of the Old Guard. He was there to see that the seventy-two men put on the roll by the National Committee were seated and their votes counted, and he performed that duty to the end. Those seventy-two men had been selected by the National Committee for the purpose of voting according to instructions, so as to confirm the theft of the convention, and they, also, performed that duty to the end. The right of each of those seventy-two men to sit as a delegate in that convention was under formal contest, which it would become the duty of the convention itself, after it had been organized, to determine. In permitting them to vote on the temporary organization, involving the adoption of the temporary roll submitted by the National Committee, Mr. Rosewater constituted those seventy-two men judges in their own cases, and permitted their votes to decide those cases. It was a procedure essentially repugnant to the spirit of American institutions, and a mockery of right and justice. The result showed that they had to do it, in order to achieve the purpose of the Old Guard. For the count, including the seventy-two fraudulent votes, gave Mr. Root 558 and Governor McGovern 501, with 20 scattering or absent. Twelve of the scattering were cast for Judge Lauder, of North Dakota, by delegates from Wisconsin, showing the real La Follette strength in that delegation, and its bitter determination not to do anything that might help Colonel Roosevelt.

Mr. Root's narrow majority showed that the National Committee had not stolen any too many votes, for a shift of half of those seated by the theft would have changed the result. We learned later in the convention that that fact did not escape the attention and consideration of some delegates who were not involved in the scheme of the Old Guard and had no representative in the group that was managing the Taft plot.

Five days of constant fighting, all along the same lines as that of the opening battle on the temporary chairmanship, were required to complete the permanent organization of the convention and adopt the platform. During all that time the extremist element in the Roosevelt forces, led by the Californians under Governor Johnson, kept up their demand for an immediate bolt. At times it even seemed likely that Governor Johnson would walk out, anyway, at the head of his own delegation alone, if no others would follow. Colonel Roosevelt was obliged to exert his influence to the utmost to prevent this.

At one stage of the proceedings, even Colonel Roosevelt wavered, for a time, in his determination to make the record complete before leaving the convention. That was soon after the meeting of the Committeee on Credentials. The Old Guard had, of course, in that committee the same proportionate majority that it had in the National Committee, by virtue of the seating of the seventy-two stolen delegates. When the Credentials Committee met, it appointed a subcommittee to prepare a set of rules for its own procedure. The report of this committee was so flagrant as to inflame even those Roosevelt men who had not been willing to follow the California lead and make an immediate bolt. Hugh Halbert, of St. Paul, the Minnesota member of the committeee, at once made an earnest argument against the rules proposed by the subcommittee, and moved to amend them in several particulars. But Frank Heney, of San Francisco, one of the hottest-headed of the California delegation, jumped up and started a bolt from the committee. As he walked out of the room, he called for all the Roosevelt men to follow him, and one by one most of them did so, although several of them, including Mr. Halbert, were reluctant to do so.

They all came down to the Congress Hotel and at once went to the conference rooms. Colonel Roosevelt was there, with a number of his friends and advisers. Instantly there was an explosion. The Colonel declared that this action capped the climax and settled the course to be taken from then on. There was, of course, tremendous excitement, and some one proposed that we should at once organize a convention of our own in Orchestra Hall and proceed to nominate Colonel Roosevelt for the presidency. The Colonel seemed inclined to agree to that, and two or three men started off post-haste to see about securing the hall.

The conference room was a maelstrom. It was crowded to the limit, and everybody was trying to talk at once. Only Senator Dixon seemed to retain his composure. He went into the Florentine Room, where the Progressive oratory was going on at an unusually fiery pitch, and sat on a table at the back of the hall, swinging his legs and looking on with amusement, apparently quite unexcited and content. Senator Bristow, of Kansas, came into the conference room for a few minutes, but took no part at first in the discussion. George B. Cortelyou, who had been in Mr. Roosevelt's Cabinet, and was a close friend as well as an astute politician and cool-headed adviser, was endeavoring to do something to calm down the crowd a little, but not having much success.

It seemed to me that a bolt at that juncture would be wholly ruinous to our side. It would be desperately premature, and could not be defended or explained away.

The fact was that the bolt from the Committee on Credentials had occurred before any definite and conclusive action had been taken by that committee, merely upon the presentation of the report of its subcommittee on rules of procedure, and after Mr. Halbert had offered his amendment to those rules. Suppose, after the Roosevelt men had left the committee room, the other side adopted the Halbert amendment, but in the meantime the entire Roosevelt force bolted the convention. Then we should be in the absolutely untenable position of having sat in the convention and endured one high-handed outrage after another, without bolting, only to bolt upon the first act of justice and honesty shown us.

At once, upon my presentation of that view to Mr. Halbert, he agreed with it, and began to urge the return of the committee members to the meeting-room. I tried to present this view to Colonel Roosevelt, but was unable to get to him. So I tried it on Senator Bristow, who promptly agreed with it, and undertook to endeavor to get it to the Colonel. Then I appealed to Mr. Cortelyou, Senator Dixon, and several others. Only Dixon declined to do anything. He simply refused to become excited, and replied, with a laugh, that it was best to let the crowd in the conference room blow off steam for an hour or so, and there would be time enough then to prevent mistaken action.

Apparently the Senator was right, for after an hour or so of this angry discussion and protest, the committee members were induced to return to their meeting. There they found that exactly what I had suspected had happened, and that the Taft forces had adopted the Halbert amendment almost entirely. Whether or not it was just a trick to trap the Roosevelt men by enticing them into a premature bolt, I never knew. But if it was, it came very near succeeding.

LVII

DURING all the time that the fight over permanent organization was grinding its slow way toward the end, the Old Guard kept giving one line of indication that it was beginning to feel some uneasiness about the result of its actions. This was in the 'feelers' that were constantly coming to Colonel Roosevelt as to whether or not he would accept a compromise and support the nominee of the convention, if the two sides could agree on some other man than Mr. Taft or himself. The Colonel's response to all these feelers was exactly the same, and was of a kind to furnish no reasons for satisfaction or congratulation to the Old Guard. It was that if the roll of delegates were purged of fraud, and the convention honestly organized, he would support its nominee, whoever he might be. The Old Guard, however, had no intention whatever of purging the roll, for they perfectly understood that such action would have two results. In the first place, it would be a public confession of their own guilt, and, in the next place, which was undoubtedly the major consideration with them, it would have been certain to result in the nomination of Mr. Roosevelt.

They were willing, however, to throw Mr. Taft overboard if by doing that they could induce Colonel Roosevelt to support a compromise nominee. For the effect of that would be tantamount to condonation on his part of the action of the National Committee, at the same time that it gave them some one else than Roosevelt to head their ticket. So they sent emissaries to try to ascertain how he felt about a compromise. At first these emissaries approached one or other of the Roosevelt Committee managers, who, of course, reported the matter to the Colonel. At length the Old Guard tried more direct methods. One day Governor Hadley came to him with the report that he himself had been approached. The Colonel saw Governor Hadley in his private rooms, not in the conference room, and there was present, besides the two men, only the Colonel's young cousin, George Emlen Roosevelt.

'They have offered to nominate me,' Governor Hadley said to the Colonel.

'Are you certain that it is a genuine offer?' was the Colonel's question in response.

They talked it over, and Governor Hadley told Mr. Roosevelt just what had occurred. When he thought over the conversation that had been had with him, he could not satisfy himself that it had been an honest offer, and he admitted as much to Colonel Roosevelt. But it had certainly been an approach designed to convey the impression that a genuine compromise would be acceptable to the Taft forces, and that he might be the choice for nominee if such a compromise could be arranged with the Roosevelt side.

The Missouri Governor was not in rugged health at that time, and in the talk with Colonel Roosevelt he mentioned the possibility that the presidency, if he should be nominated and elected, might kill him. The Colonel replied that in his judgment it was worth the sacrifice; that the presidency of the United States was the greatest task that could be laid upon any man, and that to fulfill it worthily was paramount to every consideration of personal welfare.

But he warned Governor Hadley to remember that that convention, as it then stood, and as it seemed likely to be confirmed on permanent organization, was essentially crooked in its composition, and that no honest man could afford to accept its nomination. Then he said, explicitly, that if the roll were purged and Governor Hadley should be nominated, he would be very glad to support him. Or if any other honest man of Progressive views should be named, he would support the nomination. The Colonel said that because he had received word that Senator Borah was at that moment waiting in the conference room to see him, and he understood that Borah had come to submit to him a proposition on behalf of Senator Cummins, of Iowa, exactly like that submitted to him by Governor Hadley on his own account.

The result of the conference with Hadley was that the Governor went away to endeavor to find out whether the approach to him had, in fact, meant a genuine offer to accept him as a compromise nominee, and also whether there was the least possibility of purging the fraudulent roll.

When the Governor had gone, Colonel Roosevelt saw Senator Borah, and at once confirmed his impression that this was another compromise proposition, like the one he had just heard from Hadley. He had very much the same conversation with the Senator that he had had with the Governor, and Borah left on an errand similar to that of Hadley.

While these approaches directly to Colonel Roosevelt were being made, all sorts of similar approaches were being made to different members of the Roosevelt organization. The air was full of talk of compromise, but none of it, so far as I heard, went far enough to consider the purging of the fraudulent roll, and that was the Colonel's irreducible minimum. That had to be accomplished before he would

HERBERT S. HADLEY

consider anything else, although he was open in his promise
that, if that were done, he would support the convention's
nominee, provided that nominee was not Taft.

The last of this series of attempts to reach the Colonel
with a proposition for compromise happened to be made
through me, and I have always thought it was genuine and
honest. It did not come from any one of the Old Guard
crowd, but emanated from a little group of delegates who
were not among the tainted seventy-two, and who had been
instructed for Taft by their districts. This occurred on the
fourth night of the convention, when the fight that had
been going on ever since Tuesday noon had reached its
climax of anger and bitterness, and it was apparent that
the course being followed by the Taft forces was certain
to wreck the party and bring it to disastrous defeat in
November.

When I went up to the Roosevelt headquarters offices,
after dinner that evening, I found a man there who was
waiting to see Senator Dixon. I did the best I could, by
messenger and by telephone, to locate the Senator, but
without success. Dixon was about worn out by the long
contest, and he had found some place where he could get a
little rest without being interrupted. After half an hour or
more of this fruitless effort on my part, my caller said:

'Well, never mind. I only wanted to send a message to
Roosevelt, and I guess you could take it to him, couldn't
you?'

I replied that I certainly could, and would be glad to do
so. Thereupon he said:

'I represent a group of about thirty delegates, partly
from my own State — Michigan — and partly from others
that have a good chance of going Republican at the
election. We were all sent down here to beat Roosevelt,

but this thing that is going on is beating the Republican
Party, and we are not for that. We have been talking the
situation over among ourselves, and have made up our
minds to submit this proposition to Roosevelt. We have
noticed that, on every roll-call thus far, the Taft side has
won by a majority so small that, if we had voted the other
way on any one of them, Taft would have lost. That puts
more on us than we had counted on. We are all instructed
for Taft, but this is going beyond our instructions. So this
is what we'll do. We will watch the roll-call on nomination, and, if it is going the same way that the others
went, we will vote for any man you folks say, provided you
will give a few votes to the same man, so that it will look
like an effort to compromise. That will prevent Taft from
going over on the first ballot, and I guess I don't need to
tell you any more. Now, can you take that to Roosevelt?'

He certainly did not need to say any more, for everybody in the United States, who knew anything about that
convention, knew that if Taft were not nominated on the
first ballot, he never would be nominated. It was first or
not at all with him. His failure to go over on the first ballot
would certainly be followed by the break-up of his forces
and a rush to Roosevelt. I hurried down the iron stairs to
the conference room filled with exultation. The fight had
been so long and so bitter that I was ready, by that time,
for almost anything that would give our side the victory,
and I was certain that this proposition would do it. This
was something that evidently was not engineered by the
Old Guard, but had been suggested in spite of them. This
came from men in the ranks, and certainly seemed to
promise that it would be carried out in good faith, if undertaken.

I found the Colonel in the conference room, surrounded

by a crowd of excited and enthusiastic followers. After some time and effort, I succeeded in getting him into another room, alone, and began to present my story. But before I had the proposition half stated, the Colonel saw what was coming.

'No! No! No!' he broke in, 'I won't hear it! I won't have it! You needn't talk to me at all! You go back and tell your man that I won't have anything to do with it. You tell him that this is a crooked convention, and I won't touch it with a forty-rod pole. You tell him that the first thing they've got to do is to purge the roll. You tell him that if they will purge the roll, I will support any man they want to nominate except Taft. I won't support Taft. But, until they purge the roll, neither I nor any other honest man, can touch this convention. Now, you go tell him what I say.'

'But, Colonel —' I began. I wanted to argue the point a little. It seemed to me that this proposition, if accepted, would surely mean the nomination of Colonel Roosevelt and his complete control of the convention. It would permit the purging of the roll and the rewriting of the platform, for once the Colonel's side had control enough to make the nomination, everything else would have to follow. But he simply wouldn't have it, and would not listen.

'You go tell him what I say!' he roared, and bounded back into the conference room.

So I climbed dejectedly back up those four flights of iron stairs to face the man so eagerly waiting in my office room. I can see him now, sitting there on the edge of his chair, with one large hand on each knee, and an expression of alert expectancy on his face. He believed his group had found the solution of the trouble, and he was keen to go back and tell them that it was all right.

When I reported my conversation with the Colonel, my caller's face went absolutely blank. He seemed completely dazed. His lips parted, as if he were trying to take in the meaning of the words I was uttering through the mouth as well as the ears. When I had repeated all the talk with the Colonel, the emissary of compromise sat silent for a few moments, staring blankly at me. He was a huge bulk of a man, and it was comical to see him so utterly dumbfounded. At length he exclaimed:

'Say, say that again.'

So I repeated the conversation in Colonel Roosevelt's room. The man from Michigan sat looking at me, through it all, with an expression of utter uncomprehension on his face. He did not move for some moments. Then he fetched a deep sigh and ejaculated:

'Say! Don't that beat hell!'

He rose and walked out of the room like a somnambulist or a man in a dream. And that was the end of that hopeful proposition.

To my mind that is the complete and final answer to the charge that the nomination from that Republican Convention was all that Colonel Roosevelt wanted, and that in seeking it he was actuated by personal ambition. It was distinctly offered to him, then and there, and he would not listen to the offer. He threw that nomination away, with angry refusal even to consider it. It is true that his nomination by that convention undoubtedly would have been followed by a large bolt of stand-patters, and many, who probably would not have bolted openly, would have voted against him on election day or failed to go to the polls. But it is also true that his nomination there would have given him the official support of the party and made him formally its leader again. No one would contend that the nomination which he accepted later from the Progressive faction could have the possibilities of success at the polls that this one, which he rejected, had. He was too good a politician not to appraise such a situation correctly. His action was absolutely incompatible with a motive of personal ambition.

A long time after that exciting night at the Chicago Convention, I brought that incident up again in conversation with Colonel Roosevelt.

'You surely surprised me, that night,' I said.

'Why?' he asked.

'Because,' I replied, 'in all my experience and acquaintance with you, you had "played the game." You had described yourself as a "practical" man, and I went down to you that night, thinking only of the chance to win that fight, which had been so hard and bitter. I was thinking of the practical politics of the proposition, and of you as a practical politician who would play the game at that time.'

'Yes,' he said, 'I am a practical politician, and I have played the game. But that was something very different. There was a question of simple honesty involved in that fight at Chicago, the principle of right and wrong. It had gone far beyond a mere question of expediency or political shrewdness. It was a question of fundamental morality.'

He went on to talk about that incident and all its bearings for some time, and out of that talk I got a new impression of Colonel Roosevelt. It took me back to the many months he had spent in Africa, the first period in many years of his busy, active life when he had the experience of detachment from contact with his fellows and their affairs. Then, for the first time since he had quit his North Dakota ranch, he had had opportunity for quiet reflection, and had had the advantage of perspective, which distance and solitude only could give him, on his country and his own relation to it. It was in that period of comparative solitude in Africa, when even his own son did not share his tent, that Colonel Roosevelt had the time for that introspection and reflection which were the real reasons why he refused to 'play the game' that June night in Chicago.

The Roosevelt who came back from Africa was the same physical being who went there, but in other and greater respects he was permanently changed. The experiences of his camp life, followed by his contact with the crowned heads and courts of Europe, as well as with the plain people there, had developed and enlarged him. He came home with a passion for service that outweighed other considerations, and made that of self the least and last of all.

LVIII

AT once upon the completion of the permanent organization of the convention, which confirmed the theft of the seventy-two seats by the National Committee, Colonel Roosevelt announced his desire that his name should not be presented to the convention. He had given very careful consideration to the course to be followed when the piracy of these delegates should have been completed. His decision was that immediately after the last of the reports from the Committee on Credentials had been confirmed by vote of the convention, this announcement should be made on his behalf by Henry J. Allen, of Kansas. He wrote out a brief statement, which Mr. Allen was to read, and in which the whole case of the Progressives, with regard to those seventy-two delegates, was summarized and made absolutely plain. The Colonel asked all those who had been elected as Roosevelt delegates to refrain from voting on any other matter before the convention, after the adoption of the reports of the Credentials Committee. That committee had been submitting sectional reports, dealing with one State or district at a time, and it had taken many hours to pass on them all. The Colonel distinctly stated that he did not release any delegate from the obligation to vote for him, if he voted at all, but his request was that they refrain from taking any part in the convention after the theft had been confirmed.

About three hundred and fifty of the Roosevelt delegates conformed exactly to this request, and this action gave Mr. Root, who had been made permanent chairman, the opportunity personally to gain three votes for Taft on

the roll-call on nomination. Some of the Roosevelt delegates felt that, having been elected at primaries which
carried definite and legal instructions, they were obligated,
by their State law, to vote, and accordingly the record of
the convention will show that some hundred or more did
vote for Roosevelt. But his name was not formally before
the convention, and the great body of his delegates complied strictly with his request.

When Massachusetts was reached, on the roll-call on
nomination, one of its delegates challenged the announcement of its vote, and there was a poll of the delegation. It
happened that, in three cases in that State, a Roosevelt
delegate and a Taft alternate had been elected at the same
primary. This peculiar result, showing as it did the failure
of the voters at a primary to discriminate on the issue involved, and their tendency to act on mere personal considerations, was one of the events that started me on a
consideration of the whole primary system, which has led
to the conclusion that it is wrong in principle and subversive of the original plan of representative government
adopted by the framers of the Constitution.

When the poll of the Massachusetts delegation reached
the first of these three Roosevelt men, he answered, 'Present and not voting.' It is customary at national political
conventions to adopt for their government the rules of the
National House of Representatives with occasionally some
modifications. At this convention no permanent rules were
ever adopted. On the first day there had been adopted, as
temporary rules, the rules of the preceding Republican
National Convention, which were based, as usual, on those
of the House of Representatives. When the Committee on
Rules submitted its report on permanent rules, the minority offered a substitute. That substitute was laid on the

table, and then, without adoption of the committee report, the convention went on to other business. So, if any rules were in effect in the permanent organization, when the roll was called on nomination for President, they were those of the preceding convention, based on those of the House. Frequently in the National House of Representatives members respond 'Present' when their names are called on a record vote, and, during twenty or more years of my observation of procedure there, I have never seen such a response challenged.

But when the Roosevelt delegate responded, 'Present and not voting,' Mr. Root directed the calling of the name of his alternate. What right or authority an alternate has to vote, when the delegate for whom he is alternate is present, does not appear. In this case the alternate voted for Taft and Mr. Root directed the recording of that vote. The other two Massachusetts cases were identical.

The temper of the crowds in the galleries and of some of the delegates on the floor had been at the boiling point for a long time. Mr. Root's course as chairman had been greeted constantly from the galleries as well as from the floor by hoots and cat-calls, and cries of 'Steam roller' varied with shouts of 'Toot, toot!' 'Choo choo!' and other evidences of extreme disapprobation. But he never displayed any annoyance at personalities aimed at himself. He did not hesitate in the least over the Massachusetts incident and the tumult that it raised. He went through with his part in it as calmly as he ever made any appearance in court, and gave every evidence of taking the storm that he aroused as quite what he had expected.

LIX

FORMAL plans for the organization of the Progressive
Party began just as soon as Colonel Roosevelt decided not
to permit his name to go before the Republican Convention. Orchestra Hall was obtained for the Saturday night
on which the Republicans were due to adjourn, and the
throng of Roosevelt Progressives were jubilant. Their
mood and bearing were very different from those of the
Republicans. Realization of what they had done seemed at
last to have taken hold of the delegates to the Taft convention, whether or not it had come home to the leaders of
the oligarchy who had directed that performance. They
were resorting, in shoals, to that source of solace and comfort which has since been put under the ban of constitutional amendment and statute law, and it was a wobbly
and uncertain course that they were weaving in and about
the corridors of the hotels, while the jubilant Progressives
were singing and shouting and giving every evidence of
happiness over the result.

After the Orchestra Hall meeting was over that night,
and the lobby of the Congress Hotel was almost deserted,
I was sitting there talking over the week with one of my
old associates on the 'Times,' when an old friend from one
of the Western States tacked solemnly and warily in. He
progressed slowly from one pillar to another, stopping at
each to get a good rest and straighten himself up for the
next spurt in advance. At length he arrived opposite me,
and with his back well braced against a pillar looked down
and said, with a weird attempt at a smile:

'Oshcar, I'm not 'shcouraged!'

'No,' retorted my 'Times' friend, 'the headache will come later.'

The gathering in Orchestra Hall that night was not a convention; it was simply a mass meeting that gave one more opportunity for vehement denunciation of the action of the Republican Convention and uproarious endorsement of Colonel Roosevelt. The amazing enthusiasm that the Roosevelt Progressives had been showing, during ten days of uninterrupted oratory in the Florentine Room, was not in the least decreased. If anything it was greater, although that seems impossible. Colonel Roosevelt's appearance on the platform was greeted with roars of cheering, and his announcement that if, at a regularly organized convention, to be held later in the summer, and at which the States casting Republican electoral votes were duly represented, he should be nominated for the presidency, he would accept that nomination, literally seemed to be the summit of ambition for the entire crowd.

Even Governor Johnson seemed actually happy, at last. The fight that he had been hoping for had come in earnest, and there was no doubt that he would have just as active a part in it as he was willing to take. For one summer and fall Hiram Johnson was not going to lack opportunity for political battle.

With all their enthusiasm and exuberance I do not believe there were many men in Orchestra Hall that night, if, indeed, there were any, who were under the least illusion as to the result in November. It was plain that the Republican Party was split wide open, and that the much greater faction was on our side. But there was not the slightest prospect of winning the election on such a split alone. There must be a similar division in the Democratic Party in order to furnish any real possibility of victory in

November. Without such a split, the Democrats would carry not only the Solid South, with its hundred and thirty or more electoral votes, but many Northern and Western States as well. There were very few States in the Union where the Republican vote was in such preponderance as to stand a wide-open split in the party and still permit one faction to win over the Democrats.

But some of us in the Roosevelt organization were not without hope that the Democratic Party would be split also. Its convention was coming on at Baltimore in a short time, and Champ Clark, of Missouri, then Speaker of the National House of Representatives, had obtained a large lead over other candidates in the pre-convention campaign. The indications at Chicago were that Clark would win at Baltimore.

William Jennings Bryan had attended the Republican Convention in the capacity of a newspaper correspondent. He had had several conversations with Colonel Roosevelt and Senator Dixon, and some also with me and others in the Roosevelt Committee. Senator Dixon and I had both gained the impression, from Mr. Bryan's talk with us, that he expected to be defeated at Baltimore. He was going there to oppose the nomination of Clark. In addition to other objections to Clark, the support of the Missouri man by Tammany Hall was more than enough to make Bryan fight with all his might.

Dixon and I also received from Mr. Bryan the impression that, in case he did meet, at Baltimore, the defeat he anticipated, he expected a split in the party to follow, and he himself would support Colonel Roosevelt. Colonel Roosevelt never repeated to me any of the conversation he had with Bryan during that convention, but I knew that he, too, as well as Dixon and myself, had this impression as to what would happen, if Clark were named by the Democrats as their candidate for the presidency.

At that time Bryan still had a very large following in the Democratic Party. If he led a bolt and supported the Progressive ticket, there would be a fair chance of victory for us at the election, and even a possibility of bringing about that year the realignment of parties which so many felt ought to be effected. For, with the Bryan wing deserting the regular Democratic nominee, there would be a tendency on the part of the conservatives who were left in both parties by this situation to get together on one or the other of their nominees, so that the campaign would develop into a contest between Roosevelt and either Taft or the nominee of the Democratic Convention. The easy possibility of this occurring was shown by the fact that fall that regular Republicans, publicly estimated by Mr. Taft to number more than a million, voted directly for Wilson in order to insure the defeat of Roosevelt.

A split in the Democratic Party, between progressives and reactionaries, would facilitate very greatly the development of two white parties in the South, since it would bring into the field a new party that would not be tainted in that section of the country with the negro question, as the Republican Party is. Between the time when the Republican Convention at Chicago adjourned and the Democratic Convention at Baltimore ended its contest with the nomination of Woodrow Wilson, a professed Progressive, there did seem to be a strong possibility that that year would see the long-desired readjustment between American political parties, and that thereafter the alignment would be liberals on one side and conservatives on the other. There would be a difference of principle between those two parties, such as there had almost ceased to be between the Republican and Democratic Parties.

But to his own surprise Mr. Bryan won at Baltimore. Whether it was because he was making a fight for some one else than himself or not, he made a harder fight than usual, and, when it was successful, all chance of the sort of split that we had been looking forward to was ended. From that moment it was clear to us at Progressive headquarters that there was no practical possibility of victory for us at the election. Colonel Roosevelt himself was never for a moment deceived as to the result in November.

But personal success was the least of his considerations. He really did not want another term in the White House, at least at that juncture in public affairs. What he did want was the establishment of the Progressive, or Liberal, movement. He made the very best fight during that campaign of which he was capable, simply with that object in view. There was a chance that, if we secured a large preponderance of votes over the Republicans, the result might be the recognition of the Progressive Party as the chief contender with the Democrats. That was bound to result, ultimately, in a new political alignment between liberals and conservatives.

Mr. Bryan went into that campaign with gay enthusiasm, apparently wholly unconscious that he was proceeding toward his own political extinction. When it was over, Mr. Wilson recognized his obligation by taking Bryan into his Cabinet long enough to enable himself to win away from his chief supporter the party which, up to that time, Bryan had and Wilson did not have. Then he threw Bryan out, unceremoniously, and thereafter he had both office and party.

LX

WITH the clearing-up of this one element of uncertainty in the situation, the ex-Republican Progressives were left free to proceed with their organization as vigorously and promptly as possible. The chance of a Democratic split had made advisable delay until that was determined, because, if such a split did occur, it should have recognition in the new organization. The call for the Progressive National Convention went out over the country early in July, signed by a long list of those who had been prominent in the Roosevelt fight at Chicago, including several members of the new Republican National Committee. At once there was immense activity in preparing for this convention.

Headquarters were opened in New York, in the Manhattan Hotel, where the Republican National Committee also had located. We had headquarters, too, in Chicago, in the La Salle Hotel, with a direct wire connecting the two offices, so arranged that it could be operated either for telegraph or telephone service. It was agreed between the two headquarters that neither should take any action involving a general matter without consultation of the other. A violation of this agreement by the Chicago office led to an unending lot of trouble before the campaign was over.

The Progressive National Committee was promptly filled out by the election of a member from every State, and, in a few days after the convention call was issued, we began to receive notice of the selection of delegates. It was at once apparent that there was tremendous enthusiasm for the new movement all over the country. State after State notified headquarters that it was not satisfied with the limited number of delegates to the convention provided for in the call. They doubled, trebled, and quadrupled their quotas, dividing the vote per delegate accordingly, so that many a man or woman sat in that convention with half or a third or quarter of a vote.

Colonel Roosevelt spent most of the interval between the Republican Convention and ours at his home at Sagamore, and we at Progressive headquarters in New York had frequent consultations with him, usually at Sagamore, as to details of the organization work. He was busy preparing the speech that he was to deliver at the convention, and consulting friends in all directions about its contents. He determined to include in it not only a comprehensive review of the Republican Convention and the action of the Republican National Committee, but his own programme fully set forth; the issues for which he stood, and the matters of national legislation which he would recommend as President if he should be elected.

Even before this speech was completed, a question arose as to the time at which it should be delivered, and the settlement of that question led to one of the liveliest battles with Colonel Roosevelt in which I ever participated or which I ever saw. At headquarters, both in New York and Chicago, we naturally wanted the Colonel to speak on the second day of the convention, in response to the nomination. But the Colonel thought otherwise. He said that since the meeting in Orchestra Hall, at which he had promised to accept the nomination if it were made at a regularly called and organized convention representing the whole country, he had developed some ideas that were included in his speech, and which might be regarded by a good many of his adherents as more radical than they could support. He was determined, therefore, to make his speech as soon as he arrived in Chicago, so that, if it did prove too radical for any of his friends, they should have ample opportunity before the meeting of the Progressive Convention to determine what action they would take about it. They might want, he thought, to select some other man for the presidential nomination.

The possibility that the Progressive Convention might want to nominate some one else than Colonel Roosevelt made those of us at headquarters laugh, but that did not in the least affect the Colonel's determination as to the delivery of his speech. The Chicago headquarters was making all arrangements for the convention, which was to be held in the same hall where the Republican Convention had met, and with headquarters at the same hotel. The discussion with the Colonel about the time for his speech went on, in desultory fashion, until just a few days before the date of the convention, which was set for August 5th, just three months before election day. Neither side yielded or gained a point.

At length the speech was completed, and put into proof. The Colonel sent a set of these proofs, printed with extra wide margins, to headquarters, for submission to a number of his friends and consultants and their suggestions. Probably twenty men read it, and each one of them had several suggestions to make, either as to contents or phraseology. All these suggestions were noted on the margins. When they had all come in, I took the proof down to Sagamore Hill to go over it with the Colonel and explain the suggestions that had been made.

The Colonel received me in his library, the same room in which he had talked with me about the Kaiser when I had taken the Hale letters to him four years before. His Secretary, Frank Harper, was with him. Harper was a young Englishman, with all the traditional respect of an Englishman for persons in authority, and he had not yet learned much about Colonel Roosevelt's ways with those around him. He seemed not even to have learned that the one thing which the Colonel always demanded of a friend was that he should fight for his own ideas. I doubt if there was any other way of so promptly losing Colonel Roosevelt's respect as to make him think that you were yielding your own judgment to him without a struggle simply because he was Colonel Roosevelt, and without regard to the merits of the proposition involved.

The Colonel took the proofs, with all their suggestions, and began at once to go over them. He worked very rapidly. When a suggestion was obvious, he immediately either accepted or rejected it, and went on to the next. Occasionally he would ask who had made it, and sometimes he wanted to know why it had been made and what was back of it. Always upon receiving the explanation, his decision was immediate. Sometimes he accepted the phraseology suggested, and sometimes it suggested other phraseology to him. Once or twice wholly new points came to him as a result of this talk, and he wrote in two or three new paragraphs.

At length, after two or three hours' work, the proofs were finished. The Colonel handed them to me saying:

'There you are, O. K. How soon will it be printed?'

I thanked him for his promptness, said it would be ready in a couple of days, and added:

'This speech is to be delivered at the convention, on Tuesday afternoon, after the nomination has been made.'

Colonel Roosevelt looked up at me with a grin, and pounded the desk in front of him with his doubled-up fist.

'It is not!' he declared, with regulation Rooseveltian

emphasis. 'This speech will be delivered by me just as soon as I reach Chicago. I shall go to the hotel from the train, walk out on the balcony, just where I spoke at the Republican Convention, and deliver this speech.'

'I am sorry to hear you say that, Colonel,' I replied, 'for it is our unanimous judgment at headquarters that it should be delivered in the convention, after the nomination.'

The Colonel swung around so that he faced the desk and pounded it with both fists.

'And it is my unanimous judgment that it will not!' he exclaimed, accenting every word with a resounding thump of the desk.

Harper, who had been taking dictation of some notes as the Colonel worked over the proofs, sat beside him open-mouthed. Apparently he had never seen any one venture to differ with the Colonel before, much less take on a real and vigorous controversy with him.

But it was simply out of the question to agree with the Colonel about that speech. His reasons for wanting to deliver it as soon as he reached Chicago were all sound and did him credit, but they were not so important as our reasons for having the speech in the convention. And, after all, the whole convention was simply for the purpose of nominating him, whatever he believed, or said, or did. His followers were of the Colonel Nelson stripe. They were with Roosevelt, through thick and thin. They wanted his leadership, and if he proclaimed a journey to the moon they were in a hurry to engage passage.

So I went at it, and for half an hour we had it back and forth, with all the emphasis we could develop, and without either side giving or gaining an inch. At length the time arrived when I had to hurry to catch my train back to the city, and the discussion had, perforce, to be ended. Each fired a last shot as we parted at the door of Sagamore, and each fired his own gun.

There was great disappointment at headquarters when I reported my complete inability to shake the Colonel's determination on this point. But it was decided that we had better wait a day or two before tackling him again on the subject. When we had the completed speech ready to give him, we could take it up again.

However, we found that we couldn't wait that long. The convention was to meet on Monday. On Thursday evening, just as we were sitting down to dinner at the headquarters hotel, a telegram came from the Chicago headquarters saying that, in order to get the convention programme printed in time for distribution on Monday morning, they must have the decision as to when the Colonel was to speak. If they did not have that in Chicago on Friday morning, the programme would have to be printed without including the Colonel.

So, immediately after dinner, Senator Dixon, Mr. Perkins, Henry Stoddard, and I drove out to Sagamore. It was raining, and not many cars were on the road. Mr. Perkins's chauffeur had made that trip so often that he knew every pebble in the road, even in the dark, and we made the trip in an hour and eight minutes, just a fraction over thirty-four miles, from the door of the Manhattan Hotel to the door of Sagamore Hill.

Colonel Roosevelt had not finished dinner when we arrived. He came to the door to greet us, and received us with a cheerful grin.

'To what new affront am I indebted for this formidable invasion?' he inquired, leading the way into the library. He knew there was a battle toward.

Mr. Perkins replied that we had come down for a final consultation with him as to the convention programme, and instantly the Colonel retorted that he was going to speak as soon as he reached Chicago.

Then we sat down, the smokers lit their cigars, and we went to it. One after another we stated our case, and re-stated it. To each one the Colonel made just the same reply that he had made to me that first afternoon. It was his unanimous judgment not to delay five minutes after reaching Chicago before speaking.

The discussion continued without interruption or consideration of any other subject for about three hours. Our side was exhausted. We had used every argument that any one of us had been able to think of, and without the least success. The Colonel was walking back and forth, along the bookcase that lined one side of the library, pounding out his replies with one clenched fist on the other, and his teeth clicking at every word. We were about ready to give up and go when there occurred to me a way of putting the case that had not been used.

Senator Beveridge had agreed to serve as temporary chairman of the convention, and he had prepared an extremely effective speech to be delivered when he took the chair. It was of great importance that this speech should have the fullest chance for publicity. It was bound to be very helpful to our cause, and it was imperative that our programme should be so arranged that nothing would interfere with or limit its effect.

The Colonel was walking toward the door of the library, away from me, when that idea struck me.

'You see it's this way, Colonel,' I cut in; and he paused in his walk and looked back at me over his shoulder. 'We have a six-inch gun and a sixteen-inch gun to fire at this convention. We must not fire the sixteen-inch gun first, or we shall lose the effect of the six-inch gun. Its report will be lost in the reverberations of the sixteen-inch gun.'

The Colonel swung around to face me. 'I don't know but there's something in that, O. K.,' he said.

Instantly, Dixon, Perkins, and Stoddard were on their feet with me.

'Thank you, Colonel,' said Perkins.

'Good-night, Colonel,' said the rest of us, grabbing our raincoats from the rack in the hall.

The Colonel laughed. 'You villains!' he called, as we swarmed out of the door and into the waiting motor-car.

That was the end of that fight, which showed that sometimes Colonel Roosevelt could be induced to change his mind, under argument. He spoke on the Tuesday afternoon, after the nomination.

LXI

THE Progressive National Convention was marked by a
fervor almost religious in character. It was held in the
same great hall where the Republican robbery had taken
place. The floor was filled with delegates and alternates
from every State and district in the Union, and the galleries were crowded to the utmost. The atmosphere was
charged with emotion akin to prayer. Old newspaper men,
hardened by many years of experience, made cynical and
skeptical by constant contact with human deceit and in-
sincerity, came to scoff, and went away filled with wonder
and amazement, to write such things of a political convention as they had never dreamed.

Social and industrial justice was the Progressive battle-
cry. The exaltation of the rights of property, which had
marked for years the steady course of the Republican Old
Guard, was challenged at last by eager demand for consideration of the rights of humanity. The devotion to
special privilege that had been so long the guiding principle
of political reaction was brought into head-on collision
with a keener devotion to the 'square deal' and equality
for all before the law.

It is not my purpose to attempt a political history of
that period, or to go into a detailed description of that
convention. That is part of the well-known record of those
days. But there are some incidents of that convention
which have never become known, and which it now seems
may be of some interest. One of them was of such seriousness, although not without its comical side, as very greatly

to threaten the peaceful completion of the convention itself, which, for a few minutes, was on the very verge of
disruption. Even at the climax of its marvelous enthusiasm, when the thousands who crowded the vast hall to the
limit of its capacity, were wildly cheering the two nominees, Roosevelt and Johnson, who stood together on the
platform, one of the strongest elements of support of the
whole movement was leaving the hall in complete disgust,
determined upon withdrawal from all participation in the
new party that had just been so triumphantly launched.
It required the most vigorous exercise of his supreme skill
by Colonel Roosevelt to avert that disaster and repair the
breach.

This trouble arose over the platform, and the imminent
danger of a break was precipitated by an error on the part
of the chairman of the Committee on Resolutions, in reading as part of its report to the convention a plank which
had been considered by the committee, but not adopted,
another plank on the same subject having been chosen in
its place.

The question had to do with amendment of the Sherman
Anti-Trust Law. There was no division whatever on the
proposition that that law should be amended in such a way
that the people of the country should be enabled to obtain
for themselves the benefits of combination. There was
complete recognition of the utter preposterousness of the
proposition, which is the heart of the Sherman Law, that
the only way to protect ourselves from the dangers and
evil effect of combinations is to prohibit them entirely.
This is an absurd denial of the intelligence and efficiency of
the American people. It is a declaration that they have
not the ability to control great aggregations of capital and
great combinations of men, in such a way as to prevent

them from promoting their selfish purposes at the expense of exploitation of the people.

In many of his public addresses since his return from Africa, Colonel Roosevelt had dealt exhaustively with this subject. Notably in his speech at Briceville, Tennessee, in the fall of 1910, he had handled the matter with a thoroughness and a fairness that had attracted wide attention throughout the country. It was quite natural, therefore, that the Progressive Convention, made up as it was of his enthusiastic followers, should be ready for something practical and effective in the way of dealing with this problem.

But just as soon as the Committee on Resolutions met, it became apparent that it was divided sharply on the question of procedure involved in amending the Sherman Law. One side wanted to catalogue the acts that were to be denounced by the law and to describe them in detail. The other side contended that such procedure would only serve to promote evasion of the law. It would enable lawyers of the alertness and acute intelligence of Mr. Root, for instance, promptly to devise ways and means of getting around these specific provisions. This side contended that what was necessary was a comprehensive definition of the character of act that was to be prohibited, leaving to the courts the determination whether any specific act complained of did, or did not, come within that definition. This side contended that it was impossible to make up an all-inclusive list of specific acts to be prohibited, and that the attempt to do so would, in fact, facilitate evasion and violation of the spirit of the law because it would necessarily have the effect of legalizing every act not specifically prohibited. The result would be the immediate invention of a new class of acts, violative of the spirit and intention

of the Sherman Law, but not illegal, which it would require further legislation by Congress to correct.

All this, it was argued by this side, could be avoided by
the adoption of a simple amendment to the Sherman Law
which would describe broadly and generally, so as to be
very widely inclusive, those acts of combinations the tendency of which would be detrimental to the public interests.

The whole Progressive Party was made up of enthusiasts,
and of course the Committee on Resolutions was similarly
composed. Every member of it believed, with the utmost
sincerity, in his own proposition. There was only a tattered
minimum of possibility of compromise in such a committee.
They fought all day over this Sherman Law proposition,
and they fought all night. They remained in the committee room, and had their meals brought to them there.
They argued and discussed and debated. They wrote out
their ideas in a thousand phraseologies. But they could
not agree.

Meanwhile the other work of the convention was going
on serenely, and without interruption or untoward incident. The reports from the Committee on Resolutions
greatly disturbed Colonel Roosevelt. The matter was so
clear to him that he had thought of it as easily soluble. He
was for the broad definition of the class and character of
acts to be prohibited, but some of his stanchest friends in
the committee were on the other side.

At length the Colonel brought together in his room at
the hotel a little group of his confidential friends and talked
the matter over with them. Several of them tried their
hands at phrasing the proposed plank. It was not at all
difficult to get together in that little group, for they were
all of the same view that the Colonel held. At length
Colonel Roosevelt himself wrote out a plank to which all

the others present agreed, and asked Senator Dixon to take it to the committee and submit it as the one which the Colonel personally favored. Senator Beveridge was asked also to attend the committee meeting for the purpose of explaining the Colonel's views and supporting this plank.

That was on the morning of the day on which the nominations were to be made, and the convention was then ready for the report of the platform committee. It was easy, however, to mark time in that convention, for its supply of oratory had by no means been exhausted, and its eagerness to hear the Progressive doctrine expounded was not in the least diminished. But when the Resolutions Committee continued to delay its report, it was at length decided to proceed with the nominations and hear the platform report later.

So Colonel Roosevelt was named for the presidency to the accompaniment of such cheers as one hears on board a warship when the battle-flags are broken out. Thereafter he delivered the famous speech — his 'Confession of Faith' — about which we had had such a contest with him at Sagamore. Then Governor Johnson was nominated for the vice-presidency, and when he appeared on the platform with Colonel Roosevelt, and the Colonel exclaimed: 'The Progressive Party has nominated for the vice-presidency a man fit at the moment to be President of the United States,' the climax of all that long period of enthusiasm was reached.

Just then William Draper Lewis, Dean of the University of Pennsylvania Law School, who was chairman of the Committee on Resolutions, appeared with the committee report. There had not been time to have it typewritten all in one document, and he had a mass of slips of paper carry-

ing the different planks. It was necessarily in some confusion, and he read it with no little difficulty.

George W. Perkins, whose determined support of Colonel Roosevelt had done more than any other one thing to
make the Progressive Party possible, and who was looked
upon from all sides, not only to see that the necessary
finances for the campaign were provided, but to contribute
also his own undeniably great genius for organization, was
sitting on the platform while Dean Lewis read the resolutions report. Mr. Perkins was one of those who believed in
the Colonel's method of handling the Sherman Law problem. He believed it with all his extraordinary tenacity,
and he was supported in his belief by some of his close
and wealthy friends, on whom he was relying for effective
assistance in obtaining money for the campaign. He had
been eagerly following the fight in the committee, and,
having been also very much occupied by the general work
of the convention, was just about as nearly worn out physically as the committee members, with his nerves, consequently, just about as near the ragged edge as theirs.

Mr. Perkins listened with close attention as Dean Lewis
read, and when the plank on the Sherman Law was
reached he leaned forward in his chair to catch every word.
I was sitting next him, and as the plank was read I saw an
expression of blank amazement come over his face, for it
was the plank favored by the side that wanted to list the
prohibited acts, and not the one prepared by Colonel
Roosevelt that morning.

As Dean Lewis concluded reading that plank, Mr. Perkins shoved back his chair, rose, and left the platform.
Two or three of his close friends went with him, and it was
all too evident to me that there was extremely serious
trouble right ahead. Colonel Roosevelt was standing, with

GEORGE W. PERKINS

Governor Johnson, on the platform, and I could not reach him. I left the platform and started back toward the hotel, not with any clear idea of what to do, but full of the conviction that something had to be done, and very promptly, or the whole convention would go to smash. As I was leaving the hall, I met James R. Garfield, who was just coming in from the hotel. In a sentence or two I told him what had occurred on the platform. Mr. Garfield had been in the Committee on Resolutions. He was immensely surprised when I told him the plank that Dean Lewis had read.

'But that wasn't the one adopted by the committee,' he said. 'The committee adopted the one that the Colonel sent in.'

I begged Mr. Garfield to go at once to the hotel, find Mr. Perkins, and explain the situation to him, while I went back into the convention hall to get the word to Colonel Roosevelt as soon as possible. That did not take long, and as quickly as he could the Colonel left the hall and went back to the hotel.

Conferences with Senators Dixon and Beveridge, and with other members of the Committee on Resolutions, including Dean Lewis, followed rapidly, in order to establish, with certainty, just what had happened in the committee. Mr. Lewis found that he had in the papers that he took into the convention both planks on the Sherman Law, the one that had been rejected as well as the one adopted, and it had been wholly by mistake that he had read the wrong one. The fact was that he was near the point of physical exhaustion, as were most of the other committee members, from their long struggle over the platform, and the wonder was not that one mistake had been made, but that there had not been more.

As soon as it had been made clear that the wrong plank

had been read to the convention, Colonel Roosevelt directed me to undertake to secure correction in the reports of the platform to be published, and especially to see that the newspapers had the correct version before they went to press. I sent word immediately to every Chicago paper that an important correction on the platform was coming, and then went to the press associations. The head of the Chicago office of the Associated Press was a man I had known for several years, having worked with him in the Far East and on the same assignment two or three times in this country. But he was not handling the convention story personally, and I was unacquainted with the man in charge of that. He was an extremely cautious individual, which is an excellent thing in an Associated Press correspondent, but it made me a lot of difficulty that night. He required more showing than any man from Missouri I had ever met, before he would accept my statement of the case. However, he did, at length, accept it, and the version of the Sherman Law plank sent out by the A.P. was the correct one. The other press association men made no difficulty about it at all. One glimpse of the mass of papers Dean Lewis had taken into the convention hall showed them how easily an error could occur. There was some 'joshing' about the way in which a convention will adopt, with unanimous acclaim, whatever report its Committee on Resolutions renders, and how easy it would be to get a declaration in favor of wholesale murder of the other side, but that was about all. The reports that went to the newspapers had the platform right. One or two of the Chicago papers ran little paragraphs about the incident, but no particular attention was paid to it, and I thought it was all ended.

But there I reckoned without consideration of the tenacity of some of the Progressive brethren. There were men in that committee who believed so thoroughly in the proposition that had been defeated that they were ready also to believe that it had been beaten by a trick. One of the most certain of them was the member from Wisconsin. He had been associated with La Follette long enough to imbibe from the Senator, if, indeed, it was not native to himself, the feeling of suspicion toward everything that does not exactly suit him, which marks so many of La Follette's public actions and utterances. Consequently, we had not gone very far with the campaign before I began to hear mutterings from Wisconsin about this Sherman Law plank in our platform. At first I only laughed at this, because there were so many perfectly sincere and honest men who knew all about the matter, and who had been in the committee along with the Wisconsin agitator, that I assumed they would presently be able to convince him.

But either they did not try, or he would not be convinced. At any rate, he broke into print about it at length, and supplied the newspapers with a long story in which he charged me with having executed what was in effect a double cross on the convention and the whole Progressive Party. That brought Colonel Roosevelt into action again. Right after election we had a second Progressive National Convention in Chicago. This one was not for the purpose of nominating candidates, but was a get-together meeting, to jubilate over the successes we had won in the election, and to formulate plans for the permanent organization and firm establishment of the party. Delegations were present from every State in the country.

Colonel Roosevelt took the platform matter directly to this meeting. He wrote a statement completely covering the case, and describing exactly what had occurred, which was read at a crowded session. This was followed by personal statements by several of the men who had been in the center of things at the August convention. That settled the matter, so far as public criticism was concerned, but it did not convince our friend from Wisconsin. I think he held to his belief — or his suspicion — to the day of his death.

LXII

ANOTHER little incident occurred soon after the adjournment of the August convention, which had a rather humorous side, and which illustrated the same attitude of suspicion that our Wisconsin man had shown about the platform. It was always interesting to me to see how these earnest and very sincere Progressives, especially those in what the Colonel called the 'lunatic fringe,' held to their principles and their prejudices. At the same time it was interesting to see how, occasionally, one of the extreme 'high-brows,' of the lofty, altruistic type, would come forward with a suggestion that would rather shock even a seasoned and hardened practical politician.

A meeting of the new Progressive National Committee was held in the Congress Hotel the morning after the convention adjourned. It was called chiefly for the election of an executive committee, and the transaction of the important business of organizing the campaign which had to be handled immediately. We had just three months before election, and, although a great deal of work had been done in some of the States, in many of them we were without effective organization.

It developed right away at this meeting that there was opposition to the selection of George W. Perkins as chairman of the Executive Committee. That eminent Kansas Progressive, William Allen White, editor of the Emporia 'Gazette,' who is so progressive that he is never long in any one place, politically, seemed to be the leader of this opposition. He had the courage of his convictions, too, and he spoke right out in meeting. Thereupon some one suggested that Mr. Perkins might leave the room during the discussion, in order that he might not be embarrassed by what was said. Mr. Perkins replied with a request that everybody should feel perfectly free to go right ahead and say whatever he had to say. It would not embarrass him at all to hear what was said, and he should be much better able to reply if he knew, from hearing it, exactly what had been presented to the meeting.

The opposition were obviously much more disconcerted by this than Perkins was. They hadn't had his experience of red-hot fights in meetings of boards of directors, and were evidently not accustomed to the man-to-man style of handling such situations. The Perkins habit of speaking 'from the face out' was new, strange, and disturbing to them.

After a few moments of awkward silence, some one remarked that, of course, everybody there knew of Mr. Perkins's great ability as an organizer, and was delighted that the Progressive Party was to have the benefit of his services in that capacity. But at the same time it was suggested — very delicately, of course, but nevertheless quite plainly — that, in view of Mr. Perkins's widely known connection with Wall Street and 'the interests' to which the Progressive Party was so much opposed, it did seem that it would be better if he were not to occupy so important a place in its organization as chairman of the Executive Committee.

Mr. Perkins replied with a frank statement of the situation from his point of view. He was tremendously interested in the success of the Progressive movement. He had severed all his connections with Wall Street or any other active money-making enterprise, and was devoting himself entirely, for the remainder of his life, to public service. He was a great believer in Colonel Roosevelt and the things for which the Colonel stood. The chance to secure the benefit of the Colonel's principles for all the people of the country lay in making this Progressive Party a real and effective organization, which could ultimately win elections and come into power so that it could enact needed legislation and enforce honest administration.

The fact that he was an earnest supporter of Colonel Roosevelt was well known to all the country. It did not seem to him that his open connection with the executive direction of the campaign could add anything to whatever of detriment to the cause his connection with it might have been. It seemed to him that whatever damage could result from such a situation must have resulted already, and was not likely to be increased by continuance of that situation. On the other hand, it was plain that there was general reliance upon him to see to it that the money with which to finance the campaign was provided. He was ready to undertake that task, and himself to contribute to the funds, as well as to endeavor to secure substantial contributions from some of his friends. But certainly, if he was to see that the funds were provided, he must be in a position to exert some influence over their expenditure. That seemed to him to be only natural and wholly fair.

That frank presentation of the case by Mr. Perkins spiked some of the guns of the opposition, but not all of them. It was at once approved openly by the majority of the committee members, and there was a rather outspoken demand that the committee proceed to other business. But some of those who did not like the Perkins chairmanship idea were not satisfied to let the matter drop. California came into the discussion, with a frankness equal to that of Mr. Perkins, and it became apparent that there

was a reasonable expectation of friction with Governor
Johnson before the campaign ended.

The discussion started off again *de novo*, and rambled
on for some time. At length the gentleman from Boston,
that eminent center of lofty political ethics, pleasantly
inquired why it would not be entirely feasible for the party
to have the undoubted benefit of Mr. Perkins's great
abilities without incurring the disadvantage of his open
connection with the Executive Committee. Mr. Perkins
could do his work quietly and in the background. He
could always be available for consultation, and even for
direction, but some other and less objectionable names
could be on the public roll of the Executive Committee.

Blank silence greeted this suggestion for a moment.
Then a long, lanky chap from Arizona heaved up his
towering bulk, and remarked, with a slow, soft drawl, that
somehow emphasized his words:

'We believe in toting guns down our way. But we don't
carry 'em concealed.'

There and then the Perkins debate ended. He was
elected chairman of the Executive Committee, not unanimously, but with no votes in opposition. Those who
didn't like it apparently believed in carrying 'em concealed,
for they did not come out in the open and vote 'No.'

A couple of weeks later, at headquarters in New York, I
got a sample of the Perkins quality in overcoming obstacles
and raising money. We had prepared an edition of three
million copies of Colonel Roosevelt's convention speech for
general distribution. It was to bear on the front page
pictures of the Colonel and Governor Johnson, the two
Progressive candidates. There was a tremendous call from
local Progressive committees all over the country for these
speeches, and we were in a great hurry to get them out.

One morning the man who had charge of the printing came to me with a proof of this speech. I noticed that the pictures bore the name of a Chicago studio, and were copyrighted. I asked him if he had secured the permission of that studio to use the pictures, and told him that the copyright law fixed the penalty for use of photographs without permission at one dollar a copy.

He gasped at the thought. 'Lord, no,' he replied. 'I never thought of that. Three million dollars! What's left for the campaign?'

I picked up the proof and went into Mr. Perkins's room with it. The instant I had explained the situation he summoned his stenographer and said:

'Take this telegram: "Blank Studio, Chicago. We are planning to issue an edition of three million copies of Roosevelt's speech, with pictures of Roosevelt and Johnson on the front page. This will be a great advertisement for the photographer. What will you give us to use your pictures. Rush answer."'

In less than an hour we had a reply from that studio. 'We have never done this before, but under the circumstances we will give you $250.'

Ten minutes later the presses were humming with the Roosevelt speech, and the wire was carrying back to Chicago a message from Perkins saying that it was a ridiculous offer for such an advertisement, but we were in a hurry and would accept.

LXIII

BEFORE we left Chicago, after the Progressive Convention, Colonel Roosevelt personally assigned me to take charge of his own speaking trips during the campaign, and of those of Governor Johnson. Although I had had no experience in publicity work, it had been rather tacitly understood, because of my newspaper connection, that I was to have charge of that. But this assignment from Colonel Roosevelt very soon occupied almost all of my time, and it quickly became apparent that I was not going to be able to handle the publicity also. However, I did have a part in one phase of it, which attracted very widespread attention before election day arrived.

A day or two after we had returned to New York, Frederick Palmer came to see me at headquarters, to volunteer his services for six weeks during the campaign. He suggested his own assignment, and it was a good one, but we were not yet ready to act upon it. One of the charges made by Colonel Roosevelt and other Progressive speakers was that there existed understandings between the bosses of both the Republican and Democratic Parties, in many places, under which there was a practical division of spoils, and that the public were exploited for the benefit of the bosses and their henchmen. Mr. Palmer's idea was that he could spend some time in each of several cities, which we should select, and investigate this condition of bi-partisan control. He would make a separate report for each city.

The next day Richard Harding Davis dropped in and offered his services as a writer during the campaign. But still we were not prepared to take advantage of the offer, and had nothing definite to suggest for him to do.

A day or two later, Will Irwin came in with a similar proposition. He was ready to volunteer his services for the campaign, but he naturally wanted to be directed as to what to do. I told Irwin, as I had Palmer and Davis, that I had nothing definite to suggest as yet, and Irwin was going away, when it occurred to me that, if these three had volunteered, there probably were others who would do so. I asked Irwin if he knew how the writing fraternity generally felt about the political situation. He replied at once that most of them were for Roosevelt.

'Then,' said I, 'why can't we get together a number of them and organize a Progressive syndicate to furnish political articles all through the campaign?'

'Of course we can,' he answered. 'I'll bet I can get fifty in two days, if you will give me a stenographer and a place where I can dictate the letters.'

At once a room was placed at his disposal, with a stenographer, and he began that morning the organization of the proposed syndicate. The responses came in shoals, and, before a week was out, we had the very great majority of all the well-known magazine writers in the country on our list. It was immediately evident that this was going to be a job far beyond the range of the ordinary publicity office, and a special force was organized to handle it. Elaborate preparations were made. Special sheets containing the list of writers were printed, with what the newspaper men call 'obits' of each writer attached — that is, brief sketches of their careers — for the information of newspaper editors, and always there was included a statement of the prices these authors were getting for their articles when editors purchased them.

Then a special letter was prepared, offering a daily service by this combined list of writers, free and exclusive to one morning and one evening paper in every large city and considerable town in the country. The papers picked to receive the first offer were, as far as possible, the leading newspapers of the opposition, such as the New York 'World' and the Louisville 'Courier-Journal.' These papers were constantly assailing Colonel Roosevelt with the utmost vehemence and bitterness, and we sought deliberately to counteract their editorials by the use of their news columns for our articles and reports of meetings. We believed that even reports of Progressive political meetings would be used by such newspapers, when they were written by Richard Harding Davis, George Ade, or men of such reputation, and that political cartoons by John McCutcheon would be sought, eagerly, by the opposition press, even though they struck hard for Roosevelt.

We found, very quickly, that we were not mistaken in our judgment. The opposition editors decided, promptly, that they could not afford to let such a series of articles go by, especially when they came in free. Of course, in cities and towns where there were strong Progressive papers, like the Kansas City 'Star,' Chicago 'Evening Post,' and New York 'Evening Mail,' we had to furnish these articles to our own supporters. We also increased their desirability to the newspapers by making them exclusive to one paper in the locality where it was published. We got out two series of articles, one for morning and the other for evening newspapers, and took pains to see that they did not overlap.

It was a tremendous lot of work, before we got through with it, but it was great fun. It certainly was amusing to see the New York 'World,' and other papers of that ilk, printing in their news columns red-hot Progressive stuff which they were assailing, vigorously, in their editorials.

LXIV

WE had hardly opened headquarters at New York when there was a flood of demands for speeches by Colonel Roosevelt and Governor Johnson, and I had my hands more than full making out tentative schedules for them. But, first of all, the general plan of campaign had to be determined. That required a great deal of consideration, involving several conferences with Colonel Roosevelt at Sagamore, and much consultation with Chicago headquarters. While this was going on, individual requests for dates, especially for Colonel Roosevelt, piled up rapidly.

The general plan of campaign at length determined upon involved extensive trips, by both Colonel Roosevelt and Governor Johnson, across the continent at first, with a swing by each through his own territory at the close. This would take Colonel Roosevelt to the Pacific Coast at the beginning of the campaign, and give him a turn through New England and the Middle Atlantic States for the latter part of October, with the last few days of the campaign in New York. The Middle West would be covered partly on the way out to the Coast, and some stops might be provided on the way back. There would also be time for a rapid run through some of the big Republican States north of the Ohio and east of the Mississippi after his return from the Coast, and before he started on the New England and Middle Atlantic trip. It was a comprehensive plan which involved a tremendous amount of very hard work on the part of the Colonel.

This scheme was balanced by bringing Governor Johnson to the East at the start, with a trip through the Middle

Atlantic States and New England, where he would speak at a number of Progressive State Conventions. Then he would go into the Middle West, and probably would be there about the same time as Colonel Roosevelt, so that we should be able to make a vigorous campaign in that territory with our two candidates speaking at the same time. After that the Governor would go back to the Coast, arriving in time to make two or three stops in Washington and Oregon before returning to California.

As soon as this plan for the two candidates had been determined, I wired Governor Johnson, who had gone back to California, asking him to come to New York for consultation before entering on his regular speaking trips. We wanted to talk the whole plan over with him, and to see that everything connected with his share in the campaign was arranged as nearly as possible to his satisfaction. We didn't know him very well, but had the impression, from the enthusiastic things the West Coast men said about him, that he was about the same sort of a fighter that we knew Colonel Roosevelt to be. Chester Rowell, editor of the Fresno 'Republican,' and one of the Governor's closest friends, had written us a sketch of him which fostered that impression by giving a vivid picture of Johnson making an open-air campaign for the governorship, touring the State by automobile and speaking from fifteen to twenty times a day, always up and going, and never wearing out. The Governor replied to my telegram that he would leave Los Angeles for the East on a specified date, 'and thereafter for sixty days shall be wholly at your service.' We took that to mean that he placed himself entirely in our hands, just as Colonel Roosevelt had done.

Our friends all the way across the continent were asking for speeches by Governor Johnson on his way East, and I

HIRAM W. JOHNSON

agreed that he should make four or five stops. One was in Utah, and another was to be at Lincoln, Nebraska, where he would have opportunity to speak at the State Fair, with a crowd of from fifty to sixty thousand persons seeing and hearing. From Lincoln he was to come directly to New York for the general consultation that we had planned.

But Governor Carey, of Wyoming, wanted Johnson to stop at Rock Springs. I refused, because that involved leaving the train about two o'clock in the morning. Carey appealed directly to Johnson, who agreed to make the stop. That stop put him two days behind his scheduled arrival in New York.

The Governor got down to Lincoln and sent me a telegram saying that he 'declined to be put in competition with big-bellied bulls and prize porkers' at the State Fair.

Then our Chicago headquarters shot our plans for Johnson all to pieces. Without a word to Eastern headquarters, and in complete disregard of the agreement, made when the leased wire was installed between the two offices, Chicago billed the Governor for speeches in several States of the Middle West, and as far north as Minnesota and South Dakota. Meantime we had arranged to have him speak at the New York Progressive State Convention at Syracuse. So, when we heard, at length, about the dates promised by the Chicago office, it was necessary to cut out the consultation at New York headquarters, and to turn the governor back from Syracuse to make those Middle West dates. It was agreed that more damage would be done by breaking those promises than by omitting the consultation and changing the original plan of campaign.

Governor Johnson was furious, and he had a right to be. He felt that a deliberate slight had been put upon him. Not only had he been billed to make speeches in places

where he did not want to go and without any consultation
with him, but, as he declared with bitter emphasis, no
adequate or decent arrangements had been made for his
personal comfort. Colonel Roosevelt had started West in
a private car, and with a flock of men with him to see that
he had everything he desired and to help the publicity part
of his trip. But no one had been assigned to accompany the
Governor. He had no private car, and was even compelled
to look out for his own transportation arrangements
and secure his own Pullman accommodations. He was
thoroughly bitter about it.

But his bitterness, a large part of which was certainly
justified, seemed to be directed wholly at New York headquarters, whereas the discomfort to which he had been
subjected was due almost entirely to the interference of
the Chicago office with the original plan. We had provided
proper accommodations for the Governor on his trip from
Los Angeles to New York, and, if he had made it according
to schedule, he would have been well taken care of. But his
own stop at Rock Springs and the subsequent complete
upsetting of the whole plan by Chicago created a situation
of extreme difficulty, in which he was put to a great deal of
personal inconvenience and discomfort.

LXV

GOVERNOR JOHNSON did not know the kind of reputation as a campaigner which had preceded him in the East. Apparently he was not aware of the publicity sketch that his friend Rowell had written about him, and which had been used everywhere that we could get it printed. Mr. Rowell's picture of the Governor, charging up and down California from early morning until late at night, day after day, with never a sign of weariness or hesitation, made us all think of him as just the kind of campaigner we knew Colonel Roosevelt to be.

But the Governor's earnest, personal desire was to get on the east side of New York City and preach the doctrine of social and industrial justice. He kept insisting on that up to the very end of the campaign, and the fact that, although that part of New York City is its most densely populated section, it contains a smaller proportion of voters than any other, seemed to make not the slightest difference with him.

When he was sent back through Illinois, Ohio, and Indiana, scheduled for from ten to fifteen stops a day, he rebelled. He cut some dates, slighted others, and did not exert himself to vary his speeches, so that the newspaper men with him either criticized openly, if they represented the opposition press, or sent appealing messages to head-quarters, if they were for Progressive papers.

The climax came on the day when the Governor was scheduled to go to Milwaukee. The La Follette strength in Wisconsin had been divided by the formation of the Progressive Party. Some of the men who had been among the stoutest La Follette adherents had come over to the

Progressives, and were heading the new organization in the Badger State. Henry Cochems, of Milwaukee, was one of them. He was the Wisconsin member of the Progressive National Committee. He was a great friend of Governor McGovern, whom he had been endeavoring to persuade to join the new party. At length McGovern had indicated that he would do so. Then it was arranged that there should be a luncheon at Milwaukee, presided over by Governor McGovern, and at which Governor Johnson should speak. McGovern was to announce his adhesion to the Progressive Party at that time. After the luncheon they were all to go out to the State Fair, where there would be a throng of many thousands in attendance and Governor Johnson was to make another speech.

But Johnson had been stumping through Indiana and Illinois just ahead of his Milwaukee date, and was tired. Moreover, he didn't care for the new assignment. He had already indicated to me, by that telegram from Lincoln, his antipathy to meetings at State Fairs. The opportunity, which such occasions afforded, to address huge crowds did not appeal to him. He merely saw himself as being put up to compete with the agricultural exhibits, and was extremely frank in his disapproval.

So he remained in his room in his hotel in Chicago. The train on which he was due to reach Milwaukee arrived there, with no sign of the California Governor, and no word from him. So did the next train. The luncheon crowd assembled, without its chief speaker, and Governor McGovern did not make his announcement. They went out to the State Fair, but there was no address by the Progressive candidate for the vice-presidency.

Governor Johnson took the three o'clock train that afternoon for Milwaukee. When he arrived, his reception lacked something of the enthusiasm which would have greeted him in the morning. A few of the committee dined, informally, with him, and afterward took him to the auditorium, which was only partly filled. There he delivered his speech. He was sarcastic about the cool reception, and displeased because there was not a crowd at the auditorium. He complained about the arrangements and the lack of publicity, and it was an unhappy occasion for all concerned. The Wisconsin Progressives were angry, too. They declared that the campaign in their State had been hit about the hardest blow that could have been delivered, and by their own candidate for the vice-presidency.

When, at length, the Governor got to New York City, the time for the kind of consultation originally planned had long gone by, and new plans had to be made. We listened to his complaints and criticisms, and did what we could to repair the damage that had been done. A private car was provided for his further journeying, and a man of his own selection was secured to travel with him and attend to the publicity work. A schedule through New England was made out, with which he seemed to be fairly well satisfied. He limited his work to two meetings a day.

LXVI

MEANTIME Colonel Roosevelt was working through his Western trip. It had been my intention not to give him any special stops in the East or Middle West on his way to the Coast, leaving that section to be covered on a later trip, after the campaign had developed more character. But the demand for him was so earnest, especially from Iowa, that we yielded to it, to the very great subsequent regret of both ourselves and the Iowa Committee. The Republican State Convention of Iowa had formally repudiated the Taft nomination, and the Progressive State Committee believed that an early Roosevelt meeting in the State would have an important effect. So his itinerary was arranged to include Iowa on the outward journey. He went from there up to St. Paul and west over the northern route; turned back from Portland, over the Oregon Short Line, down into Utah; thence west to San Francisco; down through California, thence east to Kansas City, and so on back to New York.

The trip required about a month, and should have had greater preparation than we were able to give it. Our campaign started so late, however, that we had to hurry over numerous matters that should have had more time, and the Roosevelt trips were in that category. We had to send him away from New York long before his itinerary for half the trip was complete, and every day there was extensive correspondence with him by telegraph on the subject. A representative of the railroad on which his journey began sat in my office every day and worked with me on the schedule. Matters were complicated very much by the way in which towns and committees along the route would insist on stops that had not been scheduled, and would take their cases to Colonel Roosevelt himself. He always desired to accommodate every committee that he could, with the result that I frequently received word that a stop had been agreed to by him, which was the first I had heard of it. One such stop produced decidedly unpleasant results. It was arranged entirely without my knowledge, and my first information about it was in the receipt of two messages, one announcing the fall of a part of the grand stand, with injury to several persons, and the other a hot protest from Colonel Roosevelt himself about having such a stop in his schedule.

Before this long trip was half through, we began to receive word from some of our newspaper friends that the Colonel was going stale, and was rehashing old stuff to such an extent that there was difficulty in getting away news stories that the papers would carry. It was too late, of course, to do anything about that for that trip, beyond trying to change schedules somewhat so as to give Colonel Roosevelt a little rest. But we talked it over a great deal at headquarters and made careful plans to prevent a similar situation on the next trip.

It was evident that the Colonel's immediate party on that Coast trip had not been prepared to supply him constantly with new campaign material, or to stimulate him in the most effective manner. Colonel Roosevelt was an extremely hard worker, and a great reader. He always took with him on such journeys a supply of books, most of which had nothing to do with politics or campaigns. They would include volumes on scientific subjects, two or three French and German works, a story or two of Dickens, a volume or two of poetry, and some miscellaneous works.

On that Coast trip the Colonel had no material whatever about Mr. Wilson, who was his chief antagonist in the campaign. He should have been furnished with a complete record of Mr. Wilson's public activities, copies of Wilson's speeches on political subjects, and all such material that we could gather. We had begun the collection of that material just as promptly as we could, but did not have it in hand until the Colonel had reached the Coast. Then we decided to keep it for the second trip, and, just as quickly as we could, to get the Colonel home, for a rest at Saga-more, so that he should be refreshed and in first-class shape when he started the swing through the Middle West, which we regarded as his real campaign.

As soon as he was back at Sagamore, we began a series of visits to him there for general consultation on all the phases of the campaign. One of the first of such meetings with him occurred on a day when the New York 'Times' had printed an editorial attack on him, under the caption 'What's the Use?' This editorial referred to some charges that had been made against him, and which had been shown to be unfounded by the publication of a letter from him to a friend, written at the time of the incidents on which the charges were based. This letter made the whole matter entirely clear. The 'Times' complained that if a committee of the Colonel's most distinguished and reliable neighbors were to visit Sagamore and find the dismembered remains of his grandmother, boiled in oil, in the cellar, it would be no use assailing him about it, for he would come out with a letter to some friend, written long before, that would show the whole thing to have been entirely innocent.

A group of us from headquarters dined with the Colonel at Sagamore that evening. There was lively general con-versation at the table, and once, when there was a little pause, I asked the Colonel to explain why it was that he had cut up his aged and respected grandmother and boiled her in oil in his own cellar.

He turned toward me, very gravely, while Mrs. Roosevelt, at the other end of the table, looked on in astonishment, and said:

'Well, O. K., she was a highly reprehensible old party, who ought to have been drawn and quartered and boiled in oil long ago. Now, what is it all about?'

None of the Roosevelt family had seen the 'Times' that day, and so the editorial had not come to their notice. There was a shout of laughter when it was read. The talk about it brought out the fact that the numerous great boxes of Colonel Roosevelt's letters were then at Sagamore. Mr. Perkins was greatly concerned about that, and before the evening was over arrangements had been agreed upon for getting them into safe storage, where there would be no danger of their destruction by fire or their loss by theft.

It had long been Colonel Roosevelt's habit to write to some confidential friend, at the time, in full detail, about every event of any importance in which he was concerned. The publication of some of his letters by Joseph Bucklin Bishop has disclosed something of the extent to which he carried this practice, and has revealed the length and detail of such letters. They form an invaluable and practically complete informal record of the events of his official life, and constitute an unexampled source of authoritative information for future historians.

In preparing for the second Roosevelt trip, which was to take him through the Middle West, it was determined that I should accompany the Colonel and have charge of the party. Philip Roosevelt, the Colonel's young cousin, was also to go, and his particular task was to see that all newspapers at every place where we stopped were procured at once, so as to enable the Colonel to keep track of what Mr. Wilson was doing and saying. Dr. Terrell, of Texas, a throat specialist, who had been on the Western trip, was engaged for that trip also, and Cecil Lyon, the Colonel's old Texas friend, was to go too. Henry Cochems, of Wisconsin, who was intimately acquainted with La Follette and his record, and who had studied the Wilson record a great deal, was the other member of the party in the Colonel's private car. Two stenographers from New York headquarters, John W. McGrath, and Elbert Martin completed the party.

By this time we had procured at headquarters an elaborate report on Mr. Wilson. It was about eighty thousand words long, and was divided into sections dealing with the different features, such as tariff, labor, woman suffrage, finance, trust control, and so on. We had a great many copies of each section made, so that every member of the party had several copies of the whole record. Each one was instructed always to have some part of this Wilson record in his pocket, to familiarize himself with it very thoroughly, and be able to talk about it at any time.

Only one Wilson topic was taboo. There had come to us at headquarters, while we were obtaining the Wilson record, a scandalous story concerning the Democratic candidate. It was reported circumstantially, and was accompanied by the assertion that it could be substantiated wholly by documents in the shape of letters that were alleged to be in the possession of a certain individual from whom we might be able to obtain them. Senator Dixon and I at once objected to the use of this story, unless and until the complete documentary proof had been obtained and was in our possession. With that we were willing to use the story, but in its absence we took the position that it did not exist, and that it was unfair and dishonest to use the story. Moreover, its use, unsubstantiated, would be bound to react to the disadvantage of the side that used it.

There were some members of our committee, however, who were very desirous that we should put out this story. We had some lively discussions at headquarters about it. But Senator Dixon's insistence on the position he took from the first prevented use of it on our part. The Democratic National Committee heard of the story, of course, and displayed an amusing curiosity as to what we were going to do about it. Several times one or other of us at Progressive headquarters was approached, very cautiously, with inquiries obviously intended to draw us out on this subject. But as a matter of fact, no proof ever developed that there was any foundation for the story, and knowing what we did about the manner in which such scandalous stories circulate, wholly unfounded, until they come to be accepted generally throughout the country as the truth, as was the case with the tale that Colonel Roosevelt was a hard drinker, we refused absolutely to have any part in spreading the tale.

Colonel Roosevelt never talked scandal, and so far as I know this Wilson story was never repeated to him. I never heard him mention it, and I know that, during all the discussion at our headquarters as to whether or not it should be used, care was taken to see that no one mentioned it to the Colonel.

Besides getting the Wilson record complete and arranging for a constant supply of newspapers along the way, we arranged to have Mr. Wilson's speeches reported to us on our train by telegraph, whenever he said anything that, in the judgment of our committee wherever he spoke, might be of service to Colonel Roosevelt. Our itinerary was furnished to our committees wherever Mr. Wilson was to be, so that we could be reached in the shortest time.

We also made preparations for advance distribution of Colonel Roosevelt's speeches, and he undertook to write several of the most important ones, so that they could be handled by the press associations several days in advance of the dates of their delivery. Chicago headquarters arranged with the 'Tribune' there to receive these advance speeches by wire, so that, as soon as the Colonel finished a speech while *en route*, we telegraphed it to the Chicago 'Tribune.' Then headquarters in Chicago saw that copies went at once to the press associations and other media of distribution.

LXVII

THE effect of our preparations for this second trip was observable immediately. Colonel Roosevelt was greatly refreshed by his stay at Sagamore, and the consultations we had had while there had furnished him much new campaign material. But the Wilson record gave him his chief subject, and his party saw to it all the time that Wilson was the main topic of conversation in the car. When we sat down to a meal, and the Colonel began to talk about any subject under the sun, it would not be many moments before something he said would remind one or other of us of something in some part of the Wilson record. Then the conversation shifted to that topic, and out of one pocket or another would come the particular section of the Wilson record dealing with that subject. The Colonel would pick it up and read it, and as soon as he rose from the table he would call McGrath or Martin and begin dictating his comment on it, for some forthcoming speech.

He worked all the time. Whenever the train stopped long enough to permit him to show himself to the crowds that always gathered about his car, he would do so. On most of these occasions he had four or five minutes in which to appeal to them for support of the Progressive ticket, or for a shot at Wilson. He almost never spoke of Taft or the Republicans. From the beginning to the end, he pounded Wilson. Once in a while he enlivened the occasion by interjecting a remark about himself, and the charge that the Republicans were harping on, that he wanted to be a king. That always amused him.

'Good Lord,' he would say, 'I know kings. Nothing would induce me to become one.'

By the close of the second day of this trip, the Colonel had dictated several of the speeches that were to be delivered at later points, and as fast as McGrath and Martin could transcribe their notes, and the Colonel had revised them, they were put on the wire to the Chicago 'Tribune.' Before the first week was over, the chief speeches for all the remainder of the trip had been written and sent to Chicago for distribution. There was no repetition of the same idea or argument to the point of weariness and exhaustion of publicity values. The Colonel was constantly stimulated by discussion and argument in his own party, and by the reports that we received, steadily and promptly, from Mr. Wilson's meetings. Repeatedly he replied the same day to something that Mr. Wilson had said, and the effect of his steady pounding of the Democratic candidate was becoming clear in the increasing irascibility of Mr. Wilson's utterances. It was all the time becoming more and more plain that the fight was between Wilson and Roosevelt, and Taft was steadily fading into the background. Wilson had started out on his campaign by making the Republicans his chief opponents, but before the Roosevelt trip had lasted three days, all that was changed, and Mr. Wilson was directing his energy and his assaults chiefly at the Colonel.

We, in the Colonel's party, were jubilant at the result. We were distinctly making progress, and the Colonel was in the finest fettle. I had never seen him so well, so vigorous, or so interested. And the longer we kept it up, the better it became. It was Wilson, Wilson, Wilson, all the time in the private car, and nothing but Wilson and his record in the Colonel's talks. We believed we were on the way to drive Wilson into one of his characteristic explosions, with result that could only be detrimental to his campaign. Mr. Wilson seems to have recognized this danger himself, for the moment that the Colonel was put out of the campaign by the assassin's bullet at Milwaukee, he came out with his offer to cease campaigning.

The crowds all along the route were larger, more enthusiastic, and more determined to get at the Colonel than any I had ever seen, even on the wonderful Middle Western trip of 1910. Police protection of the Colonel seemed to be out of the question in most places, and so we organized a method of protecting him by his own party. The crowds even invaded railroad stations, and they always flocked around the hotel entrances, wherever we stopped, so that it became a matter of football tactics to get through them. On such occasions we formed a ring of our own men around the Colonel, and pushed, shoved, and hauled until we got him from his car to the motor that was to take him to the hotel, and again from the motor into the hotel. We had a regular routine, so that the same men almost always took the same station near the Colonel, and it was extremely difficult for any one to get at him without first encountering one of us.

The campaign had become so bitter, and the assaults on the Colonel were of so virulent and inflammatory a character, that we were seriously afraid of attempts at assassination. It was hard work to be always sure of the guard in such crowds. Our arrival at Duluth was especially difficult. The police had done nothing at all there in the way of clearing the path from the private car to the automobile at the station, and at the hotel the street was jammed and the lobby was crowded to the utmost.

We formed our ring around the Colonel as he got out of

the motor in front of the hotel, and started to jam our way into the lobby. The crowd, yelling and cheering, pressed against us, demanding a sight of the Colonel and endeavoring to touch him. All that many of them seemed to want was just to get a hand on him, to pat his shoulder, or something of that sort. It took several minutes of the hardest kind of football rushing to get through this crowd and up the main stairway of the hotel, into a place of comparative quiet and ease. Then we found that part of the Colonel's coat had been torn off, and the whole garment ruined.

The door of his room was no sooner closed on him than a throng assailed it, demanding to see him, while down in the lobby the crowd was chanting, over and over again:

'Teddy! Teddy! We want Teddy!'

I managed to force my way down to the desk to demand that something be done to clear out the place, so that the Colonel could have a little rest and quiet. As I wormed through the throng, I heard some one say:

'Did you see that? He was so drunk they had to carry him upstairs.'

We had heard this drinking story, of course, a great deal. It had become, in fact, so widespread that the Colonel had determined to take legal action about it, whenever we should find it repeated by a responsible person, against whom it might be worth while to proceed in court. The Republicans were making it a part of their campaign, but its use seemed to be confined to salaried 'spellbinders' any of whom it would be worse than a waste of time to prosecute or sue.

The Duluth incident was interesting as showing how the story spread, and with what complete lack of foundation it progressed. Another similar thing occurred a few eve-

nings later at Oshkosh. We arrived there late in the afternoon and reached the hotel just in time to have dinner
before the evening meeting at which the Colonel was to
speak. The proprietor of the hotel gave our party a room
by itself, and we dined there all together. Colonel Roosevelt had, as he frequently did, a large glass of milk with
his meal. It was served, for some reason known only to
the hotel people, in a blue glass. Others in the party drank
tea or coffee, and those, with water and the milk for the
Colonel, were the only beverages brought into the dining-
room.

It was my custom on this trip not to attend the evening
meetings. We always received a great many letters and
telegrams during the day, and as soon as the Colonel
started for the hall to deliver his speech I went back to the
car, with McGrath or Martin, to handle the day's correspondence and make our reports to headquarters. That
evening in Oshkosh I had put in a long-distance call for the
Chicago headquarters, and, while I was waiting for it in
the hotel lobby, I noticed a group in one corner of the room
talking earnestly together. There were half a dozen men
in the group, and at length one of them raised his voice, so
that it carried across the room, and declared that he himself had seen Colonel Roosevelt take a drink in the dining-
room that very evening.

I walked over to them at that, and asked the man if he
had dined with Colonel Roosevelt or was a member of the
Colonel's party. He replied that he was not with the party,
but had seen the Colonel take a drink.

'Oh,' I said, 'then you dined with him?'

He admitted that he had not, but insisted on the drink.
When I asked him how he could be so sure of it, he replied
that he had seen it taken into the Colonel's dining-room.

'How many were in his party?' I asked.

He did not know.

'How do you know some other member of the party did not get the drink that you think you saw go in?'

He admitted that he could not be absolutely sure, but he had asked the waiter for whom that drink was intended and had been told it was for the Colonel.

'Do you happen to know the proprietor of this hotel?' I asked.

He said he did, and would believe what the proprietor told him. I said I was a member of the Colonel's party, and knew of my own knowledge what the Colonel had to drink that evening. But I would not ask him to believe me. I had not said anything to the hotel proprietor about the matter, and if some of them would call him over, from where he was standing at his desk, and ask him what beverages were sent into the Colonel's dining-room that evening, it ought to settle the question.

That was done at once. The hotel man replied that tea, coffee, and milk had been ordered, and that Colonel Roosevelt drank the milk.

'Now, what do you say about it?' I asked the man who had done the talking.

'Well, I certainly saw something going in there in a big blue glass that looked mightily like a drink of something more than milk,' he replied.

He declined to be satisfied, even when the hotel man told him that the milk for the Colonel had been served in a big blue glass, and I have no doubt went right on spreading the story that he had seen Colonel Roosevelt take a drink, just as soon as he got away from that party which had seen him called down for it.

LXVIII

FROM Oshkosh we went to Chicago, where we arrived on Saturday morning, October 12th, and were brought immediately face to face with a serious situation. The Progressive State Committee of Iowa was there, almost in a body, to meet us, and to insist that Colonel Roosevelt should go back into that State for another speech, or that some other man, next to the Colonel in prominence, should be assigned to them. The alternative was the resignation of the State Committee and the abandonment of the campaign. Here was the fruit of the premature routing of Colonel Roosevelt through Iowa, on his way West in September, and it was bitter fruit.

It developed that the Iowa Progressives had secured Friday, of the following week, as Progressive Day at the meeting of the State Dairymen's Association at Waterloo. These Waterloo meetings of the dairymen are always great political occasions. The cattle men from all over the country take their finest stock to Waterloo and put it on exhibition. Then, every day from noon until three o'clock, they get together and talk politics. Very prominent speakers, from all parties, are secured, and they make the most of a special opportunity, while the dairymen from all the country listen and talk it over among themselves.

Friday is always regarded as the best day of the week, not only because the crowd is likely to be better than on other days, but because the man who is to speak has the opportunity to reply to whatever may have been said by those who preceded him. Saturday is get-away day, and the political discussion ends with Friday's meeting.

Our Iowa Committee demanded a good man for their
meeting, and they were entitled to have him. The speakers' bureau at Chicago had not been able to furnish one, and
the matter had dragged along until, now, within a week of
the meeting, the Progressive Committee found themselves
not ready to announce their speaker for that great day.
Fortunately for me, I had nothing to do with any of the
speakers except Colonel Roosevelt and Governor Johnson.
They gave me quite all I needed to keep me wholly occupied, so that I had not heard of this Iowa situation until
then. I knew, of course, there had been a demand for more
of Roosevelt in Iowa, but that had been answered peremptorily by the statement that Iowa had had him and he was
needed in other States where he had not been.

We spent a good part of Saturday morning in conference with the Iowa committeemen, and Colonel Roosevelt showed his sympathy with their situation by directing
me to telegraph to Senator Beveridge, who was campaigning in southern Indiana, to see if he could, by any possibility, make the Waterloo date. Beveridge was recognized
everywhere as an extremely forceful campaigner, and was
always second in demand only to Colonel Roosevelt.

That afternoon Colonel Roosevelt spoke to a great meeting held in a tent out on the lake side. The flaps of the
tent were raised, so that those who could not get inside
might catch something of his speech. There was a raw
October wind blowing, and the Colonel's voice, strained
greatly by his long and hard campaign, was brought to the
verge of breaking by this effort.

That night he attempted to address a meeeting in the
Coliseum, the great hall where both the Republican and
Progressive National Conventions had been held. There
his voice broke, and he had to give up the effort before he

could complete his speech. He got back to the hotel unable to do more than whisper.

We were in despair, for Dr. Terrell would not promise anything, and kept repeating his orders that the Colonel must not speak aloud at all, and must not even whisper if it could possibly be avoided. He would not attempt to estimate the length of time during which the Colonel would be out of the campaign, but said only that it would depend on the care with which the Colonel guarded himself from that time on. That was the cheerful situation when we turned in on Saturday night.

Next morning I had the reply from Senator Beveridge. He said that he was billed to speak on the following Friday at the home town of Senator Hemenway, chief of the Old Guard of Indiana, and leader of the Taft campaign in that State. The Republicans had been saying that Beveridge had kept away from there because he was afraid of Hemenway. If now he were to cancel his date there, in order to go to Waterloo, it would seem to give weight to that charge. Nevertheless, he was in the hands of the National Committee, and, if we thought it best for him to go to Iowa, he would go.

When I showed that to Colonel Roosevelt, he read it carefully, and then said to me, in a whisper:

'Tell him by no means would we ask that of him. He is right to stay there. Call up Governor Johnson [who was then at Pittsburgh], and say to him that you are speaking for me. Tell him why I do not talk to him myself. Explain the case to him and ask him to go to Waterloo. Make it my request.'

Governor Johnson was scheduled for the following Friday in Illinois, where several meetings had been arranged for him. Before putting in my long-distance call for Pittsburgh, I saw Chauncey Dewey, the Progressive State Chairman for Illinois, and obtained his consent to release the Governor for Friday. Then we arranged speakers for all the meetings thus cancelled. After that we worked out the train schedule to Waterloo, and reserved accommodations for the Governor's party. We arranged so that the Governor could start from Waterloo for California. When everything had been thus prepared, I put in my call. After a long time I got a connection with McCabe, the Governor's private secretary, who told me that the Governor was still asleep. It was then eleven o'clock in Chicago, Sunday morning, October 13th. McCabe said he would give the Colonel's message to the Governor as soon as he woke, and would forward the reply as promptly as possible. About ten o'clock that evening I received the following telegram:

Awfully sorry, but impossible to change schedule. Must return to California before the twenty-fifth.

ALEXANDER McCABE.

Next morning we loaded on Chauncey Dewey the task of securing a speaker for the Waterloo meeting, and went ahead with our own plans for the remainder of the Colonel's trip. He was still unable to speak above a whisper, and he was due that evening at a meeting at Milwaukee. The Colonel insisted, despite the vehement protest and direct orders of Dr. Terrell, that he was going to show himself in Milwaukee that evening. He was not going to do anything to heighten the effects of Governor Johnson's action in September. If he could say a loud word when he got to the auditorium, he would do so, and if he couldn't, he would whisper as loud as he could, and let his friends in Milwaukee see and hear for themselves just what his condition was. Meantime we must arrange with some other speaker or speakers to go along with him, on his car, on the trip to Milwaukee, to tell the crowds at the five-minute stops, several of which had been arranged, about his misfortune.

Representative Henry A. Cooper, one of the original Wisconsin Progressives, was in Chicago at that time, and we arranged with him to go up to Milwaukee with us that afternoon, and do the rear platform talking for the Colonel. Then we notified Milwaukee headquarters of the situation, and told them to do as they thought best about making it public.

We were sitting at luncheon, in the dining-room of the Colonel's quarters in the hotel, when the mail was brought in that day. There was, as usual, a large batch of letters, and as I looked them over I handed on to the Colonel such as seemed to require action by him. Presently I came to one from a man of whom I had never heard before. It was written with a pen, and obviously his own work. It enclosed a clipping from 'Iron Ore,' a weekly newspaper of Ishpeming, Michigan, in which the charge was made that Colonel Roosevelt drank frequently and heavily, and that all his friends knew it. The writer of the letter said that this paper was owned and published by George A. Newett, of Ishpeming, who was a responsible man. Then he expressed the opinion that Newett should be prosecuted and the hope that the Colonel would do so.

I passed this letter over to the Colonel, with the remark that here, at length, seemed to be the responsible man for whom we had been looking. The Colonel read the letter and nodded his approval of my suggestion.

'Let's go at him,' he whispered.

We left Chicago for Milwaukee about three o'clock, and on the train, on the way up, I dictated a telegram to Henry

M. Wallace, the Progressive National Committeeman from Michigan, at Detroit, asking him to engage a competent lawyer, see the issue of 'Iron Ore' containing that paragraph, and prepare to bring proceedings against Newett on both civil and criminal counts.

So the Marquette libel suit was started, and Colonel Roosevelt undertook to meet, during his lifetime, this scandalous and unfounded charge against him.

LXIX

THERE were several stops on the way up to Milwaukee, at each of which a great crowd gathered around the Colonel's car. Each time Colonel Roosevelt went out on the rear platform and shook hands with a few of those whom he could reach from the car. Then Congressman Cooper made a brief explanation of the Colonel's condition, and put in a few words for the Progressive cause. We got to Milwaukee about six o'clock, and were met by a large committee, which said that arrangements had been made for a rather extensive parade through the streets to the hotel where accommodations for the party had been reserved.

After leaving Racine, the last stop before reaching Milwaukee, we had had a consultation on the car, as a result of which it had been determined that the Colonel should dine on the car, and go from it straight to the Auditorium. This was solely on account of his condition and in order to protect his voice. He intended to say a few words at the meeting, and then have the speech which he had written for the occasion read by some one of his party.

The Milwaukee committee protested vehemently at the decision to dine on the car, and began to importune the Colonel to go up to the hotel. Dr. Terrell at first declined to enter into any discussion with them about it. He said that the Colonel's condition was the first consideration, and flatly refused to consent to his going to the hotel.

To this, I added the argument that it was not Milwaukee alone which was to be considered, but that the Colonel was due at Indianapolis the following night, with a noonday meeting at Champaign, Illinois; that he was to be at Louisville on Wednesday evening, and from there was engaged for every other night of the campaign. It was the whole Progressive campaign which was at stake, and, even if it was hard on Milwaukee, it was a matter which we could only regret, but could not help. Milwaukee and Wisconsin must be generous, and give some thought to the other parts of the country and to the rest of the campaign.

Thereupon the Milwaukee chairman replied bitterly that Milwaukee seemed to be picked out to get the worst of it. He referred to the tremendous disappointment which Governor Johnson had caused them, and talked in such a discouraged way that the Colonel interfered, and asked him if he really thought it would do any special damage for him to dine in the car and not go to the hotel.

At that the whole Milwaukee committee joined in urging the Colonel to carry out the programme as it had been arranged.

I protested again that there was always a great crowd, under such circumstances, through which the Colonel had to force his way; that it was very wearing on him; that he was extremely tired and needed rest, and that he should not be asked to go through another such experience just then.

But when the committee renewed its urging, and added that already the delay would be causing inquiry, the Colonel looked up at me and said:

'I want to be a good Indian, O. K.'

That was at once taken by the Milwaukee committee as evidence that the Colonel was willing to go, and that only the objections of his party were restraining him. The chairman declared that it would be a tremendous help to their campaign if the Colonel would carry out the programme, and several of the committeemen started to leave the car, as if it had all been settled.

But Dr. Terrell came back to the attack once more. He wanted to know what sort of police protection had been arranged, both at the station and at the hotel, and insisted that he would not consent to have the Colonel leave the car unless there was certain to be adequate police protection. He did not propose to have the Colonel have to fight his way through crowds from the car and into the hotel.

The chairman at once assured us that there would be complete protection, and that we should not have to contend with any crowd anywhere. The streets around the hotel would be cleared and kept cleared, he declared, and the Colonel would be entirely comfortable throughout the evening. So Colonel Roosevelt said he would go.

We left the Mayflower — the private car — and drove through a mile or more of streets, well lined with crowds on both sides, who gave the Colonel a very enthusiastic reception. He replied by lifting his hat, but did not rise in his car, as he sometimes did, nor did he try to say anything in response to the greetings.

At the hotel we found that the police protection was as good as had been promised. The crowd had been kept beyond the middle of the street, so that there was plenty of clear space for the cars to drive up in front of the hotel, and the sidewalk was clear so that there was no crowd to fight through. Inside the hotel there were fewer people than in any other place we had been, and there was no difficulty in getting the Colonel to his room. We had a few minutes before dinner, and the Colonel took a little nap sitting in a rocking-chair in his room. It was the only time, in all the campaign trips I made with him, that I ever saw him sleep before bedtime.

The hotel corridors were kept clear all the time, so that

there was no difficulty in going down to the dining-room or back to the Colonel's quarters after dinner. The police work was so good, in fact, that it threw the Colonel's own party a little off their guard and made possible the shooting that followed. It is a curious fact that it was too good police protection which enabled the assassin to get his chance.

The Colonel rested a few minutes, in his room, after dinner, and then started, with most of his party, down to the waiting automobiles to go to the Auditorium. I had a good deal of work to do at the Mayflower, and intended to go directly back to the car, with McGrath, as soon as the Colonel had gone to his meeting. Just as the Colonel started, Dr. Terrell was taken with nosebleed. He stepped into the bathroom to endeavor to check it, and McGrath and I waited with him.

The automobile for the Colonel was waiting at the door of the hotel. He walked down toward it, with Martin and Cecil Lyon just ahead of him. Cochems walked with the Colonel, and Philip Roosevelt just behind him. They were not bothered by crowds in the corridor or on the sidewalk and reached the automobile easily. There the freedom from crowds made just the little change in our usual procedure which gave the assassin his opportunity.

Ordinarily, when there was a press of men around the car, Cochems or Martin got in first, and went to the far side, standing next to the crowd while the Colonel took his seat. But this time there was freedom for the little politeness which the crowds usually prevented. Martin opened the car door, and Cochems stepped back to permit the Colonel to enter first. Cochems followed him into the car, and Philip Roosevelt started to get in. Lyon stood near the driver, and Martin was at the car door. Fred Luet-

tich, a big chap who was employed at Chicago headquarters as doorman, and had accompanied us on that trip,
had walked out from the hotel as the Colonel did, and was
standing at the hood of the motor.

When the Colonel entered the automobile and took his
seat, the crowd began to cheer. The Colonel stood up,
faced toward the throng at the rear of the car, and lifted his
hat with his right hand. As he raised his arm, a man standing in the front rank of the crowd near the automobile, and
on the side away from the curb, suddenly threw up a big
revolver and fired at him. It was point-blank range, and
almost impossible to miss. The Colonel was wearing his big
army overcoat, and in that position, standing up in the car,
between the assassin and the light, he made a perfect
target. The shot staggered him just a little, and he sank
back on the seat of the car.

Martin, standing by the automobile door, saw the swing
of the assassin's arm as he raised his revolver. Martin was
a burly, powerful man, short and stocky, but extremely
muscular. He had been a football player, where action is
instinctive and instantaneous. To this day he cannot tell
how he did what he did at that emergency. But somehow
he threw himself right over the middle of that seven-
passenger touring car, head first at the assassin. They
struck, breast to breast, and as they went down, under the
impact of that terrific blow, Martin got his right arm
around the assassin's neck.

Almost as they hit the pavement Luettich landed on top
of them. He, too, had come, on the instant, right over the
automobile, by what means he never knew, but straight at
the assassin. Lyon came, too, with a murderous automatic
revolver in his hand, eagerly seeking an opening through
which he could shoot the assassin without hitting one of his
own men.

Blind, unreasoning rage possessed Martin. The assassin had tried to use his gun again as they went down, but Martin had seized it with his left hand and wrenched it from him. Now, with a half-Nelson grip on the man's neck, Martin put his knee in the small of his back and strove with all his power to bend his neck back until it should break. All he wanted was to kill the fellow with his hands.

As the Colonel sank back into his seat after the shot, Cochems threw his arm around him and asked if he were badly hurt.

'He pinked me,' replied the Colonel.

Then, without further reply, he stood up. As he rose, he looked over the side of the car and saw Martin doing his best to kill the assassin then and there, single-handed and alone.

'Don't hurt him!' the Colonel called to Martin. 'Bring him to me!'

That command penetrated Martin's rage-befogged brain, and he instantly obeyed, as automatically as he would have responded to a signal from the quarterback in a football game. He shook Luettich off his back, got to his feet, and with his arm still tightly around the man's neck, and the gun still in his left hand, he dragged the assassin to an upright position. He handed the gun to the Colonel, and, with the left hand thus freed, twisted the assassin's face around so that the Colonel had a full view of it.

LXX

IT takes some time to write this, but it required only a very few seconds in the doing. The police, confident in the perfection of their arrangements, were taken off guard. But they responded to the emergency instantly. As the shot rang out, the crowd, as if moved by the same impulse that pulled the trigger, surged forward. Automatically the police line stiffened and threw the crowd back. Every policeman there had his own work cut out for him right in front of where he stood, and went at it. In an instant two or three men of the detective squad, none of whom had been close to Colonel Roosevelt because of the freedom from crowding and the near presence of his own party, got through to where Martin had the assassin. But they were met by Cecil Lyon's big automatic and his savage threat instantly to shoot any one who came near, and they discreetly retired to a safer distance. They saw that all that could be done had been done, and there would be no call for them until a little later.

The report of that revolver instantly stopped Dr. Terrell's nosebleed. McGrath jumped to the open window and looked out.

'The Colonel's shot!' he shouted, and on the instant he and Terrell and I dashed down the stairs, and somehow bored through the crowd to the automobile. The police, who had been holding back the crowd in the street, were not enough to handle those on the sidewalk, too, and a throng had gathered around the car, trying to get at the Colonel to see how badly he was hurt. We succeeded, with oaths, imprecations, and violence, in getting them back a

little and cleared a passage around the car. Then police
reserves came up and cleared the sidewalk. Martin turned
the assassin over to them, and they promptly took him
away, out of the reach of the crowd.

The Colonel sat down again, after seeing the assassin,
and at once gave orders that the car should start for the
Auditorium. But Dr. Terrell had reached him by that
time, and insisted on seeing the wound. Cochems urged
the Colonel to go to the hospital, and Terrell called to the
driver of the automobile, who sat at his wheel through it
all, to get to the hospital at once.

But Colonel Roosevelt peremptorily refused to go, and
called to the driver to take him to the Auditorium. To
Terrell and Cochems he declared that he was not hurt, and
that he would permit nothing to prevent his delivering that
speech. Something, the wound, the excitement, or whatever it was, had brought his voice back, apparently as
strong as ever.

'No, Colonel,' pleaded Cochems. 'Let's go to the hospital!'

'You get me to that speech,' replied the Colonel, with a
savage rasp in his tone. 'It may be the last one I shall ever
deliver, but I am going to deliver this one.'

To my frantic appeal that he take the sane precaution
of having the wound examined at once, he replied as savagely as he had to Cochems, and it was apparent that
nothing could be done with him. Philip Roosevelt urged
the family appeal, with the same result.

So, with his whole party surrounding him, in the automobile or walking beside it, the car started for the Auditorium. We went slowly through the crowded streets, the
people constantly cheering tumultuously as they recognized the Colonel. Word of the attempt on his life had not

yet reached them, and they behaved only as such crowds do on political occasions like that. All the way to the Auditorium, Dr. Terrell kept insisting on seeing the wound. But at first the Colonel refused absolutely.

'No,' he said, 'this is my big chance, and I am going to make that speech if I die doing it.'

As soon as the car reached the Auditorium, we went into one of the retiring-rooms, where the Colonel took off his big overcoat. The Auditorium is so arranged that we drove in from the street, and the Colonel stepped out of the car to a platform on the same level. He had found the bullet-hole in his overcoat and seemed more interested in that than in the result to himself. In the retiring-room he consented, at length, to have Dr. Terrell look at the wound. But at first he refused to permit any one else to see it. But upon my suggestion that if no one but the physician with the party saw the wound, it might create the impression that we were attempting to conceal the real situation, he agreed to have in some of the local men.

We were naturally a little late in arriving at the Auditorium, and the stage was filled with members of the local committee and guests, while the big hall was crowded. I went to the stage and asked the Progressive County Chairman, who was there, whether there was a physician present. To his inquiry as to what was wanted, I replied that the Colonel had been shot at the hotel, but we thought not seriously.

The chairman turned to the stage and beckoned to a man, who proved to be Dr. R. G. Sayle, of Milwaukee. Then he summoned two others, Dr. Stratton, one of the surgeons on the staff of the Emergency Hospital of Milwaukee, and Dr. Sorenson, of Racine. They all went at once into the retiring-room, where Dr. Terrell was already looking at the wound. The Colonel had unbuttoned his coat and vest and pulled up his shirt, so as to disclose the place where the bullet had struck him.

He put his hands on his chest and drew in a deep breath, expelled it and breathed again.

'It's all right, Doctor,' he said, to Terrell. 'There's no perforation. I don't get any pain from this breathing.'

The wound was about a half-inch under the right nipple. It was bleeding slightly, the blood-spot on his white shirt being about the size of a man's hand. The doctors examined the wound closely, and asked the Colonel several questions to develop symptoms which would indicate the extent of the injury, and whether or not there had been a penetration of the chest wall.

Colonel Roosevelt kept insisting that he felt no pain, and that he was all right. He was absolutely determined to deliver his full speech. The doctors tested his breathing, and found no difficulty with it. Thereupon they concluded that it was only a flesh wound, and that he might go on, as he was determined to do. A temporary bandage was made, of a fresh handkerchief, and the Colonel went immediately upon the stage, walking with all his customary vigor.

LXXI

MR. COCHEMS was to introduce Colonel Roosevelt. It was agreed that he should be very careful not to cause undue alarm about the Colonel, and the result was he was so cautious that he did not make the crowd understand what had happened. He began by asking the audience to be calm upon the receipt of the news he was about to give them, and then said that, as Colonel Roosevelt was leaving the hotel, a man had fired a shot at him. He did not indicate, however, whether the shot had struck the Colonel or not. The audience did not seem to grasp the full meaning of what Cochems had said.

As soon as the cheering had died down, Colonel Roosevelt began his talk, saying at once that he did not think the audience fully realized that he had just been shot, and adding:

'But it takes more than that to kill a bull moose!'

A gasp of astonishment and dismay ran around the audience, and then there was a tremendous burst of cheers as they realized that Colonel Roosevelt was all right, even if he had been shot.

When the hall was quiet again, the Colonel reached into the breast-pocket of his coat for the manuscript of his speech. He had begun to speak, and was proceeding as easily as if nothing had happened to him. McGrath and Martin, sitting close behind him, were both making stenographic notes of what he said. As he drew the manuscript from his pocket and looked at it, he hesitated ever so slightly, and repeated part of one sentence. That was the only evidence he gave of realizing how close the call had been. For he saw, in that glance, the fact that it was probably that manuscript which had saved his life.

Colonel Roosevelt had the habit of having the manuscript that he intended to use in the delivery of a speech prepared on small sheets, with extra spacing between the lines This one was on rather heavy, glazed paper, and made fifty sheets. He had folded them once, in order to get it all in his coat-pocket, so that there were a hundred sheets of that stiff paper through which the bullet had had to go before it struck him. In penetrating that mass of paper, the bullet had driven the sheets closely together, and they slipped just enough to deflect it, very slightly, upward. That deflection changed its course enough so that, instead of going between ribs straight into his heart, it hit a rib and was stopped. It lodged on the fifth rib, which was cracked by the blow, but not badly injured.

A sound like a deep sigh came from the audience as the Colonel drew out that paper, for every one saw, as he did, the bullet-hole through it, and sharp realization came to them all of what had happened. It seemed to me, as I sat there watching him, that the Colonel really suffered a greater shock, as he saw that manuscript, and, comprehending the stopping power of that mass of paper, understood how narrowly he had escaped, than he did when he was hit. Dr. Sayle, who sat near me and was also watching the Colonel very closely, had the same feeling about it. It was the only time I ever saw anything seem to stagger Colonel Roosevelt, but he rallied instantly, and began to read the speech.

After speaking for a few moments, the Colonel unbuttoned his vest and disclosed to the audience the blood-stain on his shirt. Again that gasp, like a deep sigh came, from the crowd, and one white-haired old lady stood up

~~grateful. I deserve to no less now.~~

Friends, it is curious how history too often
repeats itself. The times and the men of today are smaller
than the times and the men of '64; but the situations run
curiously on all fours. In 1864 Abraham Lincoln had been
nominated for the Presidency as the then Progressive Candidate; and the only alternative to his election was the election
of the reactionary candidate. Yet there were certain Progressives, some of them actuated by selfish motives, others men
of good character, men like Freemont, and Wendell Phillips,
who for various reasons, sometimes because they thought Lincoln
had not gone far enough, or had not come quickly enough to adopt
advanced positions, sometimes for personal pique, actually proposed to run a separate candidate against him; they actually
endeavored to throw the victory into the hands of the representatives of reaction, of the enemies of all progress. I doubt if

LEAF FROM ROOSEVELT'S TYPEWRITTEN SPEECH CARRIED FOLDED IN HIS
COAT POCKET AT MILWAUKEE AND SHOWING HOLES MADE BY THE BULLET

and appealed to him to go to a hospital, saying that the audience was suffering, and would feel much better at knowing that he was being taken care of properly than at hearing his speech.

The Colonel thanked her for her interest, but assured her that he was all right, and intended to finish his speech.

'If you could see me on horseback right now,' he said, 'I am sure you would agree that I was quite all right.'

When the Colonel had been speaking for ten or fifteen minutes, and seemed to be making exceptionally good going of it, I left the stage to send reports to headquarters at Chicago and New York, and to talk to some of the newspaper men about the affair. It had happened that not one of the correspondents with our party had been present when the shot was fired. They had all gone to the telegraph office from the station, and were at their own dinner when the Colonel left the hotel. Of course, they were greatly upset, and they wanted the most minutely detailed account of the shooting that they could get. Consequently, it was some time before I got through with all their questions and returned to the stage. When I did so, I asked Dr. Terrell if any effort had been made to get the Colonel to stop. He replied that nearly every one in the party had tried it, but without success, and that apparently nothing would check him.

It seemed to me, as I watched the Colonel very closely, that he had lost color and was laboring very hard to go on. So I stepped up to him, and put my hand on his left arm. He paused in his speech, and swung around on me with an expression on his face that can be described accurately only by the word 'ferocity.' He had a trick of contracting his eyes until they were little larger than points, and he glared at me in that way then. It was the Roosevelt fight-

ing face that he showed me, with more combat in it than
I ever saw at any other time, even during his cave-man
performance at the Saratoga Convention in 1910.

'What do you want?' he demanded.

'Colonel,' I replied, 'I want to stop you. You have
spoken thirty-five minutes. Don't you think that is long
enough?'

'No, sir,' he said. 'I will not stop until I have finished
this speech. You can't stop me. Nobody can stop me!'

Long afterward, when I told him that that was the only
time he had ever spoken angrily to me, he replied that he
had not been angry then, but only in deadly earnest. But
if that was mere earnestness, I never want to see anger.

He turned from me to the audience again, and went
on with the speech. Before very long he began to be obviously somewhat unsteady on his feet, and we were afraid
he would pitch forward off the stage. So we had a few good
strong men take places as near the stage as they could get
and directly in front of him, ready to catch him if he should
fall. He noticed the precaution, and kept a little farther
back from the front after that.

On one occasion, when he was interjecting something
into his prepared speech, he laid his manuscript down on
the table near which he had been standing. Martin at
once picked it up, in the hope that that would stop him.
But the Colonel fiercely insisted on having it back. Then
he turned to the audience and said that his party was trying to prevent his completing the speech, but he meant to
go on until he had delivered it all.

A little later he asked how long he had spoken. The
answer was forty-five minutes.

'Very well,' he said, 'I will speak fifteen minutes more.'

But as a matter of fact he kept on for another forty-five

minutes, resting only while he had a Milwaukee man read
for him an article from 'La Follette's Magazine.' He sat
down while that was done.

Nothing showed the indomitable determination of Colonel Roosevelt more than his action when he happened to
mention Senator La Follette. He started to say something,
which he regarded as important for that occasion, concerning the Wisconsin Senator.

'I am very sorry that Senator La Follette —' he began,
but the crowd broke in with an outburst of cheers. When
the interruption ended, he began the sentence again.
Again the crowd cheered, interrupting at the same point.
Again the Colonel waited for quiet and repeated his words.
For the third time the crowd stopped him with cheers. But
he stood there, patiently waiting for silence, and when it
came delivered that sentence exactly as he had started out
to do. The crowd recognized his determination to say it,
and let him do so without further interruption.

At length, after having spoken for an hour and a half, he
concluded his manuscript. He had thrown the pages down
on the floor, one at a time, as he read them, and they had
been picked up, so that the whole manuscript was preserved. Afterward it was divided among his friends, and
two pages, each with its ragged bullet-hole, are now in my
possession.

As he neared the end, it was plain that he was growing
weaker rapidly, and when he ceased speaking he was very
weary. Without noticing the cheers and applause of the
crowd, he turned to Dr. Terrell as he threw away the last
page, and said:

'Now I am ready to go with you and do what you want.'

It required only three or four minutes to get him back
into the automobile and away for the Emergency Hospi-

tal. Dr. Sayle and Dr. Stratton, with Dr. Terrell, rode in
the car with him, and the others of his party followed in
another car. At the hospital he waited for a few moments
in the reception-room before being taken to the operating-
room. There he asked a few questions about what had been
done and what messages had been sent. He dictated some
messages of his own, and asked that some one should
surely telegraph his old friend Seth Bullock, at Deadwood.
He was particular that the message to Bullock should include the detail that the gun with which he had been shot
was a thirty-eight on a thirty-eight frame. He knew Bullock would appreciate that reference to the old days of the
ranching time.

LXXII

On the way out to the hospital, and again in the reception-room there, the Colonel spoke to me about his reasons for insisting on delivering his speech, even before he had his wound examined. He said it was in accordance with what had been, for a good many years, a settled rule of his life. When he went into the Spanish War he realized, of course, he said, that he might be shot. He determined then that if he were shot, and the shock did not stop him at once, he would do the best he could to go on straight through with whatever he happened to be doing when he was hit. Afterward, that appealed to him as the right rule to follow in any case. In his public life he was always the center of a great deal of controversy, and he came to the presidency as the result of the assassination of McKinley. That increased, with him, the realization that he might be shot himself. During the campaign he was then making, the extraordinary bitterness and savagery of the attacks upon him had made him realize that, at any time, some lunatic might be inflamed to the point of trying to kill him. That had made him think more of this old rule of life of his than he had in years. So, when the shot did come, his first thought was to get on with what he had been about, which was that speech. He did not know how badly he was hurt, and didn't want to know until after the speech. Nor did he have time to make all this explanation, then, to his friends. He just wanted to get to the Auditorium and on with his work. Moreover, he thought it an exceptional opportunity to drive home one of the lessons he had been preaching throughout the campaign, that against the 'envy of the haves by the have nots,' as he phrased it.

He was ready, now, for the examination and such treatment as the doctors might find necessary. But he insisted that the wound was not serious, and he hoped he would be permitted to go on and keep his engagement to speak in Indianapolis the next night. He regretted that the delay at the hospital might force him to cut out his noon engagement for the next day at Champaign, Illinois.

As soon as the Colonel went to the operating-room for thorough examination of the wound, I got the Chicago headquarters on the telephone and reported the situation with us. At the same time we discussed what was to be done in Chicago. It was agreed that we should go back to Chicago with the Colonel, just as soon as the doctors would permit him to return to his car, and Medill McCormick, with whom I was talking, undertook to have Dr. John B. Murphy and Dr. Arthur Bevan, ready to meet the Colonel on his arrival there.

Philip Roosevelt, the Colonel's young cousin, who felt a tremendous responsibility through all this because he was the only representative of the family present, had managed to keep a good, Rooseveltian grip on himself during all the excitement thus far, but the delay at the hospital, while we were waiting for the report from the operating-room, obviously began to get on his nerves somewhat. He began talking about perforation of the chest wall, and penetration of the lung cavity, and other things that sounded as if they might be of medical or surgical importance, but none of us knew whether they were or not. We had great confidence in Dr. Terrell, whom we knew to be a calm, self-reliant man, and I, personally, was quite sure that he would give me the right advice as to what to do, when the examination was over.

But a wholly unexpected and extremely disturbing thing

occurred. It happened that one of our Wisconsin State committeemen, who lived in Milwaukee, was receiving at that time a visit from his brother, who was one of the distinguished members of the surgical staff of Johns Hopkins Hospital, in Baltimore. This man's reputation was such that I was very glad when he came out to the hospital and went into the operating-room to join in the examination of the Colonel. But when he came out, he walked up to me and said, quietly, but very earnestly:

'Get him out of here just as quickly as you can. This is no place for him.'

I asked him what was the matter, but he did not say. He only repeated his advice to get the Colonel away from that place just as quickly as we could.

By that time the anxiety of waiting, piled on top of the excitement of the evening, had begun to get the nerves of Harry Cochems, also, and he, too, was talking, as Phil was, about perforation of the chest wall and such unpleasant possibilities. Also the telegraph had had time to work, and messages had begun to pour in on us from all quarters of the United States. Some of them were from men of influence and prominence in the Progressive organization, who were entitled to replies. And as soon as we finished one conversation with Chicago headquarters, the jingling telephone bell summoned us to another.

There wasn't anything I could do about the Baltimore surgeon's advice until the Colonel was released from the operating-room and I had a chance to talk to Dr. Terrell. But before that occurred, Philip Roosevelt and Harry Cochems had pretty well made up their minds that the thing to do was to keep the Colonel right there, and have Doctors Murphy and Bevan come up from Chicago to take care of him.

When the Colonel came out of the operating-room, he was in fine spirits. His color had come back and he looked better than he had at any time since leaving Chicago. The doctors said that he had been feeling very well from the time he entered the operating-room. He had sat on the operating-table, joking with them, while they examined the wound, and while they were consulting about it he was dictating telegrams to Mrs. Roosevelt and others.

By this time Dr. Janssen, the Roentgenologist, who had been sent for as soon as the Colonel reached the hospital, arrived, and the Colonel was moved into the X-ray room, where two pictures of his chest were taken. Dr. Janssen then went to his office to develop the plates and chart the results, and the Colonel dressed and walked down to the automobile which was waiting at the door. We drove carefully, but rapidly, to the station, where the Colonel walked, unaided, from the automobile to the Mayflower, climbed aboard, and went into his own room. Dr. Sayle accompanied us to the station, and he and Dr. Terrell went with the Colonel into his room. They wanted to get him to bed as promptly as possible.

But it was Colonel Roosevelt's habit at that time to shave himself, and he always did so just before retiring. So, as soon as he reached his room, he called his servant and asked for hot water. Terrell and Sayle undertook to protest, but it was of no more use than it had been trying to stop him from speaking before he finished what he had to say. So the Colonel shaved, humming softly to himself as he manipulated the razor, and acting just as if nothing in the world had occurred to disturb him or change his plans. When he had finished shaving, he climbed into his bed, and, in two minutes, was sleeping as easily as any child.

Then Dr. Terrell came out and said to me that we could start for Chicago.

But by this time Dr. Janssen had come down to the car with his X-ray plates. He was uncertain whether or not they showed a perforation of the chest wall, but Doctors Terrell and Sayle did not think they did. Philip Roosevelt and Harry Cochems, however, were positive that they did, and Phil immediately assumed the responsibility of changing all the plans. He gave directions that we should remain at Milwaukee, and the Colonel should go back to the hospital. He dashed up into the telephone room above the ticket office in the station, and hastily called up Chicago headquarters. He was countermanding the direction for Doctors Murphy and Bevan to meet us on arrival there, and directing that they come at once to Milwaukee by special train.

The situation was saved by John Ferguson, of the Passenger Department of the Northwestern Railway. We had come up from Chicago, in a special train, on that road, and it was waiting to take us back. Mr. Ferguson always made it a point to be on the train whenever Colonel Roosevelt was anywhere on the Northwestern System, and he was in charge, for the railway, of that train. When he saw how things were going that night, he came over to me and said quietly, so that no one else could hear:

'When you're ready, O. K., just give me the word, and we'll go. These boys on this train will take my orders.'

So, when Dr. Terrell told me we could start, I turned to Ferguson, and said: 'All right, John, we'll go now.'

Phil Roosevelt was still busy up in the telephone room. Ferguson stepped out on the rear platform of the Mayflower and swung a lantern, at the same time calling 'All aboard,' after the manner of passenger conductors. He aimed the call directly at the telephone room.

The engineer had been waiting for that sign, and was ready. Slowly, and without the least jerk or vibration, the train began to move. I looked out of a car window and saw Phil coming downstairs four steps at a jump. He dashed across the station platform and caught the rear of the May-flower as we pulled out. He was too much out of breath when he got inside to say anything in particular, and just sat down to talk over with Cochems the showing of the X-rays.

I took Martin and McGrath into my room, with a machine, and began to dictate a full report of the events of the night, for transmission to Mrs. Roosevelt. A shoal of telegrams had come, and these had to be looked over also. One, from Mrs. Roosevelt, had arrived just as we were pulling out, and after the Colonel had gone to sleep. Dr. Terrell would not waken him to deliver it. It was a wonderful message, showing that the woman who wrote it lived on the same plane with the man to whom she sent it.

'Don't you think you had better come to Sagamore right away?' she asked, and followed it with the argument that 'you always rest so well here.'

LXXIII

IT was four o'clock on Tuesday morning, October 15th, when we pulled into the old Northwestern station at Chicago. Mr. Ferguson had sent us there so as to avoid the noise and bustle about the new station, which was used for all passenger service. We had made the quietest run down from Milwaukee that I ever experienced on any railroad. There had been no noise, no yanks or jerks — just smooth, quiet, steady progress. No whistles blew or bells rang. Those railroad men were giving Colonel Roosevelt every chance they could to rest and sleep. As we drew into the yard at Chicago and slowed down for the stop, we passed a light engine standing on the next track. It was blowing off steam. Our engineer leaned out of his cab window and spoke softly to the man in the other cab. Instantly that engine ceased its noise, as if it had been human and understood the emergency.

An ambulance from Mercy Hospital was waiting for us with Doctors Murphy and Bevan, but the Colonel was still sleeping quietly, and there had been no unfavorable development. Doctors Terrell and Sayle had watched him, closely, all the way down from Milwaukee. The four doctors all agreed that sleep was the best thing for him, and that he should not be wakened. It would be time enough to take him to the hospital when his sleep was ended. So the ambulance waited. Doctors Murphy and Bevan went home, to get some rest for themselves, while Terrell and Sayle stood watch at the Mayflower, ready to call them when the Colonel woke.

With a great bundle of telegrams for acknowledgment,

and my own reports of the night's events to file, I took McGrath and Martin and hurried up to our headquarters in the La Salle Hotel. There I tried first to get Senator Dixon, the Chairman of the Progressive National Committee, on the telephone. But he had turned in after hearing that we had left Milwaukee, and it took some time to get him. Then I tried Mr. Perkins, but he had gone to his suburban home and could not be reached. While I was waiting for Senator Dixon, I went at the great pile of telegrams that had been received at that office. Among them was one from Governor Johnson, who had been campaigning in eastern Ohio that day. It merely expressed his shock, regret, and indignation, and made no suggestion about meeting the emergency that confronted us.

There was also a telegram from Senator Beveridge, dated at a town in southern Indiana. After expressing his grief and shock, he put himself wholly in the hands of the National Committee, to do whatever they thought best for the remainder of the time before election, cutting short his own campaign for the governorship of Indiana if the committee so chose.

I looked at those two telegrams from Johnson and Beveridge for a moment, and then, without waiting to talk with New York, wrote a message to Beveridge asking him to come to Chicago, at once, for consultation, and to wire me the time of his arrival. I sent that message immediately and solely on my own responsibility.

Soon after that I got Senator Dixon on the telephone, and talked with him for the best part of an hour, going over in detail all the events of the night and discussing what was to be done next. We had a very difficult situation to meet. Colonel Roosevelt was scheduled for every day and evening of the remainder of the campaign. All those meetings were cancelled automatically by the shot that struck him down, and of course the committees everywhere would recognize that fact. But at the same time they would be coming at us, all together, for other speakers to fill those dates, and there would be clamorous demand for Governor Johnson and Senator Beveridge, and some others. Beveridge had already signified his attitude, but our experience with Governor Johnson, only two days before, when Colonel Roosevelt had asked him to go to Waterloo, Iowa, left us in some doubt now.

Dixon confirmed my judgment in asking Beveridge to come on for consultation, and agreed to see that everything possible was done from New York to fix up the Eastern dates of Colonel Roosevelt, so that a minimum of damage should result. The Indianapolis Committee would have to do the best it could for the meeting there that night, and I was to get some one to go to Louisville, where the Colonel was due on Wednesday night, and deliver the speech that the Colonel had prepared for that occasion. His Indianapolis speech also was ready, and it could be read there.

After talking with Dixon, I turned back to the steadily increasing pile of telegrams, and presently found one from Henry M. Wallace, of Detroit, the man to whom I had telegraphed, the previous afternoon, starting the libel action against Mr. Newett, of 'Iron Ore,' Mr. Wallace said:

I assume that the events of the evening do not alter Colonel Roosevelt's determination to proceed with the libel case. I have retained Judge James H. Pound, one of the best men in Michigan, for such purposes, to represent him, and if plans are uninterfered with, we will come over to Chicago, on receipt of word from you, for consultation. Judge Pound does not think criminal action advisable.

One thing about that message was characteristic of the manner in which Progressives, all over the country, took the shooting of Colonel Roosevelt. The moment they were assured that the wound was not likely to be mortal, they took it for granted that he would demand the active and vigorous continuation of the campaign, and they gave themselves to new plans accordingly. Consequently, it was with genuine surprise that we received the message from Mr. Wilson offering to stop his own campaign and withdraw from the stump until Colonel Roosevelt should be able to resume. The first thing the Colonel did that day in the hospital, as soon as the doctors permitted him to indulge in any political activity, was to dictate a statement declining the Wilson offer, and pointing out that the issues and principles, on which the campaign was based, were not personal or individual, and were not affected by the life or death of any man. They continued, and the fight should go on to its conclusion, just as it would in case of battle, even though the commanding general might be struck down.

Senator Beveridge arrived about six o'clock that evening, weary and travel-stained. He had started immediately on receipt of my telegram, and had been obliged to make the journey in sections, partly by trolley car, in order to get through that day. I took him at once to Mercy Hospital, where the Colonel had been taken early that morning. As soon as their first greeting was over, Colonel Roosevelt picked up his personal copy of the Louisville speech and handed it to the Senator, asking him to go to Louisville and fill his date there for him.

'I should like to have you read that speech,' said Colonel Roosevelt, 'and, of course, say whatever else you think best under the circumstances.'

Beveridge knew that, in order to get to Louisville in time for that meeting, he would have to start immediately. Our meeting with the Colonel was therefore cut short and we returned to headquarters. Without waiting for dinner, or any further consultation than had been possible while going to and from the hospital, Senator Beveridge started for Louisville. I told him that Dixon and Perkins were talking the situation over that day in New York, and that Perkins might come to Chicago in a day or two. Just as soon as possible definite arrangements for the rest of the campaign would be made. Colonel Roosevelt had already expressed his own thanks for the Senator's offer, and I took the responsibility of adding those of the National Committee generally.

During the day we had received word that Theodore Roosevelt, Jr., was coming to Chicago by the first train, and that Mrs. Roosevelt would follow as soon as possible. So I wired Mr. Wallace, in Detroit, that the libel action would go on, and, as soon as members of the Roosevelt family reached Chicago, I would telegraph him, so that he and Judge Pound could come over to meet them and discuss the case.

Governor Johnson was scheduled during the week in Ohio and Indiana, and was due in Illinois on Friday. He cut his schedule for that day, so as to bring him to headquarters on Friday afternoon, and asked some of his friends to meet him there, for a personal consultation.

Except in certain outstanding particulars, such as the consultation with Senator Beveridge, the talk with Dixon, the message from Governor Johnson, and the libel case, my recollection of the events of that day has never been very clear. It was a day of tremendous confusion, with an unending shower of telegrams and telephone calls, and constant demands for personal conversation with callers who insisted on being seen. I had been under extreme nervous strain for seven and a half months, since the opening of the fight for the nomination of the Colonel in the Republican National Convention. Instead of an opportunity for sleep the previous night, there had been the climax of the long draft on nervous energy. The result was a sort of numbness, in which I did my work mechanically, but without particular sensation. I was blessed with a kind of automatic alertness, which enabled me to carry in mind the myriad things that demanded attention. But no matter what they were, from the time I knew that the Colonel's life was not in danger, hardly anything seemed to be of the least concern to me.

Somehow or other we got through our work. We patched up the holes in our programme, as best we could, I do not remember how. My impression is that Mrs. Roosevelt came to Chicago at once, but I am not sure of that. I know that she was there some time before the Colonel was discharged from the hospital, for it soon developed that she was the only one who could efficiently protect him from the demands of those who insisted on seeing and talking to him. He felt so well, and was so tremendously interested in the campaign, that he would willingly have taken, from his hospital bed, an active part in its direction. But Mrs. Roosevelt smilingly and pleasantly, gently, but always firmly, supervised all that, and it was only when there was real occasion for his decision that any political conference with him was permitted.

LXXIV

EARLY on Friday afternoon, Governor Johnson came to headquarters, with several friends. They went into the room which I had been using as my office for their conference. Harry Cochems, who was personally familiar with what the Governor had done to our campaign in Wisconsin, was at headquarters that day, but he was not invited to this conference. Neither was I, although my room had been taken for it without consultation with me. William Allen White, of Emporia, was present, and so was Francis J. Heney, who was at that time one of the Governor's stanchest California supporters.

After the conference had been going on for some time, Cochems asked me what they were talking about. I replied that I didn't know. Cochems thought we ought to go in and see. He wanted a chance to have it out with Johnson about the Wisconsin case. So he and I went in. Cochems took a chair near Heney, and I went to my usual place at my desk.

Governor Johnson was speaking as Cochems and I entered. He paused for a moment or two, as we sat down, and then resumed, apparently going right on with what he had been saying. It was a general condemnation, in vigorous language, of the conduct of the campaign, especially by New York headquarters. I do not recall any feature of the work that pleased him, and there seemed to be no person connected with the New York organization who was satisfactory to him. It seemed to make no difference what the previous political affiliations of any one in the New York office had been, the Governor either found

fault or sneered. He scoffed at an old stand-patter like
Frank Munsey and an ardent Progressive like Gifford
Pinchot, alike.

The campaign had been mismanaged, or not managed
at all, from the start. The speaking trips of Colonel Roosevelt and himself came in for a fine denunciation, and he
exploded again about being put in competition with bulls
and pigs at State Fairs. The publicity work was wretched.
Wholly inadequate preparation for it had been made, and
advance effort, especially where he had been concerned,
had been omitted until he secured his own man to attend
to it. The whole reliance seemed to have been on working
him and Colonel Roosevelt to death. God knew he was
willing to work! He had been making a dozen to fifteen
stops a day, and such meetings as the committees had
given him! It was ridiculous to ask a candidate to make
most of the meetings he had been forced to make, with no
proper preliminaries, no assurance of crowds, and no publicity groundwork.

So he railed along for some time. Then he shifted his
ground, and, from general attack upon the work and the
plan of campaign, went into specific denunciation of in-
dividuals. He spent some time describing George W.
Perkins, and commenting particularly on one pamphlet
which had been distributed from New York headquarters
which dealt with the charges that had been made against
Mr. Perkins. With open scorn he quoted from that pamphlet and sneered at its distribution.

From Perkins the Governor turned to Beveridge, and
assailed the selection of the Senator to deliver Colonel
Roosevelt's speech at Louisville. He was going on about
that when I interrupted him.

'I am responsible for that, Governor,' I said. And then

I told the story of how Colonel Roosevelt had asked the Governor to make the Waterloo speech which should have been delivered that very day. I went into all the circumstances, and repeated the message in which the Governor had had his secretary refuse the one request Colonel Roosevelt had made of him during that campaign. Then I said:

'You see, gentlemen, after that, when Colonel Roosevelt was shot, and his place at Louisville had to be filled, it simply did not occur to me to ask Governor Johnson again to do anything for him.'

Blank silence fell over the room at that. Governor Johnson sat staring down at the floor, without a word, and no one else spoke. I have wondered, sometimes, whether the Governor had ever considered just how his refusal to go to Waterloo must seem to Colonel Roosevelt. I am sure none of those in that room at the La Salle Hotel, that afternoon, had had any inkling of this situation. Presently one of them got up and left the room. Then another went out. Then Cochems went, without having had an opportunity to get in a word about his Milwaukee trouble. After a while only the Governor and I remained.

In the days that had preceded this conference, it had been agreed with New York headquarters that I was to ask Governor Johnson to take up the unfilled part of Colonel Roosevelt's schedule, and to complete the campaign for him. In talking it over with Dixon and Perkins, by telephone, the full situation had been discussed very frankly. Both of those gentlemen knew the criticism and complaint that had rolled in about the Governor's campaign work and realized its justification. Both thought that Senator Beveridge would make a more effective appearance, in the Colonel's place, than Governor Johnson would. Beveridge had had a wonderful meeting at Louisville. He had delivered the Colonel's speech as it was written, and then had added a speech of his own, of extraordinary power and sympathy. His own exceptional emotionalism had been stirred to its depths by the shooting of the Colonel, and the result was a most unusual appeal, even for so practiced an orator as Beveridge. This fact had, of course, to be considered in determining whether to ask Governor Johnson or Senator Beveridge to fill out the Colonel's schedule.

It was recognition of the fact that the country would naturally expect Governor Johnson, as the nominee for the vice-presidency, to take up the Colonel's work, that led to the decision to ask him to do so. I was instructed, however, to have a frank talk with him in presenting this request, and to say plainly that he would be expected to alter his course, and to follow, as closely as he could, the line that Colonel Roosevelt would have taken if he had not been shot.

So I took that opportunity to ask the Governor whether or not he would assume the Colonel's schedule. At the same time, I delivered the message that I had been instructed to give him, as to what would be expected of him in case he took up the Colonel's work.

Without replying directly to the request, he asked what I meant by changes in his course. I said that he would have a good many more short stops to make than he had been making, when he would have to greet crowds from the rear platform of his car, and would be expected to make little five- or ten-minute talks to them; that he would not be scheduled for more than two important meetings a day, and as far as possible such meetings would be limited to one a day, in the evening, with possibly, and even probably, a meeting of secondary importance at noon. This would involve, I said, considerably more than he had been doing.

'Well,' he interjected, 'what do you think I have been doing?'

'I think you have been making two meetings a day,' I replied, 'and delivering the same speech too frequently for good publicity.'

At that the floodgates of Johnsonian wrath were opened, and our battle was joined in dead earnest. I stuck to my point and held close to my instructions. The Governor was thoroughly angry, and we did not make much progress. We adjourned for dinner, under agreement to meet again that evening.

During Friday evening, all of Saturday and Sunday morning, this struggle with Governor Johnson continued. I do not know what his objective was. That never was clear to me. Mine was to get him to agree to take up the Colonel's schedule and work on it with something like the Colonel's habit. Throughout this discussion I kept harping on the fact that, all through the East, the Governor had the reputation of being a second Roosevelt, and that that was why we expected him to work like one. It has occurred to me since that perhaps he didn't like being called a 'second Roosevelt,' and that was one of the things which made him angry.

In the end he agreed, either in response to my argument or to some reason of his own that did not appear to me. But he took the fast train for New York that Sunday afternoon, and for the remainder of the campaign was in the East making dates that Roosevelt would have made if he had not been shot. I think he did manage to get in one or two meetings on the East Side, in New York City, where voteless aliens predominate.

Colonel Roosevelt recovered rapidly from his wound. He returned to Sagamore Hill after a few days in Mercy

Hospital, and made one more appearance in the campaign, at a monster meeting in Madison Square Garden, just before election.

So, between the disarrangement of the plans for Governor Johnson and the bullet of a lunatic assassin at Milwaukee, the wonderful scheme of a balanced campaign with which we opened the contest was pretty thoroughly broken up before it ended. But we had made a good showing. It was plain, some time before election, that we were going to poll a larger vote than the Republican ticket would, although we knew we had no chance of victory.

In point of fact we carried, as I now recall it, all the States that we thought, just before election, we could carry, except one. We did think we should win in Illinois, but were disappointed there, although by only a narrow margin. We had had a good deal of fun at New York headquarters during the campaign, and especially in its later weeks, over the erection of an imaginary asylum for the residence of some of our overenthusiastic friends. Dixon, Perkins, and I used to get together after dinner, and assign quarters in this asylum to different persons. When Governor Johnson got back from his New England trip, he was so confident about Maine that we gave him a whole wing for himself. And Perkins and I had a bit of special fun of our own with Dixon about North Carolina. We manufactured a lot of telegrams in our own office, giving most encouraging reports from the Senator's old State. But I was never quite sure that he did not see through the game, although if he did he played it very well.

LXXV

THE result of the election was cheering in some respects, but in the main very disappointing. Roosevelt polled a considerably larger popular vote than Taft, and thus seemed to justify our contention, throughout, that the will of the Republican voters had been thwarted by the Republican National Committee and the June Convention at Chicago. We carried six States, with eighty-eight electoral votes, just eleven times as many as Taft, who carried only Utah and Vermont. But it takes the election of a horde of men to minor offices, all over the country, to establish a political party as a going concern nationally. In that respect the Progressive Party failed by a wide margin in the campaign of 1912. Part of it was due to the fact that there had been so little time for organization. In only a comparatively few places did we have the local and county tickets in the field, which should have been up everywhere. And in the Congress fight we did not make anything like the showing that we should have made, or that might have been made if we had had more time, or had given more attention to it in the time we did have.

Nineteen Progressives were elected to Congress. But the Republicans elected about a hundred, and were therefore in position to claim recognition in the House as the official opposition. We did our best to obtain this recognition on the strength of our larger popular vote, but, of course, that failed, as it deserved to do.

It would have been good strategy for the Progressive National Committee to see to it that there was a Progressive candidate for Congress in every district, and,

wherever there did not appear to be a fair chance of electing him, to do everything possible to elect the Democrat,
so that we should come into the new House with a larger
membership than the Republicans. But very little thought
was given to the Congressional election, and thereby we
lost the best chance we had to gain firm ground in the solid
establishment of the party.

Mr. Taft took his disastrous defeat with apparent good-
nature, and showed that he is a good, sportsmanlike loser.
But he made occasion, several times, to remark publicly
that hundreds of thousands of Republicans had voted directly for Wilson, in order to prevent the possible election
of Roosevelt. No doubt there was some vote of that kind,
and it may have been large. But no one could tell how
large, and, unless the Republican National Committee received some very special reports from its own organization, it does not appear how it could justify the estimate
of more than a million Republican votes for Wilson which
Mr. Taft made. Naturally, he got some comfort out of
that, for, by adding that million to his own vote, he could
figure himself as having made a much more creditable
showing in the division of Republican votes throughout
the country.

The bitter personal assault on Colonel Roosevelt, that
had been growing more and more savage as the campaign
went on, was stilled for a time by the attempt on his life.
But it was renewed very promptly after the election, when
the analysis of the vote began to charge him with the whole
responsibility for the defeat of Taft and the disaster to the
Republican Party.

Such talk was, of course, as it is still, nothing but nonsense. It is a product of that blind partisanship which
resolutely refuses to see the plainest facts. Only a man

who can say that Mr. Taft had not conducted an increasingly unpopular administration can honestly charge Mr. Roosevelt with defeating the Republican Party. Only a man who can ignore the events of 1910, when the Colonel exerted himself to the very utmost in behalf of Taft and his party, can say, with the appearance of truth, that he believes Taft could have been elected by Roosevelt's support in 1912.

Such talk is the veriest twaddle, all 'bunk and peanuts,' as the lady says in the play. From the instant when he knew he had been elected, on that November evening in 1908, Mr. Taft determined to differentiate himself from Roosevelt. One way of doing that was in the treatment of the Roosevelt policies, to which he was so thoroughly pledged. From the moment he was inaugurated, he followed a course that was as certain to drive away from him the largest part of the vote that had elected him, as if it had been designed deliberately for that purpose. Almost at the outset of his administration, on the day when Congress met, when he had been less than two weeks in office, he openly aligned himself with the most vigorous opposition to Roosevelt in the party, and steadily thereafter his alliance with that faction grew stronger.

The election of 1910 gave no warning, either to President Taft or to those who were leading the forces with which he had associated himself in Congress and in the Republican Party. Then, on top of a record of unpopularity such as had not been built up by any man since James Buchanan, whom, in fact, Mr. Taft in his presidency much resembled, he proceeded to pile the performance of the National Committee and the June Convention.

We assigned special quarters in our private asylum at Progressive headquarters to our enthusiastic friends who thought we were going to win. The entire asylum would not be adequate recognition of the political optimism of the genius who really believed, in the spring of 1912, that there was a possibility of the reëlection of Mr. Taft, even if he could have commanded the hearty support of Colonel Roosevelt.

Only one thing could have been accomplished by Colonel Roosevelt that year in supporting Taft. That would have been the complete and effective alienation of his own following. They showed him very plainly in 1910, and any one else who took the pains and had the mental equipment to watch, that they were for Roosevelt himself, just as they had been right along, but not at all for some other man for whom he asked them to vote. They cheered him to the echo that year, wherever he went, and applauded his efforts in behalf of the Republican candidates, then went straight to the polls and voted as they pleased — but not for the Republicans.

But there is something about political partisanship which seems to affect a man's ability to distinguish the truth when he meets it or a fact when he sees it. Results as plain as a house are placidly ascribed to causes ridiculously false, and plans for future action are based on such deductions. It is a waste of time and breath to talk with that kind of politician or about that kind of politics. The ostrich and the mole are towering geniuses by comparison.

LXXVI

In the conference which followed the election, at Progressive headquarters in New York, it was determined by the National Committee to make the most of what successes had been gained at the polls, and to endeavor to build up, in Congress, general recognition of the permanency of the Progressive Party. As Secretary of the National Committee I was instructed to open offices in Washington and to furnish a special news service from the capital to the several hundred small Progressive newspapers that had been established in various parts of the country. Our supporters everywhere were militant and enthusiastic, and looking forward to our next campaigns with a good deal of confidence. Local committees were busy making preparation to get Progressives into the county, township, and municipal offices, and all the talk was about thorough and permanent establishment.

The spring of 1913 brought city, village, and township elections in several States, and in some of them the Progressives made a remarkably good showing. An element of real encouragement was the result. There were enough Progressive newspapers, large and small, around the country by this time, to enable us to maintain a steady publicity service, and we began the publication at Washington of a 'Bulletin' that soon had a considerable paid circulation.

It was the delegation in Congress that furnished the first real rift. It had been joined by Victor Murdock, of Kansas, who had been elected as a Republican, and had not previously affiliated with the Progressive Party. Murdock had served several terms in Congress, and was a member of the Committee on Ways and Means, which would be charged, in the special session called by President Wilson, with the preparation of the new tariff bill that was to replace the unpopular Payne-Aldrich Law.

After a good deal of discussion of the tariff situation, at headquarters, and with leading Progressives in different parts of the country, it was decided that we should make an effort, through the Progressive delegation in the House, to impress the Progressive point of view upon the country. Mr. Underwood, the chairman of the Ways and Means Committee, was already holding hearings on the tariff, and making preparations to write his bill. It was evident that the methods followed in making the Democratic bill would be exactly the same, in principle, as those followed in making the Republican bill. There were constant confidential conferences between the men specially concerned in the rates to be adopted and those who were making the bill, just as there were under the Republican régime. The real bill was made in secret, just as much as the Payne-Aldrich Bill had been, and there was just as much logical reason for objection to it on that ground.

The question with us was how to bring this objection so strongly to the attention of the country that it would raise a storm of protest against the bill. In the discussion of that question, some one suggested that the Progressives in the House should be asked to refuse to vote on the bill, for that reason. There were three possible ways to vote, 'Aye,' 'No,' and 'Present.' If our men all voted 'Present,' and each one explained, in casting his vote, as he had the right under the rules to do, that he voted that way because of the total lack of information as to why the actual rates fixed by the committee had been adopted, and of the secrecy surrounding the making of the bill, we believed it would be an effective protest that would arouse the whole country.

Accordingly, a meeting of the Progressive delegation in the House was arranged. It was held at the Columbia Country Club, of which I was at that time a member. Senator Beveridge and I were the only ones present not members of the delegation. Senator Beveridge rehearsed, in a good deal of detail, the fight made by the Senate Insurgents against the Payne-Aldrich Bill, and explained our view of the way in which a vote of 'Present' on the Underwood Bill would be received by the country as a dignified and forcible protest against the methods by which it had been made. We pointed out, also, the obvious fact that the nineteen Progressives could not, in any way, affect the passage of the bill. If they all voted for it, that would not add, appreciably, to the Democratic majority for it. If they all voted against it, that would not make the least difference in the final result. Absolutely the only way by which they could make themselves felt on this bill was the one we had suggested.

That suggestion raised a veritable storm about our heads. We were immediately and very plainly denounced as 'Bosses' attempting to dictate to free and untrammeled representatives of the people in the performance of their sacred duty. It was an unthinkable thing for a real Progressive to do. It was the lowest kind of practical politics — and much more of the same sort. One devoted young man, from Pittsburgh, thumped himself on the chest and grandiloquently announced that 'NEVER' would he consider such a thing.

So that very practical and hopeful plan for making that little group of nineteen Progressives a real and effective

force in the House was swept away even as it was launched.
And when the roll was called on the vote on the bill, our
merry group split all three ways. Some voted for the bill,
some against it, and one voted 'Present.'

But before the bill got through the House, we made
one more effort to force the unfavorable attention of the
country upon it. This time we tried to employ tactics that,
I firmly believe, might be just as well employed against
any tariff bill made under the conditions that now obtain
in tariff-making, and that will continue to obtain until
there is a very radical revision of the whole method of dealing with tariff legislation.

Under the present system, there is never any real consideration of a tariff bill in the open house. There is always a period of several days set aside for what is called
'general debate.' In this time members have opportunity
to deliver speeches on any subject which pleases them, and
it is all 'home consumption' work; that is, the speeches are
made for distribution among their constituents, as part of
the 'Congressional Record.' After general debate is ended,
the bill is taken up in Committee of the Whole, and is then
read, line by line, under the five-minute rule. By that rule
each member of the Committee on Ways and Means has
five minutes, if he desires to use it, on any point that is
raised. Any member of the House may move an amendment, and on doing so has five minutes to discuss it. One
member may be recognized for five minutes to oppose the
amendment. When all that time has been exhausted, further time may be obtained only by unanimous consent,
which, of course, one objection prevents.

Our second plan was to attack the Underwood Bill,
under the five-minute rule, with a sustained demand for information as to the reason why rates had been fixed at the

figures adopted by the committee. We knew that, at the outset, this demand would not attract any particular attention, either from the House or the country, but we believed that, if it were kept up throughout the consideration of the entire bill under the five-minute rule, it would arouse a fierce and general outcry against the bill.

The procedure proposed was simple, but somewhat arduous. It was merely that, as soon as the clerk reading the bill reached the first item carrying a rate of duty, one of our members was to rise and move an amendment, by which he would obtain the floor. Then he was to ask the committee member, in charge of the particular schedule under consideration, what information the committee had which led it to fix that particular rate. We believed that most of the rates were either fixed arbitrarily, or in conformity with the representations of some person or persons specially interested, exactly as was done in the Payne-Aldrich Bill. We saw no difference whatever, in principle, between having a cotton manufacturer from New England, for instance, write the cotton schedule and having a cotton importer from New York write it. Each was obviously considering, chiefly, his own interest, and that of the class he represented.

Mr. Murdock, the Progressive floor leader, seemed to regard this plan of attack on the Underwood Bill as a good one, and I thought he was keen to carry it through. So when the bill came up I was in the press gallery of the House, waiting to see the result. Reading of the bill started, but our plan did not get under way until the item of boracic acid was reached. Then Sammy Smith, of Michigan, jumped up and moved to strike out the last word. That is the technical, or *pro forma*, amendment, commonly used to get the floor under the five-minute rule.

Mr. Smith employed his five minutes in reading extracts of letters from Thomas Jefferson to prove that Jefferson was a protectionist. It had nothing whatever to do with the question of the rate on boracic acid, which had been reduced from three cents a pound, as provided by the Payne Aldrich Law, to three quarters of one cent.

When Mr. Smith's time expired, Mr. Murdock rose to oppose the Smith amendment, which gave him the floor for five minutes.

'I should like to ask the gentleman from New York (Representative Francis Burton Harrison) who is in charge of this schedule (the chemical schedule) what information the committee had which led it to fix this rate?' said Murdock.

Mr. Harrison rose, unsuspicious and confident, and, with a toplofty air, countered with a question of his own. 'Does the gentleman think the cut has been too severe?' he inquired. There was a note of satisfaction in his voice that showed he had no thought that any trap had been laid for him.

'I don't know whether it is too severe or not,' replied Murdock. 'That is one reason why I ask the question. I think the people of the country are entitled to the facts upon which the rates in a tariff bill are fixed. I believe the members of the House are entitled to know what the information is on which their committees take definite action such as this. I am certain that members of the committee are entitled to this information. So I ask the gentleman in charge of this schedule what information the committee had on which to base this rate?'

Mr. Harrison's manner changed abruptly. A so-called 'expert' had been employed by the Ways and Means Committee to 'assist' in drafting the chemical schedule. That fact was well enough known to members of the committee, but no doubt many members of the House did not know it, and certainly the country at large did not know it. Moreover, it was something more than a good guess that even members of the subcommittee drafting the chemical schedule did not know just why the expert fixed this or that rate. It was all just a hit-and-miss procedure, based, professedly, on Mr. Underwood's avowed purpose to make a competitive instead of a protective tariff.

So Mr. Harrison was placed in difficulties by Mr. Murdock's question and the obviously fair and courteous manner in which it had been put to him. He was not in position to answer. He could not give the information, for he didn't have it himself, and he couldn't summon his 'expert,' for that would betray the manner in which the schedule had been prepared. So he resorted to the well-known and time-honored device of 'stalling,' and managed to use up his own five minutes without getting anywhere near a responsive reply.

The chairman of the Committee of the Whole banged the desk with his gavel and announced that 'the time of the gentleman from New York has expired; all time has expired.'

'Mr. Chairman,' interposed Murdock, 'I ask unanimous consent for five minutes more, so that the gentleman from New York may answer this important question.'

'I object,' said Mr. Underwood, promptly. He had been observing the proceedings very closely, and did not at all like the drift of things. He knew enough about tariff-making to understand that, if that question were pushed home, it would surely make trouble for the bill, and so he used his privilege, under the rules, to shut it off then and there.

Mr. Murdock sat down with a smile of evident satisfaction, as if he had demonstrated the case completely by that one question. The clerk went on reading the bill. I sat there in the gallery expecting Murdock to repeat the performance on the next item, but he did not. Nor did he try it again on any other rate. He let it go with one question.

Thus our second plan for establishing the Progressive group in the House as a center of forceful leadership failed miserably, just when it gave most promise. Thereafter the nineteen House Progressives went their own way, uninterfered with by suggestions from the National Committee, and most of them lost their official heads at the ensuing election.

Sheep respond to leadership, but goats do not. A flock of sheep, called or frightened, will run all in a bunch. But under similar circumstances a flock of goats will run just about as many ways as there are goats.

LXXVII

IN the early part of 1913, Colonel Roosevelt's libel suit against Mr. Newett came on for trial at Marquette, Michigan, before Judge Flanagan. We knew that Mr. Newett had been making great efforts to obtain witnesses who would testify to the truth of his assertion that 'Colonel Roosevelt drank heavily, and all his friends knew it.' Mr. Newett's attorneys, who were assisted by the legal representatives of one of the large corporations which has headquarters at Cleveland, had taken a good many depositions in different States, but mostly in Ohio. They found a number of persons who were willing to say, in such a deposition, that they thought the Colonel was under the influence of liquor on the occasion of his delivery of a speech in their town in the primary fight in 1912.

Cross-examination of these witnesses developed the fact that they all referred to the same occasion. Judge Pound, for Colonel Roosevelt, then brought out the fact that the Colonel had spoken for an hour and a half or more, and that during that entire time he had stood on top of the stone railing which guarded the steps up to the public building in front of which he delivered the speech. When that piece of stone was measured, it was found to be about fifteen inches long by twelve wide. Mr. Newett's attorneys concluded, therefore, that testimony to the effect that a man was under the influence of liquor, who had stood for an hour and a half, or more, on so small a stone as that, while he delivered a political speech, was not worth very much in court.

But that was the best the Newett lawyers could find,

and there was no denying their ability or their eagerness to get the evidence if it was to be had. Newett was a fighting man. He had received his information as to the Colonel's alleged bibulous habits from friends in whom he was entitled to trust. It was told us at Marquette that one of Mr. Newett's informants was a United States Senator, who had said that he himself 'had been drunk with Roosevelt before ten o'clock in the morning.' But that particular Senator was very careful to keep out of Michigan, where a subpœna might bring him into court to testify under oath.

Under the Michigan law, Colonel Roosevelt was permitted to put in his side of the case first. Judge Pound began with the Colonel's cousin, Emlen Roosevelt, who had known him, intimately, from his childhood. One after another of the Colonel's close friends followed Emlen Roosevelt on the stand, and all testified to the same thing, that they had never known the Colonel to drink hard liquor, but had seen him take an occasional glass of wine at dinner, and that wine was often on his table.

Judge Pound varied this procession of friends of the Colonel by going to the press table and summoning to the witness stand some of the working newspaper men who were reporting the trial, and who had made one or more campaign trips with Colonel Roosevelt. Their story was just the same as that of the intimate friends.

When this had been going on for two or three days, the Newett lawyers began to show signs of distress. The trial began on Monday. On Wednesday, when the noon adjournment was taken, James R. Garfield, who was in the Roosevelt party, was approached by one of the Newett attorneys and questioned, very guardedly, as to the prospects of a compromise. Mr. Garfield reported this to the

Colonel at once, and was immediately instructed to see that Newett lawyer and find out just what he meant, and how far Newett was willing to go.

That afternoon, while the taking of testimony continued, Colonel Roosevelt held a general conference with all his friends there, in the consultation-room adjoining the courtroom. He asked what each one thought he should do. All were for acceptance of the Newett proposition, providing it were of the right sort, except Judge Pound. He was furious at the suggestion. He insisted that the Colonel had an impregnable case, on which he was bound to win a verdict, and he demanded that the case go on to the end. Pound had disregarded the original instructions to the extent of bringing suit for $10,000 damages instead of $5000, and he was now eager to get that $10,000. He seemed quite unable to see that Colonel Roosevelt did not want money from Newett, but only the verdict of the jury that he was not a drunkard. Ten thousand dollars was evidently a lot of money to Judge Pound. He knew Newett could pay, if the case went against him, and he stuck to his point so insistently that I began to suspect there was some personal feeling concealed about him.

Meantime Mr. Garfield had had further talk with the attorney who had first approached him, and reported that Newett was ready to go on the stand and confess that his charge was unfounded, and that he had searched the country for six months in the effort to obtain witnesses who would swear to its truth, but without being able to obtain one.

Thereupon Colonel Roosevelt decided to accept the compromise, and himself to ask the court to direct a verdict for nominal damages. He asked Mr. Garfield, Gifford Pinchot, and me, to take the draft of the statement which Mr. Newett was to make on the stand, and to go over it carefully to see whether or not there was anything in it which was not acceptable. Such a draft had been prepared by the Newett lawyers and was ready for us at once.

Colonel Roosevelt and his party were stopping at the home of George Shiras III, in Marquette Mr. Garfield, Mr. Pinchot, and I took the statement into a room by ourselves and went over it, line by line and word by word. We edited it, just as newspaper editors handle copy, striking out words, phrases, or sentences and making such substitutions as seemed to us right under the circumstances.

While we were doing that, the Colonel came into the room, picked up a couple of sheets of blank paper, took out a stub of a pencil, and wrote out the statement to the court which he intended to make as soon as Mr. Newett left the stand. The originals of both the Colonel's statement and the first draft of the Newett statement are now in my possession.

The draft of the Newett statement, as edited by Garfield, Pinchot, and myself, was taken up to Ishpeming that evening by Mr. Garfield and submitted to the Newett side. All our alterations were accepted at once by them. It was then taken to Judge Flanagan for his information. The original draft had included a sentence, in which Mr. Newett declared that he had printed the objectionable paragraph in good faith, and not believing that it would damage Colonel Roosevelt. When we edited the draft, we called the Colonel's attention to that sentence, and asked if he desired it stricken out. He at once said no. It might be true that Newett had believed it, and had not thought its publication would damage him. So he was for letting it stand. But Judge Flanagan declared promptly that it was impossible any man could believe the publication of such a statement would not damage any person about whom it was made, and that no man could say such a thing about Colonel Roosevelt in his court. So Newett struck it out.

The trial was in the week which included Memorial Day, and, of course, court did not sit on that day. That permitted the completion of all arrangements for the compromise. The day afterward testimony on the Roosevelt side went on for a while, and then Mr. Newett took the stand, and read his statement. As soon as he concluded, Colonel Roosevelt stood up and asked permission to address the court. When that was granted, he said:

'In view of the statement of the defendant, I shall ask the court to instruct the jury that I desire only nominal damages. I did not go into this suit for money. I did not go into it with any vindictive purpose. I went into it, and, as the court has said, made my reputation an issue, because I wished, once for all, during my own lifetime, to deal with these slanders, fully and comprehensively, so that never again will it be possible for any man, in good faith, to repeat them. I have achieved my purpose, and I am content.'

Judge Flanagan then instructed the jury as the Colonel had requested, saying, however, that but for that request he should have charged the jury that, if it found for the plaintiff, the full amount of damages sued for should be awarded. The jury immediately returned a verdict for six cents, and the Newett libel suit was over.

LXXVIII

IN 1913, Colonel Roosevelt went to South America, in the eager hope of being able to carry out some of the geographical work in which he was so keenly interested. The Progressive Party was left to worry its way along as best it could without his intimate leadership. He had been growing restless under the demand for this leadership, some time before he left the country. For it had become more than evident that the Progressives, everywhere, were more like goats than sheep. They had an individuality and a penchant for self-determination that made leadership, even that of Colonel Roosevelt, largely titular instead of practical. Their fierce antagonism to 'boss rule' made them as impatient of leadership in their own party as they had been of control in any other.

This general disregard for the value and effectiveness of team-work made it evident very soon that the Progressive Party as an organized force in American politics was doomed to early extinction. Moreover, it had an extremely difficult situation to face. For both the other parties promptly appropriated to themselves most of the items in its programme, and both professed to be more genuinely progressive than the Progressive party itself. One of the most ridiculous spectacles in American politics was furnished by the Republican remnant, made up as it was of stand-patters and reactionaries, solemnly professing to be progressive. This eagerness of both the old parties to appropriate Progressive ideas helped to make the Progressive Party the most effective, as it was about the shortest-lived, in United States political history.

The Democrats, under the leadership of Woodrow Wilson, not only professed progressivism, they made headway with it. There was real response to leadership in that party, and Mr. Wilson promptly displayed a willingness to dominate, to dictate, and to drive, fully equal to that displayed by any 'boss' ever known. He was not only willing to impose his will, absolutely, on his party, but to denounce publicly any and all who dared to oppose it. Opposition to the Wilson instruction was advised from the first that it could take the consequences, and Mr. Wilson did his best to make those consequences as painful as possible for his party opponents. He did not hesitate to single out men of his own party and fight their renomination or election, and his refusal to consult with them was made as conspicuous as possible.

Under such circumstances the wholesale robbery of the Progressive platform by Mr. Wilson and his party was quickly made effective. The resultant situation was almost as ridiculous, from the point of view of party principle, as that in the Republican remnant. For the Democratic Party under Wilson, although it still delighted to refer to itself as 'Jeffersonian,' was all the time engaged with matters that must have made the bones of the great founder of the party squirm and rattle in their grave. Mr. Wilson headed straight toward the development of a central government stronger by far than anything George Washington ever dreamed of as befitting American life, and he went as far toward that Federalist goal as, with all his energy and determination, he could drive his following.

When Colonel Roosevelt returned from South America, still suffering from the effects of the desperate illness which had stricken him down there and nearly ended his life, he was reluctant to resume the leadership of the Progressive

Party. He desired very much to keep entirely out of the campaign of 1914, and, at one time, it seemed as if he had brought out a plan that would at least permit him to minimize his connection with it.

The Progressive showing in New York State in the election of 1912 had given great encouragement to many of the men prominent in the organization, and this feeling had been confirmed by the subsequent developments. The impeachment of Governor Sulzer, and the open split in the Democratic ranks that resulted, seemed to open the way for a Progressive victory in 1914 if proper advantage were taken of it.

As the campaign drew near, the Republicans began to show signs that they thoroughly appreciated this situation. Harvey D. Hinman, of Binghamton, who had been one of the supporters of Governor Hughes in the primary fight that brought Colonel Roosevelt back into politics in 1910, let it be known that he would be glad to have the nomination for the governorship that year. He had been a steady supporter of Colonel Roosevelt up to the split of 1912, and the Colonel believed he would make a first-class Governor of New York. So Mr. Roosevelt began to sound out Progressive opinion in the State as to the feasibility of putting Hinman up in our primaries for the nomination for the governorship.

The proposition met with a sulky and unwelcome reception, but in the end it was accepted. The Colonel had a conference with Hinman, and thought that an understanding had been reached which made such a move by the Progressives practicable.

But it was soon made clear that Hinman would have vigorous opposition in the Republican ranks for the gubernatorial nomination, and it was by no means certain that he could win at the primaries. Thus it became extremely important to know, before he was put into the Progressive primaries, what he would do in case he won the Progressive, but lost the Republican, nomination.

Colonel Roosevelt asked me to go to Binghamton and talk this point over with Hinman, and I did so. He was loath at first to give an unambiguous answer to the question, and we discussed the possibilities for some time. I pointed out, very frankly, the situation in the Progressive organization. He knew, of course, and without my telling him so, that there was a reluctance on the part of a good many Progressives to follow Colonel Roosevelt in this plan, but we had had sufficient assurances of support, at headquarters, so that I was able to say, with confidence, that I was sure he could carry the Progressive primaries.

But in case he did that and lost the Republican nomination, would he then go through the campaign as the Progressive nominee or would he drop out of the race altogether? At length he decided that he would drop out, which was equivalent, of course, to saying that he would not run in the Progressive primaries. And, of course, under those circumstances, we would not have him run in our primaries.

So the Colonel's hopeful plan was defeated, and we went into a campaign of our own, in which Colonel Roosevelt was again dragged into service by the repetition of exactly the same argument that had taken him in in 1910 and 1912. The Progressive State Convention named for the governorship Frederick M. Davenport, the man to whom Colonel Roosevelt sent his telegram from Boston, in 1910, declaring his readiness to support the Hinman-Greene Primary Bill. Davenport accepted the nomination only on condition that Colonel Roosevelt should campaign the

State for him, and, in fulfillment of his promise to do that, Colonel Roosevelt barnstormed the State with Davenport, in an automobile, speaking at crossroads and country towns, and working very much as if he were a candidate for township supervisor. It was obvious that the Progressive Party was near its end.

That year the Colonel campaigned also for Progressive candidates in several other States, going as far west as Kansas, where he made speeches for Henry J. Allen, who was running for the governorship. He spoke also in Illinois, where Raymond Robins was running for the United States Senate; in Ohio, where James R. Garfield and Arthur Garford were campaigning for the senatorship and governorship; and in Pennsylvania, where Gifford Pinchot was running against Boies Penrose for the senatorship. In other States also the Colonel did what he could for Progressive candidates, although he knew very well all the time that it was a losing battle for a lost cause.

LXXIX

On a trip by automobile from Wichita to Hutchinson, Kansas, that fall, the Colonel came exceedingly close to death at a grade crossing. There had been an early meeting at Wichita, and we were driving across to Hutchinson for an evening meeting. The Wichita agent for a high-powered car was taking us over in a new machine. Hutchinson is north and west of Wichita, and the railroad between them makes a fairly straight line. The highway, instead of making all its westing at once, and then its northing, follows the railroad, and zigzags across it continually. It seemed to me that we crossed that track twenty times, and perhaps more. All were grade crossings, and some of them were as thoroughly screened from the railroad as if that had been the purpose.

We approached one such crossing going about thirty miles an hour or more. We were headed west, and to the north of the road there was a high willow hedge which completely shut the railroad out of sight from the car. The Colonel was sitting in the right-hand rear seat of the open car, singing softly to himself, and keeping time by pounding on the side of the car in front of him with his right hand. I. R. Kirkwood, of the Kansas City 'Star,' and I occupied the two small seats, in front of the Colonel. I think the man seated with the Colonel was Victor Murdock, but my recollection is not clear. Allen was campaigning in another part of the State and was not with us.

The railroad at that point carries a slight grade, down which a passenger train was sliding noiselessly, with steam shut off and no whistle blowing or bell ringing. Neither engineer nor fireman did a thing to attract attention, but slid down on that grade crossing as stealthily as if they were stalking deer. We came on the crossing without slowing down, and did not see the train until we reached the ditch beside the track. Then everybody, at the same instant, saw that engine looming over us. I never saw so large a locomotive before or since.

Our driver reached at first for his emergency brake, but, even as he started to set it, he saw that it was too late. He threw it open again and stepped on his accelerator. The big car shot forward in instant response, and we went over the track just barely ahead of the locomotive. It was so close that it seemed as if the Colonel could almost have touched its pilot from where he sat.

On free of the track we shot, with the big new car showing what speed it could make when pushed, and the Colonel going right on with his song, steadily beating time with his right hand, absolutely unmoved. He did not deviate one particle from what he had been doing, nor did he utter a word about it afterward. Kirkwood leaned over to me and muttered an imprecation on both the engineer and the driver of our car, that came from the depths of his heart. But that was all. I never heard Colonel Roosevelt make any comment whatever on the incident. His silence emphasized with me what he had said, after he had been shot at Milwaukee, about his rule of life. There was nothing he could do, sitting where he did in that automobile, and so he just went right on with his song.

During the campaigning that the Colonel did that fall, I traveled with him most of the time, looking out for the transportation and other arrangements, serving as a sort of combination secretary and courier. That put me, naturally, with him a good deal of the time, and gave op-

portunity for more talk with him than I had had since
the days when he was in the White House and I was
the 'Times' correspondent in Washington. We talked, of
course, of many things besides politics, although the
history and fate of the Progressive Party occupied its
share of the time.

The special train, or private car, stage of Progressive
campaigning was long gone by that time. The Colonel always had a stateroom or drawing-room for himself, and I
had other accommodation in the same car. We usually had
our meals together in the dining-car. He was an eager and
valiant trencherman, and I saw how it was that he had
more than two inches of flesh and fat over his ribs for the
lunatic's bullet to go through. He drank great quantities
of milk, but not much of anything else. I have seen him
eat a whole chicken and drink four large glasses of milk at
one meal, and chicken and milk were by no means the only
things served.

One day at noon, or perhaps it was a morning meeting,
he spoke at Centralia, Illinois, in behalf of Raymond
Robins. The crowd was composed largely of miners, and
the Colonel made a special appeal to them, because
Robins had been a miner, and had dug his fortune out of
the earth in Alaska. The Colonel's text that morning was
'Let the People Rule,' and he spoke with unusual earnestness and force, making an obviously strong impression on
his audience.

That afternoon we went up to Peoria for an evening
meeting. The Colonel always had a great deal of reading
matter with him, which he supplemented along the way
by buying all the new magazines. The character of magazine did not seem to make any difference to him. He took
'high-brow' and 'cheap-trash' with equal eagerness. I

have seen him again and again read a magazine from cover
to cover, everything in it, special articles, poetry, stories,
and all. And as he read he would tear out the finished
page and throw it on the floor, just as he did the pages of
his manuscript when delivering a speech.

On the way up to Peoria we fell into conversation, and
began talking about the Centralia meeting. He had
brought something into that speech about his favorite
theme of the size of families. That afternoon he began to
talk again on that subject.

'Well, Colonel,' I said, 'did it ever strike you that it
isn't quite fair for you to bear down so heavily on that
subject with such an audience?'

'What do you mean?' he demanded.

'Simply this,' I replied. 'Never in your life have you
had to give an instant's thought to the most important
question that comes to every one of those men, every day.
The thing that is right in front of them, morning, noon,
and night, is the question of where and how their families
are going to be housed, fed, and clothed. But, all your life,
you have been so situated that that question has never
given you one moment's anxiety.'

'By George, O. K.,' he replied, 'that's so, and I never
thought of it.'

He was silent for some time after that, but then he came
back to the discussion, saying that in future, when he referred to that subject, he should take into consideration
the point I had raised. It did not, in his judgment, alter
the obligation of every citizen toward the State, which was
always the main point that he desired to present, but it
was, plainly, right that each man's own circumstances
should be considered.

LXXX

LATER in that same afternoon we started a battle that lasted almost up to the time of Colonel Roosevelt's death. The Centralia speech was under discussion again, and I said, bluntly:

'It was a great speech, Colonel, but most of it was bunk.'

'You traitor!' he exclaimed, shaking both fists at me. 'What was the matter with it?'

'The right of the people to rule is bunk,' I declared. 'They don't know enough to rule. They don't pay enough attention to their own affairs to have any right to govern the affairs of others. They won't see and they won't learn.'

That was enough, and more than enough, to start the Colonel going at any time on a long journey about the intelligence and inherent solidity of judgment of the American people. He knew political history in the United States more minutely than any other man I ever heard speak on the subject, and he brought up case after case that afternoon to show how wrong I was in my hasty and general accusation. I was no match for him, of course, in such an argument, but it greatly enlivened the trip up to Peoria. Moreover, I had had sufficient experience with him to know that I must stand by my guns and do the best I could for my side, or run a great risk of losing his respect very quickly and thoroughly. If he caught an opponent in debate 'lying down' because the debate was with him, that opponent was not likely to get another opportunity for discussion.

This particular discussion developed, just as I wanted it to do, into a running debate with the Colonel on the whole subject of the primary system, of which he was so great an advocate. I had been just as enthusiastic about it as he, but such things as had been happening in several States had made me believe that the primary was not, after all, the machine that its original advocates had thought it would bo. It wao not mooting tho ovilo of booo rulo and machine control that it had been designed to meet, and it was producing other evils of its own that were worse, in my judgment, than boss rule, for they were subversive of the principle of representative government on which this Nation was founded, and on which all our institutions are based.

At the election, that fall of 1914, several things happened which seemed to illustrate and emphasize my side of this contention with Colonel Roosevelt. So I wrote to him about them. This was his reply:

There is nothing you can say about the voters at this particular election that is not justified. There is no conceivable iniquity they did not joyfully support. But don't forget that Lincoln's statement was merely that you could not fool *all* of the people all the time. He explicitly admitted that you could fool all of the people part of the time — and this is a portion of that part of the time!

That was the election at which the voters in Ohio, for instance, adopted a constitutional amendment which put the saloon into the Constitution, and admitted it to every part of the State, although seventy-seven of the eighty-eight counties of the State voted dry under the local option law. It is that lack of the power of discrimination on the part of the mass of the people against which the system of representative government designed by the framers of the Constitution would forever safeguard the country.

I kept up this debate with Colonel Roosevelt on the primaries for several years, writing or speaking to him about every incident which came to my attention that illustrated my side. At length, in the fall of 1917, a political hack in New York obtained the Republican nomination for Mayor, over John Purroy Mitchel, in a ridiculous primary contest, where, obviously, very few persons voted who were not organization regulars. I wrote Colonel Roosevelt about that, saying that, in my judgment, no Republican convention could have been assembled in Greater New York which would have given the nomination to Bennett against Mayor Mitchel. I added that the primary is serviceable only when the people are aroused, so that they will use it. But it is always something else, and not the primary itself, that arouses them. It should be retained as a corrective agency whenever a convention goes wrong and does not truly represent the will of the party.

Then Colonel Roosevelt came around to my side, and the long debate was ended. Under date of November 10, 1917, he wrote me as follows:

DEAR O. K.:
You are quite right, and what you say applies not only to the direct primary, but to the initiative, referendum, and recall. They should all of them only be exceptional remedies. It should be possible to invoke them in exceptional cases to control the boss and the machines; but they simply do damage if habitually invoked.

It was while campaigning in the Middle West, on this trip, that Colonel Roosevelt told me about his serious illness in South America, and related one phase of it which I should not mention here if it were not for the fact that it was referred to, and inexactly, by William Roscoe Thayer, in his book about the Colonel. It had to do with the

Colonel's thought, at a time when his illness seemed likely to be fatal, of hastening the end by voluntary means. As Mr. Thayer presents it, the reason why the Colonel did not commit suicide was that he found he was likely to recover, and that all the party could get out. But the Colonel told it to me in quite a different way.

'I have always made it a practice on such trips,' he said, 'to take a bottle of morphine with me. Because one never knows what is going to happen, and I did not mean to be caught by some accident where I should have to die a lingering death. I always meant that, if at any time death became inevitable, I would have it over with at once, without going through a long-drawn-out agony from which death was the only relief.

'I have had a very full life, and am not at all afraid to die. As far as I, personally, am concerned, it would have meant nothing much, beyond the separation from my family, for that sickness in the jungle to terminate fatally. And when I found myself so ill that I was a drag on the party, and it began to look as if we could not all get out alive, I began to think it might be better for me to take my morphine and end it. I could not stand the thought that my illness was likely to keep Kermit in that jungle, too. His life was all before him. He was coming out to be married, and I could not endure the idea that because of my failure to keep up he might not make it, when without me he could.

'Then the other side of it came to me, and I saw that if I did end it, that would only make it more sure that Kermit would not get out. For I knew he would not abandon me, but would insist on bringing my body out, too. That, of course, would have been impossible. I knew his determination. So there was only one thing for me to do, and that was to come out myself. It was a hard fight, but I made it.'

Colonel Roosevelt told me that quite naturally, and, I believe, without any thought whatever of self-exploitation. I know he was often accused of bragging about himself and his deeds, but in all I ever had to do with him there was never anything of that apparent. When he told this he was talking about his South American trip, and this incident, when he fought out with himself the question of life and death and decided it in favor of some one else, came perfectly simply, and along with numerous others of only incidental interest.

I know it is not the kind of thing he would like to have mentioned in any book about him. But since a wholly wrong impression was conveyed by the version given by Mr. Thayer, it has seemed better to include it here.

LXXXI

THE World War was several weeks old when my campaign trips with Colonel Roosevelt began in the fall of 1914. The invasion of Belgium had occurred, and Bethmann-Holweg's cynical reference to the 'scrap of paper' was known to all the world. Colonel Roosevelt was stirred, to the bottom of his soul, by these events, and, for the first time since he had left Washington, he felt an eagerness to be again in the White House. Here was that 'job of work' to be done, not only for the American people, but for all the world, which it would have delighted him to undertake. Firmness, vigor, and decision, always his outstanding characteristics, were needed, so desperately, in this emergency, and he felt that only flabbiness and eloquent inaction were rendered.

He discussed the situation a great deal with me, as we traveled from town to town, where he had political meetings to make, and I knew that he believed it would have been comparatively easy and certain to prevent the outbreak of hostilities by right action at Washington. On one occasion I asked him pointedly how that could have been done.

'We could have taken action that would have delayed the formal declaration of war,' he replied. 'A few days was all that was necessary to bring about an international conference that would have prevented war, at least at that time. Of course, it might not have prevented it permanently, for the Kaiser and Germany seem bent on attacking France, and possibly England also. They seem to think that the time has come when Germany can conquer the world. It is the old Napoleonic idea again. If Germany — that is, the Kaiser and von Moltke and the army war lords — really believe that they can dominate the whole world, then nothing would permanently keep them from making the effort.

'But Grey — and the whole British influence — was exerting himself, to the limit, to postpone hostilities until a conference could be held, and some kind of an agreement could have been brought about, at such a conference, that would have prevented hostilities at this time. It needed only a few days more to force that kind of a conference on Germany. We certainly could have supplied those few days if Washington had cared to do so, or had known how. Cleveland would have done it, or McKinley. I should have felt myself a criminal, if I had been President, and had not done so.'

'But how?' I asked.

'There were two or three methods that might have been used,' the Colonel replied. 'Probably more. One would have been to make the direct demand for a conference, because of our own interests in preventing the invasion of Belgium. We are one of the signatories to the Hague Conventions, and that not only gives us a right to concern ourselves in such matters, but lays an obligation upon us to do so. But with this Administration the chief concern seems to be to keep out of anything that is connected with Europe. That is only an excess of caution, based upon a mistaken application of Washington's Farewell Address, which is used to cover up what is really the Administration's timidity.

'Another method, based on the same principle, would have been to telegraph all our diplomatic representatives abroad, directing them to call the attention of the Governments to which they were accredited to the very grave concern felt by the United States over the situation, that last week in July, because of our own obligations. The message should have stopped right there, and not given, even to our representatives, any intimation of what Washington regarded as our obligations.

'That would have compelled every one of the Governments directly concerned to hesitate, at least long enough to make up their own minds as to what we might conceive to be our obligations under the circumstances. The necessary result was bound to be the few days of delay that Grey so desperately needed in order to bring about his conference. The Kaiser's haste in declaring war shows that he recognized the fact that, if he did not begin hostilities at once, he would be prevented from doing so. But if he had received the impression, in some such way as I have indicated, that, if he forced hostilities, he might have to reckon with us, as well as with Russia and France, he would certainly have agreed to a postponement, at least until Germany had been able to make new combinations to deal with the new situation created by our appearance on the scene.

'But what could be expected from an Administration that has at its head a college professor who has never had anything but an academic interest in foreign affairs, and a Secretary of State who knows nothing but ward politics and crack-brained economics? The United States lost the greatest opportunity it has ever had; Mr. Wilson has missed the chance of making himself immortal, and the world is embarked upon an absolutely unparalleled disaster. All because of crass incompetency in our Government.

'It's a pity we couldn't have had a man like Richard Olney, or John Hay, or Elihu Root in the State Department, or a man in the White House who would not have hesitated rightly to place the interest of the whole world ahead of dogmatic and futile devotion to an interpretation of a tradition that the originator of it would have been the first to scorn.'

About this time, while we were traveling in the Middle West, I received a telegram from New York headquarters saying that a delegation of Belgians, who had come to the United States in behalf of their country, was anxious to meet Colonel Roosevelt and have a conference with him. I was instructed to see if such a conference could be arranged. When I asked the Colonel about it, he replied, at once, that he would be glad to see the Belgians, but only in his individual and personal capacity, and only on condition that no publicity whatever was attached to the interview. He explained that he regarded it as his duty to do all that he could, publicly, to support the Administration. Personally he had no sympathy with the policy it was pursuing. There could be no neutrality, to his mind, between right and wrong. He felt our duty to be very clear, and, if the responsibility were his, he would undertake the performance of it without the least delay, even if it should mean our entry into the war. The American people would eagerly respond to the right kind of a call upon them, he was certain.

But he thought it the duty of every faithful American to support the Administration publicly, because it was of paramount importance that nothing should occur, at that juncture, to give the world the impression that the Americans were divided. Consequently, he could not consent to meet the Belgians publicly, or to have any publicity about such a meeting. But he was very keen to see them privately, and to hear all they had to report about conditions in Europe.

So I telegraphed the Hollenden Hotel, in Cleveland, reserving a suite there for the following Sunday morning. I also wired New York headquarters to advise the Belgian delegation of the time and conditions of the conference, and got in touch with James R. Garfield, with whom the Colonel had planned to spend that day, and invited him to join us on our arrival in Cleveland that morning. We were all to have breakfast in the Colonel's suite.

The Belgians promptly accepted the Colonel's arrangements and met us at the Hollenden soon after our arrival. There were three of them. Baron de Cartier was one, and the names of the other two I do not recall. The conversation was in French, which I do not understand, but both the Colonel and Mr. Garfield did. As they reported it to me afterward, the Belgians went over a long list of the crimes and outrages committed by Germans in Belgium, and when, subsequently, Lord Bryce issued his report on German atrocities, I recognized a good deal of what this delegation had told Colonel Roosevelt.

The conference lasted two or three hours, and, when the Belgians left, they were profuse in their expressions of thanks to Colonel Roosevelt for having received and heard them. It was not so very long after that the Colonel was making vigorous public use of the information thus brought to him.

LXXXII

THAT campaign trip ended with a night meeting at Philadelphia, in behalf of the Progressive fight generally, but with special emphasis on the contest for the senatorship between Gifford Pinchot, the Progressive nominee, and Boies Penrose, the high priest of the Old Guard. Colonel Roosevelt told me to secure accommodations for him on the train leaving Philadelphia at ten o'clock that night, as he meant to motor out to Sagamore, on arrival at New York. He was going home to rest, and he wanted to get there as quickly as possible.

The Philadelphia committee offered to look out for the transportation, and I accepted the tickets they gave me without question, having explained to them just what the Colonel wanted. But when we got down to the car we were surprised to find that we were on the midnight train. Colonel Roosevelt was much excited, for he had set his mind on getting to Sagamore that night. Some of the Philadelphians attempted to argue him out of it, saying that he would be much more comfortable on the midnight train, and would have a full night's sleep before reaching New York. But I knew what he wanted, and got in touch with some of the railroad men, who quickly effected a transfer so that we had a stateroom on the ten o'clock train.

The Colonel was in a talkative mood that night. He spent only a little time reading, and, most of the way back to New York, was discussing one phase or another of the campaign. He disclosed very clearly his feeling about much of the work that he had been called upon to do, and that feeling was very close to disgust. No one knew better than he the utter futility of it. He saw perfectly the effect of it upon himself and his own following. The crowds everywhere had been just as large and enthusiastic as ever, but it was inescapable that their enthusiasm was only for him, and not at all for those for whom he was asking them to vote. That situation always made Colonel Roosevelt decidedly blue. He felt that he was losing his influence with the American people, just at the very time when he most wanted it. For he had in mind an attempt to rouse them to an active sense of their duty in Europe, and he was more eager and keen about it than he had ever been about anything where he himself was concerned or would benefit.

It was the first time I had seen the Colonel in that mood, and it made a lasting impression on me. Afterward I saw it repeatedly, for it was a long time before the campaign, on which he embarked right after the election of 1914, began to show results in aroused public sentiment. And the longer that response was delayed, the bluer the Colonel became, and the more certain that he had lost his following among the people.

We were getting near to New York City that night when the Colonel leaned over and whacked me on the knee with his hand.

'Well, O. K.,' he said, 'I've got only a few hours more of this campaign, and then I shall be through. I'll be out of politics then for good and all, and I'll be a free man. I shall have paid every political obligation that I owe to anybody anywhere. I have done a great deal of foolish and useless work this fall, but, after all, it has been worth while from one point of view. It has paid all my debts. Hereafter no man can claim anything from me in politics. Not a single obligation is left. I have done everything, this fall, that everybody has wanted. This election makes me an absolutely free man. Thereafter I am going to say and do just what I damned please.'

That was one of the very few times I ever heard Colonel Roosevelt use the big D, and the emphasis with which he uttered it showed how thoroughly he meant it. I was glad to hear him say that. The performances of that campaign had made no appeal whatever to me. I had seen him, so often and so long, subordinate his judgment and his political skill and acumen to that of others far less able, that it had become wearisome to the utmost. Some of us at headquarters had been begging him, for months, to stop it, and to act only on his own judgment, which was admittedly the best of all in that organization. But he had stuck, religiously, to his old habit of answering the calls from those who felt that he was under some obligation to them. So he had gone through that soul-wearing campaign to the end, always cheerful in public, always with his head high, and with all his old appearance of confidence and with unshaken determination. Now he let me see the prize for which he had worked.

The Progressive Party died, intestate, with the campaign of 1914. It had little or nothing to devise, practically all of its assets having been appropriated, during its brief lifetime, by one of the other, or both, of the old parties. Its fate recalled to me an interview I had had with Senator John T. Morgan, of Alabama, nine years earlier. I was then in the Washington Bureau of the New York 'Times,' and went to the Senator seeking his views, as a political actuary, regarding the probabilities of life of the new Independence League, which William Randolph Hearst had just launched in New York.

'Young man,' said Senator Morgan, 'how many new political parties do you suppose I have seen started in my time? I don't know, but they are a great — a great many.

'And where are they now? Their history is a travesty upon the political ingenuity of their inventors.'

LXXXIII

FOR a long time Colonel Roosevelt had been writing magazine articles to increase his income. He needed the money, and his earnings from that work were large. He said to me once with a grin of good-humor:

'Let me give you one piece of good advice, O. K. Never have a daughter married, get shot, and prosecute a libel suit all in one year. They're all very expensive proceedings.'

The articles which the Colonel produced before the 1914 election did not give much promise of what was to follow. But no sooner had he been set free of political obligations than he embarked upon the course in which, I believe, he did the greatest work, and performed the greatest service, of all his life. Then it was that he started upon that campaign for unadulterated and unhyphenated Americanism on the part of all American citizens, that brought this country to the stage of mental preparedness in which the amazing solidarity that was achieved here, during our own part in the war, was possible.

But when it began, it brought to Colonel Roosevelt very little besides criticism and objection from sources which ought to have been among the first to support and applaud. Several times, during that period, when I saw him, he seemed as near despair as Theodore Roosevelt could come. Many of his old, tried friends gave him their customary eager support. But he knew he could rely on that always, and in this emergency it did not seem to count much with him. He felt, with all the intensity of his intense spirit, the paramount necessity of a great stirring of the soul in the

United States. He despised and hated the course of the Administration, and Mr. Wilson's success in leading the American people against what Colonel Roosevelt felt to be right, honest, and courageous brought him almost to the point of embittered desperation.

In 1915, Colonel Roosevelt gave an interview to Julian Street, in which he discussed this peculiar psychology of the American people. He pointed out how smooth and eloquent leadership, with plausible phrases, could induce them to put aside the thing they knew they ought to do and satisfy their national conscience with the soft words and excuses of the leader. But, on the other hand, under direct and forceful leadership they would rise with enthusiasm and eagerness to do the thing they knew was right.

But with real Roosevelt determination he battled on in the course he had marked out for himself. And gradually the effect began to appear. I was in China during 1915, and my only contact with the Colonel was the extremely remote one of correspondence halfway around the world. When we got the news, in Peking, of the sinking of the Lusitania, it did seem that, at length, the United States would assert itself. Then came the first note, and its reply, and the second note. With a missionary friend I was making a trip through northern Chih-li Province. We were cut off from all news, even from the part of the world where we were, for more than three weeks. On the way we talked out our duty in the war, and both decided that if, when we reached a point where we could get the news, we found that the United States had gone in, we should both come home, at once, to join up in any capacity we could. But when we got to Jehol, the missionary on whom we called told us that there had only been more note-writing.

Afterward, when I got home in the early part of 1916, I learned, from friends and from the Colonel himself, that that had been about the blackest period of his life. He felt that he had lost his influence among the American people, and that all his efforts had been well-nigh useless. Still he did not give up.

LXXXIV

THAT year saw another presidential campaign. The remnant of the old Progressive organization, which had been held together at New York largely through the influence of George W. Perkins, prepared to go into that contest with an earnest effort to force the Republicans to name Colonel Roosevelt for their candidate. That was a time when the Colonel would have grasped, with the utmost eagerness, the opportunity to direct the affairs of the Nation. There was the real job of work for him to do.

But the bitterness of 1912 seemed an insuperable obstacle in the way of his obtaining the Republican nomination. The country had been reacting to his preaching about our duty in the war more favorably than he himself appreciated, and there was much wider support for his nomination by the Republicans than he thought or the Republicans themselves realized. It was evident to the Progressives in New York that the joint Republican and Progressive nomination of Roosevelt would ensure his overwhelming election. But it required very little contact with the Old Guard leaders, who were still in control of the Republican organization, to know that only extraordinary strategy and tactics would bring about the desired result.

The first thing determined upon was to hold a Progressive National Convention at the same time that the Republican Convention was held, and in the same city. This would serve two purposes. It would keep the Republicans in ignorance as to the real Progressive intentions, and might make them believe that the Colonel would accept another Progressive nomination, which they knew would be tantamount to ensuring the reëlection of President Wilson. So that was done, and a good many sincere Progressives were sadly misled by it, because they came to Chicago singing, and with hearts all aglow, ready to do battle again with the old enemy under the inspiring leadership of Colonel Roosevelt.

But the Colonel never had the slightest intention of taking another third-party nomination. He was through with every kind of personal politics, unless, indeed, he might have the nomination of both the Republican and Progressive organizations, which would have been practically certain to mean his election. For there was such disaffection with Wilson in the country, and even in his own party, that there was more than a fair chance that any Republican nominee, unless there were a third ticket, would defeat him.

When the two conventions met in Chicago, there was an immediate and determined demand from the Progressives for the nomination of Colonel Roosevelt, regardless of what the Republicans might do. But the strategists in control held back, in the hope that, by negotiation, a joint nomination of the Colonel could be brought about.

The Progressives, however, were fatally weakened in a way for which there was no defense. The Republicans had information, on which they knew they could rely, that Colonel Roosevelt would not under any circumstances head another third ticket. That was all they needed to defeat him in their own convention. The Republican leaders had that information from sources so close to Colonel Roosevelt himself that it could not be denied. That was a situation which the Progressives could not meet. No bluff would work against such an inside revelation of the facts.

The persons who furnished that information to the Republican leaders of the 1916 convention have themselves to thank for its failure to nominate Colonel Roosevelt. They are entitled to all the satisfaction they can derive from the subsequent events, including the Treaty of Versailles, with its League of Nations Covenant, and the succeeding years of unsuccessful effort to bring about real peace in Europe.

So the negotiations, which carried with them all the hopes of the Progressives, failed. The Republican Convention nominated Charles E. Hughes, then an Associate Justice of the Supreme Court, by appointment of President Taft. Mr. Hughes, no doubt, could have brought about the nomination of Colonel Roosevelt if he had been so disposed. But the chance had come to him at last to obtain a presidential nomination for himself, in precisely the doctrinaire method to which he had always been devoted, and he was sufficiently human not to pass it by.

When Mr. Hughes made his first canvass for the governorship of New York, he was an active and hard-hitting, aggressive foeman on the stump. That quality in him was even strengthened by his first term, so that when he ran for reëlection in 1908, and at the same time campaigned for Taft, he was one of the most effective of the Republican speakers. That was the time when the late James Creelman described him as an 'animated feather duster,' in humorous allusion to his vivacity and his beard. But six years on the bench of the Supreme Court had deanimated, dehydrated, and almost dehumanized him. He had become an automatic dry-as-dust law machine, immensely valuable, unquestionably, on the bench, but practically worthless as a leader in a great political campaign, especially when such issues were to be met as those of 1916, which demanded, above everything else, vision, determination, and outspoken courage.

All through the days of waiting, the weary and apprehensive Progressives had been singing a mournful chant:

> Why not, why not,
> Why not nominate now?

With Hughes nominated by the Republicans, the Progressives broke their leash at last, and named their idol in one great shout. Then they nominated Colonel John M. Parker, of Louisiana, for the vice-presidency, and adjourned. The most militant of them, and the still evident 'lunatic fringe,' were enthusiastic over the fight they thought in prospect, but there were many sorely disappointed by the failure to bring about the joint nomination.

Colonel Roosevelt responded to the Progressive nomination with a determined telegram absolutely refusing to be considered as the candidate, and urging endorsement of Hughes. Colonel Parker refused to withdraw, and the Progressives faced the extraordinary situation of having their candidate urge them to endorse the nominee of another party which had another candidate for the vice-presidency.

A meeting of the Progressive National Committee was called, in Chicago, to fill the vacancy caused by Colonel Roosevelt's declination. The Colonel put himself vigorously into the effort to obtain the Progressive endorsement of Hughes, and, after an all-day fight in the committee, that was accomplished by a divided vote. Five or six of the National Committeemen declined to go with the majority, and turned, later, to the support of Wilson. Then the Colonel went into the campaign and delivered several speeches for Hughes. But they were not much to the liking of the Republican candidate, for they lacked nothing of that vigor and virility in attack upon Wilson and his Administration which Mr. Hughes never brought himself to show.

It was in this campaign that Colonel Roosevelt said, referring to Mr. Wilson's action in Mexico, 'He kissed the blood-stained hand that slapped his face.' In another speech, referring to the Secretary of War, he said, 'Nice Mr. Baker, he knits.'

There was nothing of that sort in Mr. Hughes's campaign, or, in fact, much of anything else. At the start of the campaign, the feeling against Wilson, all over the country, was so strong that, if the election had been held then, Mr. Hughes would have won by a large majority. But week after week, as he went about the country, delivering his lackadaisical and legalistic addresses, he steadily won votes for his opponent.

At the same time he demonstrated a complete lack of whatever political ability he had once possessed. Immediately after he had accepted the endorsement of the Progressives, several conferences were had with him by leaders of the Progressive movement. Their object was to inform Mr. Hughes, thoroughly, of all the spots where there was lingering soreness because of the 1912 fight. An extensive campaign trip was planned for him, which was to take him clear to the Pacific Coast. He was warned, especially, with regard to California, where for six years Governor Johnson, at the head of the Progressives, had annually defeated the Old Guard. Johnson was clearly and by far the strongest man, politically, in that State. Johnson's close friend, Chester Rowell, had a long conference with Hughes, at which the California situation was all talked over and explained.

Progressive headquarters proposed that one man from each side should accompany Mr. Hughes on this trip, for the sole purpose of being on hand whenever he entered disturbed territory, to give him information as to the situation there, and particularly to see that both sides were represented on the committees and delegations received by him. But this intensely practical proposition was ignored. Mr. Hughes went West in complete disregard of the still active dissatisfaction on both Progressive and Republican sides, and instead of doing everything he could to mollify it, seemed to be actuated by a desire to increase it.

When he reached California, he put the cap permanently on the climax. An extraordinary situation had developed in that State from the fact that Governor Johnson was running, in the Republican primaries, for the nomination for United States Senator. He was calling earnestly on every element of his old support for assistance in that fight. At the same time he was endeavoring to develop support for Mr. Hughes. Obviously, the only argument he could use with his old following was that Hughes was a Progressive, and that he was supporting the ex-Justice on that account. But Hughes, having declined or ignored the offer of a joint committee to accompany him through the State, proceeded to align himself openly with the faction that Johnson had beaten every year for six years. And, as if that were not enough, Mr. Hughes publicly greeted the leader of this oft-beaten faction as 'California's favorite son.'

By his own actions in California, Mr. Hughes created a situation in which it was absolutely impossible for Governor Johnson to help him. After the election, when the count of the votes showed that Wilson had carried the State by a

few thousand, and Johnson had been elected Senator by
something like 300,000, the Old Guard set up the howl that
Johnson had 'knifed' Hughes, or sold him out, or contrived
by some other kind of trickery to beat him. But the fact is
that it was Hughes who gave California to Wilson. And so
he prolonged the disaster to his party, to the origin of which
he had contributed so unskillfully in 1907–08.

Colonel Roosevelt fought as valiantly for Hughes as he
could. He put everything he knew or had into the campaign. Wilson alone he might have beaten. But it was
impossible to defeat the combination of Wilson and Hughes.

LXXXV

BEFORE Mr. Wilson, who had been reëlected by the slender majority that Mr. Hughes won for him in California,
had delivered his second inaugural address, it was evident
to all the world that he was about to be forced, at length,
to take the United States into the war. With characteristic German blundering, Berlin contributed to hasten the
time, and the break came when Mr. Wilson still had a
month of his first term to serve.

Colonel Roosevelt had been going straight ahead with
his own campaign for an aroused public opinion in the
United States with regard to the war and our duty in it,
and for an unadulterated Americanism. He was clearly
reaping the reward of his long effort, and there was again
an open turning to him everywhere. As he saw our own
entry into the war drawing nearer, he made all preparations for active personal participation in it. He planned to
raise a division of volunteers, mainly among the men of the
West, who would have much of the same zest for a fight
that had distinguished his Rough Riders in the war with
Spain. He had selected, from among his wide acquaintance
in the army, the men he wanted to officer the division, and
on paper he was practically ready, when President Wilson
called Congress in special session on April 2, 1917, and
asked for a declaration of war.

By the time we were actually in the war, the Colonel's
offer of a division of volunteers had gone to Washington.
Then he waited for action. It had been his plan, at the
start, to have command of the division himself. But he
modified that plan, I think before his offer was submitted,

so as to provide for a division commander from the regular army. In the modified plan he was to have one of the brigades of the division. He seemed to think that might make the plan more acceptable, or at least less objectionable, to the Administration.

I saw Colonel Roosevelt, at the Harvard Club in New York, within a day or two after he had received the information that his offer was to be refused. I never saw him in a blacker mood. He felt that his proposal was equivalent to an offer of his life, for he knew the sort of fighting that was going on in the trenches in France and Belgium, and he had not the least expectation of coming back, if he were permitted to go over. He felt that an offer of that kind was entitled, no matter from whom it came, to courteous consideration, and he had not received that. He was angered to the core. At the same time he had received some intimation that made him think that the service of his four sons also was to be refused. His bitterness at that was inexpressible.

The refusal of his offer of a division was only what I had expected, and what, it seemed to me, he also must have expected, if he were not so keenly interested in it as to becloud his otherwise exceptionally clear vision. For he knew, of course, of the supreme effort that the regular army was making to get away from the volunteer system, which had wrought disaster to the country in every war we had ever fought, from the time of George Washington down.

It happened that the fight for the draft law was partly in the hands, in Washington, of General Enoch H. Crowder, who knew Colonel Roosevelt well, and was able to understand very thoroughly the Colonel's motives in making the offer. General Crowder sympathized warmly with the Colonel's desire for active service. He wanted it earnestly himself. But he regarded the acceptance of a volunteer division as a fatal error, and as liable utterly to defeat the enactment of a draft law. Crowder favored, in fact, an adult service law, on lines somewhat similar to those followed in Germany, by which the whole population became subject to service, whether in the army, or at work in the production of such supplies as might be found to be necessary, either for fighting the war or for the continuation of our industries and the general support of the people. The General believed that it was a time when horse-racing and other sports, for instance, and such unnecessary features of our usual life, should be eliminated, and the energy that went into them devoted to winning the war. He was firmly of the opinion that the acceptance of a volunteer division from Colonel Roosevelt, even though the men in it were all over thirty-five years of age, and so beyond the limits likely to be fixed by the draft law, would be subversive of the principle of the draft law, and would work, in the end, to the detriment of our national interests. With all his might and influence, therefore, he opposed acceptance of the Colonel's offer.

But logical and well defended though it might be, for Colonel Roosevelt that refusal to permit him to undertake active service was a blow from the bitterness of which he never recovered. He threw himself into the one kind of service still open to him, and from which the Administration had no power to stop him, that of encouraging the American people to fight the war with all their might. Despite his flagging physical energy and his increasing ailments, he kept sounding that note with all the force he had. And he lived to see again general recognition of the sanity, the courage, and the truth of his leadership.

LXXXVI

THE test of success in art is the ability of the painter to present the thing which he sees so surely that others will see it as he does. I have written this book with no thought of anything but the effort to present the Theodore Roosevelt I knew in such a way that others also may see him as I saw him. My own mental picture of him is perfectly clear and convincing. As I see him, he followed, from the day I first knew him to the end of his life, a thoroughly consistent course. His chief characteristics were vision, courage, decision, instant readiness for action, the simplest honesty and the most wholesome sanity. His mental engine ran at a higher speed than that of any other man I have ever known. His foresight was uncanny. His sympathy was so quick, his emotion so intensely human, that he penetrated the feelings of others often as if by magic. His sense of humor was a keen and never-failing delight. And he was as clean-minded as a girl.

These are the causes of his popularity. They are the essential qualifications of leadership and the unfailing sources of political strength. To me it is a cause of never-ending wonderment that men who aspire to political influence and power do not see and follow in Theodore Roosevelt's path.

Many men in the United States to-day profess to be 'Roosevelt men.' But very few of them are really like Roosevelt, or seem to try to be. Leonard Wood, for instance, made his campaign for the Republican presidential nomination in 1920, largely on the plea that he was a 'Roosevelt man.' If he meant merely that he was a friend

of Colonel Roosevelt, that could not be denied. But when
he had the opportunity to show himself, in a test, he did
not measure up, and his action indicated that he had failed
to observe one of the outstanding features of the Colonel's
public course. There was a riot at Omaha, and General
Wood boarded a train at Chicago, went to Omaha, and
did a first-class piece of work in restoring order. That was
like Roosevelt. But unlike Roosevelt, Wood stopped
there. It was a double opportunity that Omaha furnished
General Wood. One was the restoration of order, and the
other was the driving home, to the American people, of a lesson they sadly need to learn. That is, that the first duty of
organized government is the protection of life and property,
and that it should be performed always and at all hazards
and costs. Wood had not a word to say on that subject.
Roosevelt would have sent a message flaming across the
country that would have burned its way imperishably into
every mind.

Being a 'Roosevelt man' is something very much more
than merely proclaiming his greatness and wishing he were
back again. There are plenty of men now in the Roosevelt
Memorial Association who were loud in their denunciation
of him in 1912. It is an easy rising band-wagon now, and
occupancy of a place on the front seat helps to conceal
earlier actions that were decidedly different.

Many suggestions have been made for memorials to
Theodore Roosevelt. None that has come to my notice
seems, to me, to disclose consideration of a factor that, in
my judgment, is fundamental and should be controlling.
That is, whether or not they represent anything in which
Colonel Roosevelt was actively interested; whether their
central idea is one to which he was sympathetic; whether,
in fact, they are really representative of the force and

spirit they are, or should be, designed to keep alive. So far as I know, they all propose the establishment of public parks, the naming of mountains or rivers after him, the building of monumental piles of brick and stone, and all that sort of thing which, I know, he regarded chiefly as waste and rubbish.

Why not erect a memorial to him through which his shining soul would go on, for all time, illuminating the path that he, more than any one else, opened between the East and West? We know that he regarded the Panama Canal as his greatest achievement; why not set, at each end of the Canal, a great pair of Roosevelt lights, marking and safeguarding the pathway for that ever-increasing commerce between the nations and that growing contact between the peoples of the world which steadily advance civilization, promote peace, and enure to the lasting benefit of all humanity?

Theodore Roosevelt's vision, courage, and decision made the Panama Canal a modern fact out of an age-long dream. How appropriate such a memorial would be, how representative of what he was, and how symbolic to all the world!

It is an interesting fact that Englishmen often have clearer vision and more certain perspective about prominent Americans than Americans themselves have. It was an English friend of Colonel Roosevelt, Sir George Trevelyan, who gave us one of the best pictures of the War of the Revolution ever produced. It was Colonel Henderson, a British soldier and military instructor, who wrote the real story of Stonewall Jackson, and gave both North and South the truth about some of the most important phases of the Civil War.

It was a British poet, Rudyard Kipling, who penned,

in the first wave of world-wide mourning at the news of the passing of Colonel Roosevelt, that immortal analysis of the true Roosevelt character and psychology, called 'Greatheart.' It may not be great poetry, but, none the less, it is a great poem, for it is marked by understanding and truth, and will never be excelled in accurate delineation of its subject.

Popularity has become the fetish of men in public life. They seek it now in every breath of popular sentiment. They bend to every ripple from any nook of their districts. Right for right's sake, alone, regardless of consequences, has almost ceased to be a motivating influence with them. Yet they prate about being 'Roosevelt men.'

The failure of present-day public men to grasp the fundamentals of popular leadership made clear by Theodore Roosevelt is the astonishing feature of American politics to-day.

'And our world is none the braver, since Greatheart was ta'en.'

THE END

INDEX

Ade, George, 344.

Adee, 'Old,' 142, 143, 144.

Aguinaldo, Emilio, 20, 21, 25.

Aldrich, Nelson W., Senator, 164, 168, 170, 203, 240, 242.

Allen, Henry J., 311, 426.

Anderson, General Thomas, 7.

André, Edouard, 11.

Araneta, Minister of Justice, 21.

Associated Press, 141, 202, 208, 334.

Asylum, our special, 404.

Balanced campaign, 345, 404.

Ballinger, Richard A., 126, 180, 181.

Ballinger-Pinchot Controversy, 180, 185.

Barnes, William, 192.

Barry, David S., 1, 2.

Bass, Governor, 227.

'Before April 9th' men, 280.

Bevan, Dr. Arthur, 388, 393.

Beveridge, Albert J., Senator, 169, 231, 232, 325, 331, 333, 366, 367, 394, 396, 400, 411.

Bi-partisan politics, 342.

Bishop, Joseph Bucklin, 355.

Boardman, Miss Mabel, 127.

Bonaparte, Charles J., 37.

Borah, William E., Senator, Prosecutor of Haywood, 34; victim of crooked indictment, 35; an eloquent outburst, 41; and Taft Platform, 1908, 74; action on Knox resignation, 187; proposes general primary, 253; action as National Committeeman, 287; sees Roosevelt about Cummins, 304.

Bristow, J. L., Senator, 169, 300, 301.

British at Manila, 17.

Bryan, William J., 25, 102, 110, 111, 316, 318.

Buencamino, Minister of Public Works, 24.

Bullene, Fred, 271.

Bullock, Seth, 165, 386.

Burgos, Marti, 22.

Burkett, Senator, 221.

Canadian reciprocity, 241.

Cannon, 'Uncle Joe,' 161, 164, 165, 168, 174, 185, 194, 240, 241.

Carey, Governor, 347.

Carpenter, Fred W., 157, 162, 178, 184.

Chichester, Captain, 14, 17, 18.

Clark, Champ, 241, 316.

Cleveland, President, 144.

Cochems, Henry, 350, 356, 374, 378, 381, 389, 399.

Coghlan, Captain J. B., 10, 13, 16.

Colby, Bainbridge, 287, 291.

Cooper, Henry A., 369, 371.

Corbin, General Henry C., 107, 108.

Cortelyou, George B., 300, 301.

Courier-Journal, Louisville, 344.

Coxe, George B., 99.

Crane, W. Murray, Senator, 65, 100, 170, 187, 189.

Credentials Committee, 299, 311.

Creelman, James, 450.

Cromwell, William Nelson, 122.

Crowder, General E. H., 456.

Cummins, Albert B., Senator, 304.

Curry, George, 27.

Curtis, Lucius, 202.

Curtis, Sumner, 77, 78, 142.

Dana, Charles A., 137, 138.

Darrow, Clarence, 40.

Davenport, Frederick M., Senator, 193, 425.

Davis, Richard Harding, 342, 344.

Delaney, Roosevelt barber, 136.

Democratic National Committee, 356.

Democratic National Convention, 317.

Democratic Party, 229, 315, 317.

Democrats assist Old Guard, 171.

Denison, Lindsay, 26.

Dewey, Chauncey, 368.

Dewey, George, Admiral, 'Autobiography,' 6; Philippines incident, 9; message to Germans, 11; war talk with Coghlan, 13; negotiations with Jaudenes, 15; Venezuelan incident, 89.

Dick, Charles, Senator, 99.

Dix, John A., 234, 236.

Dixon, Joseph M., Senator, 267, 269, 272, 274, 281, 283, 293, 300, 301, 316, 324, 331, 333, 356, 394.

Dolliver, J. P., Senator, 169, 199, 221.

Dolliver-Hepburn Law, 203.

Edwards, General Clarence R., 182.

Elliott, Jackson, 73.

Ellis, Wade, 74, 77.

Evening Mail, New York, 270, 288, 344.

Evening Post, Chicago, 344.

Favorite-son politics, 57, 65.

Ferguson, John, 391, 393.

Fifth Louisiana case, 286.

Flanagan, Judge, 417, 420.

Foraker, J. B., Senator, 99, 108, 109.

'Forcible Joinder' Bill, 174.

Forster, Rudolph, 114.

Fort Meigs incident, 108.

Foulke, William Dudley, 113, 120, 232.

Garfield, James R., 125, 126, 180, 333, 418, 426, 440.

Garford, Arthur, 426.

Gazette, Emporia, 337.

Glass, Captain Henry, 7.

Gooding, Frank, Governor, 34, 36.

Greaves, Arthur, 76, 79.

Greeley, Horace, 137.

Greene, Assemblyman, 192.

Griffin, Evening Sun man, 202.

Hadley, Herbert E., Governor, 294, 297, 303.

Halbert, Hugh, 299, 301.

Hale, William Bayard, 81, 82, 83, 85, 86, 89, 91.

Hamilton Club, 222.

Hammond, John Hays, 104.

Hampton, Ben B., 245.

Hampton's Magazine, 245, 255, 260.

Harlan, Mr. Justice, 211.

Harper, Frank, 321.

Harriman, F. H., 28, 29, 31, 259.

Harrison, Francis Burton, 414.

Hay, John, 438.

Hayes, Colonel John, 27.

Haywood, 'Big Bill,' 30, 31, 32, 36, 39, 42.

Hearst, William Randolph, 47, 60, 63, 113.

Hemenway, James, Senator, 367.

Heney, Francis J., 299, 399.

Henderson, Colonel, 460.

Hepburn, William P., 221.

Herald, Boston, 251.

Herrick, D. Cady, 28.

Herrick, Myron T., 99.

Higgins, Frank, 28.

Hill, David Jayne, 83.

Hill, George, 109, 142, 202.

Hinman, Harvey D., 192, 424.

Hinman-Greene Bill, 192.

Hintze, Flag-Lieutenant, 10.

Hitchcock, Frank H., 99, 100, 161, 297.

Holcombe, Lieutenant John H. Lee, 7.

Hooper, Captain, 10.

Hoover, Herbert, E. 254.

Howland, William B., 138, 139.

Hughes, Charles E., had caught public imagination, 45; popular out West, 46; personal characteristics, 46; rejects Roosevelt aid, 48; refused to seek Presidency, 49; attitude of New York delegation, 65; outmaneuvered by Taft men, 71; Youngstown speech, 72; reëlected Governor, 72; gets Roosevelt back into politics, 192; political aggressiveness, 194; nominated in 1916, 450; effect of bench experience, 450; action in California, 453; elects Wilson, 454.

'I and my people,' 141.

'I'll be a free man,' 442.

Illinois Primary Law, 273.

Indiana Primary, 284.

Ireland, Archbishop, 83.

'Iron Ore' Ishpeming, 369.

Irwin, Will, 343.

Jansen, Dr., 390, 391.

Japanese Treaty, 250.
Jaudenes, Captain-General, 15.
Jiji Shimpo, 250.
Johnson, Governor Hiram W., 220, 254, 284, 295, 299, 315, 331, 340, 342, 345, 347, 349, 366, 367, 372, 394, 397, 399, 401, 403, 452; at Milwaukee, 350; desire, 349; in critical mood, 400; eager for fight, 295; nominated by Progressives, 331; takes up Roosevelt schedule, 403; telegram from Lincoln, 347.

Keifer, General J. Warren, 107, 108.
Kellogg, Frank B., 287.
Kennedy, James S., 167.
Kern, Charlie, 202.
Kipling, Rudyard, 460.
Kirkwood, I. R., 427.
Knox, Philander C., Senator, Secretary of State, on Panama Canal Purchase, 119; position in Taft Cabinet, 186; resignation prevented, 189.
Kohrs, Conrad, 165.

Laffan, William M., 20.
La Follette, Robert M., Senator, 69, 220, 221, 254, 256, 263, 276, 294, 298, 335, 349, 356, 385.
La Follette's Magazine, 385.
Lane, Franklin K., 62, 238.
Lauder, Judge, 298.
Ledger, Philadelphia Public, 153, 154.
Lee, William, 292.
Lewis, William Draper, 331, 333.
Libbey, Edward W., 292.
Lindsay, Dick, 77, 78, 98, 102.
Lodge, H. C., Senator, 227, 236, 250, 266.
Loeb, William, Jr., 60, 67, 68, 78, 116, 123, 125, 139, 178, 184.
Long, Chester, 74, 77.
Lord, Chester S., 2, 4.
Lorimer, William, Senator, 222.
Luettich, Fred, 374.
Lyon, Cecil, 274, 356, 374, 377.

McCabe, Alexander, 368.
McCormick, Medill, 388.
McCullough, Charley, 231.

McCutcheon, John T., 222, 344.
McGovern, Francis E., Governor, 295, 297, 350.
McGrath, John W., 356, 359, 374, 377, 381.
McKinley, William B., 269, 271.
McSween, Angus, 136, 202.
Manila, expedition to, 4; German incident at, 6; Germans and Filipinos, 9; British action, August 13, 17; Weir advises Filipinos, 23.
Manning, Richard I., Governor, 171.
Manning, W. Sinkler, 171.
Martin, Elbert, 356, 359, 374, 381.
Maryland Primaries, 282.
Matsui, Counsellor, 250.
Meat Inspection Law, 203, 231.
Memorial, a real, 460.
Meyer, George von L., 266.
Michael, 'Jimmie,' 153, 155.
Miller, Charles R., 85, 141.
Mitchel, John Purroy, 433.
Mitchell, Edward Page, 138.
Moore's Digest, 248.
Morgan, Casey, Lieutenant, 16.
Morgan, John T., Senator, 443.
Morgan-Guggenheim combination, 181.
Munsey, Frank, 400.
Murdock, Victor, 409, 413, 427.
Murphy, Charles F., 47, 234.
Murphy, John B., Dr., 388, 393.

Needham, Henry Beach, 142.
Negro problem, 228.
Nelson, Colonel William R., 77, 150, 184, 267, 270.
New York County Republican Committee, 66, 68.
New York Governorship, 425.
Newett, George A., 369, 395, 417.
News, Indianapolis, 113, 115.
Nolan, Major Dennis E., 27.
North American, Philadelphia, 136, 202, 270.
North Dakota Primary, 275.
Norton, Charles D., 184, 239, 240.

Ochs, Adolph S., 78, 79, 82.
Old Guard politics, 57, 65, 93, 98, 100, 110, 159, 167, 192, 194, 203, 237, 240,

242, 253, 281, 286, 288, 298, 302, 327, 448.
Olney, Richard, 438.
O'Loughlin, J. C., 271.
Orchard, Harry, 39.
Oshkosh scandal-monger, an, 363.
Otis, General E. S., 20.
Outlook, The, 135, 138, 139, 195, 206, 344, 363.

Palmer, Frederick, 342.
Panama Canal Purchase, 113.
Panama-Pacific Exposition, 251.
Pardo, President of Peru, 141.
Parker, Alton B., 29.
Parker, Colonel John M., 451.
Parsons, Herbert, 66.
Payne, George Henry, 288, 291.
Payne-Aldrich Tariff, 167, 173, 176, 180, 202, 215, 231, 236, 410, 413.
Peckham, Mr. Justice, 211.
Penrose, Boies, Senator, 242, 426.
Perkins, George W., 268, 270, 289, 292, 324, 332, 337, 394, 400, 448; gets a copyright permission, 341.
'Personalities,' 281.
Pinchot, Gifford, 180, 181, 191, 258, 276, 400, 419, 426, 441.
Pound, James H., Judge, 395, 397, 417, 419.
Primary system, 432.
Progressives, 93, 191, 194, 204, 226, 255, 311, 319, 396, 448; congress delegation, 409; Committee on Resolutions, 329, 330; Executive Committee, 337; Headquarters, 319; National Committee, 319, 337, 405, 409, 451; National Convention, 229, 290, 319, 327; news syndicate, 343; oratory, 295, 315; rebel at "bosses," 411.
Progressive Party, 54, 314, 318, 330, 335, 338, 349, 405, 422.

Railroad Rate Bill, 203.
Railroad Securities Bill, 237, 239.
Recall of judicial decisions, 261.
Reick, William C., 81, 83, 85.
Reid, Whitelaw, 121, 135.
Republican, Fresno, 346.

Republican insurgency, 46, 51, 161, 170, 173, 194, 241.
Republican National Committee, 64, 253, 254, 266, 284, 291.
Republican National Convention of 1912, 56, 267, 274, 297, 317.
Republican Party, 93, 94, 195, 204, 206, 237, 241, 306, 315.
Riley, gun-pointer, 16.
Robins, Raymond, 426, 429.
Robinson, Douglas, 113, 198.
Roosevelt, Emlen, 418.
Roosevelt, George Emlen, 303.
Roosevelt, Kermit, 147, 434.
Roosevelt, Philip, 355, 374, 378, 388, 391.
Roosevelt, Theodore, first meeting with, 1; astonishing memory, 26, 230; controversy with Harriman, 29; and the third term, 45; attitude toward Taft in 1908, 49; preferred Root as his successor, 49, 54; pressure on 1904 statement, 51; why he wouldn't repeat, 52; on party realignment, 53; on negro problem, 54, 229; analysis of Elihu Root, 55; on the 1908 situation, 57; reason for supporting Taft, 58; helps the *New York Times*, 62; the 'Wall Street Message,' 70; blankets Hughes's speech, 71; comment on Kaiser Wilhelm II, 87; action in Venezuelan incident, 89; final judgment on Kaiser, 92; Old Guard opposition, 93; enters Campaign of 1908, 110; Panama Canal Purchase, 113; orders Canal papers made public, 117; Special Message to Senate on Canal papers, 123; and the Washington correspondents, 124; and the Taft Cabinet, 125; his greatest achievement, 129; his example to youth, 131; analysis of himself, 132; on sticking to decisions, 133; asked to take a newspaper editorship, 135; 'I and my people,' 143; interview with Williams, 145; attitude toward Senator Aldrich, 165; return from Africa, 191; yields to Hughes's appeal, 192; attitude toward political obligations, 193, 205; urged to take New York

leadership, 194; Western trip, 196; interview at Henderson Farm, 198; disappointed in Taft, 199; 'don't care that for Presidency again,' 200; comment on third term, 201; Republican Party facing defeat, 202; on working with the organization, 203; why he entered the campaign, 204; ostentation or furtiveness, 206; his 'attack' on the Supreme Court, 210; pressure to talk politics, 213; Kansas City speech, 214; 'Progressive,' not 'Insurgent,' 215; an amazing reception, 217; protecting himself, 218; attitude toward La Follette, 221; declines to dine with Lorimer, 222; speech at Saratoga Convention, 224; 'one chance in five to win,' 225; trust speech at Briceville, 227; result of 1910 Campaign, 228; campaigns for Beveridge, 231; New York State Campaign, 234; psychology, 246; insists Progressive fight go on, 256; reassumes Progressive leadership, 258; his motive, 259; two incompatible propositions, 260; 'hat in the ring,' 261; challenges Taft to Primaries, 272; goes to National Convention, 294; almost ready to bolt, 300; rejects compromise, 304; 'must purge the roll,' 307; 'a question of simple honesty,' 309; talks with Bryan, 316; did not consider himself, 318; his Progressive Convention speech, 321; for Sherman Law amendment, 329; writes platform plank, 330; nominated by Progressives, 331; speaking campaign, 342; correspondence, 355; never talked scandal, 357; 'I know kings,' 360; the drinking story, 362; a speaker for Waterloo, 365; voice gives out, 367; starts libel suit against Newett, 370; shot at Milwaukee, 375; takes a look at the assassin, 376; 'my big chance,' 379; tests his wound, 380; insists on speaking, 381; goes to hospital, 386; a rule of his life, 387; takes a shave, 390; on to Chicago, 391; at Mercy Hospital, 393; asks Beveridge to speak for him, 396; statement on libel case, 421; goes to South America, 422; in 1914 Campaign, 426; faces death at grade crossing, 427; a new thought for T. R., 430; final judgment on primaries, 433; on his South American illness, 434; on preventing the World War, 437; meets Belgian delegation, 439; political debts paid, 443; on leadership, 446; ready for a real job, 448; through with personal politics, 449; in 1916 Campaign, 452; refused for war service, 456; his last, and greatest, service, 457; chief characteristics, 458.

Roosevelt, Theodore, Jr., 397.

Roosevelt, Mrs. Theodore, 392, 397, 398.

Roosevelt music for Chicago, 289.

Roosevelt National Committee, 267, 270, 291, 320.

Root, Elihu, speech against Hearst, 47; preferred by Roosevelt, 50; Roosevelt's analysis of, 55; action at convention in 1912, 56; opposes recall of judicial decisions, 266; named for temporary chairman, 295; counts three alternates, 312.

Rosewater, Victor, 297, 298.

Rowell, Chester, 346, 452.

Rowell's sketch of Johnson, 346.

Ruick, district attorney, 36, 37.

Samuels, Arthur, 202.

Saratoga Convention, 223, 227.

Sayle, Dr. R. G., 379, 382, 390.

Schley, Commodore, 3.

Schroeder, Reginald, 114, 116, 118, 120, 248, 249, 250.

Sherman, James S., 28, 98, 194, 223.

Shipp case, 211.

Shiras, George III, 420.

Slemp, C. Bascom, 227, 236, 274.

Smith, Marcus A., 174, 175.

Smith, Sammy, 413.

Snure, John, 202, 216.

Sorenson, Dr., 379.

Staats-Zeitung, New York, 248.

Stand-pat trickery, 167.

Star, Kansas City, 139, 150, 262, 270, 271, 344, 427.
Steunenberg, Governor, 30.
Stimson, Henry L., 225, 244, 247.
Stoddard, Henry L., 270, 288, 324.
Stratton, Dr., 379.
Street, Julian, 446.
Strite, Lieutenant, 10.
Sun, New York, 1, 2, 135.
Supreme Court, attack on, 209.

Taft, Charles P., 113.
Taft, William H., campaign for nomination, 1908, 45; no contest with favorite sons, 65; sharp about Progressives, 93; attitude as Secretary toward newspapermen, 94; at Hot Springs, Va., 1908, 98; titular Republican leader, 98; lack of political skill, 100; his speech of acceptance, 103; 'a long, hard work,' 103; the bench and the presidency, 105; causes of the break with Roosevelt, 106; rebuffed by organized labor, 107; and the Roosevelt Cabinet, 112; changed attitude toward correspondents, 127; inaugurated as President, 150; declines to receive newspapermen, 157; calls special session of Congress, 159; supports Cannon for Speaker, 162; reason for supporting Cannon, 164; course during tariff fight, 169; swing around the country, 173; Winona Speech, 176; loses strength with Progressives, 180; action in Ballinger-Pinchot controversy, 181; revises a denial, 183; Old Guard's growing influence, 199; action on Railroad Securities bill, 240; attitude on Roosevelt policies, 241; alienation of Progressives, 242; trades for Japanese Treaty, 252; identified with Old Guard, 270; put on the defensive, 273; obtains lead in South, 280; 'even a rat will fight,' 281; controls National Committee, 293; nomination repudiated by Iowa, 352; takes defeat good-naturedly, 406; his record of unpopularity, 407.

Tang Shao-yi, 84, 87.
Tawney, James A., 173, 174, 176, 179, 272.
Terrell, Dr., 356, 367, 371, 373, 374, 377, 378, 383, 388, 391.
Thayer, William Roscoe, 433.
Thompson, Charles Willis, 60, 183.
Tighe, Matthew, 60.
Tillman, B. R., Senator, 203.
Times, New York, 30, 31, 32, 60, 61, 63, 73, 76, 78, 86, 98, 111, 119, 120, 121, 128, 135, 141, 150, 152, 153, 154, 157, 171, 177, 188, 196, 224, 227, 247, 262, 268, 292, 314, 354, 429.
'Toot, Toot! Choo, Choo!' 313.
Trevelyan, Sir George, 460.
Tribune, Chicago, 270, 271, 273, 280, 358, 360.
Tribune, New York, 135.

Underwood, Oscar W., 241, 410, 415.
United Press, 208.

Van Anda, Carr V., 31, 32, 60, 72, 79, 81, 85, 86, 121, 123, 135, 139, 145, 152, 156, 157, 177, 184, 189.
Van Hise, Dr., 264, 265, 266.
Van Valkenberg, E. A., 270.
Venezuelan incident, 84.
Von dem Bussche-Haddenhausen, 83.
Von Diedrichs, Admiral, 10, 18.
Von Holleben, Baron, 88, 89, 90.

Walker, Captain Asa, 10, 15.
Walker, Ernest G., 251.
Wallace, Henry M., 370, 395, 397.
Warren, Francis E., Senator, 195.
Weir, John, 20, 23.
White, Henry, 119, 122.
White, Lieutenant, 10.
White, William Allen, 337, 399.
Wickersham, George W., 186, 188, 238.
Wilhelm II, Kaiser, 81, 84, 87, 89, 92, 436.
Williams, *Times* reporter, 145, 147, 183.
Wilson, Woodrow, 317, 354, 356, 359, 360, 396, 410, 423, 438, 451.
Wood, General Leonard, 458.
Woods, Judge Fremont, 42, 43, 44.
World, New York, 113, 115, 344.
Wright, General Luke, 116, 117, 118.